BEYOND BOMBSHELLS

THE NEW ACTION HEROINE IN POPULAR CULTURE

Jeffrey A. Brown

UNIVERSITY PRESS OF MISSISSIPPI • JACKSON

www.upress.state.ms.us

Designed by Peter D. Halverson

The University Press of Mississippi is a member of the Association of American University Presses.

Chapter Six, "Sex, Romance, and the Teenage Superheroine," was originally a keynote lecture delivered at the 10th Annual University of Florida Conference on Comics and Graphic Novels: "A Comic of Her Own: Women Writing, Reading and Embodying Through Comics."

Copyright © 2015 by University Press of Mississippi
All rights reserved

First printing 2015

Library of Congress Cataloging-in-Publication Data

Brown, Jeffrey A., 1966–
  Beyond bombshells : the new action heroine in popular culture / Jeffrey A. Brown.
    pages cm
  Includes bibliographical references and index.
ISBN 978-1-4968-0319-1 (hardback) — ISBN 978-1-4968-0320-7 (ebook)
1. Women heroes in literature. 2. Women in popular culture. 3. Women heroes in motion pictures. 4. Mass media and women. 5. Action and adventure films—History and criticism. 6. Comic books, strips, etc.—History and criticism. 7. Heroines in literature. I. Title.
  PN56.5.W64B76 2015
  809'.93352042—dc23   2015008901

British Library Cataloging-in-Publication Data available

For Anastasia and Sydney, the strongest heroines I know.

CONTENTS

INTRODUCTION 3

1. Torture, Rape, Action Heroines, and *The Girl with the Dragon Tattoo* 24

2. Teams, Partners, Romance, and Action Heroines. 54

3. Ethnicity and New Action Heroines 78

4. Panthers and Vixens
   Black Superheroines, Sexuality, and Stereotypes in Contemporary Comic Books 119

5. Supermoms?
   Maternity and the Monstrous-Feminine in Superhero Comics 136

6. Sex, Romance, and the Teenage Superheroine 152

7. Girl Revolutionaries
   Neoliberalist, Postfeminist, and Feminist Heroines 167

8. Pretty Little Killers 197

CONCLUSION. Still Wondering about Wonder Woman. 232

WORKS CITED. 242

INDEX 255

BEYOND BOMBSHELLS

INTRODUCTION

COLLOQUIAL TERMS USED TO DESCRIBE FEMALE BEAUTY AND SENSUALITY have a tendency to categorize sexually desirable women as dangerous. For example, women are routinely described in the media and everyday life as having "killer looks," being "drop-dead gorgeous," "stunning," a "man-eater," a "knock-out," or "on fire." The clear implication is that beautiful women embody an innate threat to men. Female sexuality is imagined as potentially lethal in and of itself. The phrase "bombshell," in particular, has a long tradition in the media as a concise description for an extremely sexually attractive and potentially explosive woman. In 1933, Jean Harlow played the title character in Victor Fleming's *Bombshell*, and was ever after identified as a blonde bombshell in the press. In the 1940s, when *Gilda* (1946) cemented Rita Hayworth's status as the ultimate femme fatale of film noir, it was widely reported that a picture of Hayworth was attached to the first nuclear bomb the American military tested after World War II. Hayworth reportedly hated her status as a bombshell and destroyer of men (she also hated the story that her image was used on an actual bomb), but she was never able to move past the public's perception that her sexuality was lethal. In the 1950s, Marilyn Monroe was routinely described simply as "the blonde bombshell." Monroe's tumultuous personal life and her vapid sex-kitten screen roles resulted in an image of the ultimate bombshell that still defines her legacy today. The bombshell designation has continued over the years as a way to describe sex symbols such as Sophia Loren, Ann Margaret, Raquel Welch, Farrah Fawcett, Pamela Anderson, Jennifer Lopez, Salma Hayek, Megan Fox, and Scarlett Johansson. The simultaneous appeal and threat of their curvy bodies and smoldering personas is easily understood as perilously explosive. It is the irresistible sexual allure of the bombshell that marks her as dangerous to heterosexual men. Her beauty gives her power over men helpless to resist her, men who are willing to do anything to be with her. The double meaning of "bombshell" neatly encapsulates the dual perception of women as beautiful and dangerous. As a descriptive term, "bombshell" is a characterization that has been applied to sexy women by the very men who feel threatened by their sexuality.

In contemporary popular culture, the association of women with bombshells takes on a much more literal meaning. Though no less sexy than the bombshells of the past, contemporary female characters are far more likely to be actually lethal—to take men's lives with a gun or a sword—than to merely ruin men through their passions. Modern bombshells may not be just sexpots; they may also be explosives experts. The pixie-sized Fiona Glenanne (Gabrielle Anwar) on the long-running television series *Burn Notice* (2007–2013) would just as soon blow up a car, house, or boat than rely solely on her sexuality. As Fiona says in one episode, after hiding out under a parked car: "You have no idea how painful it was to be under that car and not wire it to explode" (season 3, ep. 7). Fiona's passion for explosives makes her one of the most dangerous members of the *Burn Notice* team, and makes all of her hardened male allies nervous. When one of her teammates, Sam Axe (Bruce Campbell), an ex-Navy Seal, pleads with her, "Easy on the explosives, Fi. We're trying to nail this guy on corruption charges. Could be tough if he's in little pieces," Fiona casually points out: "We'll save on shipping" (season 3, ep. 1). In another episode Michael Westen (Jeffrey Donovan), a blacklisted spy and Fiona's on-again/off-again boyfriend who always tries to reign in her violent tendencies, is in danger of being caught by the police with explosives. Fiona tells him: "This is a valuable lesson for you. C-4 is meant to be *used*, not stored. I'm serious. All those times you told me to make the explosion smaller. . . . I shouldn't have listened to you" (season 3, ep. 2). Fiona is certainly beautiful, and the series often finds reasons for her to use her sexuality on missions (I return to this issue in Chapter Two), but she is always presented as dangerous first and sexy second. The quirky, forthright, and violent Fiona Glenanne quickly became a favorite character for many *Burn Notice* fans and inspired countless websites and blogs dedicated to her passionate use of explosives. An article in the *New York Times* praised Fiona's skills—"she can build explosives the way the rest of us make toast"—and argued that Fiona steals the show, turning it "into a winning post-feminist revenge fantasy. Fiona fights for us all" (Bellafante, January 30, 2009). Female characters in modern action films and television, like Fiona, are redefining what a bombshell is. The modern sex bomb may also be a bomb expert. Sex and feminine wiles are no longer the only weapons in a woman's arsenal. Modern heroines may literally be armed to the teeth rather than just dressed to kill. Though it has been long in development, women are assuming lead roles in action narratives on a fairly regular basis. The action heroine is steadily becoming a viable role for women.

Fig. 0.1. Fiona Glenanne is more bloodthirsty than her male teammates on *Burn Notice*.

The Hollywood action heroine is a character who has finally established a record of popularity and profitability after years of uneven success at the box office. Fictional women in contemporary popular culture are just as likely to be super-spies, superheroes, monster slayers, avengers, detectives, kung fu masters, and revolutionary leaders as they are damsels in distress or romantic leads. For feminist film studies, the figure of the action heroine has proven an especially interesting character because she occupies a position so closely aligned with cultural conceptions of ideal masculinity. The modern action heroine can fight, shoot, solve mysteries, and save the world as well as Rambo, James Bond, or Indiana Jones ever did. This progressive development in acceptable depictions of female heroism has led to an impressive amount of scholarly consideration and debate about the gendered and cultural significance of action heroines (see, for example, McCaughy and King 2001, Inness 2004, Mizejewski 2004, Schubart 2007). As female characters assuming a masculine-identified role within a genre (or a range of subgenres) deeply rooted in masculine fantasies of empowerment, the action heroine provides an access point for reconsidering changes in both gender and genre. The recent success of such blockbuster series as the *Kill Bill* films (2003, 2005), the *Underworld* films (2003, 2006, 2009, 2012), the *Resident Evil* films (2002, 2004, 2007, 2010, 2012), and the initial movies based on the book trilogies *The Girl with the Dragon Tattoo* (2012) and *The Hunger Games* (2012) suggests that the action heroine is here to stay. Other blockbuster films like *Salt* (2010), *Hannah* (2011), *Brave* (2012), and *Snow White and the Huntsman* (2012) have likewise challenged the assumption that action movies are a strictly male domain. There has been a parallel growth in successful television series featuring tough female leads, such as *In Plain Sight* (2008–current), *Nikita* (2010–current), *Covert Affairs* (2010–current), *Homeland* (2011–current), *Revenge* (2011–current), *Revolution* (2012–current), *The Blacklist* (2013–current), and *Killer Women* (2014–current). On the printed page, comic book superheroines like Supergirl, Batgirl, Captain Marvel, and Spider-Girl have begun to rival their male counterparts in monthly sales. And young adult books have seen a huge boon thanks to the strong adolescent heroines in series like *City of Bones* (2008), *Paranormalcy* (2011), *Firelight* (2011), *Divergent* (2012), *Delirium* (2012), and *Dustlands* (2012). It would seem that female characters have finally established more than just a foothold in action genres. The action heroine is no longer just an anomaly or a novelty, she is a full-blown character type and a financially dependable one at that. Audiences in this new millennium have demonstrated that they want to see women kick ass, and they are willing to pay to enjoy the heroic exploits of female characters.

The action heroine's dramatic increase in popularity through the first two decades of this century is an indication of changing cultural, gendered, and economic conditions. Women continue to make great strides in politics and business, chipping away at the patriarchal and misogynistic bedrock of Western culture in the real world. The increased presence of fictional action heroines is regarded by many critics and commentators as a dramatic and exciting analogy to real world changes, as heroines like Katniss Everdeen, Lisbeth Salander, and Tris Prior challenge the male-dominated fictional ideal of heroism. The increased visibility of these modern action heroines is a progressive change and models for viewers and readers an image of strong femininity, as well as a belief that women can in fact be their own heroes. But, as with any wide-ranging trend in popular culture, the figure of the action heroine also needs to be considered as more than just a harbinger of evolving gender politics. The current crop of action heroines reveals a number of cultural concerns about femininity that still influence media representation and still need to be negotiated. The action heroine exists at the center of a precarious set of beliefs about gender, sex, ethnicity, age, violence, and power. In a previous book, *Dangerous Curves: Action Heroines, Gender, Fetishism and Popular Culture* (Brown 2011), I argued that the action heroine is a "contestable figure," that she could mean many different things to many different people, and that depictions of action heroines could not simply be understood as either positive or negative characters. Much of my focus in *Dangerous Curves* was on the various ways that action heroines negotiate and redefine the boundaries of normative feminine behavior. I was particularly concerned with the way action heroines performed a type of transgressive femininity and the myriad ways that she is fetishized as a sexual fantasy and as a commodity under a patriarchal system. While I do not think these factors are any less important today, the incredible increase in the number and success of action heroines in the few short years since *Dangerous Curves* was published has foregrounded other important topics that deserve attention. The chapters in *Beyond Bombshells: The New Action Heroine in Popular Culture* address new issues related to heroines and further develop some of the themes I explored in *Dangerous Curves*. While the sexual fetishization of heroines is still an important factor, in this collection I focus more on some of the common narrative variables that have developed and influence how the action heroine is understood as an emblematic character type. Factors like the preference for youthful heroines, their relations with central male characters, and the sometimes extreme levels of violence associated with heroines all help illustrate how the current wave of action heroines is redefining femininity through a struggle with stereotypical and historical ideas about womanhood.

The popular and financial success of action heroine vehicles like *The Hunger Games* ($410 million) and its sequel *Catching Fire* ($450 million), *Brave* ($238 million), *Snow White and the Huntsman* ($156 million), and *Salt* ($120 million), has been taken as cause for a celebration of an acceptance of strong female characters. And we are certainly seeing far more action heroine projects being made and widely promoted than ever before. The media has been quick to praise this developing trend. An article in the *Atlantic* entitled "The Rise of the Female-Led Action Film" (Meslow, Jan 20. 2012) argued that these new characters are "torchbearers of a promising, relatively new genre trend: the era of big-budget action movies starring women" (para. 2). Likewise, a piece in the *Huffington Post* entitled "Brave, Prometheus, and the Rise of Female Action Heroes" (Satran, July 2, 2012) claimed that "while these aren't the first action movies ever to feature female protagonists, the heroes of these films are different than most. They are killers first and knockouts second" (para. 7). But the future of action heroines is still precarious enough that an article in the *New York Times*, headlined "Hollywood's Year of Heroine Worship" (Scott, December 6. 2012), both praised the emergence of strong female characters and argued that "the rush to celebrate movies about women has a way of feeling both belated and disproportionate" (para. 10). These characters still have to grapple with being turned into sex objects, with being compared to male heroes, with being described as gender transgressive, and perhaps worst of all, with failing at the box office, television ratings, or at the cash register. The increased success of several notable heroines does not mean that putting a female lead in an ass-kicking role guarantees success. There have been at least as many notable failures over the last half-decade as there have been breakthroughs. The Academy Award-winning director Steven Soderbergh failed to turn mixed martial arts champion Gina Carano into an A-list action star in *Haywire* (2011), despite adding a stellar supporting cast made up of Michael Douglas, Ewan McGregor, and Antonio Banderas. Likewise, the Zack Snyder-directed *Sucker Punch* (2011) was written off by fans and critics alike as vapid titillation and earned back less than half of its $82 million production costs, even though it was widely promoted by its studio. And *The Mortal Instruments: City of Bones* (2013), based on the best-selling book series, bombed at the box office and put the studio's plans for a *Hunger Games*-like franchise on hold. On television, a 2011 reboot of *Charlie's Angels* was much anticipated but was canceled after only four episodes. Also in 2011, an American version of *Prime Suspect* was critically praised but garnered low ratings and was canceled by mid-season. The public may be more accepting of action heroines, but they are not indiscriminate. Like with male heroes, the characters and the stories they appear in have to be well developed.

Mass-media entertainments—including Hollywood film and television, music recordings, book publishing, comic books, and the gaming industry—are all part of popular culture in that we interact with them everyday, they shape our worldviews, and they in turn are shaped by our changing beliefs. But the mass media is a business first and foremost and the commercial viability of heroines is crucial to their continuation and development in mainstream media. The fact that audiences are willing to pay for movie tickets, for books, and to watch (or binge view) television series is proving better for the health of strong female characters than any fictional superpower. In some cases, fans can push a heroine from the realm of profitable box-office returns into the domain of a cultural and marketing phenomena. For example, the success of Suzanne Collins's *The Hunger Games* book trilogy—and the critically acclaimed feature films based on those novels—resulted in a wave of merchandising (T-shirts, mugs, games, dolls, bags, etc.) that is usually reserved for live-action superheroes and children's animated characters. Financial success breeds imitation more than critical adoration. Thus, despite some notable failures to turn best-selling young adult book series into blockbuster films (*Beautiful Creatures* 2013, *The Mortal Instruments: City of Bones* 2013, and *Vampire Academy* 2014), Hollywood is throwing the full weight of its marketing and merchandising power behind the feature film *Divergent* (2014), an adaptation of Veronica Roth's book trilogy, in the hope of cashing in on the success of young dystopic sci-fi heroines. Dozens of other feature film adaptations of young heroines from best-selling books are in the works, including Moria Young's *Dustland* novels, Sophie Jordan's *Firelight* series, Marie Lu's *Legend* trilogy, and Tahereh

Fig. 0.2. Fans demonstrated their desire for strong female characters with record-breaking support for the *Veronica Mars* movie.

Mafi's *Shatter Me* books. If any, or all, of these projects succeed the young action heroine's bankable status in Hollywood will be bolstered.

The most notable proof that audiences are interested in strong heroines is the remarkable story of how the short-lived television series *Veronica Mars* (2004–2007) was brought back to life by fans for a feature film of the same name in 2014. Veronica Mars was a breakthrough teenage heroine, equal parts brainy, witty, jaded, brave, sarcastic, tenacious, and passionate. Moreover, as played by Kristen Bell, Veronica was classically beautiful but still the complete antithesis of the shallow pretty kids she went to high school with. Armed with her formidable investigative mind, her acerbic tongue, and a can of pepper spray, Veronica was a pint-sized hard-boiled detective. The *Veronica Mars* television series was a critical darling and attracted a devoted fan base, but its relatively meager average of 2.5 million viewers per episode resulted in a disappointing cancellation after three exciting seasons. Rob Thomas, the series' creator, lobbied the networks to renew the program with a change in format but to no avail. For years after the show went off the air, *Veronica Mars* fans (dubbed "Marshmallows") petitioned for its return; their hopes were bolstered by regular comments by both Rob Thomas and Kristen Bell that they too would love to see the character brought back to life. After a few failed attempts to interest the networks in a *Veronica Mars* project, Thomas convinced Warner Bros. to back the film's development and release on the condition that he could raise the bulk of the financing on his own and prove that there was an audience for a potential movie. To do so, Thomas, with the assistance of Bell and other actors from the show, launched a now-legendary Kickstarter campaign in the spring of 2013 with a goal of raising $2 million in thirty days. The use of crowdfunding to launch a studio production was unprecedented, and *Veronica Mars* made headlines around the world when it reached its $2 million goal in less than eleven hours, and broke records by raising close to $6 million by the end of its thirty days. Film production began almost immediately, and the *Veronica Mars* movie was given a limited theatrical release simultaneously with a video-on-demand release within a year. Countless media stories have focused on how unprecedented the crowdfunding of *Veronica Mars* is, and the overwhelming evidence that fans are willing to pay to see a strong heroine in the media if she is well done.

Despite being made quickly and on a relatively small budget, the *Veronica Mars* movie did extremely well upon its release. Advanced screenings in select locations quickly sold out and additional showings were added. The studio had to rent out 290 theatres on their own in order to have a small theatrical release (theatre chains would not show the film because it was being released simultaneously on video-on-demand), but the movie still earned over $2 million on its opening weekend. Likewise, video sales and rentals were reportedly very high even though most of the Kickstarter backers received a complimentary digital copy of the film. Reviews were predominantly positive: the *Guardian* referred to the film as "a momentous return" and "worth the wait" (Patches, March 9, 2014). The *New York Daily News* addressed fans directly, claiming: "Veronica's return is everything you've hoped it would be. It's so much fun you may want to put a few bucks aside for a sequel" (Weitzman March 13, 2014). And *Total Film* magazine wrote of the film: "An emotionally rewarding reunion tour for established fans and a taut, sharp-tongued, character-driven thriller for all, *Veronica Mars* makes a compelling case for its heroine's continued existence" (Simpson, March 10, 2014). As most critics point out, the *Veronica Mars* movie represents a new model for feature film production and distribution in an increasingly digital age, but it also represents a fervent desire by audiences to see carefully constructed and well-rounded heroines in the media. Though nothing has been announced officially yet, the success of *Veronica Mars* may allow the character to continue in a series of film sequels or in several television miniseries (she is already set to appear in her own book series).

While the unconventional path taken by *Veronica Mars* from canceled television series to feature film is unique, the character of Veronica Mars is, in many ways, very typical of current action heroines (though she is really more of a detective, a close cousin of the action heroine). Like many of the heroines discussed throughout this book, Veronica is young, white, smart, middle-class, American, heterosexual, and pretty. In my previous book about action heroines, *Dangerous Curves*, one chapter focused on teenage and pre-teenage heroines constructed as postfeminist narratives and commodities. But, as the action heroine has developed, youthfulness has increasingly become one of the most common characteristics. Young action heroines have come to dominance in films like *The Hunger Games*, *Divergent*, *Hanna*, and *Sucker Punch*; superhero comic books like *Supergirl*, *Spider-Girl*, *Young Justice*, *The Young Avengers*, and *Avengers Academy*; as well as countless young adult book series. Correspondingly, several of the chapters to follow focus specifically on the importance of the heroines' youthfulness. The shift to younger heroines is partly grounded in a general cultural obsession with youthfulness, and in the related marketing desire to appeal to young consumers with disposable income and a voracious appetite for popular culture. But the marked increase in adolescent heroines is also an indication of a younger generation's acceptance and desire for strong female characters. The perception that we now live in a postfeminist era—where women can be heroic and independent, where they can do whatever they want, and where they can overcome oppressive patriarchal systems—is well served by the fantasy of teenage adventurers who can readily kick ass. Much of "postfeminism" is a marketing ploy or a carefully scripted rhetoric about freedom of choice for women. Despite the optimistic premise of "postfeminism" as it is commonly used as a catch-all phrase in public discourse, the reality is that feminism is still very much needed and the world has a long, long way to go before real gender equality is achieved. Still, the teenage action heroine taps into a *belief* that exists in young viewers that women are capable of being their own heroes, and this belief is fostered and promoted via these fictional narratives that present fantastic examples of women capable of amazing things. The young action heroine still grapples with discrimination, sexism, and gender expectations, but she presents a fantasy of overcoming all these factors that try to limit her.

The youthfulness of action heroines has become a common feature at the expense of imagining women of different ages being actively heroic. Some actress, like Milla Jovovich, Kate Beckinsale, and Salma Hayek, have managed to performed action roles successfully into their early forties, but by and large the action genre is a young woman's game. In feature films, male action heroes are less restricted by advanced age. Actors like Bruce Willis, Sylvester Stallone, Arnold Schwarzenegger, Liam Neeson, and Harrison Ford have remained popular action stars well into their sixties and seventies. These elderly male action heroes, who were iconic in the 1980s, literally embodying the masculine tough-guy political ethos of the Reagan era (see Jeffords 1993, Tasker 1993), have successfully reemerged in the new millennium primarily by returning to the heroic roles that defined their earlier careers. Most notably, Bruce Willis returned as John McClane in *Live Free or Die Hard* (2007) and *A Good Day to Die Hard* (2013), Sylvester Stallone revamped both Rocky Balboa in *Rocky Balboa* (2006) and John Rambo in *Rambo* (2008), and Harrison Ford took another turn as Indiana Jones in *Indiana Jones and the Kingdom of the Crystal Skull* (2008). As Philippa Gates (2010) argues, these former hardbody heroes found success as older action stars by following the model established by Clint Eastwood and embracing their advanced age as a physical limitation to be overcome, and by focusing on paternal relationships rather than romantic ones. "While Stallone, Willis, and Ford's bodies are not as frail as Eastwood's, in their recent films, they are presented as less powerful than they were at their peak (i.e., in the '80s)—and all three star in films that thematize their being undervalued because of their age" (Gates 2010, 278). Moreover, Gates stresses these older "heroes focus their emotional efforts instead [of romance] on shoring up damaged relationships with their own children" (278). In the continuation of these film series, paternity facilitates a desirable older action hero. But paternity does not seem to be a perquisite for the older action hero's popularity as each of these actors, and other older male stars, have gone on to other successful action roles devoid of familial relationships. Willis played the tough guy again in two *Sin City* (2005, 2014) and two *Red* (2010, 2013) movies, Schwarzengger in *The Last Stand* (2013) and alongside Stallone in *Escape Plan* (2013). Most remarkably, *The Expendables* series of films (2010, 2012, 2014) has proven incredibly profitable with an ensemble cast of aging male action stars including all the performers listed above, as well as Jean-Claude Van Damme, Dolph Lundgren, Mel Gibson, Wesley Snipes, Jet Li, Antonio Banderas, and others. The male action hero certainly seems to have conquered the restrictions of age and is appealing to new and younger viewers as well as the audiences that grew up watching their original exploits.

The success of *The Expendables* franchise has led to rumors of a female version with two "yet-to-be-developed" projects in the works, one tentatively entitled the *Female Expendables*, the other *The Expendabelles*. Numerous older actresses associated with the action genre have been mentioned as possible cast members, including Pam Grier, Sigourney Weaver, and Linda Hamilton. But it seems that studios are not rushing to support projects headlining older action actresses in the way they did with the men. Interestingly, producers also seem to recognize the difficulty of promoting a film based on older actresses, and younger performers have been tentatively associated with the projects as well, including Gina Carano, Katee Sackhoff, Sharni Vinson, and Maggie Q. The one real exception to the youthfulness of action heroines in recent years has been the character of Victoria Winslow in *Red* and *Red 2*. Played by Helen Mirren, who was sixty-five in the first installment and sixty-eight in the sequel, Victoria is a rare image of a glamorous older woman who is also a ruthless assassin and a skilled fighter. A retired special agent, like the rest of

Fig. 0.3. Helen Mirren's Victoria in *Red* and *Red 2* is the rare exception to the belief that all action heroines have to be young.

the otherwise-all-male team ("Red" is spy-speak for "Retired and Extremely Dangerous"), Victoria relishes violence and can hold her own against adversaries less than half her age. When a young male interrogator for MI-6 taunts the handcuffed Victoria, saying, "They say you're a legend around here. I've never heard of you. Must have been a bit before my time," Victoria frees herself from the handcuffs and easily beats him unconscious, telling him, "Well, you've heard of me now." Mirren reportedly relished cutting loose in an action role after playing so many serious characters over her long, Academy Award-winning career, and expressed an interest is revisiting the character as often as possible. While promoting the first film, Mirren was quoted in the *Telegraph* proclaiming: "I'm dying to be a full-time action movie heroine" (Evans, September 23, 2011). Likewise, when the sequel was released, an article in the *Daily Mail* pointed out that Mirren "revels in her newfound status as an action heroine," and quotes Mirren declaring: "I love being a badass, it's just the best!" (Lipworth, July 20, 2013). Unfortunately, despite the success of the *Red* films, and Mirren's scene-stealing role as Victoria, other older action heroines have yet to emerge in a time when teenage girls with guns are far more profitable than older women with weapons.

The choice of Mirren to play Victoria Winslow in the *Red* films is an interesting one since she is best known for her role as Inspector Jane Tennison in the long-running BBC miniseries, *Prime Suspect* (1991–2006). An enormously popular television drama, based on the books written by Lynda la Plante, Mirren's powerful performance of Tennison also made the character a favorite subject for feminist analysis (see, for example, Thornham 1994 and 2003, Jermyn 2003, Hallam 2005, Sydney Smith 2007, Piper 2009, and Cavender and

Jurik 2012). Walton and Jones (1999) claimed: "The *Prime Suspect* miniseries and its sequels constitute one of the most significant depictions of a professional female investigator to be aired on prime-time television" (249). Interestingly, *Prime Suspect* covers Tennison's police career, from her early struggles to prove herself in a misogynistic profession, to her final case before retirement. Given this career-spanning narrative, Charlotte Brunsdon (2013) has astutely argued that the older figure of Tennison came to represent a feminist and a female detective of a particular era that paved the way for other women on television but also reveals many of the negative perceptions of second-wave feminism in a contemporary context of postfeminsim, as well as the logical and unfortunate way older female detectives are regarded as out of place in police work. Brunsdon points out that the final season of *Prime Suspect* portrayed the once-groundbreaking feminist character as a burned-out alcoholic, to the chagrin of many fans. "Gone is the brief camaraderie with prostitutes witnessed in *Prime Suspect* 1, or the later breakthrough in that case achieved through Tennison's ability to listen to Maureen, her junior colleague," writes Brunsdon. "Instead, Mirren plays a woman who has given her life to the police force, and now faces a lonely retirement, unable even to judge when a water-cooler beaker of water is full" (387–88). The iconic Tennison becomes a cautionary tale in her later years, and an image of older women who are no longer acceptable in the media landscape of female detectives. Brunsdon contrasts the final season of *Prime Suspect* with two other female-led detective series, *Murder in Suburbia* (2004–2005) and *Ghost Squad* (2005), to reveal how the younger, "more girly" detectives who now live in a presumed postfeminist climate are dismissive of older women like Tennison. Both *Murder in Suburbia* and *Ghost Squad* had storylines featuring a Tennison-like female superior who is portrayed as less capable than the younger heroines. Brunsdon argues: "These are the women who have now come to represent fuddy-duddy feminism, who have sacrificed their femininity and their niceness in their journey to the top. They are 'old school'—but their very presence testifies to their historical and psychic importance for the identity of the new girls. And in each series, we see enacted a formal repudiation of these women who are imagined, incontrovertibly, through the figure of Jane Tennison" (385). Both Tennison as an older detective and the earlier feminism she represented are regarded as out of place in today's environment. As Brunsdon concludes: "In dramatic terms, putting young women into traditionally male character slots works as long as they stay 'young' (i.e., without responsibilities to families). Amy, Ash, and Scribbs [the heroines of *Murder in Suburbia* and *Ghost Squad*] can provide a fantasy of 'hot babes' who solve crimes—as long as nobody has to go to the supermarket" (2011, 389). No wonder Helen Mirren embraced the chance to portray an action heroine after completing her tenure as Jane Tennison.

The relative youth that Brunsdon identifies as crucial to the current wave of fictional female detectives is even more crucial a component of the modern action heroine's persona. At least women in the police force have to be old enough to be employed full-time; many of the action heroines are still teenagers or even preteens. The action heroine's youthfulness guarantees that she is "without responsibilities to families," as Brunsdon puts it. She may feel the weight of protecting family members, as Katniss does in the *Hunger Games* when she volunteers as a tribute to save her younger sister from certain death, but the young action heroine is more likely to be designated as a daughter than as a caregiver. This shift is a notable one because protective maternal instincts have long provided a justification for women kicking ass in popular culture. Maternity was framed as a strong motivation for such landmark women in action as Ellen Ripley (Sigourney Weaver) in *Aliens* (1986), Sarah Connor (Linda Hamilton) in *Terminator 2: Judgment Day* (1991), and the Bride in the *Kill Bill* films. Likewise, pregnancy and maternal protection have been worked in as plot devices near the series end for the television programs *Xena: Warrior Princess* (1995–2001) and *Alias* (2001–2006). And the most recent installment of the *Underworld* film series, *Underworld: Awakening* (2012), saw the vampire heroine Seline (Kate Beckinsale) fighting to protect the vampire/lycan hybrid daughter that she gave birth to while being held captive in suspended animation. Recently, though, Hollywood has concentrated far more on the plight of heroic fathers saving their children. Films like *War of the Worlds* (2005), *Taken* (2008), *Edge of Darkness* (2010), *Erased* (2012), *Prisoners* (2013), *Snitch* (2013), *3 Days to Kill* (2014), and *Homefront* (2013) have all used the hero's quest to save his child as the prime excuse for a lot of gut-wrenching action. Chapter Five picks up on how paternity is depicted as heroic while maternity is derided by looking specifically at the treatment of pregnancy and motherhood in recent superhero comic books.

In contemporary popular culture, fatherhood has become a heroic act. In action narratives, protecting one's children at any cost is a clearer demonstration of hypermasculinity than the ability to defeat countless hordes of enemy soldiers. But where protective and ruthless paternity has become a common action trope, the popularity of mothers kicking ass has waned. Tellingly, when Angelina Jolie replaced Tom Cruise as the lead for *Salt*, the creators claimed that they did very little tinkering with the script to accommodate the gender change—but significantly they did drop the subplot of Salt having a child to save. Another example of heroic paternity being valued over maternity can be seen in the contrast between the film *Taken* and the television series *Missing*

(2012). *Taken* features Bryan Mills (Liam Neeson), a retired CIA agent who undertakes a brutal quest to find his teenage daughter after she has been kidnapped during a trip abroad. Mills uses what he famously refers to as his "very particular set of skills" to cut a bloody swath through the underbelly of the European sex trafficking trade and rescue his daughter. The sparse but violent movie is a straightforward story summed up in the promotional tag lines used on the film's posters: "They have taken his daughter. He will hunt them. He will find them. And he will kill them." *Taken* became a huge success, turned Neeson into a top-tier action movie star at the age of fifty-six, spawned a 2012 sequel (with another planned for 2015), and a host of imitators. One of the most obvious works inspired by *Taken* was the 2012 television series *Missing*, starring Ashley Judd as Becca Winstone. Early hype for *Missing* was very positive, as it featured an A-list actress who had never done television before and was using a longer format to tell basically the same appealing story as *Taken*. Winstone, like Mills, is an ex-CIA agent whose child goes missing while he is studying abroad. As the series' promotional tag line makes clear: "She will stop at nothing to find her son." Winstone uses her old contacts scattered across Europe, her espionage skills, and her fighting abilities to track down the people who kidnapped her son and rescue him. Unfortunately, despite high production values, *Missing* failed to attract an audience and the ratings quickly dwindled after the premiere episode. Numerous press reviews and viewer postings online only seemed interested on commenting about how puffy Judd's famously beautiful face appeared and speculating about the effects of aging and/or whether she had undergone bad cosmetic surgery. Judd publicly responded by pointing out how sexist and ageist the comments were, but in the end *Missing* bombed. It would seem that audiences prefer to see older fathers heroically and violently saving their daughters rather than middle-aged mothers heroically and violently saving their sons. Maternal instincts are far less of a rationale for female violence now that youthfulness has become a defining characteristic for action heroines.

The heroines that I focus on in this book are characters primarily from American action and detective films, television, literature, and comic books—though non-American heroines, like Lisbeth Salander from the Swedish *The Girl with the Dragon Tattoo* novels and film adaptations, and various Hong Kong-based kung fu heroines, are also discussed at length. It is important to note that strong heroines have emerged and succeeded in non-American-produced entertainments. British television has an established tradition of capable heroines, including the above-mentioned landmark character of detective Jane Tennison from *Prime Suspect*. British television is rife with strong female detectives and special agents in other popular programs including

Murder in Suburbia, *Ghost Squad*, *The Fall* (2013–current), *Scott and Bailey* (2011–current), *The Bletchley Circle* (2012–current), *Hit & Miss* (2012), *Hunted* (2012–current), and *Broadchurch* (2013–current). Many of these British programs have developed a worldwide following, as have television series from other nations featuring strong heroines, such as *Spiral* (2005–current) from France, *The Killing* (2007–2012) from Denmark, *Annika Bengtzon: Crime Reporter* (2012) from Sweden, *King* (2011–current) from Canada, and *The Bridge* (2011–current), a Swedish and Danish coproduction. Moreover, action heroines in films from outside Hollywood (and Hong Kong) have achieved global popularity in movies, including *The Nest* (2002) from France, *Chocolate* (2008) from Thailand, *My Girlfriend is an Agent* (2009) from South Korea, *Jodhaa Akbar* (2008) and *Chandni Chowk to China* (2009) from India, and *Rosario Tijeras* (2005), a Mexican, Colombian, and Spanish coproduction. Many heroines who originate from a variety of non-American nationalities share traits with their Hollywood counterparts. These women are all strong, resourceful, beautiful, and violent, like the Hollywood heroines, but they also reflect a range of different cultural and national beliefs about gender, politics, and crime. The difference between how action heroines are depicted in entertainments from different nationalities is an underdeveloped area of cross-cultural research, and one that is beyond the scope of this book. A few scholars have explored violent women in foreign cinemas; for example, Gopalan (1997) and Virdi (1999) have written about avenging women in Indian film, and Pobutsky (2005) has discussed Mexican heroines, and there is a vast amount of work written about Hong Kong film heroines. But cross-cultural analysis is a notoriously difficult undertaking when critics are not indigenous to the cultures in question. In any case, the rise in the number and popularity of strong female characters in the media from a wide range of nations is an indication that action heroines are achieving success well beyond the narrow confines of Hollywood.

The first chapter deals with one of the most internationally successful heroines of all time. The figure of Lisbeth Salander became a controversial worldwide phenomenon, through Stieg Larsson's best-selling book trilogy *The Girl with the Dragon Tattoo* (2004), *The Girl Who Played with Fire* (2007), and *The Girl Who Kicked the Hornet's Nest* (2009). The gripping story of *The Girl with the Dragon Tattoo* captured a generation of readers. The heroine Lisbeth Salander, an antisocial and punkish computer hacker, teams up with Mikael Blomkvist, an investigative journalist, to solve a decades-old missing-person case and bring down a torturer and killer of women. The books were so popular, thanks primarily to the innovative character of Salander, that all three of the stories were turned into award-winning Swedish movies in 2009, as well as a high-profile Hollywood feature film in 2011. Salander survived a lifetime of abuse at the hands of men, and her personal story is one of graphic revenge against individual men and against a corrupt system of misogyny that contributed to her sufferings. Some critics regarded Salander as a feminist avenger, while others saw the stories as misogynistic themselves, accusing Larsson and the various film versions of dwelling on scenes of violence against women for pure titillation. The catalyst for most of the controversy surrounding Salander and *Dragon Tattoo* is the infamous scene where Salander is raped by her court-appointed guardian early on in the story, and her subsequent revenge when she tortures and rapes him. Neither the Swedish nor the American film versions shied away from these moments of rape and revenge, depicting them as brutal assaults which many viewers could not bear to watch. Chapter One considers how the issues of rape and power, so central to all three versions of *The Girl with the Dragon Tattoo*, are configured according to gendered scripts in narratives featuring strong female characters. The ability to withstand torture has long been a hallmark of heroism for men in popular fictions, allowing strong male bodies to be put on display without feminizing the characters as helpless victims. The male hero's triumph over torture allows him to reconfirm his superior masculinity and to exert his power over his captors. Torture scenarios featuring female victims, on the other hand, have traditionally been far more sexualized with the erotic implications of helplessly bound beautiful women filmed for maximum visual appeal. Contemporary action heroines often blur the lines between eroticized depictions of women being tortured and courageous depictions of men being tortured. The first chapter explores how these divergent gendered perceptions of torture have been reinforced in popular culture, and how Lisbeth Salander's rape and revenge lays bare the sadistic power relations involved in torture and rape that have little to do with gender. Ultimately arguing that torture in action narratives, of both men and women, is shifting to a recognition that maleness and femaleness are separable from conceptions of victimizer and victim, powerful and powerless.

The second chapter deals with the common presentation of action heroines as members of a team and in pairings with male partners. The relationship between men and women in action film and television is important for understanding how strong female characters are used to both reinforce practices of sexual objectification and to challenge stereotypes about gender norms. When action heroines function as part of a team—for example, Fiona in *Burn Notice*—their toughness is routinely tempered by their primary role as a token female presence and their key role as a sexual distraction on missions. Time and again, heroines in films like *Mission: Impossible: Ghost Protocol* (2011) and *The Avengers* (2012) are reduced to playing the "Honey Pot" figure who seduces the villain to keep him occupied while the men of the team complete their mission. Women on action teams are described within the narratives as being just as lethal and just as important as the male characters, but they are representationally overburdened as sex objects. Strong female characters have fared much better in recent film and television portrayals, often being framed as the smarter, more reliable, and more badass than their male colleagues. Female/male partnerships have become a standard formula in action and detective narratives, both on the big screen in vehicles like *Mr. and Mrs. Smith* (2005) and *Knight and Day* (2010), and on the small screen in series like *Chuck* (2007–2012), *Bones* (2005–current), and *Castle* (2009–current). The female/male partnership evolves out of the popular male/male buddy-cop films that dominated film and television in the 1970s and 1980s. When the thinly veiled homoeroticism of the buddy-cop formula became too problematic, the shift to a female partner was a natural change. The new female/male partnerships play into the same themes found in buddy-cop stories about characters who are extreme opposites who come together in mutual support for the greater good of catching the bad guy, and learning to appreciate each others' differing methods. But the change in gender dynamics from same sex to opposite sex partners also overlaps with the formulaic pattern found in romantic comedy films, where two desirable characters initially dislike each other but gradually realize that the other person is a soul mate who makes them a better and happier person. The female/male partnership in action and detective stories merges the buddy-cop and the romantic comedy formulas so that the odd-couple pairings result in a seamless professional and personal relationship. In these partnerships, the heroine is allowed to be both professionally strong and romantically feminine; she can combine characteristics that have been coded as masculine (police work) and as feminine (beautiful love interest), becoming a fully rounded character in the process.

Chapter Three takes the ethnicity of action heroines as its main topic. The current crop of heroines is predominantly white, as embodied by actresses like Jennifer Lawrence, Milla Jovovich, Kate Beckinsale, and Angelina Jolie, as well as countless others. This contemporary overwhelming preference for white protagonists discounts the historical importance of the ethnically identified characters who first popularized the image of women kicking ass on screen and thus opened the door for the current action heroines. The ethnicity of women in the media has always been subject to racial stereotyping of the worst kind, but some of the specific stereotypes of black, Asian, and Latino women led to an acceptability in relation to violence in a way that earlier depictions of white women were never permitted. Chapter Three reviews the history of strong ethnically identified women in earlier Blaxploitation and kung fu films in regards to specific stereotypes, including the black jezebel, the Asian dragon lady, and the Mexican spitfire. This chapter considers how these stereotypes influenced the development of action heroines in general, and how racial markers are deflected by current heroines. A major focus is given to the few contemporary heroines of color who have carved out a small niche in action films and on television. As case studies, I look in detail at the careers of Zoe Saldana, Maggie Q, and Jessica Alba, all of whom are of a mixed racial heritage, in order to discuss the way mixed race identities allow action genres to tap into ethnicities but also to temper them as partially white. The characters played by these actresses facilitate a certain "spicing up" or "exoticizing" of modern action heroine roles, a mobilizing of specific racial stereotypes, without completely sacrificing the dominant template of white women as the preferred contemporary heroine.

Whereas Chapter Three addresses the mixed race tendencies of contemporary action heroines in film and television, Chapter Four, "Panthers and Vixens: Black Superheroines, Sexuality, and Stereotypes in Contemporary Comic Books," focuses specifically on depictions of African American women as superheroes in two recent storylines. Following a general review of the "Orientalist" logic that has long characterized black women as the uncivilized, animalistic, and hypersexualized Other to the idealized image of white womanhood, I focus on two successful recent comic book miniseries headlined by black superheroines: DC Comics' *Vixen: Return of the Lion* and Marvel Comics' *Black Panther: Deadliest of the Species*. Both stories were published in monthly issues in 2009 and then immediately republished as trade paperbacks. Both were also the first comics to be headlined by either female character (the original Black Panther had his own series, but this was his sister taking over the role), and featured similar storylines. Vixen and Black Panther are both African nationals, and these adventures take place on the plaine and in the jungles of Africa, both involve a degree of sexualizing the heroines, a link to magical or voodoo powers, an alignment of the heroine with wild animals, and both stories are ultimately tales about learning to trust oneself and the value of self-sacrifice. While both series employ a range of stereotypes about black women, they also move beyond those stereotypes in many regards and intentionally construct empowered and empowering images of black female heroism that are rarely seen in popular media forms.

Continuing a focus on comic book superheroines, Chapter Five explores how issues of maternity and the pregnant body are derided within the superhero genre. As a genre, superhero comics present idealized images of powerful men and women who literally embody cultural ideals about physical and sexual perfection. Superheroes are handsome men with chiseled physiques and beautiful women with toned but extremely curvy bodies. The superhero body is also ideally impervious to physical assault, able to deflect punches, bullets, lasers, and anything else that seeks to harm it. Given this emphasis on idealized and impervious bodies, the issue of pregnancy is treated as an abject horror. The superheroine body that becomes pregnant challenges the fantasy of perfect and impervious sexual bodies. Sexually fetishized characters like Catwoman and Witchblade fail to conform to traditional sexual ideals if they are dressed in their revealing costumes while in the third trimester. The pregnant superheroine body becomes what Kristeva refers to as "grotesque," as "monstrously-feminine," a body that does not respect borders, that transforms and reproduces. And while superheroines may physically return to perfection, their roles as mothers are derided as selfish, as a weak point, and as irresponsible. Moreover, there is a greater misogynistic message that maternity is an untenable position for strong female characters and they must either give up the child or their heroic persona in order to carry on. Conversely, paternity is valorized within the genre as a heroic act that reinforces the overall theme of superhero stories about the righteousness value of embracing patriarchal ideas of law and order. This relatively minor theme in comic books regarding pregnancy and maternity reveals a larger cultural lesson about the continued gender restrictions placed on strong female characters and naturalizes the realm of herodom as a continuing masculine arena.

Chapter Six, "Sex, Romance, and the Teenage Superhero," is from a keynote lecture delivered at the tenth annual conference on comics and graphic novels held at the University of Florida entitled "A Comic of Her Own: Women Writing, Reading and Embodying Through Comics." This talk focused specifically on teenage superheroines and how the characters are used to explore issues of gender and sexuality for a young audience. As I explored previously in *Dangerous Curves*, adult women in comics are depicted as excessively hypersexual with bodies and costumes that cater to a male fantasy of erotic spectacle. This core fantasy of powerful but sexy women reveals the clear theme of castration anxiety that persists in the comic book industry. Thanks to their nominal status as underage characters, teenage superheroines are not illustrated or portrayed in as sexually gratuitous a manner as their adult counterparts. The toned-down sexual appearance of teen superheroines makes her a more accessible proxy for both young female and male readers to identify with. Correspondingly, the stories told about adolescent superheroines involve the usual world-saving adventures, but they also focus a great deal of attention on interpersonal issues of concern for young readers. In particular, teenage superheroines reveal a concern with romance and budding sexual desires that can act as guidance for young consumers. Characters like Batgirl, Supergirl,

Stature, and X-23 are anxious about crushes on hunky superpowered boys, they embark on relationships, they suffer heartbreaks and breakups, and they fall in and out of love. And where adult superhero characters casually enter into numerous sexual relationships, teenage superheroines are seen contemplating their first sexual encounters and what the emotional and physical result of sex might be. For the most part, teenage superheroines lead rewarding romantic lives, but the stories do not ignore some of the darker outcomes of sex and romance. Characters have endured stalkers, unplanned pregnancies, abusive boyfriends, and becoming HIV positive. Teenage superheroines shift the focus of superhero comics from the dominant terrain of hegemonic power fantasy to a relatively thoughtful parable about the twists and turns of sex and romance for young people.

Chapter Seven, "Girl Revolutionaries," considers the role of teenage action heroines as reluctant revolutionary leaders in dystopic fantasy settings. In films like *The Hunger Games*, *Snow White and the Huntsman*, and *Divergent*, and the television shows *Revolution* (2012–current) and *The 100* (2014–current), teen heroines are forced into a Joan of Arc-like role as revolutionary catalysts. These heroines pick up bows and swords to battle corrupt totalitarian systems, and inspire masses of downtrodden citizens to rise up against oppression. Metaphorically these revolutionary tales play out a youthful rebellion against parental control writ as epic battles for freedom. And while the heroines of these stories are beautiful and find romance, the narratives challenge traditional ideas about beauty as a superficial power. Their youthful innocence reinforces a postfeminist belief in a woman's ability to become anything she wants without sacrificing desirability. On the positive side, these tales are encouraging myths of young women who can, and do, fight for themselves and for larger social causes. They are messages of empowerment for everyone, made all the more effective because the spark of revolution comes from a young girl, a seemingly unthreatening character. On the negative side, the fantastical settings of these stories imply that this type of female adventure is only the stuff of fairy tales. Moreover, the dystopic settings may provide a great backdrop for dramatic action, but can girls only be strong in a world that has completely gone to Hell anyway?

I return to the important issue of youthfulness for action heroines in Chapter Eight, "Pretty Little Killers." The focus of the chapter is on three recent films, *Kick-Ass* (2010), *Sucker Punch* (2011), and *Hanna* (2011), each of which stars young action heroines that differ significantly from the girl revolutionary types discussed in the previous chapter. The heroines of these films raise important and controversial issues related to the depiction of young women as violent, sexualized, and under patriarchal control. The violence that has become culturally acceptable to witness adult women dishing out in action movies is brought into question when a character—such as the eleven-year-old Hit-Girl from *Kick-Ass*—is seen gleefully slicing dozens of armed men to death. Likewise, the standard sexualization of adult heroines is a cliché of the genre but the visual fetishization of teenage girls, like the five heroines of *Sucker Punch*, raises questions about exploitation and sexually appropriate roles for young women. The youthfulness of these heroines also reveals a degree of patriarchal control that can easily be read as misogynistic rather than liberating. The image of teenage or preteen heroines executing perfect backflips, wielding huge swords, or handling machine guns against slimy men may be a powerful fantasy of escapism or redemption in a postfeminist sense, but it also needs to be understood within the larger media cultural context where young women are still treated simultaneously as innocents in need of protection and as blossoming sex objects. All three of the films use action and adventure as an exciting metaphor for the girls coming of age in unusual circumstances. The transition from violent but innocent girl to sexually aware and powerful woman marks the allure and the threat underlying young action heroines.

1

TORTURE, RAPE, ACTION HEROINES, AND *THE GIRL WITH THE DRAGON TATTOO*

ONE OF THE MOST IMPORTANT MOTIFS FOR MALE CHARACTERS IN ACTION films is the convention of torture, and the hero's ability to withstand it. Torture is also a key component for action heroines but the often brutal on-screen torture of female characters foregrounds issues of sexualized violence, rape, power, and gender in a manner very different than with male characters. Heroes can triumphantly turn the tables on their torturers and thus prove their superior manliness. But when heroines are victimized in torture scenes, often to the point of actual rape, the films risk eroticizing images of violence against women, even if the women do eventually triumph over their torturers. The pivotal rape scene in Stieg Larsson's controversial, but incredibly popular, novel *The Girl with the Dragon* Tattoo (2005) was cause for a great deal of debate among critics and many of the books' readers. Was the graphic and prolonged description of the heroine Lisbeth Salander's horrific anal rape misogynistic? Or was it necessary to reveal the brutality and inhumanity of the act, and to justify her violent revenge? The debates were renewed when both the Swedish version of the film (2009) and the subsequent Hollywood version (2012) each depicted the rape in graphic detail. When considered within the larger context of torture in recent Hollywood film and television action genres, the torture and rape of Salander in all three versions of *The Girl with the Dragon Tattoo* reveals a complex understanding of victimization and redemption that cuts across traditional gender boundaries. Unlike earlier action movies or rape-revenge films, contemporary depictions of torture and rape lay bare the tenuous links assumed in our patriarchal culture between notions of power and powerlessness, masculinity and femininity.

The torturous rape of Lisbeth Salander in *The Girl with the Dragon Tattoo* sparked a heated public debate about whether the story should be heralded as a groundbreaking feminist tale of empowerment or as yet another example of the lurid sexualization of male violence against women. A review in the *Independent* described Salander as "a vision of female empowerment . . . a kind of goth-geek Pippi Longstocking" (Gibbs 2008, para. 7). The *Boston Globe* praised Salander as a remarkable character: "Her life is full of abuse violence, and familial woe, but her resilience and her peculiar moral stance give the book most of its thrill" (Morris 2010, para. 2). On the more critical side, when *Entertainment Weekly* ran a cover story about the incredible popularity of the book trilogy, they included a sidebar by Missy Schwartz entitled "Did Larsson Have a Problem With Women?" She emphasizes the brutality of the attacks against female characters, and condemns Larsson for "exploiting it [savage misogyny] in graphic detail for titillating storytelling purposes" (Schwartz 2010, 42). Similarly, a *Bitch* magazine article, "The Girl Who Doubted Stieg Larsson's Feminism," argued that "Larsson's vivid scenes of sexual violence against women, particularly Salander, occur so frequently that it's hard not to question whether they're there as much for titillation as for social commentary" (Taraneh 2010, 9). A book review in the *Guardian* entitled "The Girl with the Dragon Tattoo: Feminist, or Not?" summarized the debate: "The book divided critics. Some saw Lisbeth Salander (the tattooed private investigator of the title) as a feminist avenging angel. Others criticized Larsson's graphic descriptions of the abuse and mutilation of women, judging the whole effort 'misogynist'" (Groskop 2010, para. 2). Yet, regardless of the visceral reactions that critics and readers/viewers had to the violent events in the story, specifically Salander's rape and her subsequent revenge against individual rapists and systemic misogyny, this scene and the controversy it inspired crystallizes the sexual and the gendered nature of torture.

TORTURE AND THE MALE ACTION HERO

Torture scenes have long been a staple of action-oriented films featuring male heroes, from the early swashbuckling films of Douglas Fairbanks and Errol Flynn to hard-boiled detectives played by the likes of Humphrey Bogart and Dick Powell to the iconic action heroes of the 1980s personified by Arnold Schwarzenegger, Sylvester Stallone, and Mel Gibson. Over the years, the intensity of torture scenes has increased dramatically. For example, the torture of James Bond in *Goldfinger* (1964), where he is bound spread-eagle with a laser slowly burning its way towards his crotch, seems incredibly tame compared to the prolonged beating Bond experiences in *Casino Royale* (2006), as the villain brutally assaults his genitals with a knotted rope. While the intensity of the tortures endured by male heroes has changed, the symbolic and the narrative reasons for the convention have not. Torture is a concise and effective means to establish both the heroism and the unassailable masculinity of the characters. The primary function of male torture at the narrative level is to demonstrate the exceptional strength, nobility, and endurance of the protagonist. Real heroes never crack: they never give more than their name, rank, and serial number to the torturers. Gary Cooper as Lieutenant Alan McGregor in *The Lives of a Bengal Lancer* (1935) will never give up the details about a British ammunitions delivery no matter how many hot bamboo shoots are inserted under his fingernails. Likewise, fifty years later, Sylvester Stallone as John Rambo in *Rambo: First Blood Part 2* (1985) refuses to tell the Viet Cong and the Russians about American military operations, despite repeated electrocutions and scarring by a hot knife. As viewers, we know that heroes like these will remain stalwart and endure whatever pain they must in order to safeguard their comrades. We also know that, as real heroes, they will eventually triumph over their interrogators. When Martin Riggs (Mel Gibson) is chained from the ceiling and electrocuted in *Lethal Weapon* (1987), he still manages to break his torturer's neck with his legs and then bursts in guns-a-blazing to save his partner Roger Murtaugh (Danny Glover) just as the villain claims: "There are no more heroes." But as Riggs proves, and as we in the audience know, there still are heroes. At least in the world of action movies, there still are men who can withstand any torture and rescue themselves and others.

Yet, as critics like Steve Neale (1983), Kaja Silverman (1992), Susan Jeffords (1994), and David Savran (1992) have argued, the incessant and spectacular depiction of male torture in action movies functions to both eroticize the male body and to deny that very eroticism. Ever since Laura Mulvey (1975) first identified the dichotomous ways that gender is represented in cinema with the dominant gaze coded as masculine and the object of that fetishizing gaze being feminine, it has been commonplace to understand prolonged looking at male bodies as a potentially feminizing erotic act. In visual forms of media, men are coded as voyeurs and women as exhibitionists, thus any time the male gaze of the camera dwells on a male body there is a symbolic risk of emasculation. Even a character as undeniably masculine as James Bond can run the risk of being feminized by the camera gaze if a display of flesh seems unmotivated by anything other than erotic contemplation. When Daniel Craig's Bond emerges from the surf halfway through *Casino Royale* clad only in tiny European swimming briefs, the camera lingers appreciatively on his taut and muscular body. So atypical was this unmotivated male erotic display that critics and fans were quick to point out that this scene turned the tables and treated Bond as a Bond girl, most notably Ursula Andress's Honey Rider, whose bikini clad body was a focal point of the first Bond feature film *Dr.*

No (1962). *Casino Royale* ultimately returned Bond to a more typical realm of male display through the controversial torture scene, which we will return to in detail below, torture being the most common of conventions which have developed to compensate for the fetishization of male bodies in the media. Visual media forms use a variety of techniques to justify looking at the male body without implying emasculation. For example, Richard Dyer (1982) has detailed the techniques employed in photographs of male pinups, such as the male subject looking away from the camera in disinterest or staring back at the viewer challengingly, and creating a ridiculously hypermasculine mise-en-scene via exercise, muscles, weapons, or tools. Similarly, Neale argues that "male heroes can at times be marked as the object of an erotic gaze," thus "it is not surprising that 'male' genres and films constantly involve sado-masochistic themes, scenes, and phantasies" (1983, 13). Building on these theories in her analysis of 1980s action movies, Susan Jeffords argues that "the chief mechanism in mainstream cinema for deferring eroticism in the heterosexual male body is through establishing that body as an object of violence, so that erotic desire can be displaced as sadomasochism" (1994, 51). The torture of male action heroes, more than any other compensation technique or sadomasochistic phantasy, allows the camera to appreciate the shirtless and bound bodies of male ideals as they valiantly writhe in pain without any feminizing or homoerotic implications because the narrative makes it clear that these male bodies are only being displayed under duress. The tortured male body is not a passive and inviting spectacle; it is a body that demonstrates strength and resilience even when it is at its most vulnerable point.

The tortured male body in film is a way to display and to deny feminization of the body. Its resistance to torture demonstrates not just the heroism of the character and his strength but also that the body is not passive or penetrable. On the occasions when the body is penetrated, it is usually still able to repair itself. For example, when Rambo is wounded by shrapnel in *Rambo III* (1988), he is resilient enough to force the piece of wood straight through his body and then cauterizes the wound by igniting it with gunpowder. The male body may not be completely impervious (though in the case of Superman it is) but rarely is it irreparably scarred. Even when the torture of male heroes ends in death, their valiant endurance can still win the day, as when Mel Gibson's William Wallace is tortured and disemboweled in *Braveheart* (1995) but his suffering unites Scotland to fight their oppressors. To be penetrable and passive is to be coded as feminine, and the suffering of male heroes carefully denies feminization. So common is the depiction of male heroes being tortured and subjected to prolonged suffering that it seems willfully masochistic. In fact, the extensive suffering that seems to be embraced by heroes like Rambo, Bond, and any character played by Mel Gibson (for more on Gibson being tortured, see Brown 2002) can be understood as a form of reflexive masochism. Others may be the actual agents of the hero's physical torment, but the persistent spectacle of heroic suffering that is common in action films suggests that it is ultimately a willful form of self-punishment undertaken to solidify a masculine position and eradicate any hint of passivity or feminization. According to Kaja Silverman, "because reflexive masochism does not demand the renunciation of activity, it is ideally suited for negotiating the contradictions inherent in masculinity. The male subject can indulge his appetite for pain without at the same time calling into question . . . his virility" (1992, 326). No matter how spectacular the display of the male body is in torture, it refuses feminization. For example, in his analysis of the Rambo films, David Savran argues that "these ordeals [Rambo's exaggerated sufferings] must be seen as self-willed, as being the product of his need to prove his masculinity the only way he can, by allowing his sadistic, masculinized half to kick his masochistic, feminized flesh 'to shit'" (1992, 201). Any hint of feminization is symbolically eradicated through a momentary embrace of masochism and the hero's ability to overcome whatever tortures are heaped upon him.

For some critics, masochism is as fundamental to filmic depictions of masculinity as are displays of strength, intelligence, and sexual conquest. Gaylyn Studlar (1992) argues that the central appeal of visual pleasure in cinema for male spectators may not be rooted in identification with control and power but in an alignment with masochistic fantasies. Directly countering Mulvey's theory about the powerful and controlling male gaze, Studlar claims that masculine pleasure "contains passive elements and can signify *submission to* rather than *possession of* the female" (1992, 183, italics in original). Tim Edwards (2008) convincingly argues that Hollywood movies from *Spartacus* (1960) and *Ben-Hur* (1959), to *The Terminator* (1984) and *Die Hard* (1988), to *Fight Club* (1999) and *Casino Royale*, "centrally and fundamentally construct masculinity around *heroism* which is then in turn dependent upon suffering, endurance and the spectacle of masochism for its resolution into happiness" (169, italics in original). While Studlar sees erotic identificatory possibilities in the masochistic submission to females as key to visual pleasure, Edwards argues that masochism is fundamental to our basic understanding of heroic masculinity because it confirms the hero's strength, fortitude, and commitment to an ideal. So central is the issue of masochism in relation to masculinity that some critics see it as foundational even in genres like rape-revenge movies (a genre that we will return to in more detail below) that foreground female suffering at the hands of men and the woman's subsequent vengeance against those men. In an interesting divergence from the conventional theories about gender identification in rape-revenge, Peter Lehman (1993) theorizes that masochism of the most extreme sort may be at the core of male enjoyment of this genre. Lehman reasons that rather than male viewers deriving pleasure from identifying with the avenging female heroine, they may be indulging in "a male masochistic fantasy so extreme that even brutal death can be part of the scenario" (193). Thus, erotic fantasy and violence can merge in a masochistic version of masculine ideals.

Whether erotic, heroic, or a combination of both, torture and other forms of masochistic suffering are an integral part of filmic depictions of masculinity. And while in extreme cases male characters may be tortured to the point of death, the far more common pattern is for the hero to reconfirm his masculinity by enduring the torture and triumphing over his assailants. While the potentially feminizing or eroticizing torture scene has received a significant amount of attention in film studies, it is the requisite triumph of the hero in the end that reestablishes the dominance of hegemonic masculinity. In his insightful chapter "Eastwood Bound," Paul Smith (1994) addresses the potential eroticization of the male body that is displayed in torture and the narrative disavowal of any feminizing implications. Smith then focuses on the larger third stage found in films where the hero rises Phoenix-like from his moment of torture to defend his masculinity and to restore social order. Smith contends that even in the films where heroes suffer an incredible amount of violence, there is "a process of narrativization in which a masochistic moment is but part, a single element caught up in the machinery of the proferring of significance" (1994, 164). In other words, within the overall context of the film, the masochistic moment of torture does not subvert or undermine cultural standards of masculinity. Instead, these masochistic moments reinforce the perception of hegemonic masculinity as invincible precisely because they are endured and because the hero always manages to reestablish the prevailing status quo.

TORTURE AND THE FEMALE ACTION HEROINE

While the torture of male heroes—and their subsequent victories—has long been a staple of action and adventure films, women have typically been relegated to the damsel-in-distress role with merely the threat of bodily violation—which the hero always manages to rescue them from anyway. But in recent years, as action heroines have come to prominence as leading characters in their own right, torture has become an increasingly common trope for heroines as well. In *The Long Kiss Goodnight* (1996), the amnesiac spy Samantha/

Charly (Geena Davis) is tied to a mill wheel and repeatedly lowered into freezing water while being interrogated. The opening scenes of *Salt* (2010) depict CIA agent Evelyn Salt (Angelina Jolie) being bound, beaten, and waterboarded in a North Korean prison. The first time we see the Black Widow (Scarlett Johansson) in *The Avengers* (2012), she is tied to a chair as several generic European bad guys punch and slap her. On television, Sydney Bristow (Jennifer Garner) of *Alias* (2001–2006) was often captured and tortured in various ways including teeth-pulling, waterboarding, and electrocution. Likewise, the two heroines of the most recent TV version of *Nikita* (2010–current), Nikita (Maggie Q) and Alex (Lyndsy Fonseca), have each been subjected to multiple torture scenes. In fact, by the second season of *Nikita* the CW network lured audiences with advertisements featuring the heroine bound to a metal chair while her nemesis points a gun at her with the tag line: "Nikita: Discovered. Tortured. Betrayed." And while Lisbeth Salander's rape in all the versions of *The Girl with the Dragon Tattoo* is not torture in the sense of pain inflicted for the sole purpose of deriving information, it is still clearly presented as a torturous experience as she is bound, gagged, and beaten in addition to the grueling anal rape. Defining torture in film and television is more open-ended than legal definitions of torture are. For the purposes of this book, "torture" incorporates scenes that dwell on the hero's or heroine's physical and emotional pain for prolonged periods when the character is bound or helpless and can not resist being victimized by the villain. Scenes like the lengthy opening black and white sequence of *Kill Bill* (2003) featuring an extreme close-up of the Bride's (Uma Thurman) bruised, bloody, and tear-stained face as she is taunted by Bill is no less a torture scene than are clichéd portrayals of violent military interrogations.

Fictional film and television depictions of torture often share many of the same conventions and serve similar narrative goals whether the protagonist being tortured is male or female. Where they do differ greatly, depending on the gender of the sufferer, is in relation to issues of eroticization. While the torture of action heroes strives to offset or negate the sexualization of the male body, the torture of action heroines risks eroticizing the victimized female body. Because women are already so heavily coded as sexual objects in the media and subjected to the dominant male gaze, valued primarily for their "to-be-looked-at-ness" as Mulvey (1975) refers to it, female torture scenes can be understood as more overtly sexualized. Women in Hollywood films are so thoroughly eroticized and objectified that it becomes difficult to present them, or read them, through any other perspective. For example, the simple and overused cliché of introducing attractive female characters with scenes that dwell on the spectacle of their beauty function to confirm for viewers that these women are first and foremost sexual objects. The first shot of Gilda (Rita Hayworth) in *Gilda* (1946) establishes her destructive beauty as she flips her hair back, smiles at the camera, and coyly asks, "Am I decent?" In *The Mask* (1994), we get our first glimpse of Tina (Cameron Diaz) through the hero's eyes as she walks in from the rain and seductively adjusts her dress and shakes the water from her hair. In *Desperado* (1995), the first depiction of Carolina (Salma Hayek) is of her walking in slow motion down the street in a revealing outfit as cars crash behind her, the drivers so distracted by her oozing sexuality. A list of establishing erotic scenes of female characters could go on and on. My point is simply that from the very start certain female characters are marked as undeniable sexual spectacles. In this context, it is easy to see the initial introduction of Black Widow in the blockbuster movie *The Avengers* as an eroticized torture scene. As if the superheroine was not eroticized enough simply by being played by reigning sex symbol Scarlett Johansson, this establishing scene is stylishly filmed with Black Widow dressed in a revealing little black dress and nylons, with her arms bound behind the back of a chair so that her chest is thrust out, her hair carefully tousled. Black Widow is roughed up by the men interrogating her, but she remains beautiful and confidently flirtatious during the beating, demurely asking her captors: "Do you think I'm pretty?" She eventually beats all of the bad guys to a pulp (while still tied to the chair, no less), but the scene is designed to eroticize her more than it is about her endurance of torture. That the establishing scene for Black Widow in a family friendly movie like *The Avengers* is so thoroughly fetishistic reveals just how much our society is accustomed to objectifying women in ways that overlap sex with violence.

As a superheroine, Black Widow's erotic torture scene is rooted in the decades old comic book tradition of binding sultry heroines. Like pulp novels before them, superhero comics have always managed to capitalize on the erotic illustration of heroines bound in tattered clothes and held helpless by male villains. Wonder Woman, the archetypal superheroine, is perhaps the most famous example of routine bondage in the comics. From her very inception, it was established that if Wonder Woman is bound by a man she loses all of her formidable powers. Several websites are even devoted to the countless depictions of Wonder Woman tied helplessly as she is threatened by some type of phallic object (such as missiles, lasers, or swords). Unfortunately, this comic book cliché is as popular today as it ever was. Wonder Woman is still often portrayed being bound and tortured, as are such other iconic superheroines as Catwoman, Batgirl, Supergirl, Power Girl, and Spider-Woman. A recent issue of Marvel's series *Heroes for Hire* (#13) received a slew of criticism for its cover image of the three main heroines bound to a pole, their breasts thrust out and their hips posed seductively, as a long (and obviously phallic) tentacle approached them. Critics pointed out that the cover image alluded to the "tentacle rape" genre of Japanese manga comics, and is clearly not appropriate for the typically young male audience of superhero comics. Even when a comic book superheroine torture scene is not blatantly misogynistic, it is difficult for the genre to separate the sexual overtones from the violence. For example, at around the same time that Marvel Comics was being criticized for its *Heroes for Hire* cover, the company was being lauded for its "realistic" depiction of torture in their *Ms. Marvel* series. Issue #32 of *Ms. Marvel* tells the story of the heroine fighter pilot, Carol Danvers, before she developed superpowers. Danvers is shot down and captured during a mission in the Middle East and is subjected to several days of interrogation by torture, including electroshock, sleep deprivation, and fingernail-pulling. The possibility of rape is put aside at the start of her ordeal when the villain tells her: "I stop my men from having their way with you because that is an act of the weak-minded." And while Danvers does eventually free herself and beat up her captors after they smash her arm with a sledgehammer, the reader does get eleven pages of her clad only in bra and panties as she is tortured. Danvers's self-rescue is heroic in a manner usually reserved for male superheroes but the generic conventions mean that there is also an awful lot of sexual display. The consistent problem in popular culture is that female vulnerability and sexuality are yoked together.

The current popularity of the "torture porn" subgenre of horror films explicitly links together the premise of torturous violence with the exploitative erotic thrills of pornography. It is no surprise that the majority of victims in torture porn are women, their beauty and pain spectacularized for viewers (see Lowenstein 2011). Less extreme than torture porn, but perhaps more influential, is the kinky erotic symbolism of BDSM that originated in fetish subcultures and has achieved mainstream acceptability. Contemporary Western culture is flooded with images of women enjoying sadomasochistic play. Erotic thrillers like *9 and ½ Weeks* (1986) and *Basic Instinct* (1992), which were controversial successes in the 1980s and 1990s, have given way to acclaimed explorations of submissiveness in films like *Secretary* (2002), *Unfaithful* (2002), and *Kinky Boots* (2005). Likewise, mild bondage commonly appears on television in shows like *Buffy the Vampire Slayer* (1997–2003), *Desperate Housewives* (2004-2012), *Castle* (2009–current), and *The Client List* (2011–current). Sexy sadomasochistic scenarios are common in advertising for everything from cars to clothes to shoes. To promote voter registration, young sex symbols like Jessica Alba and Christina Aguilara appeared in print advertisements bound by black duct tape and wearing fetish muzzles. The fetish photography of Ellen Von Unwurth, Sebastian Faena, and Bob Carlos Clarke appear regularly in fashion magazines. Turn on the radio and you can hear Rihanna singing "sticks and stones may break my bones, but chains and whips excite me" in her song "S/M." Other pop stars like Britney Spears, Katy Perry, and Lady Gaga have likewise made careers based on fetishistic images. E. L. James's book trilogy *Fifty Shades of Gray* (2012) has become a bestseller chronicling the heroine's increasing submissiveness to her sadistic lover and includes numerous erotic scenes of bondage. Charting the mainstreaming of sadomasochism, Eleanor Wilkinson (2009) argues: "Since the 1990s we have seen a proliferation of SM images in western cultures, leading some to claim that representations of BDSM are everywhere" (182). Specifically, these images of female sexuality in the media routinely combine objectification with the symbols of sadomasochism. Is it any wonder that the standard costume for action heroines is skintight leathers? Brian McNair (2002) refers to the increased commonness of this fetishistic type of images as "porno-chic." These mainstream images, McNair argues, are "not porn, then, but the *representation* of porn in non-pornographic art and culture" (61) and that "porno-chic replaced the traditional demonization of porn with, if not always approval or celebration, a spirit of excited inquiry into its nature, appeal and musings" (63). Similarly, these common, glossy, and often-sanitized images of fetishism and sadomasochistic play can be understood as "bondage chic" or "torture chic." They represent the trappings of bondage and torture in a highly stylized and unthreatening manner that flirts with fantasies of domination and submission but always with a message that it is good, sexy fun, and implies that women are always aroused by these scenarios. The omnipresence of BDSM imagery in the media is presented as postmodern playfulness and minimizes any threat of real violence. "Ultimately," Wilkinson points out, "there is no escaping the fact that SM has been made 'safe,' toned down and commodified" (2009, 185).

The increasingly prevalent image of torture chic in popular culture shifts the perception of torture scenes featuring action heroines. In a culture that normalizes female sexuality as submissive, filmic torture scenarios with victimized women are likely to eroticize them as much, or more than, to validate their strength. For male action heroes, torture can deny their feminization, but for female action heroines torture confirms femininity. The longstanding cultural assumption that masculinity is active and powerful, while femininity is passive and powerless, extends to a belief that male sexuality is naturally sadistic and female sexuality is naturally masochistic. Freud established this gender binary in "The Economic Problem of Masochism," in which he argued that masochism is an exclusively male pathology because it casts the afflicted in a feminine position. In other words, masochism is only pathological for men because it renounces subjectivity and control and is feminizing (hence

Fig. 1.1. Nikita is strong, capable, and can rescue herself . . . but she still looks beautiful while being tortured.

all of the filmic strategies to deny the hero's feminization), while masochism is natural for women. In her thorough discussion of masochism, Kaja Silverman points out that this gendered way of thinking assumes masochism "is an accepted—indeed a requisite—element of 'normal' female subjectivity, providing a crucial mechanism for eroticizing lack and subordination" (1992, 189). This binary logic that assumes masochism is a natural or normal condition of femininity means that when strong women are tortured in the media it is not a transgression but a reaffirmation of their inherent femininity. That so many of these scenes are eroticized, like the torture of Black Widow described above, only reinforces the objectification of women and its association with violence. Even when dealing with real-life survivors of sexual assaults, the media frequently frames the discourse according to this logic. In their analysis of rape coverage in the media, Alcoff and Gray argue that the media "often eroticize the depiction of survivors of sexual violence to titillate and expand their audiences" (1993, 262). Torture and rape are, at their core, more about power than about sex, but because torture and rape are so heavily laden with sexuality in filmic representations, they are usually far more disturbing when the victim is female.

In action film and television, torture scenes can work narratively in a manner parallel to depictions of male torture. Like the male hero, action heroines usually endure the pain with only grimaces of discomfort, lots of brave wisecracks, and promises to exact revenge. Ultimately, the heroines prove their superiority by escaping and killing or wounding their torturers. When Charly/Samantha is strapped to the mill wheel in freezing water in *The Long Kiss*

Goodnight, she refuses to give up information and instead says, "I feel dirty, time for a bath." When she is lowered into the water again, she frees her hand and retrieves a gun from a corpse, then kills her captor. Later, when she is locked in a subzero meat locker, she promises her nemesis that she will watch him "die screaming," which she does after escaping and foiling a terrorist plot. The pilot of *Alias* (episode 1, "Truth Be Told") is structured around Sydney Bristow's torture at the hands of foreign terrorists. Sydney is bound to a chair as they beat her and pull her teeth out. Her torturer taunts her by calling her just a "pretty, pretty girl," but Sydney taunts him right back before freeing herself and subduing dozens of armed men. In the first season of *Nikita* (episode 11, "All the Way"), the heroine has been captured by the ominous unit called "Division" and is suspended by her arms in a barren room, chained to the concrete ceiling. Nikita is promised impending torture by knives, needles, and electricity after she is tormented with a video detailing the murder of her lover. Though visibly distraught, Nikita responds with, "You should be wondering who is going to save you," just before her pre-planted bomb explodes. Nikita pulls herself up on the chains and rips them from the ceiling before assaulting her captors and escaping. And, in a revealing example, when Jordan (Demi Moore) in *G.I. Jane* (1997) is bound, beaten, and nearly raped after her squad has been captured during a training exercise, she ends up beating her assailant to the ground and then galvanizes her unit by taunting him with a chant of "Suck my dick!" In cases like these, as the *G.I. Jane* example makes abundantly clear, the torture scene serves the same function as for male heroes. It proves that the heroine who is the toughest, the most resilient, and the most resourceful is the one who wields the phallus and all of its assumed power. But, even in these scenes, the threat of sexual violence is closer to the surface than it is when men are tortured. Samantha/Charly is clad only in a flimsy nightgown that becomes relatively transparent in the water, and in both cases she is being tortured by men she has slept with. Sydney wears a tight black sweater, leather pants, and a spectacular red hairstyle, and is taunted for her beauty. Nikita is dressed in a tight undershirt and pants that show off her curves, and the lighting accentuates her flawless beauty. And, of course, the attempted rape of Jordan reveals that sexual assault is always more of an imminent threat to females who have been captured and bound.

THE RAPE OF LISBETH SALANDER

The combination of Hollywood's persistent objectification of women, the implicit eroticization of these types of scenes, the omnipresence of torture chic, and the heroine's physical vulnerability means that the possibility of rape is always an underlying current for action heroines. The heavy-handed fetishization of action heroines (Brown 2011) always implies the prospect of sexual acts, even if it is forced on the heroine. The emphasis on the heroine's sexuality is so common a theme that Marc O'Day (2004) refers to the subgenre as "action babe cinema," wherein generic expectations "demand an actress who is 'young' (usually in her twenties or early thirties), slim, shapely, often (though by no means exclusively) white and marketed as of primarily (though not necessarily wholly) heterosexual orientation" (205–206). It is within this context that the rape of Lisbeth Salander in *The Girl with the Dragon Tattoo* is problematic. The story is narratively more of a mystery, a thriller, or even a rape-revenge tale, but the character of Salander is so original, so competent, so intelligent, so strong, and so active that she was quickly categorized as a new type of action heroine. For critics, readers, and viewers, Salander is a character who embodies action heroism in a non-action narrative and who subverts the traditional expectations of beauty. "The success of the heroine Lisbeth Salander suggests a hunger in audiences for an action picture hero," writes Roger Ebert in the *Chicago Sun-Times*, describing her as "thin, stark, haunted, with a look that crosses goth with S&M, she is fearsomely intelligent and emotionally stranded" (2011, para. 2). A cover story in *Entertainment Weekly* called her "the inscrutable, androgynous, and explosive heroine," a "sleek, spooky avatar of payback," and "a stone-cold female badass" (Harris 2012, 26, 28, 30). In *Psychology Today*, Robin S. Rosenberg (2011) argues that while "there is a sense in which Salander is an action hero," her persona also elevates her to the level of being a "superhero" (para. 1). Salander may be understood as an action heroine—and she is certainly tough, smart, active, and self-reliant—but her depiction in both film and print is far more realistic than is the norm for action heroines. She does not have crazy kung fu skills or superpowers (though she is unsurpassed in computer hacking); she is not a master of swordplay or archery; and she is not conventionally beautiful with a Hollywood perfect body slinking around in a tight black leather outfit. Both the character of Salander and the narrative of *The Girl with the Dragon Tattoo* are grounded in realism rather than the fantasy world of unquestionable empowerment offered in action films. Salander's torture and rape is also more disturbingly realistic—there are no witty and confident rejoinders, no feats of remarkable skill to free oneself from chains before sexual assault can take place. She may be a tough action heroine, but the reality of sexual violence and victimization is laid bare rather than glossed over as teasing and stylish torture chic.

The novel and both film versions of *The Girl with the Dragon Tattoo* features a complicated narrative that weaves together three different stories. The central story deals with disgraced journalist Michael Blomqvist attempting to solve the mystery of a young woman, Harriet Vagner, who disappeared from her wealthy family's island estate forty years ago. Blomqvist is a skilled researcher but when he discovers just how complicated the case is, and how it may be intertwined with the rape and murder of dozens of women over several decades, he asks Lisbeth Salander, a formidable investigator in her own right, to help him. Together, they solve the mystery and locate the now-grown Harriet Vanger, who had fled her family home to escape her brother who had been raping and murdering women (including repeatedly raping Harriet) just as their father had been doing before. Ample time is also given to Blomqvist's own tale of losing a libel suit brought by a corrupt business magnate due to an accusatory expose written by Blomqvist and published in his own magazine. In the end, thanks in large part to Salander's computer hacking, Blomqvist is redeemed and publicly destroys the businessman in a scathing book. But it is the character of Salander who really fascinated readers and viewers the world over. Salander is a withdrawn, antisocial, and hostile young woman covered in tattoos and piercings who dresses in an aggressive punk style. Salander has been declared incompetent, spent her youth in a mental institution, and is thus a ward of the state who must answer to a court-appointed guardian. It is the abuse she suffers from her newly assigned advokat, Nils Bjurman, that provides most of the controversial points of the story. Bjurman sexually assaults her twice. The first time Salander meets with him in his office, Bjurman forces her to perform oral sex on him before he will grant her access to any of her own money. The second time, Bjurman brutally rapes Salander after insisting that she must come to his apartment if she wants any more money. But the third time Salander meets with Bjurman, she exacts her revenge by tasing him, tying him down, and raping him anally with a butt plug, just as he had done to her. She then tattoos "I am a sadistic pig, a pervert, and a rapist" on Bjurman's stomach and blackmails him into obedience with a video that she had clandestinely recorded when he had raped her previously. It is Salander's story that is at the heart of the narrative and all of the controversy that surrounds *The Girl with the Dragon Tattoo*. The subsequent two books/films in the *Millennium Trilogy* (*The Girl Who Played with Fire* and *The Girl who Kicked the Hornet's Nest*) reveal Salander's lifelong sufferings at the hands of men protected by the government, as well as her eventual revenge, with Blomkvist's help, against her abusive father, her abusive psychiatrist, and the entire system of men who had been responsible for her abuse and the sex trafficking of other women.

The driving motivation for Salander's quest is revenge, a common provocation for modern action heroines used explicitly in films like *Enough* (2002),

Kill Bill, *Salt* (2010), *Colombiana* (2011), *Haywire* (2011), and television series like *Nikita* and the aptly titled *Revenge* (2011–current). More specifically, Salander's story is about revenge for the sexual abuses she (and other women) have suffered and aligns closely with the subgenre of rape-revenge films that emerged in the 1970s and 1980s, such as *The Last House on the Left* (1972), *I Spit on Your Grave* (1978), *Ms. 45* (1981), and *Extremities* (1986). Rape-revenge movies have made a bit of a comeback in recent years with remakes of *The Last House on the Left* (2009) and *I Spit on Your Grave* (2010i) and lauded European art-house films like *Irreversible* (2002) and *Baise Moi* (2000). During the first wave of rape-revenge films, Pam Cook (1976) argued that while these and other exploitation type films allowed for new representations of women, the "stereotype of the aggressive positive heroine obsessed with revenge" (124), they undermined feminist messages of rape by framing the assaults with titillating nudity, numerous seduction scenes, and by sexualizing the female victims. The ongoing tendency in Hollywood films is to suggest that female victims are somehow complicit in their rape because they have been flirtatious or hypersexual. In films like *The Accused* (1988), *Lolita* (1997), and *Jennifer's Body* (2009), the women are depicted as asking for it. But Salander is not overtly sexualized or flirtatious, her past abuses have left her seething with animosity, and her unusual appearance is carefully constructed to scare people away, especially men. Likewise, her revenge is not tinted with eroticism or sexuality; instead, it is about violence and retribution both for herself and on behalf of other women.

The controversy in the popular press, and on the Internet, over Salander's rape stems from the assumption that scenes of graphic sexual violence always eroticize the act and perpetuate or normalize violence against women. But Salander's rape scene in the book and both movies is anything but eroticized. The degree of the violence and the number of other sexual assaults documented in the story have a cumulative effect and risk a narrative indulgence in the gory details. This concern is a valid one, but by not glossing over the brutality of sexual assault, *The Girl with the Dragon Tattoo* distinguishes itself from making light of the reality of violence against women in torturous scenarios. Moreover, the horrendous nature of the act has to be apparent so that her brutal revenge is justified narratively. Still, the reaction many had to the anal rape scene in the novel reveals the shock that realistic violence contains in a media environment where we have all gotten used to female torture scenes that tease but do not really lead to the logical level of sexual assault. The editorial in *Bitch* magazine argued that the book "dwells on Salander's rape in indulgently gory detail" (Jerven 2010, 9). In fact, in the book, the description of the rape is less than a page long (the earlier oral rape is even shorter). The particulars of Salander's physical and mental pain after the assault and the steps she takes to recover are given more time and detail than the rape. The description of her revenge on Bjurman, on the other hand, is over eight pages long, with far more information given for how she tasers him, binds him, rapes him with an anal plug, blackmails him, and tattoos him.

The filmic representations of Salander's rape, in both the Swedish and the American versions of *The Girl with the Dragon Tattoo*, are powerful scenes that carefully avoid eroticizing the assault. They each make it clear that this is a perverse violation of Salander's body, that it is violent, painful, dehumanizing, and a twisted exertion of Bjurman's state institutionalized power over her. The Swedish film directed by Niels Arden Oplev stars Michael Nyqvist as Mikael Blomkvist and Noomi Rapace as Lisbeth Salander. Rapace's powerful performance as Salander was universally praised for the emotional depth and strength that she brought to the complicated and unconventional character. Like the novel before it, Oplev's *The Girl with the Dragon Tattoo* captured audiences around the world and became one of the most successful non-Hollywood films ever produced, despite its disturbing subject matter and gut-wrenching moments of sexual assault. Roger Ebert describes the sexual violence in the Swedish film as "having a ferocious feminist orientation," arguing that while "there are scenes involving rape, bondage and assault that are stronger than most of what serves in the movies for sexual violence, but these scenes are not exploitation" (2011, 2). When Bjurman (Peter Andersson) rapes Salander in his apartment, there is no hint of titillation, only the pain of her suffering. Salander kicks at Bjurman; she flails and tries to rip the handcuffs from the bed frame; she screams in anger even after he shoves a rag in her mouth and wraps a belt around it. The review of the Swedish film version in *Ms.* magazine emphasizes the emotional force of the pivotal rape: "While the scene isn't pornographic, the vehemence of her excruciating struggle renders it horrific enough to still set my heart racing. One feels her desperate determination to be angrier than her attacker is strong, and it's stunning that her ferocity fails to save her" (Traywick 2010, para. 5). The scene is more violently shocking than in the book because we are forced to bear witness to the assault. There is nothing erotic about it; it is filmed from Salander's perspective as Bjurman's deranged face descends on her, intercut with close-ups of her terrified face, eyes wide in terror, and her desperate cries of anger and then pain. The scene is raw, violent, terrifying, and—as it should be—difficult to watch. As numerous critics pointed out, it is not the type of artfully lit and eroticized scene that we are used to seeing in films even when the sexual act is an assault.

When it was announced that David Fincher would be directing the inevitable big-budget Hollywood remake of *The Girl with the Dragon Tattoo*, there was a great deal of concern that an American version would eroticize the violence and portray Salander as more of a sexpot. With James Bond himself, Daniel Craig, on board as Mikael Blomqvist, rumors began circulating about A-list actresses famous for their beauty being considered for the role of Lisbeth Salander, such as Scarlett Johansson, Anne Hathaway, and Natalie Portman. The relatively unknown Rooney Mara eventually won the role, and Fincher promised to deliver an unwavering take on the story in the same manner he had for films like *Se7en* (1995) and *Fight Club* (1999). When a shocking teaser poster for the film was released in the fall of 2011, it raised concerns both from conservative groups and from fans of the book series. The poster featured Craig's Blomqvist standing behind Mara's Salander with his left arm wrapped around her shoulders. Salander is topless in the photo, with her breasts exposed beneath Blomqvist's arm, pierced nipples and all. The only text was a semi-transparent date of release and the tag line: "Evil Shall With Evil Be Expelled." The forthright nudity earned predictable condemnation from religious and conservative watchdog groups, but the bulk of the controversy surrounding the poster came from fans who took the image as an indication of Salander's impending Hollywood transformation. Countless bloggers and media critics decried the presentation of Salander, a tough and resilient survivor of sexual violence, being offered as a sexual spectacle. They also took issue with the suggestion that she needed Blomqvist as a protective figure. A critical essay from the website "Oh No They Didn't" surmised: "This one image immediately coded him as the troubled girl's tough protector," while Lisbeth becomes "the objectified and sexualized heroine, the goth punk Bond girl saved by 007 himself" (Anon. 2011, para. 10). Both the stars and the director defended the controversial poster but it was clear that potential audiences were aware of Hollywood's tradition of overtly sexualizing female characters and that doing so with this film would be unacceptable.

When the American version of *The Girl with the Dragon Tattoo* hit theatres, most fans and reviewers were relieved to find that not only was Salander not oversexualized in the film, but that the sexual violence was still presented as horrific. The English-language remake may have had a bigger budget, more star power, and higher production values, but it was still a gut-wrenching depiction of violence against women. Peter Bradshaw in the *Guardian* declared that Fincher's take on the story "is sleeker, smoother, sexier than its Swedish predecessors," and that "it is a muscular, overwhelmingly confident movie—and its brutal violence is thus even tougher to take" (Bradshaw 2011, para. 3). The rape scene is filmed in a manner very similar to the Swedish version. When Salander visits Bjurman's (Yorick van Wageningem) apartment, he leads her to the bedroom where she assumes he wants oral sex again. When

Bjurman grabs her hand and slaps a handcuff on it, she is shocked and fights to reach the door. We get glimpses of her struggle intercut with a retreating shot of the bedroom door from the hallway outside, as the ominous music pulses under her muffled screams. Then there is a close-up of Salander's face as she regains consciousness on the bed to find herself bound and spread, face down, with a gag already in her mouth. She wails and thrashes in terror as Bjurman rips her clothes off, asks her if she like anal sex, and then penetrates her as she screams. There is no hint of titillation, no suggestion that Salander, wanted it, deserved it, or enjoyed it. There are no snappy comebacks or eleventh-hour rescue; there is nothing but violence and victimization, although, ultimately, Salander rejects being victimized.

In all three versions of the story, Salander's rape is difficult for readers/viewers to experience, precisely because we do "experience" it with her. We identify with her horror and her helplessness. We vicariously empathize with her being exploited just as much as we thrill to her brutal revenge against Bjurman. Salander's rape is undoubtedly one of the most controversial and painful scenes ever to appear in mainstream cinema. The laborious realism of sexual violence in *The Girl with the Dragon Tattoo* sets the story apart from the earlier wave of rape-revenge films, and Salander's gritty appearance and ruthless demeanor distinguish her from the unbelievable stylized glamour of traditional action heroines. Critics and fans have characterized Salander as an action heroine, or even a superhero, born from real world violence. The brutality of her rape is jarring because it confronts viewers with the ugly reality of sexual assault, rather than glossing over it or fading to black to avoid depicting such upsetting moments. The tone and style of the rape in *The Girl with the Dragon Tattoo* is similar to *Monster* (2003), another progressive film about sexual violence and its consequences. Lisa Purse (2011b) astutely argues that the vicious rape of Aileen (Charlize Theron) by Corey (Lee Tergesen), which sets her on a murderous path, is filmed in a way that "interrupts" the usual cinematic landscape of sanitized images of female violence played out by beautiful actresses. Purse contends that the rape scene in *Monster* "feels 'too close,'" like an invasion of one's personal space. The staging prevents a clear view of what is being done to Aileen's body: we access the violence not through its spectacle (which risks sensationalizing or eroticizing the event) but through glimpses of Corey's instruments of torture and, much more importantly, Aileen's facial reactions; her struggle for comprehension; her silent cry as she experiences the physical and mental agony of the rape" (2011, 192). Salander's rape in both Oplev's and Fincher's movies functions in much the same way, not because it is filmed in an excessively choppy or claustrophobic manner but because we have been situated to identify with Salander. She is never ogled before the rape, the camera never treats her as sexual object, and we know just enough about her before the event to sympathize with her. Like with Aileen, Salander's rape is not an eroticized spectacle but a horrific event that audiences, both male and female, *experience*.

While every reiteration of *The Girl with the Dragon Tattoo* depicts Salander's rape as a vile and torturous experience perpetrated by a sadist with physical and institutionalized legal power over her, the story ventures into rape-revenge territory because she refuses to define herself as a powerless victim. It has become common knowledge that Stieg Larsson's creation of Lisbeth Salander stemmed from his guilt-ridden memories of witnessing a gang rape of a young girl when he was fourteen. Larsson did nothing to save the girl and carried that burden of helpless complicity with him for the rest of his life. Larsson became a political activist and reporter as a way to struggle against routine misogynistic violence, like the atrocity he had witnessed. The book's original title, *Men Who Hate Women*, was a stark assessment of the systemic violence that Larsson realized was ever present for women. Salander's stunning revenge against Bjurman (and, in the later books, against the entire patriarchal system that had exploited her and other women) was Larsson's redemptive fantasy for the young woman, also named Lisbeth, whom he had seen raped. In the book and both films, Salander's retributive torture of Bjurman is presented with far more detail. Knowing full well that the legal system will not believe her nor help her, Salander refuses to be a mere victim. She carefully plots and prepares for her revenge and makes Bjurman suffer the same physical pains that she endured (binding and anally raping him) and sets in place safeguards (promising to distribute the video of her being raped if he does not do exactly as she says) to protect herself from any retribution he might think of, and to prevent him from assaulting other women (tattooing "I am a rapist and a sadistic pig" on his torso). In effect, Salander proves herself a far more successful torturer than Bjurman. She not only turns the tables on him, but she also demonstrates her ability to exert power over him without the aid of physical size or institutional support. Salander shows Bjurman that rape is about power, not sex, and that power can be exercised by women as well as by men.

"I WANT YOU TO HELP ME CATCH A KILLER OF WOMEN"

Salander's story is clearly rooted in rape-revenge fantasies, but where earlier films focused entirely on the woman's revenge against her own rapists, Salander ties her personal revenge against men to a larger agenda of retribution against violent misogyny. Salander's is a deeply personal quest grounded in

Fig. 1.2. Lisbeth Salander and Michael Blomqvist work as equals to uncover a serial rapist and murderer of women.

her own experiences of abuse, but it also becomes a crusade on behalf of women in general. Salander initially refuses to help Blomqvist with his murder investigation when she first meets him, but as soon as he explains that he is asking her to help catch a rapist and killer of women, she readily agrees. Ultimately, she is instrumental in figuring out that Harriet Vanger's brother, Martin, has been torturing, raping, and killing women for decades. Salander is also the one who breaks Martin's jaw just in time to save Blomqvist from being tortured, and then chases after Martin until he dies in a fiery car explosion. In *The Girl Who Played With Fire* and *The Girl Who Kicked the Hornet's Nest*, Salander's quest continues as she hunts down and kills her villainous father, half-brother, and other men involved in a sex trafficking organization, and she helps expose a clandestine government organization that had aided her father, and destroys a reputable psychologist who had tortured her as a child and was involved in child pornography. The stories' project of exposing and dismantling a variety of sexually abusive men struck a chord with audiences worldwide. Hundreds of blogs cheered Salander's emergence as a realistic fantasy of a feminist avenger. Femmagazine.com wrote: "Ms. Salander is a bona-fide badass. I believe she appeals to women because she operates under a code of justice that gains revenge for victimized women everywhere" (Anon. 2010, para. 2). Zeldalily.com refers to Salander as "a stone cold feminist" (Loud 2010, para. 1). Media reviewer Susan Toepfer at trueslant.com calls her a "tiny terminator," and declares "Lisbeth is a super-heroine for our time, a feminist avenger" (2010, para. 3). Likewise, feministing.com calls her "basically a feminist avenger" (Anon. 2010, para. 2). Christina Konig at the *Times* argues the story is "a contemporary feminist polemic with a good old fashioned thriller" (2010, para. 2). Opinonessoftheworld.com says: "Salander is a ferocious feminist, crusading for women's empowerment" (Anon. 2010, para. 4). And forbes.com claims that "what's significant—and utterly awesome—is that Lisbeth is not a victim. She's a revenger seeking payback and justice" (Silverstein 2010, para. 6).

Because Salander can be so readily understood as a realistic feminist avenger, fighting on behalf of women everywhere who have been victimized by men, she represents a far more radical challenge to sexism than the standard Hollywood action heroine who may beat up men but always looks like a beauty queen while doing it. David Denby (2011) writes in the *New Yorker* that "everything that happens to Lisbeth is a real enough danger in the world—it has happened to many women. She's a genuine possibility, not a cartoon, and therefore far more serious as a pop-culture figure than the super-killers played by Uma Thurman in the *Kill Bill* movies or by pouting, vogueing Angelina Jolie in her kick-groin roles" (34). Salander may be the most visible feminist-influenced character in popular film but she is not completely alone. In an era in which female empowerment in the movies is still grounded in an overvaluation of female beauty, when tough women are more likely to look like the sexy fantasy figures embodied by the five young heroines of *Sucker Punch* (2011) than the punkish and antisocial but realistic Salander, there have been a few other exceptions. Most notable is perhaps the character of Hayley Stark (Ellen Page) in the revisionist rape-revenge film *Hard Candy* (2005). In the critically acclaimed film, Hayley is a very young teen who meets up with a suspected pedophile, Jeff (Patrick Wilson), after flirtatiously chatting with him online. Jeff takes the young girl back to his house and gives her alcohol but seems resistant to her clumsy advances. Things immediately change when Hayley drugs Jeff and then spends the rest of the film interrogating him, taunting him, torturing him, and eventually convincing him to kill himself. *Hard Candy* is a rape-revenge film that shockingly does not portray the initial rape, nor does it present any sexualized images of women or victims at all. The film thus manages to avoid any complicity in perpetuating images of sexualized violence against women that might be titillating. Despite Jeff's protests of innocence, even after Hayley has convincingly performed a mock castration (which Jeff believes is real thanks to a bag of ice and a deceptive video monitor), he eventually confesses that he had been involved in the torture, rape, and murder of a missing girl. In her fascinating analysis of *Hard Candy* (and *The Brave One* [2007], starring Jodie Foster), Rebecca Stringer (2005) argues "the character of Hayley Stark is more clearly drawn as a feminist avenger—a vigilante acting directly on the basis of feminist principles" (277). There is no clear connection between Hayley and the girl who was killed, and no explanation why she took it upon herself to hunt down and destroy Jeff for his sexual abuses (she also claims to have killed his accomplice). At the end of the film, when Jeff begs Hayley to tell him who she really is and why she is doing this, she vaguely replies: "I am every girl you ever watched, touched, hurt, screwed, killed." Though she eschews certain feminist principles like non-violence and collective action, Hayley is, like Salander, an agent of female anger and vengeance against not just specific men but an entire culture that normalizes sexual violence against women.

Likewise, realistic "based-on-true-story" films likes *The Whistleblower* (2010) and the documentary *The Invisible War* (2012) have explored the systemic sexism of the military that has resulted in the sexual abuse of female soldiers and the exploitation of female civilians. Inspired by true events, *The Whistleblower* is the story of Kathryn Bolkovac (Rachel Weisz) who serves as a U.N. peacekeeper in postwar Bosnia. Kathryn uncovers a conspiracy of sex trafficking allied with American military personnel and powerful international business concerns. The film follows her harrowing experiences of trying to rescue the female victims and expose the men (and women) behind the exploitation of the impoverished girls. The film is a damning indictment of the systemic misogyny that runs rampant in male-dominated organizations that wield an incredible level of militaristic, financial, and political power. Perhaps even more shocking than the dramatized story of *The Whistleblower* is the award-winning documentary *The Invisible War*, which thoroughly exposes the epidemic of sexual abuse suffered by women in the American military at the hands of their fellow male soldiers. Effectively told with cold, hard facts and news footage, as well as with first-person accounts from numerous victims, *The Invisible War* reveals the extreme levels of misogyny and sexual violence that are endemic to the American military system. The documentary makes it clear that this epidemic of rape against our own female soldiers is a systemic problem rather than just the actions of a few disturbed soldiers. Most alarmingly, *The Invisible War* also illustrates that the upper echelons of the military and government are criminally complicit in the dismissal and cover-up of these routine rapes. These two films depict a horrendous real world situation of female exploitation and sexual abuse perpetrated by contemporary male-dominated institutions, but the fact that Hollywood films and documentaries can even address the issues and bring them to a wider audience is an indication of increased public scrutiny and a cultural recognition of the unacceptability of this type of institutionalized sexual violence.

Salander's revenge against her rapist, Advokat Bjurman, is a solitary and personal act similar to the basic structure of rape-revenge narratives. As powerful and shocking as Salander's confrontation with Bjurman is, it is over before the book or the movies are even a third of the way completed. The larger project of *The Girl with the Dragon Tattoo* and the entire *Millennium Trilogy* is her struggle to uncover who has been torturing and raping women for decades, and then to avenge and dismantle the state sanctioned organization that has been involved in exploiting young women, herself included. These overarching plots truly cast Salander as a feminist avenger writ large instead of just a singular agent of rape-revenge. Importantly, Mikael Blomqvist is her partner in vengeance against systemic sexual violence. As almost every reviewer points out, Blomqvist is clearly written as a fantasy version of author Stieg Larsson. He is an intelligent and well-respected crusading journalist; he is also unabashedly heterosexual and apparently irresistible to women. Blomqvist sleeps with numerous women throughout the stories, including Salander, and has a long-standing sexual arrangement with his married business partner, Erika Berger. But Blomqvist is an important factor because the revulsion he shares with Salander regarding the exploitation of women clarifies that systemic sexual violence is not just an issue for women. Larsson's point is that this is a cultural problem that requires deep structural change, and should be addressed by everyone regardless of gender, class, or sexual orientation. In *The Girl with the Dragon Tattoo*, Blomqvist's character is also crucial for revealing that torture and sexual violence is not gender specific. Being male or female does not matter when torture and rape are reduced to situations of being in power or being powerless.

Lisbeth Salander is undoubtedly one of the most original and spectacular fictional characters to come along in years and has become the focal point of the *Millennium Trilogy* phenomenon, but Mikael Blomqvist is a sympathetic male presence that broadens the gender politics of the stories. For all his competencies as an investigator and as a romantic partner, Blomqvist is cast in a melodramatic tradition as a "fallen man," for whom we can feel pathos and cheer for redemption. Whereas the stereotype of the "fallen woman" most commonly found in film noir and melodrama usually arrives at her lowly status due to the misfortunes of love and sex, fallen men lose their way for any number of reasons. Though love and sex are often involved, Janet Staiger (2008) argues that "plot devices lure a man into wayward paths because of his lack of control. These lures may be drink or gambling or even blind ambition" (73). The ability to control one's life, to control any situation, is a key feature of our cultural definition of masculinity. To lose control is to lose masculine stature and to lose one's way. Blomqvist is established as a fallen man at the onset of *The Girl with the Dragon Tattoo* through the detailing of his conviction for slander when he is unable to substantiate his accusation against a corrupt industrialist. Indeed, he only takes on the assignment of investigating Harriet Vanger's disappearance because he is unable to work for his own magazine and the case allows him to hide away in the country while he awaits his brief prison term. As in so many

Fig. 1.3. Victimization, torture, and rape are not gender specific.

action movies, Blomqvist must redeem his masculine identity, which he does in the end by publishing a damning and thoroughly documented account of the industrialist's illegal activities. And, like action heroes, part of Blomqvist's redemption is written on his body as he suffers torture at the hands of the story's villain. But unlike the Rambos, John McClanes, and Martin Riggs of action movies, Blomqvist is unable to save himself.

In the novel, Blomqvist is captured by Martin almost immediately after he figures out that Martin has been abducting, torturing, and killing young women and is the reason for the disappearance of his sister Harriet. Martin takes Blomqvist at gunpoint into his personal torture chamber in the basement of his expensive home, handcuffs him, and uses a throat collar attached to an eyelet in the floor to bind Blomqvist while he beats him. Feeling safe in the knowledge that he has complete control over Blomqvist, Martin explains the pleasure he takes in kidnapping women and then keeping them captive while he tortures and abuses them for days on end, even videotaping the assaults. Then, in between bouts of hysteria and homicidal glee, Martin suspends Blomqvist from the ceiling by a leather noose, rips most of his clothes off, and prepares to rape him. Just before the final violation, as Blomqvist is gasping for a last few breaths of air, Salander arrives. She beats Martin viciously with a golf club, breaking many of his bones, before she takes a moment to free Blomqvist from the noose. Martin makes a desperate run for it, driving off in his car, but Salander pursues him on her motorcycle until he crashes and dies in a fiery explosion. Both film versions of the story present this scene of Blomqvist's torture and near death in a manner very true to the book except that Martin is eerily calm as he explains what he has done to women in his dungeon. The Swedish film has Salander come to Blomqvist's rescue sooner than in the book or the American film, just moments after he has been strung up, thus cutting the scene short before there is any suggestion that Martin will rape Blomqvist. The American film does not shy away from Martin's intent to rape Blomqvist. Martin explains that he "feels himself getting hard" as the hope drains from Blomqvist's face, as it does when he watches his female victims, then he cuts off Blomqvist's shirt and undoes his pants, relishing having a man as a victim for the first time. Salander arrives to save Blomqvist and simply asks, "May I kill him?" before chasing Martin to his death.

The use of Daniel Craig, the current James Bond, as Mikael Blomqvist in the American adaptation of *The Girl with the Dragon Tattoo* is an especially fortuitous bit of casting. Craig's identification with the role of 007 does risk bringing Bond's famous hypermasculinity—his toughness and his sexual desirability—to the character of Blomqvist. The fear that many had when they saw the teaser poster for the film was that Salander would basically be just another Bond girl for his sexual conquest and in need of his protection. But Craig's version of Bond, especially in the widely praised rebooting of the franchise *Casino Royale* (2006), represents a different take on ideal masculinity and the vulnerability of the hard male body. "Above all, *Casino Royale* is a story of remasculinization," argue Susanne Kord and Elisabeth Krimmer (2011). "Surprisingly, although the popular notion of Bond suggests otherwise, Craig's Bond is ideally suited for such a narrative. The new Bond is a paradoxical hero who embodies both hypermasculinity and vulnerability" (130). Craig's Bond is still in the formative stages of his super-spy career, only earning his "double-o" status in the film's pre-credit sequence. This Bond makes mistakes; he gets bloodied and bruised; he is more introspective than glib; he is victimized and needs rescuing. An important shift in gender representation was noted by many critics when Bond himself is positioned as more of a sexual spectacle than are any of the women in the film. In her discussion of historical changes to Bond and to the Bond girls, Lisa Funnell (2011b) notes that "through cinematography and mise-en-scene, *Casino Royale* places continuous and intentional emphasis on Bond's body" (463). Funnell also argues that "emphasis is placed on Daniel Craig's exposed muscular torso rather than his sexuality, libido, and conquest" (462), thus positioning this Bond as a sexual object more than a sexual subject. In one striking example, Craig's Bond in essence becomes the Bond girl, the object of the camera's sexual gaze, in the scene where he emerges from the water in a skimpy pair of swim shorts. The scene begins with a long-distance shot of a woman riding a horse on the beach in just her bikini, and sets us up to expect a typical Bond girl moment. But, instead of a close-up of her, the camera switches to Bond in the water; it is his body that the gaze lingers on and admires. Audrey Johnson (2009) rightly identifies this moment as part of a larger trend in the film to "move away from gratuitously displaying the female body in favor of putting the male body on display" (125). In addition to presenting Bond as a sexual spectacle, the foregrounding of Craig's exceptionally muscular body in *Casino Royale* revisions Bond as more rugged, serious, and believably tough than his predecessors. But while his body is presented as strong and hard, it is also more vulnerable than any other Bond's. In *Casino Royale*, as well as in the later Craig films *Quantum of Solace* (2008) and *Skyfall* (2012), the physical affects of his struggles are written on his body. Unlike earlier Bonds, who rarely wrinkle their tuxedos, this Bond is constantly bruised and bloodied.

This shift to a more realistic Bond whose version of masculinity bears the physical and emotional scars of vulnerability is nowhere more evident than in *Casino Royale*'s infamous torture scene. The villain's torture of Bond has long been a convention of the series, from the classic scene of Sean Connery's Bond strapped to a metal table in *Goldfinger*, as a laser slowly burns its way towards his groin, to Pierce Brosnan's Bond being tied to an antique strangling chair device in *The World Is Not Enough* (1999). But where Connery's Bond bluffs his way out of the death trap with cool quips, and Brosnan's Bond actually has sex with the villainess while bound, Craig's Bond is tortured in a far more realistic, painful, and emasculating way. When Bond is captured by Le Chiffre (Mads Mikkelsen), the evil financial dealer of *Casino Royale*, he is stripped naked and bound to a bottomless chair. Le Chiffre proceeds to interrogate and torture Bond by repeatedly pummeling his testicles with a large, knotted rope. Unlike earlier Bond tortures that established the hero's superior masculinity, Johnson argues that the scene "brings us up close to the torture of Craig's Bond" (2009, 119). As Johnson describes it: "An establishing long shot shows a naked Bond in the bottomless chair, and, as it proceeds, the scene contains close-ups on the expressions of pain on his face throughout. Just as we see the physical presence of Bond, we hear his pain since he does not try to remain stoically silent but instead exhales and howls loudly" (2009, 119). Still, in traditional heroic fashion, Bond endures the pain and refuses to divulge any of the information that Le Chiffre is after. Bond also manages to verbally best Le Chiffre when, despite the excruciating pain, he laughs at the villain and tells him: "Everyone will know you died scratching my balls!"

But the scene was shocking to many fans, and painful to watch, because it diverges so much from traditional torture scenes with heroic male ideals. First, Bond is fully naked, not just shirtless, and his genitals are explicitly the location of the torture; in other words, Bond's preeminent phallus is literally being destroyed and along with it all of the mythos about masculine impermeability. Second, the scene may not be an actual rape but it is clearly presented as a sexual violation and does not shy away from the threat of male-on-male rape. Le Chiffre touches Bond in a sexual manner, admires his physique, and commends him on the wonderful shape he has kept his body in—before making it clear that none of Bond's physical strength matters now that he has been put in a position of powerlessness. The third, and most realistic divergence, is that Bond is rendered incapable of triumphant self-rescue. He cannot free himself from the bonds and he cannot bluff or fuck his way out of the torture; indeed, he blacks out from the pain and is only saved when an assault team bursts in at the last minute and kills Le Chiffre. Moreover, he does not miraculously recover from the wounds inflicted upon him. Bond spends months confined to a hospital bed and a wheelchair, and it is explained that his penis, his "manhood" itself, may never work again. This infamous torture scene does not employ any of the compensation techniques used in most action films to confirm the hero's masculinity. According to the logic of our cultural perception of gender, this scene feminizes Bond by offering his body as a spectacle and by restricting him to passivity and vulnerability. That *Casino Royale* can do this to Bond himself, and still be a huge critical and commercial success, indicates a significant shift in understanding issues of gender and victimization.

Casting Daniel Craig as Blomqvist in *The Girl with the Dragon Tattoo* may bring along an association with James Bond, but it is not the same Bond that has long been regarded as the utmost example of hegemonic masculinity. Craig's is a Bond who is realistically vulnerable to the point of sexual victimization. This is also a Bond that is aware of misogynistic violence and does not condone it. This new willingness for the stars and creators behind the mythic masculinity of Bond to address the character's position in relation to violence against women was made shockingly clear in 2011 Public Service Announcement about women's continuing struggle for equality. In the PSA, Craig's Bond saunters to the forefront of a stark black set illuminated by a single spotlight. In a voiceover, Dame Judi Dench, in character as Bond's superior M, questions Bond's love of women while rattling off a long list of alarming statistics about the discriminations and violence that women worldwide continue to suffer at the hands of men. Halfway through the spot Bond walks off screen; then Bond reappears dressed in full drag as the narration continues listing atrocities. Finally, a forlorn Bond removes the wig and earrings and walks off screen as M asks: "Are we truly equals? Until the answer is 'yes' we must never stop asking." This PSA for the "Equals?" campaign was a tremendously effective use of a fictional character long associated with some of the most rudimentary of sexist fantasies to question the real world implications of gender inequality. It also explicitly declared that this was a new Bond with a new agenda regarding gender politics. That Craig's Bond and his Blomqvist can each embody ideal masculinity and rapeable vulnerability helps to reposition our understanding of torture and rape as undeniably about issues of power rather than just gender.

Salander may be the one who is actually raped in *The Girl with the Dragon Tattoo* but the story indicates that Blomqvist can also be victimized. Moreover, in the ultimate reversal of the damsel-in-distress trope, Blomqvist is saved by a woman and never achieves his own revenge on Martin Vanger. Likewise, in *Casino Royale*, we find out that Bond's rescue is thanks in large part to information provided by Vesper Lynd (Eva Green), and he is denied the possibility of revenge against Le Chiffre. Throughout the *Millennium Trilogy*, Salander is accorded the full status of what Carol Clover (1993) refers to as the "Victim-Hero" of rape-revenge films. Salander is sexually victimized but the larger portion of the story deals with her calculated, lengthy, and violent revenge. Blomqvist, on the other hand, is only victimized. Blomqvist's redemption is restricted to his professional career not his physical being. That both Salander and Blomqvist are tortured and sexually victimized suggests that Clover is correct in her assertion that rape-revenge films can facilitate audience identification with the Victim-Hero regardless of the viewer's gender because the biology of the character is less important than the performance of victimization or revenge (which are culturally deemed as feminine and masculine, respectively). Clover insightfully argues that rape-revenge films "operate on the basis of a one-sex body, the maleness or femaleness of which is performatively determined by the social gender of the acts it undergoes or undertakes" (1993, 159). While Clover is talking about rape-revenge films specifically as a horror subgenre, her theory about gender roles being performative based on either the suffering or the retribution they enact is equally applicable to understanding torture in action films.

The slippage between torture as sexual victimization and as potential or actual rape in action movies, regardless of a character's gender, means that these films may be reworking issues of gendered assumptions about power in an increasingly progressive way. That men like Blomqvist and Bond can be depicted as powerless victims of sexual violence, as rapeable, helps to uncouple the ideological link between helpless victim and femininity. That neither of these two male characters is allowed direct revenge, nor a triumphant self-rescue, means that their masculinity is not magically restored through any of the complex compensation techniques that are so commonplace when male heroes are tortured. Nor are Blomqvist and Bond explicitly feminized through their helplessness. They may be scared and howl in pain, but they do not cry or beg for mercy. Their position as helpless victims of torture and sexual assault casts them not as masculine or feminine but as powerless regardless of gender. Likewise, Salander's rape casts her as a momentarily powerless victim who happens to be a woman. She also does not cry or beg, but lashes out and howls in pain. Salander's revenge on Bjurman for her rape can be seen as masculinizing her (she does penetrate him) but it is not a radical shift in her demeanor. She was smart and tough before the rape; the need for vengeance did not transform her from passive femininity to active masculinity. Moreover, Salander's larger revenge against men who torture, rape, and murder women raises the revenge narrative to the level of feminist politics. While popular culture may still be a long way away from truly repositioning violence and sexual assaults as not gender specific, these films are at least grappling with the deeper complexity of the issues.

In addition to revealing that torture and rape is about powerlessness and vulnerability regardless of the victim's gender, *The Girl with the Dragon Tattoo* and the entire *Millennium Trilogy* also demonstrate that sexual violence against women should be condemned and fought against by both genders. Although Blomqvist may sleep with a lot of women in the books, he is still a preferable male for his disgust with sexual violence. Blomqvist is as invested as Salander in the quest to catch Martin, the serial rapist and murderer, and the organization of men who have been abusing and trafficking in women for years. The stories make it clear that Blomqvist is out to take these men down not because it is his job, not because he was assaulted, not because he has a brief relationship with Salander, but because it is the morally responsible thing to do. Nor does Blomqvist take the lead in the struggle; he and Salander work together (even when they are physically separated through most of the last two books/films). While Salander is more than capable of handling almost anything on her own, Blomqvist is always ready to assist her because systemic sexual violence against women is something that everyone should rally against. Nor is Blomqvist the lone understanding male who helps Salander throughout the series. Numerous men directly or indirectly help Salander because they believe in her and/or they understand the sexist injustices being perpetrated. At one point, Blomqvist even dubs this group of men who aid Salander as "Knights of the Idiotic Table." Among this diverse group are: Dragan Armansky, the CEO of Milton Security, where Salander had worked; Advokat Holger Palmgren, her former guardian; and Paola Roberto, a professional boxer and Salander's ex-sparring partner. While the central revenge fantasy of the *Millennium Trilogy* is focused around Salander and her remarkable exploits, her mission is never really a solitary one in the tradition of earlier rape-revenge narratives.

In the *Millennium Trilogy*, Salander does not act entirely alone, nor does Blomqvist act alone on her behalf. They fight systemic misogyny and sexual violence both individually and together. Coincidentally, at the same time that Larsson's books and the Swedish film versions were taking the world by storm, the acclaimed American television show *Dexter* featured a season-long story arc about a man and woman working together to seek revenge on a group of male rapists and murders. In season five of the award-winning Showtime program, the titular serial killer hero, Dexter Morgan (Michael C. Hall), rescues a young woman named Lumen (Julia Stiles) who had been held captive, tortured, and repeatedly raped by a group of men lead by motivational speaker Jordan Chase (Jonny Lee Miller). Dexter may be a serial killer, but he has a heart of gold and only kills criminals, so it is no surprise that he is disgusted by the hell these men have put Lumen through. Dexter and Lumen soon discover that these men have been group raping and murdering women for years. After trying to dissuade Lumen from seeking revenge and offering to murder them all himself, Dexter realizes that her only hope of recovery is for Lumen to kill them. Dexter helps her track each of the men and capture them, showing her how to kill them without being caught. Dexter and Lumen become romantically involved but go their separate ways after eliminating all of Lumen's rapists together. Once they dispatch the ringleader Jordan Chase, Lumen is fully recovered and able to return to a normal life. Rape-revenge, it would seem, is becoming an issue for men and women to undertake together in popular culture.

This fifth season of *Dexter* was lauded by critics and fans alike for its nuanced inflection of feminist politics in a series that is typically more about the heroic exploits of the central male character. Lumen's rape and torture is not a minor plot convenience that is quickly done away with. Nor is Lumen's mental, emotional, and physical recovery from the sexual abuse taken lightly. Lumen's vengeance is presented as justified and necessary rather than a simple excuse for a female character to kick ass. Likewise, Dexter's assistance is framed as an appropriate and supportive male response in the face of such misogynistic horrors. Even a serial killer knows that this kind of abuse is unacceptable. Progressive, albeit disturbing, depictions of torture and rape in films like *The Girl with the Dragon Tattoo* and *Casino Royale*, and television series like *Dexter*, indicate a cultural shift in our attitudes towards torture and sexualized violence. The realistic brutality of the torture and rape mark the events as abusive tragedies rather than titillating eroticism; they illustrate that victimization can occur to either gender and that it is equally harmful to both; that rape and torture do not confirm masculinity or femininity; and that sexual violence, whether implicit or explicit, is intertwined with the cinematic depictions of abuse and its eradication is the responsibility of both heroes and heroines.

2

TEAMS, PARTNERS, ROMANCE, AND ACTION HEROINES

THE CONVENTION OF THE LONE WOLF OR ROGUE HERO IN POPULAR CULture is a misleading stereotype. Despite an entrenched American belief in a myth of rugged individualism, very few fictional heroes or heroines really work alone. From classical legends to contemporary films, heroic adventurers tend to have a variety of helpers, be they sidekicks, partners, team members, or background assistants. Contemporary action heroines are no exception. While some action heroines pursue their adventures primarily on their own, most function as members of a team of heroes, or as partners with varying degrees of equality. The dynamics of working with others is more complicated for action heroines than it is for their iconic male counterparts. Female characters in action genres run the risk of being reduced to the token woman on a male-dominated team or of being the sexy love interest for the male partner. Despite some significant advances for strong female characters in action film and television over the past two decades, the genre is still primarily a bastion of masculinity and Hollywood seems nervous about the inclusion of women in narratives that have traditionally been targeted at male viewers. This chapter addresses how action heroines function within a team dynamic and in partnership with male colleagues. In the worst of these situations, heroines are depicted as only superficially strong characters who are included on teams to provide a splash of sex appeal for the viewers and the fictional male heroes alike. Women may now be part of the team, but for the most part they are far from equal. Contemporary heroines fare much better in regards to equality when they are partnered with men, particularly in recent male/female detective narratives. In partnerships, the women are able to achieve the relatively equal status of buddy-partner, and these narratives often follow a heteronormative script that ultimately sees the male/female partners enter into a committed loving relationship as well.

Placing female characters on male-dominated teams, or partnering them with a male colleague, is a common strategy for including women but also tempering any threat they may pose to the ideal of manly heroism. In recent years, token female team members have appeared in high-octane summer movies like *Pirates of the Caribbean* (2003), *X-Men* (2000), *G.I. Joe: The Rise of Cobra* (2009), *The Fantastic Four* (2005), *Gone in 60 Seconds* (2000), *Kung Fu Panda* (2008), *The Losers* (2010), *The Italian Job* (2003), *Wanted* (2008), *Star Trek* (2009), *Predators* (2010), *RED* (2010), *Inception* (2010), *Mission: Impossible: Ghost Protocol* (2011), *The Avengers* (2012), and *The Guardians of the Galaxy* (2014), and on such popular action-oriented television series as *Burn Notice* (2007–2013), *Hawaii Five-o* (2010–current), *The Breakout Kings* (2011–2012), *Without a Trace* (2002–2009), *Criminal Minds* (2005–current), *Crossing Lines* (2013–current), *Alphas* (2011–2013), *Leverage* (2008–current), *The Mentalist* (2008–current), *NCIS* (2003–current), *CSI* (2000–current), *MI-5* (2002–current), and *Stargate: Atlantis* (2004–2009). Heroines have also commonly been paired with male partners in movies like *The Peacemaker* (1997), *Mr. & Mrs. Smith* (2005), *Knight and Day* (2010), *Killers* (2010), and *The Girl with the Dragon Tattoo* (2011), and even more commonly in detective-oriented televisions series like *The X-Files* (1993–2002), *Castle* (2009–current), *Chuck* (2007–2012), *Bones* (2005–current), *Undercovers* (2010), *Unforgettable* (2011–current), *Case Sensitive* (2011–current), *King & Maxwell* (2013–current), *CSI: NY* (2004–2013), *Law & Order: SVU* (1999–current), and *Elementary* (2012–current). While the heroine who is part of a predominantly male team or partnered with a male may be relatively diminished in importance, these scenarios also open up a possibility for strong female characters to present a challenge to traditional gender relations. Where gender symbolism usually remains a subtext in action narratives (albeit an obvious one), the relationship dynamics between men and women on teams and in partnerships shifts the topic of gender roles and sexuality to the forefront.

TEAMS: "BURNED MAN. SMOKING WOMAN."

Burn Notice (2007–2013) is the USA Network's most successful, and one of its longest-running, original programs. The series follows the exploits of Michael Westen (Jeffrey Donovan), a disavowed super-spy who uses his skills each week to help people who find themselves in life-threatening situations. Though the series revolves primarily around Michael, all of his adventures are undertaken with his team of specialist allies listed in the opening credit voice-over: "A trigger-happy ex-girlfriend; an old friend who used to inform on you to the FBI; family too—if your desperate. And a down and out spy you met along the way." Every member of the *Burn Notice* team has proven themselves intelligent, resourceful, adept with any number of weapons, explosives and high-tech tools, skilled in hand-to-hand combat, and great at assuming a range of undercover identities. While Michael's mother, Madeline (Sharon Gless), occasionally helps out on missions, it is the character of Fiona Glenanne (Gabrielle Anwar) who constitutes the lone female presence on the regular team. The petite but muscular and volatile Fiona is an ex-IRA member and an ex-gunrunner, whose primary function is as the team's weapons and explosives expert. She is the most ruthless member of the team, always suggesting that the easiest solution to whatever problem they face is to put a bullet in the bad guy or blow him up. Michael and Fiona have an on-again/off-again romantic relationship, and while he trusts her with his life, Michael is also a little afraid of her, as are the other members of the team—Sam Axe, an ex-Navy SEAL, and Jessie Porter, an ex-spy and counter intelligence agent. Despite being a full and valuable member of the team—equal in every way—to Michael, Sam, and Jessie, the promotional materials for *Burn Notice* occasionally, and misleadingly, reduced her to eye candy. The print advertisements for the second season depicted Michael in a suit, pulling his gun and ready to burst into action, and Fiona calmly walking straight toward the camera in a tight orange, one-shoulder dress. The tag line: "Burned Man. Smoking Woman." This reinforced the visual implication that *he* is a man of action, while *she* is just really "hot." Although Fiona is a well-rounded, undeniably tough character, every bit as valuable to the *Burn Notice* crew as are the men, the promotional perception of Fiona can fall prey to the cliché of a token beautiful woman added to a team of male heroes to provide sex appeal, a little T&A for the viewers.

So common is the Hollywood logic of adding a female to an otherwise all-male action ensemble, to allow for some sexual display, that even famously feminist directors can be unintentionally complicit in perpetuating the cliché. Both Joss Whedon, the creator of the landmark feminist television series *Buffy the Vampire Slayer*, and J. J. Abrams, the creative force behind the equally iconic action heroine program *Alias*, had to defend themselves against accusations of sexism in their respective blockbuster movies, *The Avengers* (2012) and *Star Trek: Into Darkness* (2013). Whedon's *The Avengers* is the third highest-grossing film of all time but, as many critics pointed out, the roster of heroes included only one female, Black Widow (Scarlett Johansson). Placed alongside such superpowered and hypermasculine characters as Iron-Man, Captain America, the Hulk, and Hawkeye, the tiny, curvy, powerless Black Widow in her form-fitting body suit clearly seems to have been added to the team for her sex appeal. Black Widow's diminished status on the team was compounded in some of the promotional materials that sought to market the character on her sexuality alone. Perhaps the most blatant inequality came with the film poster, which depicted the entire team striking heroic poses, ready to lunge into battle, except for Black Widow who is posed coyly with her back to the viewer and her ass thrust out. The sexist double standard was so ridiculous that a spoof of the poster depicting all of the male characters with their asses absurdly thrust out went viral on the Internet. Whedon was quick to agree that more superheroines are needed and that their visibility should not be dependent on their sexuality. The director has been very vocal about his desire to include more female Avengers in the sequels. Similarly, J. J. Abrams was forced to respond to accusations of a sexual double standard about a scene in *Star Trek: Into Darkness* in which Dr. Carol Marcus (Alice Eve) strips down to her bra and panties while Captain Kirk and the camera ogle her. Abrams had done a lot in both the original *Star Trek* (2009) reboot and its sequel to elevate the role of the lone female team member, Lt. Uhura (Zoe Saldana), to something more than the glorified space receptionist she was in the original 1960s television series. But the gratuitous display of Carol seemed included simply for the sexual appeal of showing off Alice Eve's toned body. Abrams went on Conan O'Brien's talk show to apologize and explain that the scene was supposed to be a lighthearted poke at Kirk's lecherous reputation. In any case, even in films directed by champions of strong female characters, the women on action teams are routinely burdened with the role of sex object.

In 1991, Katha Pollitt, a feminist cultural critic for the *New York Times*, coined the phrase the "Smurfette Principle" to describe the preponderance of children's television shows and movies aimed at boys that include one, and only one, female character. "Contemporary shows are either essentially all-male," wrote Pollitt, "or are organized on what I call the Smurfette principle: a group of male buddies will be accented by a lone female, stereotypically defined" (April 7, para. 4). The popular cartoon *The Smurfs* featured over a dozen joyful little blue men with distinct personalities, with only one female character, Smurfette, added to the mix. As the sole female Smurf, Smurfette is the sole repository for all things stereotypically feminine. While the Smurfs may be the most extreme example, the same principle was in effect for programs like *The Super Friends*—only Wonder Woman (1973–1986), *The Muppets*—only Miss Piggy (1976–1981), *Spider-Man and his Amazing Friends*—only Starfire (1981–1986), *He-Man and the Masters of the Universe*—only Teela (1983–1985), *Thundercats*—only Cheetara (1985–1989), *Teen-Age Mutant Ninja Turtles*—only April (1987–1996), and countless other children's shows. But the Smurfette Principle has never been restricted simply to children's fare. The same logic is in effect on adult action-oriented film and television productions, from the original TV series *Mission: Impossible*—only Cinnamon

Fig. 2.1. Fiona is the lone female on the *Burn Notice* team.

Carter (1966–1973), *The A-Team*—only Amy Allen (1983–1987), and *21 Jump Street*—only Judy Hoffs (1987–1991) to their big-screen remakes. Male characters each have their own unique personality and area of specialization, but a lone female character becomes the sole repository for femaleness, which is usually emphasized as disruptive sexuality. What the female character brings to the team is sex, the ability to seductively distract bad guys and flirt her way into and out of tricky situations. One small step in the evolution of the Smurfette Principle has been the development of what tvtropes.org defines as the "Two Girls to a Team" rule. The logic of this common trope is that any male-based ensemble can accommodate a maximum male-to-female ratio of three-to-two. Thus, the various *Power Rangers* configurations can have two female Rangers so long as there are three or more male ones. Likewise, adult programs like *NCIS*, *Leverage*, *Stargate: Atlantis*, and *The Mentalist* can each have two heroines because they have three or more male team members. This means that the types of femininity portrayed can be moderately more diverse but still tend to fall into fairly stereotypical patterns.

In action genres, the fantasy of a group of heroes who can band together to defeat whatever evil they face thanks to their well-coordinated teamwork has been a long-standing tradition—from war movies like *The Dirty Dozen* (1967) and *Force 10 From Navarone* (1978) to Westerns like *The Magnificent Seven* (1960) and *The Professionals* (1966) to contemporary action series like *The Expendables* (2010, 2012, 2014) and *Mission: Impossible* (1996, 2000, 2006, 2011). Very often, the group of heroes is somehow cut off from outside help—either they are geographically isolated or they have been disavowed by their government agencies—and they are forced to rely only on each other. Typically, the teams consist of a diverse group of colorful characters, each having their own crucial area of expertise: one is the strategist, one the demolitions specialist, one the marksman, one the con man, one the hand-to-hand fighter, one the expert driver or pilot, etc. This trope of validating the efficacy of a small group of disparate individuals who can band together to accomplish seemingly impossible tasks is a critical American belief born of the mythology of the American Revolution. It is also a central metaphor from the age of industrialization onward, offering evidence of the importance for each individual to do his best as part of the larger system. Teamwork-based films and television programs provide a heroic dream about experts working together like a well-oiled machine to defeat superior forces. In his discussion of the team aspects found in the horror films of George Romero, Barry Keith Grant (1996) dubs this convention "Hawksian Professionalism," indebted to the adventure films of director Howard Hawks. Grant describes this type of plot as "the familiar narrative situation wherein a small group is cut off from society and must accomplish a certain dangerous task" (204). Whether the story is about surviving hordes of zombies, blowing up a bridge to halt the advances of an army, or stealing a crucial document from a well-guarded building, each member of the small team must execute his portion of the mission expertly.

The inclusion of women on these teams of Hawksian Professionals in action narratives almost always reduces her to the role of sexual object. The women may have admirable skills in any area of professional expertise but as the lone female—the Smurfette among military experts—her primary use to the team is typically her sexual attractiveness. As the lone female, or at best the two-to-three ratio, her mission skill often comes down to her ability to distract the bad guys while wearing a slinky dress. As the sole repository for all things feminine and sexual, action heroines operating in male-dominated teams are stereotypically tasked with the role of being the "Honey Trap." The purpose of a Honey Trap is to use the female operative's spectacular sexuality to distract or seduce the male target while the rest of her team accomplishes their mission. This is the role repeatedly fulfilled by female team members like Kono Kalakau (Grace Park) on *Hawaii 5-0* and Sophie Devereaux (Gina Bellman) on *Leverage*. The specifics of the Honey Trap can be as simple as small flirtations or flashing some cleavage and as complex as prolonged seductions of the target to gain access to his bedroom and personal life. As a preeminent example of modern action teams functioning as Hawksian Professionals, the series of *Mission: Impossible* movies, starring Tom Cruise as Ethan Hunt, demonstrates the conventional position of the female operative as Honey Trap.

Fig. 2.2. The female spy's role is to distract the villain while the rest of her team carries out the mission in *Mission Impossible: Ghost Protocol*.

In the first *Mission: Impossible* (1996), Claire Phelps (Emmanuelle Beart) is used on individual assignments to distract men and to seduce Hunt and keep him from uncovering the real villain. In *Mission: Impossible II* (2000), Nyah Nordoff-Hall (Thandie Newton), a professional thief, is predetermined for the Honey Trap role because she is an ex-girlfriend of the main villain. In *Mission: Impossible III* (2006), Maggie Q plays Zhen Lei, a skilled agent whose most significant contribution is distracting the evil Owen Davian (Phillip Seymour Hoffman) at a formal event by wearing a very revealing red dress. By the fourth installment, *Mission: Impossible: Ghost Protocol* (2011), the capable female agent, Jane Carter (Paula Patton), is used to seduce a wealthy playboy in league with the film's villain in order to attain top-secret computer codes. So blatant is the disparity between the roles of male and female team members in the *Mission: Impossible* series that even the teaser posters for *Ghost Protocol* made Jane Carter's role as Honey Trap explicit. One promotional banner for the film made the contrast clear. The banner combined the four individual character posters of each of the team members. Ethan Hunt was depicted menacingly in a hooded leather jacket; tech genius Benji Dunn (Simon Pegg) was intensely focused on a computer; security expert William Brandt (Jeremy Renner) was aiming his gun; but Agent Carter is just posed seductively in a very low-cut evening gown. The symbolism is clear: among these elite experts, the men are active heroes, the woman is sexual spectacle.

The blatant and insistent use of female teammates as Honey Traps functions to contain action heroines within a traditional conception of gender appropriate roles. While the female team member may be just as tough as the guys, her primary value is nonetheless her irresistible sexuality. The men may be attractive, but they are rarely called upon to exploit their sexuality as part of the mission. The potential threat posed to gender normativity by action heroines who can shoot, fight, and blow things up as well as male characters can is safely realigned by stressing that even these women are, first and foremost, beautiful and seductive. At a deeper level, the use of women as seductresses reinforces the misogynistic conception of women as inherently manipulative and untrustworthy. Though the heroines are required to use their "feminine wiles" as an important part of a larger plan to defeat the villains, the implication is that this seductive treachery is something that women are naturally good at. History and fiction is full of parables about treacherous women using their sexuality to undermine men: Eve, Delilah, Cleopatra, Morgan le Fay, Salome, Carmen, Mata Hari, the femme fatales of film noir, Bond girls, etc. The action heroine as Honey Trap reinforces a masculine fear of female sexuality as dangerous and emasculating. Discussing the modern spy film, Estella Tincknell notes that "in fictional spy narratives female agents are almost always double-agents," and that their overt sexuality is "a symptom of the threat femininity poses to the stability of masculinity" (101). While the overall suspicion of female sexual trickery is bolstered by the Honey Trap scenario in team movies, the narratives often go to great pains to distinguish between the noble flirting of the heroines and the degenerate attempted seduction of heroes by villainesses. The action heroine may use her sexuality on the target but she never carries through. Typically, she lures the bad guy away from his bodyguards with the promise of sex, but then quickly discards the charade and kicks his ass. Only evil women, like the bad girl spies bedded by James Bond, are willing to fully prostitute themselves as part of their mission. While the heroines may be seductive, the narrative makes it clear that they are only mimicking sexuality (excessive femininity as a "performance" in Judith Butler's 1990 terms, or as a "masquerade" according to Mary Ann Doane in 1991). This distinction is an important one in order to visually exploit the attractiveness of female team members while at the same time preserving their status as one of the noble good guys. In her discussion of the sexual dynamics of Sydney Bristow (Jennifer Garner) on the television series *Alias*, Miranda J. Brady (2009) describes how the distinction is crucial to preserving Sydney's particularly American heroic status despite repeatedly being called upon to seduce villains: "While foreign spies will shamelessly enter into a sexual contract (including marriage) to gain information, Sydney Bristow will only emulate the use of sex for espionage, saving copulation for meaningful, conjugal relations" (114).

In contrast to feature films focused on completing one monumental mission requiring the female to fulfill the Honey Trap role, the serial and often long-running format of television programs can afford action heroines on teams to transcend the restrictions of being *just* the Honey Trap. While the promotional material for *Burn Notice* may stress Michael Westen as a "burned man," and Fiona Glenanne as a "smoking woman," the series itself depicts Fiona as a diverse character, useful to the team for a variety of skills beyond just her sexuality. Fiona is petite, beautiful, confidently sexual, and always fashionable, but she is also a fearless and resourceful operative, a superb sniper, military strategist, lock-picker, safecracker, con artist, and an unparalleled explosives expert. Fiona has no problem with playing the Honey Trap when it is needed; her beauty often allows her to simply stroll up to well-guarded men in seedy Miami nightclubs. For example, in a second season episode, "Trust Me," the team is trying to retrieve the money a friend lost to a gang of con artists. The front man for the criminals, Zeke, is a Playboy Club owner who Fiona flirts with to gain access to his well-guarded VIP area and private office. But when Fiona cannot get to the safe because she needs a magnetic key card, the team switches strategies and presents Michael as a rich patsy instead. Michael becomes the lure and Fiona helps with the mission by pickpocketing the magnetic card, placing bugs, and blowing up the gang's car. Likewise, in a seventh season episode, "All or Nothing," while undercover as a computer hacker, Fiona easily lures one of the bad guys away from the office simply by touching his leg and asking him to take her out for a drink so that Michael can access a locked room.

While Fiona is beautiful, and the only female on an otherwise all-male team of heroes, over the duration of the series *Burn Notice* makes it clear that her sexuality is the least of her skills. Like a tiny, stiletto-wearing MacGyver, Fiona can make a bomb out of just about anything. In the first season episode, "Fight or Flight," Fiona is safeguarding a woman and her teenage daughter when Michael calls and frantically warns her that a car full of hit men are coming to kill them. Fiona calmly asks where the liquor cabinet is and by the time the car arrives she casually lobs Molotov cocktails at the bad guys until they have to drive off in fear. In numerous other episodes, Fiona calmly cobles together various types of bombs from common household items while flirting with Michael or strategizing attack plans. Some *Burn Notice* episodes highlight Fiona's skills and her ability to take care of herself independently. In the fourth season episode, "Where There's Smoke," Fiona is taken captive by kidnappers, along with a socialite she is guarding. While locked in a basement, Fiona is able to pick a lock with an earring, make a small explosive from gardening supplies, play her captors against each other, send a Morse code signal to her team, and send smoke signals. Even when her team locates Fiona, she sends Michael off to save the other woman while Fiona handles her own situation. In the finale, Fiona is bound to a chair for execution, but when the kidnapper leaves the room for a moment she frees herself and quickly transforms the overhead light bulb into a makeshift bomb with vodka and a piece of chewing gum. Fiona pretends to be helpless and then stalls for time until the light bulb explodes over the head of the gun-wielding captor and she then subdues him. Episodes like this one make it clear that Fiona does not need the help of her male teammates to do the impossible. In fact, in all of their missions, the men of *Burn Notice* need Fiona's help more often than she needs theirs. There are times when Michael has to save Fiona from certain death, but she saves him from similar predicaments just as often. Fiona is the rare example demonstrating that lone sexy women on heroic teams can function as more than just a Honey Trap. Unfortunately, most action teams are so restricted by gender expectations that women are sex objects and men are active agents who only give lip service to the idea that the women are equal to the males.

Of course, there have been some very notable exceptions to the standard male-dominated team dynamic, though all-female teams usually tend to be primarily campy in tone. The landmark television program *Charlie's Angels* (1976–1981), and the feature film remakes of the series, *Charlie's Angels* (2000) and *Charlie's Angels: Full Throttle* (2003), are perhaps the most obvious deviation—though the Angels still work for Charlie. Other films, like *Sucker Punch* (2011) and *D.E.B.S.* (2004), have been less profitable at the box office. Action-oriented television series with female teams include *Charmed* (1998–2006), *The Powerpuff Girls* (1998–2005), *Totally Spies* (2001–2012), *V.I.P.* (1998–2002), *She Spies* (2002–2004), and *Cleopatra 2525* (2000–2001). In the world of superhero comic books, there has been DC Comics' all-female team *Birds of Prey* (which resulted in a short-lived TV series), while Marvel Comics has an all-female series in *The Fearless Defenders* and relaunched their signature book *X-Men* with a cast made up of only superheroines. Hong Kong-based martial arts films have several female-centered movies that have become cult classics among Western audiences, like *The Heroic Trio* (1993) and *So Close* (2002). Female/female partnerships have also appeared sporadically in action film and television, with varying degrees of success. The groundbreaking series *Cagney and Lacey* proved that female-partnered detectives could be every bit as successful as male partners. And, despite its campiness, *Xena: Warrior Princess* (1995–2001) demonstrated the popular appeal of a strong female lead, Xena, and her more sensitive female partner, Gabrielle. More recently, television has offered female/female detective partners on *Murder in Suburbia* (2004–2005), *The Protector* (2011–2012), and *Scott & Bailey* (2011–current), super-spies on *Nikita* (2010–current), and homicide detective and coroner on *Rizzoli and Isles* (2010–current). Feature films have been more reluctant to invest in serious female pairings after the moderate returns on earlier films like the comedy *Feds* (1988), the thriller *Copycat* (1995), and the western comedy *Bandidas* (2006). The most hopeful sign for female-centered adventure stories is the phenomenal box-office success of the buddy-cop parody *The Heat* (2013), starring Melissa McCarthy as a foul-mouthed Boston cop and Sandra Bullock as an uptight FBI agent. *The Heat* earned a whopping $40 million on its opening weekend and grossed well over $150 million in total. While *The Heat* is primarily a comedy, it does demonstrate the possibility of profitable female/female action films.

While female-only teams or female/female partnerships have been rarer in action narratives, and have been used primarily for comedic effect, the few instances of their success helps negate the belief that strong women need to rely on men. When female characters are depicted relying primarily on each other, it provides a wish-fulfilling parable of cooperative feminist practices. Carol Dole (2001), in her insightful analysis of female lawmen in 1980s and 1990s films, charts both the positive elements and the potential pitfalls of strong female characters working together. Dole identifies a common narrative strategy of "splitting" used with action heroines. Important intellectual and physical skills are divided or "split" between protagonists who need to work together to solve the crime or find the serial killer, such as the combined efforts and insights of Clarice Starling (Jodie Foster) and Hannibal Lecter (Anthony Hopkins) in the prototypical strong heroine film *The Silence of the Lambs* (1991). Dole's example of the 1995 film *Copycat*, starring Sigourney Weaver as criminal profiler Dr. Helen Hudson and Holly Hunter as detective M. J. Monahan, illustrates the strengths and weaknesses that can occur with female pairings. Hudson is an expert on serial killers but is extremely agoraphobic due to a horrific attack she was subjected to in the past; Monahan is a strong-willed cop who struggles against a sexist police force. The two women have to combine their distinct skills to apprehend a copycat killer who is targeting Hudson. The women's individual areas of expertise work well together and they are ultimately successful in defeating the killer. But the splitting of skills undermines the heroic status of each of them. As Dole argues:

> The teaming of two women not only provides them an occasion to conquer through cooperation but also allows the film to limit the strength

of each. Though both women are admirable, M.J. is neither muscular nor especially insightful, and Helen suffers from agoraphobia and her resulting bitterness. By positioning Helen as potential victim in a horror plot, the film invites the viewer to contemplate its hero's vulnerability as well as her strength. (2001, 91)

Where Hawksian Professionalism, at its most optimistic, validates the individual strengths and contributions of each participant, Dole's conception of splitting stresses a potentially more pessimistic viewpoint. With essential skills divided between different female protagonists, there is an implication that it takes two or more women to equal the heroic status of a single male like Jason Bourne or James Bond. Of course, the accusation that male partners like Starsky and Hutch, Tango and Cash, or Riggs and Murtaugh are somehow each less heroic because they work best together does not occur. Male heroes are assumed to be fully competent in their own right, whereas female characters face a presumption of lack.

PARTNERS: "SHE'S ARMED. HE'S DANGEROUS."

One area where contemporary action heroines do thrive, particularly on television, is in pairings with male partners. Since the mid-1990s, male/female law enforcement pairings have been very popular in prime time: *The X-Files, Castle, Chuck, Bones, CSI: NY, Law & Order: SVU, Elementary, King & Maxwell, The Killing, The Bridge, The Mentalist, In Plain Sight, Vexed, Fringe, Perception, Broadchurch* (2013–current), *Shetland,* and *Mayday*. Male/female detective partnerships have been successful in the past, from the landmark *The Thin Man* movies about Nick and Nora Charles in the 1930s to *Hart to Hart, Remington Steele,* and *Moonlighting* in the 1980s, but the proliferation of male/female partnerships has developed into a full-blown subgenre in contemporary popular culture. The more recent type of male/female crime-solving partnership allows the women to be full and relatively equal participants in the adventure and is a logical evolution of the buddy-cop genre that dominated detective television in the 1970s and 1980s, and action-oriented feature films in the 1980s and 1990s. The odd-couple premise so crucial to buddy-cop narratives, and repeated in male/female partnerships, is made explicit in promotions like the second season advertisements for *Castle* wherein the pair are pictured at a crime scene, with Kate Beckett (Stanic Kata) crouching seriously over a chalk outline of a body while Richard Castle (Nathan Fillion) smugly signs autographs for fans behind the yellow police tape. The tag line simply reads: "She's armed. He's dangerous." This odd-couple cliché is crucial for understanding the role of action heroines partnered with men in relation to the buddy-cop genre, but it also indicates a crossing with the more female friendly genre of romantic comedy. Though romance and/or romantic tensions are not essential to modern male/female partnerships, it is a common feature and allows the pairings to address love and sexuality as part of the action heroine's persona in a direct, yet formulaic, manner.

The buddy-cop genre, made popular by films like *48 Hours*, *Lethal Weapon*, *Red Heat*, *Bad Boys*, *Black Rain*, *Rising Sun*, *The Last Boy Scout*, *Tango and Cash*, *The Hard Way*, and countless other movies, follows a basic narrative formula. Two men, at least one of which is some type of law enforcement officer, are forced into an uneasy partnership in order to defeat a ruthless villain. The men are always mismatched personalities: one is by-the-book, the other a wildcard; one a family man, the other a roguish bachelor; one a neat freak, the other a slob; one a planner, the other impulsive; and so on. In most cases, the superficial personality differences are mirrored by racial and/or national differences. One of the most common conventions during the genre's heyday was the pairing of a white American cop with some type of "Other," typically a black or foreign partner. It was not until the *Bad Boys* series that a buddy-cop film featured two African American leads, and then the *Rush Hour* series united an African American and Asian lead. Still, both the *Bad Boys* and *Rush Hour* films maintained the odd-couple differences between the partners. The partners' overcoming personal differences is just as crucial a part of the formula as is defeating the bad guys. The partners may resent each other at first, but they learn to appreciate the other person's worldview—in other words, they learn to be buddies. By the end of the film, not only is the pair victorious, but each of the partners is also better off for the lessons provided by their new friendship. The buddy-cop genre is so clichéd after thirty years of overexposure that parodies (like *Showtime* [2002], *Starsky and Hutch* [2004], *Hot Fuzz* [2007], *The Other Guys* [2010], *Cop Out* [2010], and *The Heat* [2013]) are more common now than serious buddy movies.

The cultural appeal of buddy-cop movies is not complicated. The odd-couple partners learning to work together to defeat a greater evil is an example of what Robert B. Ray (1985) identifies as one of the central premises of American cinema, the magical resolution of competing cultural beliefs. Clearly analogous to the buddy-cop genre is Ray's description of requiring the union of two diametrically opposed characters: "the outlaw hero and the official hero." Though speaking in broad terms, Ray's description of the two contrasting hero types encapsulates the differences between the buddy-cops:

Embodied in the adventurer, explorer, gunfighter, wanderer, and loner, the outlaw hero stood for that part of the American imagination valuing self-determination and freedom from entanglements. By contrast, the official hero, normally portrayed as a teacher, lawyer, politician, farmer, or family man, represented the American belief in collective action, and the objective legal process that superseded private notions of right and wrong. (Ray 1985, 59)

By overcoming their differences (whether procedural, racial, or national), the buddy-cops—one outlaw hero, one official hero—embody a distinctly American belief that despite our differences we can come together for noble purposes. United we stand, divided we fall. Thus buddy-cop films exemplified a finding of common ground between reckless, suicidal cops and responsible family cops (*Lethal Weapon*), between fast-talking convicts and tough, world-weary detectives (*48 Hours*), between strict Russian police officers and boorish Chicago cops (*Red Heat*). In a less literal sense, buddy-cop films also suggested a reconciliation between white and black, Republican and Democrat, rugged individualism and communal responsibility.

As the buddy-cop genre naturally evolved, it slowly introduced female characters as the Other partner for the nominal male lead in a variety of ways. In some cases, the women were brought into the narrative as sidekicks/romantic interests, typically an amateur who gets caught up in trying to help the male police officer or government agent. Earlier action films like *Commando*, *Speed*, *True Lies*, *Eraser*, *Fair Game*, and *Broken Arrow*, as well as more recent action movies like *The Bourne Identity*, *Knight and Day*, and *The Killers*, all allow amateur women to partner up with exceptional male heroes. Yvonne Tasker points out that the female sidekick is similar to the buddy role but is also crucially different. "The distinction, though difficult to draw precisely," Tasker (1998) argues, "lies within the extent to which the film emphasizes hierarchies of knowledge and skill: the relationship between two cop partners, however hierarchical is more equal than that of the professional and the amateur in need of protection" (74). The amateur female sidekick also served the function of romantic prize for the hero as the two unequal partners usually fall in love over the course of their adventure. Another means used to incorporate women into the buddy-cop genre, without the implications of romance, is through the trope of an older male mentor and a younger female protégé. Interestingly, as Philippa Gates observes, many of these films cast a young white woman as the Other to the more central black male lead. In action-thriller movies like *The Pelican Brief* (1993), *Kiss the Girls* (1997), *The*

Bone Collector (1999), and *Along Came a Spider* (2001), the white male hero is displaced as part of the biracial buddy-cop narrative altogether. The pairing of an older black male and a younger white female in these crime dramas was a welcome diversification that illustrated that heroes did not always need to be white men. Unfortunately, these pairings can also be understood to imply that neither the black male nor the white women were heroic enough on their own to save the day. Even in its absence, the assumed white male heroic preeminence may be reinforced. Though attractive young women are part of these black male/white female pairings, these films tend to deny the fulfillment of any romantic attraction by minimalizing the black male's sexual presence. In these films, the women learn how to investigate under the male's tutelage, and take equal part in the action when needed. The women actively strive to avoid the predicament of being a damsel in distress. Another cliché utilized in action films to incorporate female characters is what Holly Hassel (2008) refers to as the "babe scientist" who serves as a "romantic interest or buddy, or a combination of the two" (191). The young and sexy female scientists in films like *The Relic* (1997), *The Peacemaker* (1997), *The Mummy* (1999), *Bats* (1999), and *I, Robot* (2004) explain complex plot devices and help the hero achieve his goals. "As such," Hassel notes, "she appears to have equal narrative significance to her male counterpart" (90). Unfortunately, the authority granted female characters with PhDs is really a chimera as the films typically show her as "too bookish" and ultimately she needs to be saved by the more impulsive hero who survives on gut instincts.

While most of these early experiments with male/female pairings in action narratives portray the women as less-than-equal partners, more recent efforts have achieved a greater degree of parity. For example, on *Law & Order: SVU* (1999–current) both Olivia Benson (Mariska Hargitay) and Elliot Stabler (Christopher Meloni) are NYPD detectives, and on *King & Maxwell* (2013–current) both Sean King (Jon Tenney) and Michelle Maxwell (Rebecca Romijn) are former Secret Service agents turned private security. Moreover, in many of the current male/female partnerships, the woman is cast as the more professional agent of law enforcement. In *The Killing*, Sarah Linden (Mireille Enos) is the grizzled homicide veteran and Stephen Holder (Joel Kinnaman) is the rookie transfer; in *The Mentalist* (also a team show), the two leads are California Bureau of Investigation senior agent Teresa Lisbon (Robin Tunney) and the consulting con man Patrick Jane (Simon Baker); in *Chuck*, Sarah Walker (Yvonne Strahovski) is a top CIA agent and Chuck Bartowski (Zachary Levi) is a geeky store clerk. The long-running and highly rated program *Castle* is perhaps the best example of this tendency for male/female partnerships to cast the woman as the primary agent of official law enforcement.

Castle focuses on the crime-solving relationship of New York homicide detective Kate Beckett and best-selling crime novelist Richard Castle, who tags along on her cases under the pretense of conducting research. She is serious and tough, and he is immature and intuitive, but they work together to solve complicated murders. As a duo, Beckett and Castle are extremely effective and equal partners but Beckett has the upper hand in their relationship because she is the legally sanctioned detective. Still, even in this contemporary type of male/female partnership, the woman's status risks being compromised in favor of privileging the man's contribution. As an amateur sleuth, Castle is as useful as the professionally trained veteran Beckett, the same as on *Chuck* and *The Mentalist*. In all three of these shows, the men are the more intuitive and emotional (feminized) characters—yet it is this unprofessional quality that usually wins the day or solves the crime. And, after all, the shows are named for the male partners. Thankfully, rare exceptions to this formula do exist, such as on *Bones*, with the male being FBI Special Agent Seeley Booth (David Boreanaz) and the woman the consulting forensic anthropologist Dr. Temperance "Bones" Brennan (Emily Deschanel). *Bones* reverses the roles and even the gender of the character for whom the show is named.

The gradual shifting of female characters from the margins to the shared center of action narratives is crucial to counteracting the barely disguised homoeroticism of the buddy-cop genre. The basic formula shared by every male/male buddy story revolves around their relationship, as they grow emotionally and physically closer over the course of their adventures. The deflective presence of wives and girlfriends as background characters, and/or homophobic jokes, are overshadowed by the homoerotic implications of the narrative. In fact, the buddy-cop formula is nearly identical to the popular, and more female-targeted genre of romantic comedies, or "romcoms," wherein a seemingly incompatible male/female pair are placed in an unusual situation, share adventures of some kind, and ultimately realize the other person is their perfect (romantic) match. As Celestino Deleyto (2003) summarizes in his discussion of contemporary reworkings of the genre: "a romantic comedy is still primarily conceived as a narrative in which a man and a woman . . . fall in love, discover that they have found their 'special person' and end up, if not always at the altar, at least promising each other eternal love" (168). Change the description from "a man and a woman" to "two men," and "eternal love" to "eternal allegiance," and you have the basic structure of the buddy-cop story. The close association of buddy-cop narratives and romcoms is alluded to by critics like Yvonne Tasker (1993), who points out that in the *Lethal Weapon* films "a range of differences are established between the two (Riggs and Murtaugh), the unlikely combination which works out is a convention of both the buddy movie and the romance" (45), and Cynthia J. Fuchs (1993) in her discussion of the biracial aspects of the genre when she notes that "the secrecy of masculine intimacy and vulnerability is sustained in these films by the 'marriage' of racial others" (203). More recently, some television series do not even try to deny their explicit homoeroticism. The long-running program *White Collar* (2009–current), which teams an FBI agent with a former con man, has a notable number of emotional scenes between the two men, and the short-lived *Common Law* (2012–2013) featured two arguing partners who are ordered to take marriage counseling to help their working relationship. Appropriately, *Common Law*'s tag line was: "It's like marriage. Only with bullets." Buddy-cop stories may have more explosions, fistfights, and car chases, while romcoms have more humorous misunderstandings and public declarations of love, but both genres are about seemingly mismatched individuals who become intimately attached to each other, with each becoming a happier, more complete person because of the relationship. The inclusion of modern action heroines as partners for male characters diffuses the homoerotic implications of the genre through a heterosexualizing of the "buddies." The resulting slippage between buddy-cop and romcom formulas allows action narratives to address conventional and unconventional ideas about romance, sex, and gender relations.

In her overview of women in various action roles in 1990s film, Yvonne Tasker (1998) insightfully points out some of the problems raised by the shift in action movies from male/male to male/female pairings:

> Such narratives offer a variant on the mismatched male partnership theme which serves to make explicit the romantic/sexual aspects of that relationship within a heterosexual context. Yet in highlighting this aspect of "partnership," the male/female action narratives come across the "problem" of (hetero) sex. The sparks which fly when male buddies banter with one another become more transparently sexual when transposed onto the male/female pair. And if the convention of the male buddy pairing is that the two will *not* kiss—though they may joke about it incessantly, or perhaps exchange tender glances, as in the *Lethal Weapon* films—it is almost inevitable that the male/female buddy pair *will* end up in an embrace. The foregrounding of romantic/sexual possibilities may be a "problem" since it potentially halts the action and generates vulnerability . . . such moments have the additional effect of "exposing" the homosexual as well as the homosocial aspects of male buddy relations, even as the contrast is maintained. . . . this movement serves at a narrative level to reaffirm the idea that women are a

disruptive force who somehow bring sexuality into the (male) world of work. (74–75)

However, as the instances of male/female pairings have increased and the formula has developed, generic expectations have shifted, as has the manner of depicting female characters in male-dominated work places such as law enforcement. Similarly, the increasingly recognizable overlap between male/female "partnerships" and romantic expectations means that the more emotional moments do not detract from the central story as much as enhance it in many of the contemporary examples.

In fact, in any Hollywood production featuring relatively equal male and female leads, audiences expect some romantic tensions, if not a full-blown love story. The generic prospects of romance are so strong that the exceptions (when beautiful and available male/female leads do not engage in romance) are notable, and somewhat frustrating to audiences. In their introductory film studies text, Lehman and Luhr (2008) observe that it is rare when films like *A Few Good Men* (1992) thwart romantic couplings despite focusing on a close working relationship between characters portrayed by the likes of Tom Cruise and Demi Moore (31). When male and female characters are shown together in tense situations and becoming increasingly vulnerable with one another, the specter of romance is bound to develop. As the Tasker quotation above declares: "it is almost inevitable that the male/female buddy pair *will* end up in an embrace." The familiar trope of "will-they-won't-they" couples on television attests to audience's generic expectations and our cultural preoccupation with (heterosexual) romantic culmination as an ultimate goal, a modern take on the "happily ever after" promised in fairy tales. That many of these "will-they-won't-they" couples come from the area of action/detective series (e.g., *Remington Steele, Moonlighting, The X-Files, Bones, Castle*) only reinforces the slippage between buddy and romance formulae. As thousands of slash fiction stories and "shippers" (relationship-focused fans) attest, viewers desire a logical romantic culmination. That all five of these "will-they-won't-they" detective pairings given as examples ended up in romantic couplings after years of teasing audiences only confirms viewers' expectations and provides a sense of logical character progression.

While earlier inclusions of women in traditionally male-centered action and/or detective narratives may have been depicted as sexually disruptive, versions in the twenty-first century of male/female partnerships treat a female presence very differently. For the most part, female police officers, detectives, FBI, CIA, Homeland Security agents, and so on are treated as comparatively equal with their male colleagues. If the heroine's gender is an issue, the narratives typically address it less as "disruptive sexuality" and more as a reflection of the outdated misogynistic beliefs of older or bullheaded male officers. In the storylines that address gender-based discrimination, the central female ultimately proves her superior abilities and begrudgingly wins over even the most sexist of detractors. On *The Closer* (2005–2012), for example, Deputy LAPD Police Chief in Charge of Homicide Brenda Johnson (Kyra Sedgwick) is initially dismissed by her all-male team of investigators because she appears to be a sweet and somewhat flighty Southern belle. But in each episode, and over the course of the entire series, even the most bitter and close-minded of her male colleagues come to recognize her superb skills as an investigator and interrogator, as she brilliantly solves case after case. Likewise, the short-lived American version of *Prime Suspect* (2011–2012) featured NYPD Detective Jane Timoney (Maria Bello) as a new addition to the all-male homicide squad that initially resents her intrusion to their "boys club" because they mistakenly assume that she slept her way into the position and that she was too opportunistic about making a play for the job after one of the men in the department dies. But, like Brenda Johnson, Jane Timoney confronts the sexism of her workplace head-on, eventually gaining their support and trust because she is excellent at her job.

For the most part, action television programs and movies featuring male/female partners address female sexuality not as disruptive or threatening to the men; instead, the adherence to conventions of romantic comedy shifts the gendered focus onto the development of a loving relationship. The professional and personal relationship between Richard Castle and Kate Beckett on *Castle* is a clear example of the way that the romantic comedy formula overrides the buddy-cop narrative with male/female partners. *Castle* is classified as a detective series, but like so many other narratives featuring male/female partners, it also utilizes many of the conventions found in romcoms. Steve Neale (1992), in his discussion of the different historical cycles of romantic comedies, identifies key conventions found in New Romances (from the mid-1980s on) and their ideological significance in perpetuating romantic exemplars of coupledom. Some of the important romantic comedy conventions followed by *Castle* include the "meet cute," the wrong partner(s), unspoken feelings, personal confidants, moments of playfulness, declarations of love, and most importantly, a learning process. The "meet cute" is a common narrative device for introducing prospective lovers in a unique manner that indicates their relationship is a matter of destiny. For example, at the onset of the series Castle and Beckett are brought together because a serial killer is reenacting murder scenes described in Castle's best-selling mystery novels. It may be a "meet cute" over dead bodies, but the comedic overtones of the

Fig. 2.3. He is the amateur and she is the detective, but Castle and Beckett are partners in crime-solving and in romance.

series make it clear that it is a "meet cute" nonetheless. Beckett resents Castle's involvement in the investigation and his irresponsible demeanor, but the two work together well enough to catch the killer. After this initial case, Castle continues tagging along with the NYPD homicide team lead by Beckett, in small part because he is using her as the basis for his new book series, and in large part because there is an obvious attraction between them. For years, the two leads flirt back and forth but never advance their relationship because they are scared to mess up their partnership and/or because one or the other of them is dating someone else. When Castle is available, Beckett is dating a doctor, another detective, or her old partner. When Beckett is available, Castle is dating an actress, his publicist, a stewardess, or his ex-wife. These relationships never amount to much because they are what Neale describes as "wrong partners": "a would-be suitor or a possible but unsuitable partner for one or other of the members of the couple" (289). These potential partners are wrong or unsuitable because they represent undesirable traits and they cannot provide what audiences understand that the member of the main couple really needs. Similarly, other members of the squad act as confidantes for both Castle's and Beckett's burgeoning romantic feelings. There are also numerous moments over the first five years of the series in which one or the other of the partners misses the opportunity to declare his or her feelings. Ultimately, at the end of season five and after Beckett is nearly killed, the two declare their love for each other.

The two intertwined romantic comedy conventions of "playfulness" and "a learning process" are the most significant for understanding how action heroines function similarly—but also very differently—in buddy-cop pairings. Neale describes the two conventions as "elements which contain both ideological and formal ingredients, and which perform both ideological and formal functions" (290). In romantic comedies, these conventions are formal plot devices that move the story forward and ideologically reinforce the belief in true love, that the man and woman are soul mates who complete each other. In romance, moments of playfulness are typically lighthearted montages of time spent exploring a city, playing dress up, having snowball fights, and so on. While playful comedic moments do occur in male/female buddy-cop pairings, the most direct version of the couple's "play" is their adventure of pursuing a killer. There are always moments of fun, playful teasing, and flirting woven in alongside moments of action, adventure, and violence. As the male/female partners play and work seamlessly together, they also learn about each other, and more importantly, about themselves. Castle learns to be more serious and responsible; Beckett learns to be less intense and more emotionally available. "There is a degree to which the learning process is mutual," Neale writes, "and to which the members of the couple learn from, and teach, one another" (293). Thus, Castle and Beckett, like many other male/female partners in action and detective narratives, achieve what Neale describes as romantic comedy's ideal of an "equal partnership." Castle and Beckett repeatedly save each other from physical dangers, but they also, like the romantic comedy couple, save each other from the emotional dangers of being alone or having unfulfilling lives.

The romantic possibilities explored by most contemporary male/female investigative pairings shifts the narrative focus away from characterizing the female detective's sexuality as disruptive or aberrant. The possible burgeoning romance between the relatively equal male and female heroic leads does not depict her sexuality as any more disruptive than his sexuality; in fact, their mutual attraction strengthens their professional relationship. Although many film and television narratives which focus on female detectives without male partners make the former's sexuality an object of investigation and punish her for it, the male/female partnered stories depict ideal coupledom and an equal partnership as the overarching theme. In earlier films like *The Accused* (1988), *Blue Steel* (1989), *Impulse* (1990), *Bodily Harm* (1995), and *Twisted* (2004), the female investigator's sexual desires and carnal history are as much the subject matter of the films as is the central crime. As Yvonne Tasker (1998) has written, these types of mysteries "all involve an exploration of the sexuality of the female investigators alongside, and complexly intertwined with, the central case itself" (93). The lone female investigator in these types of films is often sexually involved, or at least suspected of being sexually attracted to, the killer. Her sexuality thus becomes a plot point needing to be exposed and sometimes punished. In her discussion of female profilers in feature films and television series, Lindsay Steenberg (2011) argues that "where the male profiler is doubled with the killer and in danger of becoming *like* him, the female profiler is positioned as being dangerously attracted *to* the killer" (227). Moreover, Steenberg points out that female profilers like Illeana Scott (Angelina Jolie) in *Taking Lives* (2004) are professionally diminished because her "credibility and expertise are not only questioned as a result of her sexual(ized) relationship with the serial killer, but as a result of her sexuality itself" (231). But in the contemporary male/female pairings, the woman's sexuality is not given prominence, even though the characters are portrayed by conventionally beautiful young actresses. It is not the female protagonist's sexual past or a misguided attraction to the killer that is investigated; instead, it is her (and his) sexual desires and appropriate romantic attraction to the partner that is investigated.

The romantic leanings of most male/female pairings explore what a mature and fulfilling relationship of equals is like, rather than just a lurid consideration of female sexuality. Yes, the partners must find each other physically attractive, but they also must be intellectual equals, comforting of each other, patient with one another, and committed to the relationship. Romance flourishes over time out of a mutual respect and caring for each other that goes beyond an immediate sexual attraction. And, like the romantic comedy that celebrates the culmination of a perfect, loving union, male/female partnerships can, and often do, result in committed romantic relationships. As perhaps should be expected, detective and action television series that explicitly overlap with romantic comedy, such as *Remington Steele*, *Moonlighting*, *Chuck*, *Bones*, and *Castle*, go as far as seeing the couple enter into marriage. The ideal professional and romantic partnership is realized in the couple's public declaration of commitment. The marriages usually occur near the end of a series' run as an attempt to regain flagging viewership; even so, it is still a logical resolution of romantic longings and a partnership of equals.

Marriage is treated in most narratives (romantic, action, and/or detective) as a culmination of the partners finding their special person, the one who, to paraphrase *Jerry Maguire* (1997), "completes" them. It is also a cultural symbol of our presumptions about modern "happily ever afters." Very few narratives, particularly those in the area of action, are able to maintain interesting adventures once the tension of romantic possibilities is resolved. For all the romance involved in action and detective narratives, there are only a few instances of successful married male/female partners working together to fight crime. *The Thin Man* series of movies, as well as television programs like *McMillan & Wife* (1971–1977) and *Hart to Hart* (1979–1984), are among the exceptions that prove the rule that adventure seems to be reserved for couples who are courting not married. The failure of J. J. Abrams's television series *Undercovers* (2010), about a husband and wife who are reactivated as CIA agents, illustrates the difficulty of maintaining the romantic tensions that arise from dangerous adventures if the couple is already fully committed to each other. In the rare instances when action narratives successfully feature an already married male/female pairing, the marriage is initially depicted as failing and in need of excitement so the couple can remember why they are right for each other. For example, in *True Lies* (1994) Helen Tasker (Jamie Lee Curtis) is a bored middle-class wife desperate enough for adventure that she contemplates having an affair; her husband, Harry Tasker (Arnold Schwarzenegger), is secretly a James Bond-like super-spy. When Helen unwittingly gets involved in one of Harry's adventures, they each learn how valuable and exciting the other is, and the passion of their marriage is rekindled when Helen becomes Harry's professional as well as marital partner. Yvonne Tasker (1998) describes the film as a clear message about the close ties needed at multiple levels to achieve a satisfying union: "In *True Lies* it is not so much that the marriage overcomes the buddy relationship, but that Harry and Helen must *become buddies*. Harry and Helen are produced as a couple in terms of the homosocial codes of the buddy partnership . . . and the heterosexual codes of marriage" (78). The idealized view of coupledom achieved through the courtship of male/female partners as equals at all levels of the relationship is carried over into a lesson about maintaining the idyllic couple in marriage as both buddies and lovers.

A similar message is repeated in the 2005 film *Mr. & Mrs. Smith*, starring real-life couple Brad Pitt and Angelina Jolie as John and Jane Smith. In this instance, the couple is on more equal footing professionally because they are both superb assassins, though initially neither knows the other is. On the surface, John and Jane are the picture of an upper-middle-class marriage, with a beautiful home in the suburbs, high-paying (cover) careers, and a comfortable, albeit boring, daily routine. Yet they are both increasingly dissatisfied with the mundane façade of their marriage. Kord and Krimmer (2011) discuss *Mr. & Mrs. Smith* as an insightful critique of middle-class marital angst and frustration because the characters have become smothered by the ordinariness of their attempts to live according to the scripts of conventional marriage: "John and Jane struggle with the typical problems of a marriage that longs for a union of equals but remains stuck in traditional gender stereotypes and the stifling routines of suburban life" (191). Like the Taskers in *True Lies*, the Smiths entered into marriage under false pretenses, without being completely open and honest with each other about who they are and what they do for a living—that is, without being the true equals they long to be. When the

Smiths discover the truth about one another, they immediately assume the other is an enemy agent out to kill the other, and so they spend much of the film trying to kill each other. When their respective agencies decide that they must each be a traitor for marrying an enemy, they are both targeted for termination and have to work together to stay alive. It is only when John and Jane are forced to align that they begin to take pleasure in each other's lethal skills, thereby reigniting the passion of their romantic relationship. Fighting off common enemies, the Smiths become buddies and lovers—equal partners in every sense.

While the equality of these male/female partners is a positive development in the depiction of smart, strong, and resourceful women in action and detective narratives, the assumption that the equality of a professional relationship must be accompanied by a romantic relationship is troubling. The heteronormative imperative that Hollywood so often follows, and viewers expect, when men and women are paired together conveys a relatively conservative message. Professional success may be achieved—but real happiness still resides in romantic coupledom. The implication that men and women working together as equals must result in a romantic attraction undermines the possibility that women can merely be incredibly good at their heroic jobs and find enough satisfaction on a professional level. While each individual film or television series may simply be attempting to satisfy viewers' desire to experience a happy ending for the pair, taken as a repeated convention this romantic trope may only be reinforcing or shaping cultural perceptions of romance as the ultimate end game for women. Very few male/female pairings resist romantic culmination. Most famously, *The X-Files* kept Mulder and Scully's relationship purely professional, but they are really the exception that proves the rule that romance trumps adventure. Depictions of men and women as truly equal in these masculine genres are a progressive development in the depiction of action heroines in popular culture. But even more progressive will be narratives that clarify that men and women can work together as equals without romance becoming a requisite ending.

3
ETHNICITY AND NEW ACTION HEROINES

THE CURRENT SUCCESS OF ACTION HEROINES OWES A GREAT DEAL TO A DIverse range of historical precedents in popular culture, including the femme fatale of film noir, female detectives, and private eyes on television, comic book superheroines, and hard-boiled paperback heroines. But the clearest, and perhaps most important, developmental phase in the history of Hollywood action heroines was the radical image of strong women that occurred during the 1970s in B-level Blaxploitation and kung fu films. African American heroines in films like *Coffy* (1973), *Cleopatra Jones* (1973), and *Foxy Brown* (1974), and Asian heroines in such movies as *Golden Swallow* (1968), *Lady Whirlwind* (1972), and *The Tournament* (1974), paved the way for future generations of kick-ass women. Women of color in Blaxploitation and kung fu films, and to a lesser extent the spitfire stereotype of Latina women in earlier Westerns and 1960s and '70s Mexican B-movies, established many of the narrative and character conventions that would develop into the modern Hollywood action heroine. Given the importance that strong cinematic women of color have had in creating and popularizing action heroines, it is somewhat surprising how predominantly white the current wave of heroines is, and how critical discussions often overlook the historical importance ethnicity has played in the development of strong female characters. "Unfortunately," Chris Holmlund notes, "this amnesia regarding earlier female figures hampers appraisals of today's action trends: for the most part, attention remains focused on white women" (2005, 97). The oft-cited quotation from *Aliens* (1986), one of the foundational action heroine films, when Pvt. Vasquez (Jenette Goldstein) asks: "Who is Snow White?" This is in reference to the heroine, Ellen Ripley (Sigourney Weaver), and is meant to be dismissive of her blandness and apparent weakness. Of course, the film shows us just how strong a character Ripley is despite, or perhaps because, of her whiteness. Coincidentally, by 2012 the character of Snow White is herself turned into an action heroine in *Snow White and the Huntsman*. White actresses like Angelina Jolie, Jennifer

Lawrence, Kate Beckinsale, Uma Thurman, Milla Jovovich, and Scarlett Johansson tend to dominate the action genre while ethnically identified actresses are, for the most part, relegated to the margins as helpers or villains. As Lisa Purse (2011a) observes in her discussion of race in modern action films, while African American men have increasingly gained access to lead roles, "African American women are notoriously absent from action cinema" (116). Only a few action films have featured African American women in the past twenty years, such as Halle Berry's roles in the *X-Men* films (2000, 2003, 2006, 2014) and *Catwoman* (2004) or Jada Pinkett Smith in the final two *Matrix* movies (both 2003). Asian women have managed to maintain a small foothold in the action market primarily due to the Hong Kong film industry, while Latina heroines have begun to appear only sporadically.

Quentin Tarantino's *Kill Bill* (2003) employs the director's trademark style of directly referencing earlier, often low-budget films which influenced his approach to various genres. In *Kill Bill*, Tarantino's landmark action heroine, known only in this film as the Bride (Uma Thurman), alludes to the historical heroines of Blaxploitation and kung fu movies as she seeks revenge on the first two members of the Deadly Viper Assassination Squad who betrayed her and left her for dead. The Bride's first epic battle is with the African American character Vernita Green (Vivica A. Fox), code-named "Copperhead." Green may be a suburban mother now, but her swagger and attitude align her with the heroines of Blaxploitation. As Green angrily tells the Bride, who used to go by the title of "Black Mamba": "Black Mamba! I shoulda been motherfuckin Black Mamba!" After killing Green, the Bride travels to Tokyo to confront her next target, O-Ren Ishii (Lucy Liu). In the infamous House of Blue Leaves scene, the Bride brutally dispatches dozens of Yakuza gang members with her sword before facing down O-Ren herself. O-Ren ridicules the Bride: "Silly Caucasian girl likes to play with Samurai swords." But the Bride slices the top of O-Ren's head off before heading out for further revenge. In his discussion of Hollywood fantasies in modern kung fu films, Sean M. Tierney (2006) uses the Bride's defeat of O-Ren as an example of popular cinema reinforcing a conception of whiteness as innately superior: "Narrative constructions that make recurrent, implicit assignments of superiority and inferiority along ethnic lines are examples of how White superiority is inscribed, reinforced and perpetuated through film. The ability of the White practitioner to defeat Asians, using an Asian skill, in Asia, propagates the theme of ubiquitous, even inevitable White supremacy of global proportions" (614). In *Kill Bill*, the white heroine demonstrates her superiority over both the lethal black and Asian woman. In these two scenes, the white action heroine addresses and defeats the traditional strong women associated with both Blaxploitation and kung fu films. It is tempting to read *Kill Bill* as symbolic of the modern white action heroine as displacing or surpassing active women of color in a larger sense. But a few ethnically identified women have still managed to take center stage in their own action narratives. What is perhaps more interesting, though unintentional, regarding race in these two *Kill Bill* scenes is the fact that the actresses chosen to represent black and Asian are both reportedly of mixed racial heritage. Vivica A. Fox is referred to as African American and Native American, while Lucy Liu is rumored to be biracial and often plays characters who are part Chinese and part white, such as O-Ren Ishii or Alex Munday in the *Charlie's Angels* films (2000, 2003). When non-white women appear as action heroines in modern Hollywood, they are almost always portrayed by mixed race actresses.

The use of mixed race actresses in action film and television is becoming increasingly common with performers like the aforementioned Halle Berry, as well as Zoe Saladana (*Avatar* [2009], *Star Trek* [2009, 2013], *Colombiana* [2009], *Guardians of the Galaxy* [2014]), Maggie Q (*Mission: Impossible III* [2006], *Nikita* [2010–current], *Priest* [2011], *Divergent* [2014]), Jessica Alba (*Dark Angel* [2000–2002], *The Fantastic Four* [2005, 2007], *Machete* [2010], *Spy Kids 4* [2011]), Rosario Dawson (*Sin City* [2005], *Grind House* [2007]), Cameron Diaz (*Charlie's Angels* [2000, 2003], *Knight and Day* [2010]), Devon Aoki (*D.E.B.S.* [2004], *Sin City* [2005], *DOA* [2006]), Paula Patton (*Mission: Impossible: Ghost Protocol* [2011], *2 Guns* [2013]), Natassia Malthe (*Elektra* [2005], *Bloodrayne: The Third Reich* [2011]), Kelly Hu (*X2* [2003], *Arrow* [2012–current]), Thandie Newton (*Mission: Impossible 2* [2000], *Rogue* [2013–current]), Annie Ilonzeh (*Charlie's Angels* [2011], *Arrow* [2012–current]), and Gugu Mbantha-Raw (*MI-5* [2006], *Undercovers* [2010–11]). Even Lynda Carter, who so perfectly embodied Wonder Woman in the 1970s as an icon of strong American womanhood, is a racial mix of white and Latina. But while Carter can be understood as effectively passing for white, as embodying an icon of ideal white femininity, the current wave of mixed race actresses function in direct opposition to the idea of passing for white. With the possible exception of Cameron Diaz, the rest of the actresses bear physical markers of non-white ethnicity, and are marketed as non-white performers. Their value as mixed race women is not perceived as their ability to pass, but in being able to signify a tempered exotic Otherness. The current use of mixed race actresses as an alternative to specifically identifiable ethnicities reflects a shift in the conception of race itself in contemporary Western culture. By featuring actresses of mixed racial identities as heroines, the action genre is able to both utilize ethnic stereotypes about women and to sidestep other racial issues, such as discrimination or miscegenation. This chapter explores how the use of mixed race actresses as action heroines both challenges and reinforces genre conventions about ethnicity and sexuality, ultimately using racial indeterminacy as a means to capitalize on the shifting racial identities of viewers and to literally spice up the heroine's image without sacrificing white womanhood as a cultural ideal.

Until recently, the modern action genre has been a definitively masculine domain, and the default heroes (embodied by iconic actors like Sylvester Stallone, Arnold Schwarzenegger, Mel Gibson, Bruce Willis, and Chuck Norris) have been almost exclusively white. Characters of color, particularly African American ones, remained on the periphery or served as the "racial other" or "black helper" (Tasker 1993, 36) in landmark buddy-cop films like *48 Hrs.* (1982), *Lethal Weapon* (1987), *Die Hard* (1988), and *The Last Boy Scout* (1991). In the 1980s and 1990s, only a select few African American actors—including Eddie Murphy, Wesley Snipes, and Will Smith—were able to transition from playing supporting partners to the central lead. In more recent years, as the action genre has developed and as cultural perceptions about ethnicity have shifted, several mixed race actors, such as Keanu Reeves, Vin Diesel, and Dwayne Johnson, have become major action stars. As Mary Beltran and Camilla Fojas note in their introduction to the anthology *Mixed Race Hollywood* (2008): "Multiracial action heroes in fact have become a trend in their own right. Such figures often continue to serve as ethnic enigmas but are also now associated with notions of cultural mastery and other positive characteristics" (11). The popularity of mixed race action stars like Reeves, Diesel, and Johnson in such blockbuster films as *The Matrix* series (1999, 2003, 2003), the *Riddick* series (2000, 2004, 2013), and *The Fast and the Furious* series (2001, 2003, 2006, 2009, 2011, 2013, 2015) is garnering academic attention (see Beltran 2005 and 2013, Nishime 2008, Park 2008, Knee 2008, Greven 2009), and these racially ambiguous male action stars have also created a space for mixed race action heroines in contemporary film and television.

The increased visibility of mixed race actors and actresses reflects a growing cultural shift in the loosening borders of ethnic identities in Western cultures. The number of people in America who are mixed race has increased substantially since anti-miscegenation laws were struck down nationally in 1967 with the decision of *Loving v. Virginia*. By the 1990s, a period designated as a mini-baby boom of mixed race individuals, people of multiracial lineage were becoming far more common, visible, and less stigmatized than ever before. Novelist Danny Senna influentially described the trend as a dawn of a new "mulatto millennium," while others refer to it as "generation mix." The popular press even began referring to the trend as "multiracial chic," as models and actors with indistinct ethnic appearances became highly sought after. Beltran describes this shift as a "general popularity in Hollywood and U.S. popular culture since the 1990s for ethnically ambiguous looks. Mixed race actors and models in particular are being centrally featured in advertising and media productions, alongside ethnically inflected and 'multicultural' products and aesthetics. These trends have been prompted, among other catalysts, by increasing ethnic diversity and cultural curiosity in this country" (2008, 251). In addition to a trendy beauty aesthetic and a reflection of the changing ethnic makeup of audiences, mixed race performers function well for Hollywood as a means to include ethnic diversity on a superficial visual level, without completely forsaking the racial stereotyping that it has long employed as narrative shorthand for stock character types. In other words, the conventional stereotypes of black, Asian, and Latina women still inform how the characters are presented, but their status as mixed race heroines allows them to transcend racially restricted roles to a certain degree. While each of these three ethnicities—black, Asian, and Latina—continue to share characterizations as exotic female "Others" (see Brown 2011), they have also each been subject to differing stereotypes that have influenced the development of strong action heroines. The following case studies consider the action roles of three popular mixed race actresses who are generally aligned in their roles and in the press as black, Asian, and Latina. In grounding the discussion with specific action heroine roles embodied by Zoe Saldana, Maggie Q, and Jessica Alba, I want to illustrate how the histories of Blaxploitation, kung fu, and Hispanic spitfires continues to influence action heroines of color, and how their mixed race standing has tempered those stereotypical traditions.

BLAXPLOITATION MIXED WITH ZOE SALDANA

For a relatively short-lived film genre (lasting from roughly 1970 to 1975), Blaxploitation was incredibly pervasive and maintains a strong influence in American popular culture. The unprecedented success of Melvin Van Peebles's independently produced *Sweet Sweetback's Baadasssss Song!* (1971) was immediately followed by studio-backed Blaxploitation films like *Shaft* (1971), *Super Fly* (1972), *The Mack* (1973), *Black Caesar* (1973), *The Spook Who Sat by the Door* (1973), and *Three The Hard Way* (1974). Reflecting and capitalizing on the political and cultural unrest of the late 1960s and early 1970s, especially civil rights battles and Black Power movements, Blaxploitation films catered to black audiences by focusing on the violent struggles of African American protagonists in urban settings. Ed Guerrero describes Blaxploitation as "made possible by the rising political and social consciousness of Black people—taking the form of a broadly expressed Black Nationalist impulse at the end of the civil rights movement—which translated into a large Black audience thirsting to see their full humanity depicted on the commercial cinema screen" (1993, 69). Blaxploitation offered an unprecedented image of strong and cool black heroes, masters of their ghetto environments, usually resisting and overcoming white villains and corrupt police forces. Though the genre had more or less played itself out by the mid-1970s, the sixty or so films that make up the corpus of Blaxploitation were quickly and cheaply produced and distributed, flooding urban markets and making movie stars out of such black actors as Melvin Van Peebles, Fred Williamson, Jim Brown, Richard Roundtree, and Ron O'Neal. The male heroes of Blaxploitation were uniformly tough, streetwise urban warriors who could outfight and outshoot whoever they encountered. They embodied a black macho coolness, a character type dubbed "Superspade," in direct contrast to earlier passive or comedic racial stereotypes like the Uncle Tom, Stepin Fetchit, or the stoic and noble black man depicted most famously in the roles of the young Sidney Poitier. The Blaxploitation heroes were a funkier, racialized, street-level melding of James Bond, Dirty Harry, and Sam Spade, mingled together with stereotypes about black hypersexuality and political anger.

At its core, Blaxploitation—as with most action subgenres—was a masculine fantasy about a lone heroic male who can physically dominate other men and sexually dominate beautiful women. While the genre vividly challenged stereotypes of emasculated black masculinity, the bulk of the films simply reinforced characterizations of women, especially black women, as merely sexual objects. In order to bolster the image of a phallic black masculinity, women were depicted primarily as sexual conquests and routinely displayed with a lot of nudity. As Patricia Hill Collins argues, Blaxploitation "films such as *Shaft* and *Superfly* presented African American women as sexual props for the exploits of the Black male heroes" (2005, 124). Because the films were working within a culturally dominant patriarchal and heterosexist framework, the spectacular reversal of existing racial oppression via the black male hero was premised in large part on the depiction of female bodies at his disposal. The hypersexual depiction of women in these films also informed the wave of Blaxploitation features crafted around a central female protagonist. Inspired by the success of black male heroes, the low-budget industry cranked out a number of movies featuring strong women, including the previously mentioned *Cleopatra Jones*, *Coffy*, and *Foxy Brown*, as well as *T.N.T. Jackson* (1973), *Friday Foster* (1973), *Sugar Hill* (1974), *Lady Cocoa* (1975), and *Velvet Smooth* (1976). Even television got in on the trend with the short-lived series *Get Christie Love* (1974). Though a number of actresses appeared in these and other films, the most popular and visible among them were Tamara Dobson (who played Cleopatra Jones in the original film and its sequel, *Cleopatra Jones and the Casino of Gold* [1975]) and Pam Grier (who starred as Coffy, Foxy Brown, and numerous similar characters). Dobson and Grier achieved iconic status as powerful and beautiful black heroines; they maintain a cult following to this day. Likewise, as emblems of Blaxploitation femininity, Dobson and Grier have been the subjects of numerous scholarly considerations (see Brody 1999, Holmlund 2005, Sims 2006, Dunn 2008). Like their male predecessors, these heroines of Blaxploitation were cool, tough, and sexual, and they operated on the mean inner-city streets. These characters presented a version of angry, ass-kicking women that was unlike anything ever seen before in American films.

In her insightful analysis of Blaxploitation women and their nostalgic appeal for female viewers, Stephane Dunne describes this type of black action heroine as "a sexy, streetwise, tough woman who shows no fear, takes on powerful whites and men, and, according to the genre's expectations, wins" (2008, 3). Similarly, Schubart's description of the way Pam Grier was promoted in the press encapsulates the uniqueness of Blaxploitation heroines: "a sexy, aggressive, and cool super bitch, a bad mama who dished out violence in its most extreme forms: shooting, killing and castrating men; stabbing them with broken bottles, hair pins and metal hangers; hiding razor blades and guns in her high afro and serving lines like 'Have I bruised your masculinity?' Her film persona was based on aggression towards men and an unabashed exploitation of her body" (2007, 41). As both descriptions clearly imply, the Blaxploitation heroine's sexiness was as crucial a part of her persona as was her toughness. While the heroine was undeniably strong and independent, an incredible breakthrough for female roles, the extremely misogynistic visual depiction of women in Blaxploitation (and in exploitation films more generally) remained in place even when the central protagonist was female. The films still catered to a presumed male audience and found ample opportunities to reveal the women's naked and near-naked bodies. The visual emphasis on the sexual exploitation of the black heroines' bodies has meant that many critics scorn the potentially feminist and empowering aspects of these characters. Donald Bogle dismisses the films as "high flung male fantasy" (1973, 251), and Mark Reid sees them as simply "made to engage male fantasies," arguing "the penetrating male heterosexist gaze does more to disarm these heroines than their actions do to empower them" (1993, 88). While the erotic spectacle of Blaxploitation heroines is rather extreme, it is a continuation of the more general cultural desire and fear of strong female characters and the danger their sexuality is presumed to pose. Still, for many female viewers, the erotic spectacle did not undermine the message of empowerment. Just as feminists like Susan Douglas (1994) recall enjoying television programs like *Charlie's Angels* (1976–1981) and *Wonder Woman* (1975–1979), in spite of the shows' catering to a male gaze, many women were encouraged by the black action heroine's actions despite the gratuitous sex. As Sims speculates: "It is not unreasonable to assume that some African American women found admirable traits in Pam Grier and Tamara Dobson's heroines in spite of the problems of Blaxploitation films in general" (2006, 10).

The unprecedented and unabashed toughness of the Blaxploitation heroine represented a general shift in American film depictions of women. She may have been overtly sexualized but her strength and "take-no-shit" attitude was an abrupt departure from the stereotypical ways women had been portrayed in Hollywood in general, and how African American women were depicted in particular as mammies or tragic mulattos. There was no passivity to these women, no waiting around for a man to save them or to fall in love with them, no fear of speaking their mind, nor of shooting, stabbing, or choking someone to death. Even in their sexual encounters, they were aggressors. This broad shift in what women could do on screen was made possible by the very marginality of Blaxploitation films. Mainstream Hollywood would have been reluctant to create a female character of this type, but low-budget films had nothing to lose and everything to gain by shocking viewers with something new and seemingly outrageous. And because this dramatic shift in female representation happened within the confines of Blaxploitation, the characters specifically rewrote stereotypes of black women. These characters may have protected family members, but they were no mammies. These black heroines may have been desired by men, but they were no tragic mulattos. These characters "offered a significant departure from the historical representations of African American women and, through the writers, producers and directors of the genre, brought to the screen a new image of African American femininity" (Sims 2006, 26). Yet the contradictory nature of Blaxploitation heroines as excessively tough and excessively sexualized meant that at the same time they shattered stereotypes about feminine passivity and African American women's helplessness, they also reinforced and extended other stereotypes regarding black female bodies and sexuality.

Age-old stereotypes about black women as exotic racial "Others," who, in a colonial way of thinking, are the epitome of an aberrant and promiscuous sexuality that borders on the bestial (an issue discussed in more detail in the next chapter), were exacerbated by the more lascivious aspects of the Blaxploitation heroine's image. As Dunn describes the sexual exaggerations of the Blaxploitation heroine: "the stereotypical iconography mixes the primitive

African image popular in nineteenth-century European literature and the U.S. mythology of sexually wild black female slaves now evolved into the twentieth-century 'sexpot' or 'hot mamma' image of black femininity" (2008, 111–12). Because black women have been (and continue to be) overwrought as hypersexual and even "savage," compared to white women, it seemed more acceptable, or at least believable, for black women to assume a role as violent and sexual protagonists. In her discussion of the historical development of the action genre, Yvonne Tasker (1993) notes that Blaxploitation heroines were able to break new ground because: "It is in part the blackness of these heroines which opens up, through notions of black animality, the production of an aggressive female heroine within existing traditions of representations" (21). In a circular and mutually reinforcing logic, black women could be depicted as tough and sexual because they are stereotyped that way, and they are stereotyped that way, in part, because they are depicted as tough and sexual in these films. "The 'macho' aspects of the black action heroine—her ability to fight, her self-confidence, even arrogance—are bound up in an aggressive assertion of her sexuality," Tasker continues. "Simultaneously it is this same stereotypical attribution of sexuality to the black woman which generates anxiety around her representation" (21–22). For all her strength and progress, the Blaxploitation heroine is still intertwined with the specific black female stereotypes of the jezebel and the sapphire.

In media representations—and in American culture generally—black women have been overdetermined by the stereotypes of the mammy, the tragic mulatto, the jezebel, and the sapphire. Blaxploitation represented a significant shift away from Hollywood's earlier emphasis on mammy roles, but in featuring black protagonists as explicitly violent and sexual characters, the films emphasized the potential threat they posed to patriarchy. The stereotype of the black jezebel, whose unbridled animalistic sexuality is perceived as the undoing of men who are helpless to resist (initially conceived as a rationale for the sexual assaults perpetrated by white men on female slaves), and the conception of the black sapphire, whose outrageous and outspoken "bitchy" attitude is deemed emasculating, combine in the Blaxploitation heroine. These combined roles result in a female character who potentially represents a threat to patriarchy well beyond just the men within the film. As Collins describes Grier's groundbreaking roles: "Pam Grier's films signaled the arrival of a new kind of 'bitch.' As a 'Black Bitch,' Grier's performances combined beauty, sexuality, and violence" (2005, 124). Grier, like all Blaxploitation heroines, aggressively killed and fucked multiple men, used her sexuality to lure men to their deaths, and both verbally and literally castrated them. While the black action heroine was a progressive role, it also, unfortunately, solidified notions of strong black women as "bitches." Dunn describes how this "black bitch" persona combines the preexisting stereotypes of the jezebel and the sapphire:

> One of the defining traits of the jezebel's sexual aggression is its designation as both amoral and dangerous. In the wake of her wrath, she undermines the power of both black and white male and female enemies who are drawn by her sexual allure and crushed. The jezebel intersects with the Sapphire image—the bitchy and deceptive black female. This dual imagery reverberates in the presentation of a black woman virago who temporarily disturbs the supposedly fixed boundaries of the gender and racial hierarchy through her most potent weapon—her sexual body. (Dunn 2008, 115)

Thus, along with opening up a cinematic space for strong and violent female protagonists, the Blaxploitation heroine also yoked together and reconfirmed some of the more demeaning characteristics associated with African American women.

Depictions of African American women in current media forms still clearly rely on the iconography of the jezebel, the sapphire, and the "black bitch." Performers like Lil Kim, Beyonce, Rihanna, Nicki Minaj, Naomi Campbell, and dozens of others have crafted entire careers around exploiting these stereotypes. But since the heyday of Blaxploitation, African American action heroines have all but been erased, possibly because they were so thoroughly depicted as violent and sexual "bitches" in a manner that would be deemed too obviously racist in the current culture climate. The Blaxploitation heroine is such an extreme type that she is more likely to inspire parodies than serious homage. Sexy, sassy, gold-pantsuit-wearing caricatures like Foxy Cleopatra (Beyonce Knowles) in *Austin Powers in Goldmember* (2002) and Sistah Girl (Aunjanue Ellis) in *Undercover Brother* (2002) are more common than serious revisionist versions like Quentin Tarantino's updating of Pam Grier in *Jackie Brown* (1997). The dearth of African American women in contemporary action movies may be a negative consequence of the prominence of the Blaxploitation heroine in the popular imagination. The black-identified mixed race actresses Halle Berry (African American/white) and Zoe Saldana (Dominican/Puerto Rican) are the only two women to achieve any success as modern action heroines. In recent years, Saldana, in particular, has been closely aligned with big-budget action roles in *Avatar*, *The Losers*, *Colombiana*, and the *Star Trek* movies. Though Saldana is cast primarily as a black actress—for example, as iconic Lt. Uhura in *Star Trek* or as Nina Simone in

Nina (2014)—her well-publicized mixed race heritage and her unique appearance facilitate a rethinking of how her ethnicity factors into her action roles.

As two of the most visible mixed race actresses in Hollywood, Halle Berry and Zoe Saldana also represent the divergent ways that performers characterize their multiracial identity in media coverage. Berry controversially declared in the *Evening Standard* (2002) that she regards herself as black because she believes in the "one-drop rule" of race. Berry cites childhood experiences of discrimination as a factor for choosing to align with a singular race, revealing in interviews: "When we lived in the black neighborhood, we weren't liked because my mother was white. In the white neighborhood they didn't like me because I was black" (quoted in Arogundade, November 21, 2002). Berry's experiences allude to the idea of the "tragic mulatto" who has long been characterized as a liminal figure, ostracized on both racial sides. Sims describes the dual heritage dilemma embodied in the stock figure of the tragic mulatto: "Her one-percent of African American blood kept her from becoming part of the Caucasian community, and the African American community rejected her as well. Thus, the tragic mulatto became an outsider and was given the 'tragic' label because of her inability to reconcile her dual heritage" (Sims 2006, 32). Saldana, on the other hand, widely acknowledges her mixed race heritage; she also argues that her ethnicity is not really a factor, and that she has moved beyond outdated racial categorizations. On several occasions, Saldana has claimed that she is weary of the public's fascination with her ambiguous racial make up. In an interview on BET (Black Entertainment Television), Saldana lamented:

> I find it uncomfortable to have to speak about my identity all of the time, when in reality it's not something that drives me or wakes me up out of bed everyday. I didn't grow up in a household where I was categorized by my mother. I was just Zoe and I could have and be anything that I ever wanted to do . . . and every human being is the same as you. So to all of a sudden leave your household and have people always ask you, "What are you, what are you" is the most uncomfortable question and it's literally the most repetitive question. I can't wait to be in a world where people are sized by their soul and how much they can contribute as individuals and not what they look like. I literally run away from people that use words like ethnic. It's preposterous!

Berry was born in 1966, Saldana in 1978, and that twelve-year difference—and the shifting cultural attitudes towards ethnicity over time—may account for their differing beliefs about race. The positioning of mixed race performers in the media also can be a conscious strategy to garner access to racially specific roles, or to open up possibilities across different ethnic roles. Gregory T. Carter (2008) discusses how these different strategies have been employed by mixed race male action stars like Vin Diesel, who is reluctant to identify his exact racial background, and Dwayne "The Rock" Johnson, who is proudly open about his African American and Samoan heritage. Saldana's ambiguous ethnicity has allowed her to straddle different identifications. While her film roles typically present her as black, her public image is more inclusive. For example, she is probably the only celebrity to appear on both the covers of African American magazines like *Ebony* and *Essence*, as well as Hispanic magazines like *Latina* and *People en Espanol* (in addition to dozens of less ethnically specific publications).

Saldana's skin tone has typically resulted in her roles being identified as black, but her mixed race appearance has also allowed her to play other ethnicities. While her ethnicity has opened up a wide range of possibilities, it has also resulted in occasional controversies. Saldana's casting as the legendary black singer Nina Simone in the biopic *Nina* led to an outcry about the casting of a non-African American in the role. Likewise, some fans took issue with Saldana's role as the new Lt. Uhura in *Star Trek* because the original character was a landmark role for an African American woman to perform on 1960s prime time television (see Scodari 2011). At other times, Saldana's ambiguous ethnicity seems to play into the practice of Orientalism that casts all "Others" as equally and all encompassingly foreign and exotic, such as her turns as heavily computer-generated aliens—the blue-skinned Neytiri in *Avatar* and the green-skinned Gamora in *Guardians of the Galaxy*. Saldana's performance as Neytiri was her major breakthrough as an actress and catapulted her into the realm of blockbuster action movies, despite the fact that she was never depicted as herself in *Avatar*. Saldana's performance was recorded via a motion capture suit and served as the underlying basis for the entirely CGI-rendered character. Yet Saldana still managed to convey a complex and strong alien female who falls in love with the human, Jake Sully (Sam Worthington), who has been relocated into an artificial alien host body. Ethnicity in *Avatar* is transposed onto an alien race (though, tellingly, all the actors used as the basis for the Na'vi were African American or Native American), but holds true to Hollywood's conception of innate white superiority under the guise of valorizing exotic native cultures. Jake, the white human hero, learns the way of Na'vi and embraces their culture, eventually falling in love with princess Neytiri and ultimately saving their society from the colonizing humans. It is a familiar modern story of "white guilt," wherein an Anglo messiah is accepted into a foreign and mysterious culture, finds love, and eventually proves himself a better native than the natives themselves. It is the same skewed story of race relations seen in films like *Dances with Wolves* (1990), *Ferngully* (1992), *Pocahontas* (1995), and *The Last Samurai* (2003) (for a discussion of white saviors in film see, Vera 2003). Zoe Saldana may regard herself as post-racial, but her roles often seem dependent on visible ethnicity as a key ingredient.

Though her characters are an integral part of the science fiction films *Avatar* and *Star Trek*, Saldana is a supporting actress behind white male leads in both. Saldana's most significant lead roles in action movies came with *The Losers* and *Colombiana*. In *The Losers*, Saldana plays the mysterious and deadly Aisha, sharing top billing with Jeffrey Dean Morgan, who plays Colonel Clay. The titular "Losers" of the film are a misfit band of elite American soldiers, led by Clay, who have been framed as traitors and are out for revenge against an evil government official who funds terrorists. After narrowly escaping an assassination attempt, the Losers are presumed dead and left to their own devices in Bolivia. The sexy and violent Aisha seduces Clay and offers to help the Losers get back into the United States and kill their nemesis. Aisha proves herself incredibly capable with guns and fists alongside these elite soldiers, but she is also depicted as a seductress (lots of underwear scenes rolling in bed with Clay) and as a traitor (she is the daughter of a drug lord whom Clay killed). In the end, Aisha comes to the team's rescue in their hour of need and assumes a role as a full member of the Loser's group. As the lone female in the film, Aisha is repeatedly put on display in a manner that marks her as sexually aggressive and associates her sexuality with her violence. The *Film Journal International* review points out that "Saldana brings a potent mixture of attitude, ferocity and sex appeal to the role" (Alter, April 22, 2010). Indeed, Aisha first approaches Clay in a seedy Bolivian bar and takes him back to his hotel room, where the promise of sex quickly becomes a destructive fistfight. Clay only escapes being beaten by Aisha when the hotel room catches fire and they escape together and bargain for a meeting the next day. Later, back in the U.S., Aisha seduces Clay for some rough-and-tumble sex before their first mission together. And, then again, she has sex with him in another hotel room when the rest of the team busts in to attack her after they have figured out who her father was. Clad only in a skimpy pair of panties and a tight undershirt, Aisha gets into a firefight with the team and escapes through a bathroom window. Like the Blaxploitation heroine before her, Aisha's sexuality is depicted as promiscuous, devious, and dangerous. She also is characterized as both literally and figuratively castrating. When one team member, Jensen (Chris Evans), tries to flirt with her Aisha is dismissive and frightens him off when she explains that, as a child in Africa, she used to collect ears from the men she killed. And when the Losers first burst in on her postcoitus scene

Fig. 3.1. Zoe Saldana is both tough and sexy in *The Losers*.

with Clay, Aisha holds them off by pointing two guns at them—one directly at Jensen's crotch, which he loudly complains about.

In *Colombiana*, Saldana does not have to share the action spotlight with anyone. Originally written by famed action heroine director Luc Besson as a sequel to his *Leon: The Professional* (1994), which featured the training of twelve-year-old Mathilda (Natalie Portman) by a mob hitman. When Portman was unavailable, the script was altered to be the story of Cataleya, a young girl who witnessed the assassination of her Colombian father and African mother in Bogota and flees to Chicago to become an accomplished hitwoman working for her uncle. Cataleya is a catlike killer for hire; we repeatedly see her slinking through air ducts and past guards to assassinate her targets. Her ultimate goal is finding the Colombian crime lord, Don Luis, who ordered her parents' murder and is now in protective custody with the CIA. The film relishes displaying Saldana in her underwear and skintight bodysuits. The *Movieline* review points out that "in catsuits, swimsuits and skimpy underthings, Saldana is as potently elusive as a shadow can be" (Orange, August 25, 2011). *Colombiana* is a sparse story of Cataleya's revenge as she murders her way to Don Luis, and then single-handedly shoots, stabs, and blows up dozens of his heavily armed security men before literally feeding Luis to her two attack dogs. Cataleya's adult life is all about her mission; the only human contact we see for her, besides her uncle who assigns Cataleya the contracts, is her love interest Danny (Michael Vartan). Still, Danny barely knows her—he doesn't even know her real name. Cataleya just meets with him for sex whenever she feels like it, repeatedly breaking into Danny's apartment, where she immediately strips and jumps him, always leaving before he wakes up in the morning. The one time Cataleya lets her guard down with Danny, the FBI manage to figure out who she is through a series of lucky breaks. *Colombiana* fetishizes the idea of a petite, beautiful woman wielding big guns. As the film's promotional tag line declares: "Vengeance is Beautiful." And as the *Los Angeles Times* blurb used on the cover of the DVD release makes clear, the film is "a scandalous blend of action, sex and violence." Putting it bluntly, the *Washington Post* argued that for all the film's images of a strong heroine, "the filmmakers were surely thinking of the guys when they arranged for Saldana to play many of her scenes in a cat suit, a bikini or lingerie" (Jenkins, August 26, 2011). *Colombiana* is as much about displaying Saldana as an erotic sight as it is about her incredible skills as a killer.

In both *The Losers* and *Colombiana*, Zoe Saldana yokes together themes of steamy sexuality and violence more than do any of the white action heroines who dominate current Hollywood films. Clearly, white action heroines are fetishized as well (see Brown 2011), but Saldana's action roles harken back to Blaxploitation heroines by dwelling on her sexual scenes and directly linking them to her lethal abilities. As the review in the *Boston Globe* argued: "It's basically a Blaxploitation movie stretched to meaningless international proportions," with Saldana "aiming to be some kind of new Pam Grier" (Morris, August 27, 2011). Saldana's sexual presence on-screen is often described as aggressive and slinky—almost feline. Her African American appearance means that Saldana is still conceived in the same type of racialized ways that Blaxploitation heroines were. As Aisha and Cataleya, Saldana is irresistibly sexy but dangerous, a castrating jezebel. In all of her action roles, Saldana is an exotic fetish object lusted after by men. Even in *Star Trek*, Saldana's Lt. Uhura is introduced in a bar scene when the future Captain Kirk (Chris Pine) unsuccessfully hits on her. But Saldana's mixed race identity also facilitates her characters ability to move beyond the one-dimensional stereotype of Blaxploitation heroines. Within the films themselves, the ethnicity of Saldana's action characters is never dwelled upon. Where Blaxploitation heroines were derided as "black bitches," Saldana's race seems irrelevant. Saldana's action characters seem equally at home in any ethnic setting, her mixed race status allowing her to move fluidly between worlds. And while Saldana's characters are tough, her tiny body and delicate features position her as less threatening to masculine assumptions about gender relevant body sizes than the 6-foot, 2-inch Tamara Dobson or the 5-foot, 10-inch Pam Grier. Likewise, Saldana's mixed race makes her romantic pairings with white men less potentially controversial. All of Saldana's on-screen lovers are white—Clay, Danny, and Kirk pursue her, though she ends up with the Vulcan Spock (played by white actor Zachary Quinto); even in *Avatar*, Jake is originally a white human. Saldana is never depicted as a tragic mulatto; she has no trouble reconciling her different racial sides; nor is she ever seen to be rejected on the grounds of race.

KUNG FU MIXED WITH MAGGIE Q

Concurrent with Blaxploitation, foreign-made kung fu films became incredibly popular in the West during the 1970s. But unlike Blaxploitation that quickly fizzled out, kung fu films continued to be produced abroad and maintained a cult-like following in America through the 1970s. By the 1980s, Hollywood had begun incorporating martial arts and Americanizing it via white actors like Chuck Norris, Steven Seagal, and Jean-Claude Van Damme. Western audiences embraced Hong Kong-made films again in the 1990s, and they have remained popular into the twenty-first century. The first wave of kung fu started in the 1970s with the incredible international popularity of Bruce Lee. Lee's Hong Kong films—*The Big Boss* (1971), *The Chinese Connection* (1972), and *The Way of the Dragon* (1972)—helped launch an American fascination with kung fu and led to his Hollywood feature film, *Enter the Dragon* (1973). Lee's untimely death in 1973 dampened, but did not halt, the 1970s' fascination with kung fu films, which included such other international successes as *The Chinese Boxer* (1970), *Heroic Ones* (1970), *Five Fingers of Death* (1972), *Master of the Flying Guillotine* (1976), *Drunken Master* (1978), *Five Deadly Venoms* (1978), and *The 36th Chamber of Shaolin* (1978). The Western rise in popularity of kung fu films coincided with a concerted effort within the Hong Kong film industry to expand its international sales, and a symbolic remasculinization of Asian stereotypes that had characterized Asian men as small, weak, and feminine. Lee's muscular and powerful body, his defeat of larger opponents (including Chuck Norris and Kareem Abdul-Jabbar), and his narrative triumphs over foreign colonial forces was a clear example of this effort of remasculinization. "The significance of Lee's Western success," observes Tasker, "lies partly in his articulation of a tough masculinity within nationalistic films that can be read against a history of 'feminizing' Western representations of Chinese men" (1997, 322). The underdog stories of these kung fu films resonated with heroic American fantasies of rugged individualism, and the spectacular physical feats of performers like Bruce Lee, Sammo Hung, Kwan Tak-Hing, and Gordon Liu exhilarated audiences.

Just as the Blaxploitation genre provided a space for strong African American heroines to emerge, kung fu films introduced the idea of Asian women as skilled fighters in their own right. The long tradition of martial arts stories featuring women, and the premise that kung fu did not require large bodies or excessive muscles in order for a fighter to be deadly, meant that a number of women were also featured as fighting heroines. In his discussion of the history of female characters in kung fu films, Leon Hunt (2003) notes that "women warriors are nothing new in Chinese storytelling and have a much longer history than their Western counterparts. There is the warrior Fa Mulan, who drags up to replace her father in battle, *Wing Chun* legends Ng Mui and Yim Wing Chun (the one prominent female Master/Pupil pairing), White Crane exponent Fang Wing Chun, the wife of Hung Hei-kwun. Their literary and cinematic counterparts include the Maiden of Yueh (*Annals of the Kingdom of Wu and Yueh*, 1AD), the flying swordswomen of silent Shanghai cinema, Golden Swallow, the Deaf-Mute Heroine and the Bride with the White Hair" (117–18). Often the heroines in 1970s kung fu films would fight alongside male heroes, but occasionally the women assumed the lead. Actresses like Angela Mao Ying, Hui Ying-hung, Linda Lin Ying, and Sharon Yeung Pan-Pan developed cult followings around the world and held their own with, or surpassed, male fighters in films like *The Deaf and Mute Heroine* (1971), *Lady Whirlwind* (1972), *Hapkido* (1972), *When Taekwondo Strikes* (1973), and *My Young Auntie* (1979). These films, and dozens of others, presented a world where women could be just as strong and deadly as any man. For example, in *Lady Whirlwind*, Angela Mao Ying plays Tien, a stern lone warrior out to revenge her sister's death, who other characters claim "fights like a man, even better." Tien was an image of a strong and noble woman fighting in a way that Western audience had never seen before. Hunt describes Tien as "formidable bordering on invincible; she flattens everyone in her path in her quest for revenge" (2003, 126).

Still, while kung fu films presented an image of incredible female heroism, they were (and still are) subject to a range of narrative containment strategies that function to limit the idea that women can be strong in real life. Because the Hong Kong films were involved in a remasculinization agenda in an effort to redress demeaning stereotypes of Asian men and years of Chinese domination by foreign nations, the women often gave way to a male hero. Despite Tien's incredible skills in *Lady Whirlwind*, Hunt does go on to note that "nevertheless, the film cannot or will not embrace her unequivocally as the heroine" (2003, 126). Moreover, the historical and/or fantasy settings typically employed by the kung fu films featuring exceptional female warriors implies that these women are figures of the past or of another surreal world. Despite these limiting strategies, the kung fu action heroine established a prototype for violent and competent female protagonists that would influence action heroines for decades. The incredibly prolific Hong Kong film industry continued to make kung fu and other action genre movies that achieved varying degrees of success in the West from the 1980s on. Actresses like Michelle Yeoh, Maggie Cheung, Ziyi Zhang, and So-Yi Yoon have carried on the tradition of formidable kung fu women in Hong Kong films. Interestingly, one of the most popular Hong Kong warrior women post-1970s was Cynthia Rothrock. The American-born Rothrock became a major star in the Hong Kong film industry (and a cult star in the West) due to her background as a champion martial artist, and due to the rarity of a white heroine appearing in a decidedly Asian genre. Rothrock's unparalleled kung fu skills were not appealing to Hollywood in the 1980s, but they were ideal for the Hong Kong industry, leading to very successful leading roles in films like *Yes, Madam* (1985) and *Righting Wrongs* (1986), as well as the joint Hong Kong/American *China O'Brien* movies (both 1988). Rothrock eventually became a cult hit in America in low-budget, direct-to-video kung fu films, but she was never able to rise above the status of a B-movie star. Rothrock carved out a niche as an authentic martial arts actress in a Hong Kong industry that was more accepting of fictional female warriors; her success also foreshadowed the adoption of kung fu aesthetics to be used by white action heroines in Hollywood films from the mid-1990s on.

While the unequivocal strength of kung fu women has been somewhat tempered or contained by the narrative use of accompanying male heroes, as well as historical or fantasy settings, one of the most limiting obstacle for theses heroines has been the long standing stereotypes of Asian women as erotic fetishes, particularly in the patriarchal Western imagination. Since early colonial times Asian women have been conceived and depicted as the quintessential exotic "Other," both lusted after and feared by white men. Even in this modern era of political correctness and an increasing awareness of demeaning racial stereotyping, Asian women continue to be understood as passive lotus blossoms or dangerous dragon ladies. As Hunt clarifies: "The Chinese action heroine is even more vulnerable when crossing cultural and geographic boundaries; specifically to what I shall call 'Deadly China Doll' syndrome. If the martial heroine can be an empowering identification figure in one context, she can just as easily be appropriated as exotic fetish in the Western Orientalist imaginary" (2003, 119–20). The kung fu heroine's usually petite stature and the conception of Asian women as excessively feminine ideals mark her as a sexual fetish, but when combined with her lethal skills she becomes a threatening, potentially castrating, façade. As Wendy Arons (2001) notes in her study of 1990s kung fu heroines, "the genre continues to resurrect the traditional figure of the cruel and sexy 'Dragon Lady,' whose violence is framed as deviant and always punished" (31). The shadow of the dragon lady stereotype is in play no matter how heroic the kung fu heroine is. Thus, while these strong heroines offer a potentially progressive image of female strength, they also function semiotically within a racist ideological framework that limits a fully rounded depiction of Asian women. It is a double-bind that perpetuates a specific racial and sexual conception of these women as exotic objects. Fantasies of the kung fu heroine's perceived sexiness as a China doll, or her threatening sexuality as a dragon lady, may be as important to some viewers as her heroic skills.

The incredible international success (and a significant popularity in the West) of female-centered Hong Kong films from the 1990s and early 2000s led to Hollywood's explicit incorporation of kung fu heroines in its own films. The remarkable Asian warrior women featured in Hong Kong films like *The Heroic Trio* (1993), *Butterfly and Sword* (1993), *Wing Chun* (1994) *Crouching Tiger, Hidden Dragon* (2000), and *House of Flying Daggers* (2004) helped reinvigorate Hollywood action heroines and provided a more feminine template in comparison to classic American, but decidedly masculinized, heroines like Ellen Ripley in *Aliens* (1986) and Sarah Connor in *Terminator 2: Judgment Day* (1991). One Hollywood strategy was to incorporate some of the Hong Kong actresses within existing action franchises where they could showcase their kung fu performances. For example, Michelle Yeoh was cast as a Chinese spy who partners with James Bond in *Tomorrow Never Dies* (1997), and Ziyi Zhang as a villainous Triad member in *Rush Hour 2* (2001). While these films exposed Yeoh's and Zhang's kung fu skills to a wider Western audience, they also reduced these strong women to, respectively, a helpmate and romantic partner for Bond, and a sexy but treacherous dragon lady killer. A second, and far more common, strategy for Hollywood films was the increasing use of Hong Kong filmmakers, fight choreographers, and stunt coordinators in American productions. As Lisa Funnell details Hollywood's assimilation of kung fu heroines, Hong Kong creators like the Yeun brothers and John Woo directly influenced the fighting women in the successful American-made feature film series *Charlie's Angels* (2000, 2003) and *The Matrix* (1999, 2003, 2003), as well as indirectly shaping dozens of other movies featuring action heroines who utilize martial arts, including *Underworld* (2003), *Aeon Flux* (2005), *Elektra* (2005), and *Serenity* (2005). In essence, this strategy displaces the Asian heroine in favor of white women, while still co-opting the Hong Kong style and the kung fu abilities of the women in those films. Funnell argues that "Hollywood continues to perpetuate the notion that white female body performance is preferred in the action genre, and that white action women are more appealing and thus more profitable (or vice versa) than Asian and/or Asian American heroes" (2011a, 73). Thus, the dominant white action heroine of contemporary Hollywood film is directly influenced by kung fu women of the past and the present, but narratively elides a connection to the specific ethnicity of those heroines.

Lucy Liu was one of the few Asian American actresses to achieve some success with action heroine roles during the early 2000s, but her roles were often secondary to, or in partnership with, white heroines. More recently, Maggie Q has become one of the most visible Asian American actresses associated with action movies and television. As an American mixed race actress (with an Irish American father and Vietnamese mother), whose career started in Hong Kong before finding success in Hollywood, Maggie Q functions as a melding or compromise between Asian warrior women and modern white action heroines. Maggie Q was born and raised in Hawaii but moved to Tokyo on her own as a teenager where her striking biracial looks led to a moderately successful modeling career. In pursuit of other opportunities, Maggie Q moved to Hong Kong in her twenties and almost immediately found success as a model and an actress. An editorial in *Time Out Hong Kong* claimed: "Q's unique Eurasian looks—her sharp, long, flawlessly symmetrical seemingly computer-enhanced features—which had been a liability for her in Japan and Taiwan, were instantly devoured by a Hong Kong fashion and advertising scene hungry for something new" (January 19, 2011). Despite not speaking the language or knowing anything about kung fu, Maggie Q was singled out by superstar Jackie Chan as a potential martial arts performer. Chan trained Maggie Q, casting her in a Hong Kong film he was producing, *Gen-X Cops 2: Metal Mayhem* (2000), and then again briefly in Chan's American film *Rush Hour 2* (2001). The combination of Maggie Q's beauty and her convincing performance of kung fu led to several feature roles in Hong Kong films, including other action movies like *Manhattan Midnight* (2001), *Naked Weapon* (2002), *Dragon Squad* (2005), and *Three Kingdoms: Resurrection of the Dragon* (2008). Maggie Q quickly transitioned to Hollywood, where she continued to have her greatest success playing deadly martial artists in feature films such as *Mission: Impossible III* (2006), *Live Free or Die Hard* (2007), and *Priest* (2011). Her unique status in both Hollywood and in Asia has allowed Maggie Q to continue working in both industries. Her highest-profile role to date in the West is as the title character in the American television series *Nikita* (2010–2014), in which she plays a super-spy action heroine out to take down a clandestine organization of villains.

Though Maggie Q plays strong women who are better at martial arts and other lethal activities than any of the men in the stories, she is always characterized as incredibly sexy and the camera always films her body and face in a manner to accentuate her desirability. The fetishizing male gaze of the camera is explicit in most representations of Maggie Q, in both her Hong

Kong and Hollywood roles. In *Naked Weapon*, one of her most popular Hong Kong films, Maggie Q plays Charlene, a young woman who was kidnapped as a child, along with forty other young girls who showed athletic promise. All of the girls are trained by the ruthless Madame M (Almen Wong) to become ruthless assassins. The girls are taught martial arts, marksmanship, and become proficient in all manner of weapons. They also are trained in the use of makeup, style, and how to overtly use their sexuality to disarm their targets. As the girls age, they are forced to kill each other in "survival of the fittest" competitions, until only Charlene, her friend Katt (Anya), and the psychotic Jill (Jewel Lee) remain. The women become elite assassins, dubbed "The China Dolls" by the CIA officer pursuing them. The film follows Charlene's adventures, which involve completing numerous kills before she finally reunites with her long-lost mother and escapes her life of servitude. In addition to showcasing Charlene's incredible kung fu skills in several elaborate fight scenes, the film also excessively frames Maggie Q as an erotic object. Close-ups of her face and body are seen throughout the film, emphasizing that her beauty is just as dangerous as her kung fu. In one lengthy scene, for example, Charlene targets a cocaine-snorting mob boss in Spain by posing as a call girl. In a short dress and stilettos, Charlene struts past dozens of leering henchmen on her way to her target's bedroom. Suddenly, a wind machine kicks in as Charlene dances seductively in a skimpy negligee. She gyrates her hips and whips her hair around a lot, gives the bad guy a lap dance, and pole-dances on his bed frame as she slides her panties off. Throughout the entire scene, the camera focuses on Charlene's body in close-ups and slow-motion shots to clarify she is just irresistible. Charlene then has sex with the target before killing him. While *Naked Weapon* is sympathetic to Charlene, and she is portrayed as a good girl forced to do bad things, she is still clearly cast in the lineage of the seductive and dangerous dragon lady.

Maggie Q is subject to the same type of fetishization even in her first smaller roles in Hollywood films. Moreover, her presence as the only Asian character in *Mission: Impossible III*, and *Live Free or Die Hard* compounds the association of her sexuality with racist fantasies about Asian women. In *Mission: Impossible III*, Maggie Q plays Zhen Lei, an incredibly capable operative who joins Ethan Hunt's (Tom Cruise) small elite team of (male) agents out to save the world from super-villains. Despite all of her skills, Lei's biggest role is to act as a seductive "honey trap" (a cliché discussed in more detail in Chapter 3) so that the rest of the team can apprehend the main bad guy. Maggie Q's most memorable scene in the film, one repeated in all the trailers and commercials, is a clear example of her fetishization. Clad in a super slinky red dress and driving a yellow Lamborghini, Lei goes undercover as a sexy guest at a black-tie event. When Lei exits the sports car, the camera—joined by all the male characters around her—pans up her long, sleek legs, as the high slit in her skirt reveals an incredible amount of skin. Of course, she attracts the attention of the villain and everyone else at the party. Lei's beauty is distraction enough for the mission to proceed undetected. While Maggie Q's character in *Mission: Impossible III* is primarily used as a sexual distraction in the standard style of fetishizing women, especially Asian women who are regarded as excessively erotic, at least she is one of the good guys in support of Ethan Hunt's heroic exploits. In *Live Free or Die Hard*, the fourth movie in the *Die Hard* series starring Bruce Willis as the now-iconic working-class hero John McClane, Maggie Q plays Mai Linh, the main henchwoman for the domestic terrorist Thomas Gabriel (Timothy Olyphant), who also happens to be her (white) lover. Linh is a ruthless villain who does not think twice about killing anyone. Her biggest scene is a lengthy and brutal fight with McClane, where she easily thrashes him. At one point, after she has knocked McClane to the ground yet again, he xenophobically mutters: "That's enough of this kung fu shit." Undaunted, Linh kicks him out of a window. McClane only gets the upper hand when he manages to drive a car back in through the window, striking Linh and plunging her and the car into an elevator shaft. Linh is a better fighter than McClane, but his brand of rugged American masculinity and gritty persistence finally wins out. After her death, McClane's comments about Linh come off as disturbingly racist and sexist. When the villain Gabriel asks about her, McClane tells him: "Mai? Oh Yeah, little Asian chick, likes to kick people? I don't think she is going to be talking to anybody for a real long time. Last time I saw her she was at the bottom of an elevator shaft with an SUV rammed up her ass!" Later, McClane also calls her "another dead Asian hooker bitch." Asian action women like Maggie Q may be valorized as strong, but they are also pigeonholed as fetish objects and even derided with some very harsh racist characterizations.

As a mixed race actress repeatedly cast as a kung fu Asian babe in action movies, Maggie Q seems well aware of the stereotyping that she is being subjected to. Almost every interview, review, or profile in the press about Maggie Q describes how beautiful she is and credits her Vietnamese/Irish/Polish background as the source of her unique look. Unlike Zoe Saldana, who evades questions about her mixed race heritage, Maggie Q proudly talks about her mixed ethnicity and is surprised at how obsessed people are with it. She has been open in interviews about her biracial heritage and the opportunities her unique looks have created for her, even joking about having to reduce her Anglo name of Maggie Denise Quigley to simply Maggie Q because it was easier for Asian audiences to pronounce. Conversely, she has commented on talk shows about her assumed foreignness because of her appearance: "My name is Margaret Denise Quigley. I have the whitest name ever! Yet I'd walk into executive offices and they'd say, 'Your English is so good,' and I'm like, "That's a shocker.'" Despite these racial confusions, Maggie Q has benefitted from a two-nationality career. She is Asian enough for Hong Kong films, but not too Asian for Hollywood productions. Rather than being excluded from either industry, she has been embraced by both. Maggie Q's Asian appearance allows her to seem an authentic depiction of a kung fu-wielding character in both Hong Kong and American productions and taps into the long lineage, and the acceptable conception of, female kung fu heroines. But she seems intent on moving past this stereotype of the sexy kung fu dragon lady, and her relative whiteness has helped her land some less stereotypical roles. As Maggie Q told Jimmy Kimmel on his late-night talk show: "Not only do I not want to be stereotyped as this Asian girl who fights—gee, what a wonder—but also I have more to offer than that." Because Maggie Q is only partially Asian, she may be given opportunities to transcend stereotypes that other Asian actresses don't have.

Maggie Q's most recognizable role has been as the title star of the American television series *Nikita*, which aired on the CW network from 2010 until 2014. The series is the latest take on the story of an attractive young woman who is turned into an assassin by a clandestine government organization that forces her to work for them in exchange for her life. The character of Nikita was created by Luc Beeson, making her first appearance in his hit French film, *La Femme Nikita* (1990), featuring Anne Parillaud in the lead role. The success of Beeson's film resulted in an American remake, entitled *Point of No Return* (1993), starring Bridget Fonda, and a Canadian television series *La Femme Nikita* (1997–2001), with Peta Wilson in the role. Maggie Q's *Nikita* focuses on the character's life after she has broken free from the clutches of the shadowy unit know simply as the Division. Nikita works each week to take down the group that stole her life by disrupting their assignments and trying to uncover their secrets. Nikita is aided in this series by another young woman, Alex (Lyndsy Fonseca), who is a current recruit working within the Division. Nikita's former mentor and eventual love interest, Michael (Shane West), is her initial nemesis and ultimately an ally. The series is a strong showcase for both Maggie Q's physical abilities, capitalizing on her background in action and kung fu movies, and for her acting skills. Before the series aired, some fans of the character Nikita expressed a concern about casting Maggie Q because the role had previously been performed only by white actresses. The worry was that the shift in the character's ethnicity would affect her overall persona, but Maggie Q's convincing performance was well-received by fans and she

Fig. 3.2. Maggie Q is more than just a Dragon Lady in *Nikita*.

was credited with giving the character surprising emotional depth at the same time that her action scenes were thrilling and believable.

Though the series makes no mention whatsoever of Nikita's ethnicity, the initial promotional materials clearly played upon expectations of the heroine as sexy and dangerous, as a twenty-first-century dragon lady. Three advance advertisements appeared in magazines and on billboards that positioned Nikita as a sexy femme fatale. All three of the images carried the simple yet suggestive tag line: "Nikita: Looks Do Kill." In two of the advertisements, Maggie Q is posed in a curve-hugging red gown reminiscent of her featured moment in *Mission: Impossible III*, with a very high leg slit and shoulder cut-outs; in one of the advertisements, she is standing with a machine gun resting on her high-heeled leg, while in the other, she is lying suggestively on her side with her leg fully exposed. In the first two images, Maggie Q is overtly presented as a dangerous sexual spectacle, but the third image more clearly aligned the character with the stereotype of a dragon lady. In this poster, Maggie Q is dressed in a very skimpy and fetishy leather outfit, complete with strapped leather gauntlets on her arms; she is posed with guns in both hands, her long bare legs draped over a chair, and a large Phoenix tattoo fully visible on her bare hips. This modern dragon lady advertisement so explicitly linked together sex and violence that *Variety* reported that the image was banned from public display in numerous malls and on roadside billboards (Schneider, August 18, 2010). The controversy helped generate a great deal of media buzz for the show well before the first episode even aired. But it also indicates a lingering cultural uneasiness in America when the long-standing association of Asian women as personifying unconventional and dangerous sexuality is made too explicit.

With the premiere of *Nikita*, Maggie Q became one of the few Asian-identified actresses to headline her own television series in America. Some television critics observed that Maggie Q's mixed race status made her more acceptable to general audiences—white enough for everyone to identify with, Asian enough to be safely exotic. She does use martial arts when she has to fight, and she does use her sexuality when she needs to, but she also uses guns, bombs, spy gadgets, and anything else that is needed. She has no mysterious Eastern origins, but is instead a fully Americanized woman. The series itself treats Nikita's ethnicity as a non-issue; it is never mentioned and it never defines her character. However, the program does take ample advantage of Maggie Q's attractiveness, particularly in the first season. As a review in *USA Today* put it: "*Nikita* tells its story well, but its also more than willing to push it aside so the camera can linger lovingly on its stunningly photogenic star. We see her in a red bikini, worn so she can kill some bad guys at a pool party. We see her in a skin-tight gown, worn so she can kill some bad guys at a fancy fund-raiser. We see her in her bra and panties, worn so we can see her in her bra and panties" (Bianco, September 9, 2010). Despite the sometimes excessive sexualization of Nikita that visually recalls fantasies of the dragon lady stereotype, the series also presents her as a full and complex character. The extended narrative format of television means that characters can become more than just two-dimensional types. After describing how often *Nikita* depicts Maggie Q in revealing outfits, the *USA Today* review also argued: "That's no knock on the show, which knows what it is doing, and no knock on Maggie Q, who retains dignity and gravity throughout. She's being used as eye-candy, but she and her character are clearly more than eye candy, and that saves *Nikita* from feeling cheap or exploitative" (Bianco, September 9, 2010). The program manages to tap into the allure of the dragon lady, but it also moves beyond this simple and limiting stereotype.

Maggie Q's career trajectory appears to benefit from her mixed race identity. Her Hong Kong-based work presents her as a modern kung fu warrior, and her Americanness also makes her suitable for Hollywood film and television. Like most beautiful women in the media, Maggie Q is filmed as an erotic spectacle, but her half-Asian appearance and her frequent use of kung fu conjure up and perpetuate the idea that Eastern women are especially exotic and desirable at the same time they are dangerous. Overcoming racial stereotypes is a huge obstacle for ethnically identified actresses because those are the roles that are available to them, and because the stereotypes are so cultural ingrained that they are easily activated. Still, although Maggie Q has been clearly aligned with the dragon lady fantasy, she nonetheless is aware of the stereotype and has used her increasing power within the industry to try and change things. In a *New York Times* article entitled "Asian Actresses Challenge Stereotypes," television critic Mike Hale notes that in *Nikita* Maggie Q's character resonates with a common set of clichés about Asian women: "the lethal, sometimes icy Nikita, able to dispense violence while wearing skimpy and tight outfits, evokes a long line of dragon ladies and ninja killers" (Hale, December 6, 2013). But Hale goes on to argue that the actress and the writers have gone to great lengths to avoid or transcend stereotypes: "A lot of effort has gone into humanizing Nikita and making her a sisterly or even maternal figure for the younger assassin, Alex, and the emphasis on violence has decreased during the show's run." And he points out that "Maggie Q fought some battles over her costumes in the early days of *Nikita*, and she has spent progressively more time in plain, covered-up (although still closefitting) workout-style ensembles and less in skimpy red dresses." Maggie Q's unique Eurasian looks and identity may yet allow her to fully transcend limiting stereotypes about Asian women and kung fu. Like Zoe Saldana, Maggie Q's mixed race status also seems to make her romantic pairing with white men in American productions less controversial. In *Live Free or Die Hard*, she is involved with the white villain played by Timothy Olyphant, and in *Nikita*, she has several brief romantic relationships with white male characters and ultimately is paired with her former mentor and enemy, played by Shane West. This tendency to pair mixed race actresses with white male romantic partners is common for all of the modern action heroines discussed in this chapter and it is an overarching theme we will return to below.

LATINA MIXED WITH JESSICA ALBA

Where the history of Blaxploitation and kung fu films clearly position black and Asian women within a context of action movie subgenres, there is no specific history of strong Latina heroines in film. Though the Latina heroine is not a direct influence on modern constructions of white action heroines, there are aspects of common Latina stereotypes that bear discussion. Moreover, current Latina actresses like Jennifer Lopez, Salma Hayek, Michelle Rodriguez, Eva Longoria, Sofia Vergara, and Jessica Alba have been credited with overcoming racial barriers because they have achieved mainstream Hollywood success, and it is important that much of their success has come in action-oriented roles. The closest parallel to the early 1970s craze for Blaxploitation and kung fu films, was the concurrent wave of Mexploitation films from the late

1960s and early 1970s that were extremely popular in Mexico, but only garnered a small amount of attention internationally. Mexploitation films were cheaply and quickly made B-movies produced in Mexico, many of which had some element of action, although by and large they were not action movies. Most of the early Mexploitation films focused on masked wrestlers battling the likes of aliens, vampires, and werewolves; others were bawdy comedies, such as the cycle of "cine de fincheras" sex comedies revolving around female showgirls, strippers, and prostitutes. By the 1980s and 1990s, the Mexploitation industry had died out, and more action-oriented low-budget films came to the fore, particularly those by gonzo Mexican-American filmmaker Robert Rodriguez, who later became a Hollywood director.

The incredible increase in the Latino/a population in America over the last two decades (surpassing African Americans as the second largest ethnic group in the nation) has resulted in a concerted effort by the media to court them as consumers. Spanish language television channels and radio stations have become far more common, as have Latino/a targeted versions of popular American magazines like *People en Espanol, Cosmopolitan en Espanol, Latina Magazine,* and *Alma Magazine.* As Guzman and Valdiva (2004) have described it: "We live in an age when Latinadad, the state and process of being, becoming, and/or appearing Latino/a is the 'It' ethnicity and style in contemporary U.S. mainstream culture. This construction of Latinadad is transmitted primarily, though not exclusively, through the mainstream media and popular culture" (205–206). Still, despite the size and desirability of the Latino/a market in the U.S., mainstream media productions have struggled to provide Latino/a characters who are multidimensional or not grounded in long-standing stereotypes. Latino men are still commonly portrayed as uneducated, inner-city gang members, as unwashed and impoverished laborers, or as hot-blooded lovers. Likewise, Latina women are typically restricted to roles as saintly matriarchs, as domestic servants (like maids and nannies), or as hypersexual exotic seductresses. The stereotype of the feisty and sexy Latina spitfire is the most relevant to the consideration of Latina women in relation to action narratives because it is the role most commonly ascribed to Latinas and because hot-tempered spitfire implies an outspokenness (like the sapphire) and a dangerous sexuality (like the jezebel).

The spitfire stereotype was solidified in the early days of cinema primarily through the figure of Lupe Velez, and it continues to inform Hollywood's idea of Latinas in contemporary film and television. As a teenager in 1926, Velez moved from Mexico to Hollywood to pursue her dreams of stardom. She was a beautiful and talented actress, singer, and dancer but was quickly restricted to roles deemed suitable to her Mexican identity. She had some early successes in Westerns playing strong and outspoken Mexican women who win the hearts of white male adventurers in films like *The Gaucho* (1928), starring Douglas Fairbanks, and *The Wolf Song* (1929), featuring Gary Cooper. Velez's feisty, exotic screen persona soon became reinforced and overshadowed by tabloid stories about her steamy and tumultuous affairs with the likes of John Gilbert, Gary Cooper, Clark Gable, Charlie Chaplin, and Errol Flynn. On the positive side, Velez's screen characters and her active personal life can be understood as a sign of female strength and independence in an era when women were rarely offered the opportunity to act out. Rosa Linda Fregoso optimistically argues that "through her public persona and movie characters, Lupe Velez portrayed strong women who were active agents in public spaces both as career women and as players in romance and courtship" (2007, 55). But the overwhelming perception was less favorable, and by the mid-1930s Velez was considered, on-screen and off-, to be the epitome of a hot-blooded and hot-tempered Latina seductress who preyed on white men. The Velez stereotype was solidified in her most famous series of films, the eight "Mexican spitfire" screwball comedies she starred in between 1939 and 1943, in which her "characters are childish, they throw temper tantrums (often literally throwing objects across the room or pulling weapons on the men they love), they are irresistible to men, they misunderstand American customs, and they speak with exaggerated accents" (Sturtevant 2005, 20–21). Though the spitfire films were broad comedies based on a racist caricature of Velez, the idea of the spitfire came to stand for a very specific stereotype of Latina femininity. "Initially associated with Lupe's comedic performance in cinema, the term is now interpreted as an insignia for all that masculinist discourse judges as 'negative' about Velez's public persona, as synonymous with the 'sexually alluring and available . . . fallen Latin woman'" (Fregoso 2007, 57). Unfortunately, the display of strength and independence associated with the spitfire is typically undermined by the fetishized and racialized sexual exoticism of the stereotype.

All of the most visible and successful Latina actresses working in Hollywood today conform in varying degrees to the hot and sexualized spitfire stereotype. Though the term was initially associated with Mexican women like Velez, it has been generalized and applied to all Latina women regardless of their specific origins. The American-born Jennifer Lopez, whose parents are Puerto Rican, has become one of the highest-paid women in Hollywood and a top musical performer marketed primarily for her exotic beauty and curvaceous body. Lopez's famously curvy figure has been the subject of public and media fascination for over a decade. In particular, Lopez's iconic ethnic butt became a type of fetish object in and of itself, much-hyped in the media and magazine pictorials, and even the subject of several academic inquiries (see

Beltran 2002, Barrerra 2002). Beltran provides an excessive example of the media fascination from London's *Sunday Times* that praised "Jennifer Lopez's bottom, her backside, her butt, her rear, her rump, her posterior, her gorgeously proud buttocks, her truly magnificent, outstanding booty" (Goodwin, September 20, 1998). Thousands of magazine covers attest to Lopez's overall appeal as a sexual icon. The December 1998 issue of men's magazine *FHM* featured a barely clad Lopez on the cover with the headline "Ay Caramba! Jennifer Lopez is out of this world!" *People* magazine declared Lopez to be "The World's Most Beautiful Woman" on the cover of a special issue in 2011. Likewise, Salma Hayek, who was born in Mexico to a Spanish/Mexican mother and Lebanese/Spanish father, has parlayed her beauty and ethnic sensuality into a top-tier film career. Despite being listed in *Time* magazine as one of the most influential Hispanics in America, Hayek was still described as "a body with curves more dangerous than a racetrack's and a face that stops traffic" (Luscombe 2005, 18). In her analysis of Hayek's biopic of Frida Kahlo, *Frida* (2002), Isabel Molina Guzman (2007) describes the actress in her early roles as self-consciously aware of being "typecast as Hollywood's twenty-first-century Latina Spitfire" (119). Hayek played the Latina seductress to perfection in films like *Desperado* (1995), *From Dusk Till Dawn* (1996), *54* (1998), *After the Sunset* (2004), and *Bandidas* (2006). As an example of how thoroughly stereotyped the curvy and thick-accented Hayek was in her early American films, Guzman points to her character Isabel Fuentes from the culture-clash romantic comedy *Fools Rush In* (1997): "A loud, talkative, devotedly Catholic, superstitious woman, Fuentes dresses in bright, colorful, revealing clothing and when angry resorts to rapid-fire Spanish, despite having lived most of her life in the United States" (2007, 119). Both Jennifer Lopez and Salma Hayek have gone on to become Hollywood powerhouse producers as well as dependable box-office draws, yet both are still framed by the media as first and foremost "hot" Latinas.

The exaggerated eroticization of Latinas is also a common and popular cliché on prime time American television. On the award-winning comedy/drama *Desperate Housewives* (2004–2012), Mexican-American Eva Longoria achieved stardom by playing Gabrielle Solis as a spitfire who is spoiled, forthright, sultry, and a wanton trophy wife. *Rolling Stone* magazine described Longoria as "the hottest, juiciest of the Wisteria Lane housewives" (Hedeggard, December 15, 2005), and the *Guardian* called her "a hot tempered siren" (Wittstock, March 8, 2005). Eva Longoria is also the only woman to be voted by readers of the men's magazine *Maxim* as the world's number one hottie two years in a row, in their 2005 and 2006 "Top 100 Hot List." In her analysis of Longoria's conformity to stereotypes in *Desperate Housewives*,

Debra Merskin (2007) concludes with a long list of spitfire tropes: "She is sexy, sultry, promiscuous, sexually experienced, quick tempered, materialistic, devious, desiring, not inclined to work, has an Anglo love interest for whom she will risk almost anything to keep, becomes pregnant quickly, uses her wiles to manipulate men, wears flashy, brightly colored and tight-fitting clothing she hopes will be noticed" (146). Similarly, on the top-rated and Emmy-winning television comedy *Modern Family* (2009–current), Sofia Vergara (born and raised in Colombia) has come to personify the most recent example of the over-sexualized Latina spitfire with her outspokenness, thick accent, indifference to American customs, and, of course, her extremely curvaceous figure. A cover story in the April 2012 edition of *Esquire* described Vergara's character, Gloria, in such typical spitfire terms as "gorgeous, caring, opinionated, loud, and much younger" than her Anglo husband. So extreme is Vergara's image that in an article on NBCLatino.com, entitled "Stop the Sexy Latina Stereotype," Esther Cepeda (2012) complained, "I just hate that she so expertly works the dreaded, overdone 'sexy, ditzy, bombshell Latina' stereotype that many Hispanic women have worked their whole lives to overcome. Her appearance on the cover of *Esquire* magazine's April issue in frilly lingerie, with the word 'SEX' superimposed on her midsection, pretty much encapsulated the damage she adds to an overly sexualized pop-culture image of Latinos in general, and Hispanic women in particular" (August 8, 2012). The sexualized spitfire stereotype of Latinas from a variety of cultural backgrounds still dominates media representations as well as generalizing, reinforcing, and naturalizing racist and sexist beliefs.

The continued prevalence of the Mexican spitfire stereotype has been reinforced through its persistent use in popular culture and has been expanded and applied to all Latina identities, regardless of cultural or national origins. This generalization of the spitfire trope is symptomatic of Orientalist practices that symbolically categorize all non-white others into indistinctive racial categorizations. This slippage between diverse Hispanic origins is also reflective of the broad concept of a homogenizing Latinadad. The all-inclusive category of Latinadad brings together all people who share a Spanish-speaking heritage from a range of more than thirty Caribbean and Latin American countries, as well as the worldwide Hispanic diaspora. Guzman and Valdivia describe Latinadad as "an imagined community of recent, established and multigenerational immigrants from diverse cultural, linguistic, racial, and economic backgrounds" (2004, 207). While the concept of Latinadad recognizes the commonalities and shared cultural/racial issues across a range of nationalities, it also runs the risk of reinscribing and internalizing Orientalist conceptions that efface important differences. Many Chicano and Latino critics "have questioned the usefulness and effect of such labeling, for example, its tendency to homogenize peoples whose histories, language usage, and circumstances may differ significantly or to alienate U.S.-born Latinos, who may not speak Spanish or share other identifying criteria" (Mendible 2007, 4). Significantly, though, Latinadad does acknowledge the intrinsically blended nature of Latino/a identities. In the context of discussing mixed race people, it is important to recognize that "Latina" is inherently ambiguous, not a clearly delineated ethnic category. As Mary Beltran makes clear in her discussions of mixed race performers in the media, Latino/as have a long history of blended heritage recognized in the figure of the mestizaje. Beltran argues that "because of the Latino legacy of *mestizaje*: Latinos, though often not acknowledged as multiracial, are of widely mixed ethnic and racial descent with respect to indigenous and Spanish ancestry and heritage that can be traced to African and other origins. As Gregory Velasco y Trianosky notes, 'The central racial and cultural reality of Latino life is that everyone is *mestizo*'" (quoted in Beltran 2008, 251–52). Thus, while mestizo is a common identity in Latinadad, not all depictions of Latinas acknowledge this identity as a form of mixed ethnicity.

Many of the current iconic Latina actresses have been used to combine spitfire stereotypes with roles as action heroines. The resourceful, gun-wielding, and sultry Latina has been performed to varying degrees of toughness by Jennifer Lopez in *Anaconda* (1997), *Out of Sight* (1998), *The Cell* (2000), and *Enough* (2002); by Salma Hayek in *Desperado* (1995), *After the Sunset* (2004), *Bandidas* (2006), and *Everly* (2015); by Eva Longoria in *The Baytown Outlaws* (2012); and by Sofia Vergara in *Machete Kills* (2013) and *Heat* (2014). All of these action films depict the Latina as first and foremost a sexual object. Michelle Rodriguez is one of the few Latina actresses in Hollywood who has been identified with action roles without being hypersexualized. But other than her first film, *Girl Fight* (2000), Rodriguez's strong characters have been restricted primarily to smaller and supporting roles in films like *Resident Evil* (2002), *The Fast and the Furious* (2001), *S.W.A.T.* (2003), and *Avatar* (2009). Rather than a sexualized spitfire, Rodriguez has been characterized repeatedly as explicitly masculinized—as a "butch" or "Macho Latina" (Tolchin 2007, 184). All of these actresses—including those used primarily as spitfires, and even Rodriguez who is portrayed as macho—are cast explicitly as Latinas, regardless of their specific or blended cultural background.

Jessica Alba is one of the most widely recognized actresses who is of mixed race but is also primarily identified as Latina. Alba's diverse racial background is often highlighted in interviews and media profiles of the actress and has contributed to her being cast as a wide range of characters beyond traditional Latina roles. Born in California to a second-generation Mexican-American father and a mother with Danish, French-Canadian, English, and Italian heritage, Alba has been a successful actress since childhood, and media polls often rank her as one of the most beautiful women in the world. Alba's beauty and racially ambiguous appearance was a central aspect of her character in her breakthrough role as the lead on the television series *Dark Angel* (2000–2002). There, she played Max Guevera, a young woman with extraordinary abilities who was created in a futuristic genetic experiment. Max was a mixture of countless genetic strands and Alba's vague and indistinct ethnic beauty worked well to symbolize the character as a mélange of traits. Though *Dark Angel* was heavily hyped as a James Cameron production, the program's ratings struggled and it was canceled after only two seasons. Still, Alba's stunning and unique look on the series garnered a significant amount of attention and she easily transitioned from television to feature film stardom. While Alba's film roles were never restricted just to action narratives, she has appeared in a number of action films, including *Fantastic Four* (2005) and its sequel, *Fantastic 4: Rise of the Silver Surfer* (2007), *Sin City* (2005), *Machete* (2010), *Spy Kids 4* (2011), and *Barely Lethal* (2014).

In her insightful comparison of Jessica Alba with Rosario Dawson, another mixed race actress (Puerto Rican, black, Cuban, Native American), Mary Beltran (2008) points out that when Alba initially attracted a lot of media attention for her role in *Dark Angel*, there was very little discussion of her ethnicity, despite the genetic premise of the program. The mainstream media tended to focus more on how beautiful the young starlet was than on her ethnic diversity. It was not until Alba's stardom was solidified that coverage began to routinely include mention of her mixed race status. The Latino-oriented media, on the other hand, quickly claimed Alba as a celebrated Hollywood Latina and she was even awarded "Breakthrough Star of the Year" in 2001 from the American Latino Media Arts association. Before Alba became a permanent fixture on the cover of mainstream entertainment magazines, she was routinely featured on the front of publications like *Latina, People en Espanol*, and *Latin Heat*. For her part, Alba has always been open about her mixed race heritage and has actively pursued roles regardless of character ethnicity. For example, the casting of Alba in the blockbuster film *Fantastic Four* was initially considered controversial because the superheroine Sue Storm/Invisible Woman has always been depicted as a Waspy, Nordic-looking blonde in the comic books. But with the help of blonde hair dye, light-blue contact lenses, and Alba's relatively light olive complexion, she won over critics and comic books fans alike. While Alba's mixed race heritage has afforded her non-stereotypical roles as a Latina, she has also been open to discussing the difficulties inherent in being multiracial. Echoing Halle Berry's earlier comments about not fitting in with

Fig. 3.3. With her multiracial looks, Jessica Alba is not restricted to stereotypical Latina roles.

white or black neighborhoods as a child due to her mulatto identity, Alba told *Rolling Stone* about her early experiences as mestiza: "I never really belonged anywhere . . . I wasn't white. I was shunned by the Latino community for not being Latin enough" (Glock, 2005). And, for her part, Alba was ridiculed by many Latinos, and the Latino press, in late 2007 when they misinterpreted comments she made in an interview about not wanting to be labeled Latina. A February 2008 cover story of Alba in *Latina* magazine entitled "Think You Know Her? You Have No Idea!" set the record straight and allowed Alba to clarify how proud she is of her Mexican heritage. Likewise, when Alba had her DNA tested on the December 1, 2009, episode of the late-night show *Lopez Tonight*, Alba appeared shocked when host George Lopez revealed results that she was 87 percent white. Alba was offended when Lopez joked that she was more Buffy (the vampire slayer) than Dark Angel, and she reiterated the importance of her father's Mexican heritage (and questioned the specificity of the results because they characterize Spanish as white European).

Despite her good looks and celebrated sexuality, Jessica Alba has never been restricted to stereotypical Latina roles in the way other actresses have. Alba's early popularity, and her widely recognized sex appeal for male audiences, has allowed her to pursue non-racially specific roles and non-stereotypical Latina characters. But the perception of her racial status in Hollywood is a factor that Alba has had to broach in a very self-aware manner. In a cover story for *Elle* magazine, Alba revealed her struggles against Hollywood's racial typecasting: "Everyone wants to categorize you and pigeonhole you. I'm half Latin, but I grew up in the States, and I can't get roles playing a Latina because I don't speak Spanish. And I don't want to be the best friend, or the promiscuous girl, or the maid, because those stereotypes still exist with Latin roles. I wanted to be a leading lady. And I thought that because I have brown skin shouldn't make any difference. Why should only Aryan-looking girls be that girl?" (Goldman, 2008). Alba's mixed race appearance has not hindered her ability to play white characters like Sue Storm in *Fantastic Four* or Nancy Callahan in *Sin City*. Yet, while roles like these elide a Latina identity, they are still premised on Alba's "hotness"—there is much fetishizing focus on her body in a skintight outfit in *Fantastic Four*, and in *Sin City* she plays a bikini and leather-chaps-wearing stripper. In many of her roles, the ethnic or racial identity of the character is "absent" from the text; in other words, there is no mention of specific ethnicity, no presence of ethnic stereotypes, and no secondary indications of the character's racial background. Beltran argues:

> Jessica Alba's initial lack of ethnic self-labeling in her career and her light tan, not brown, skin, and perhaps even her perceived girlishness have contributed to the perception that she is ethnically ambiguous to the degree most preferred by Hollywood producers and casting directors in casting leading roles. In other words, Alba has achieved an "off-white" image, to borrow the term coined by Diane Negra (2001) to describe the liminal racial status of white ethnic actresses since Hollywood's silent film era. (Beltran 2008, 260)

While Alba has been successful at assuming an "off-white" image, her Mexican-American heritage has still been a factor in her public persona and, at times, in her film career.

Some of Jessica Alba's most explicitly Latina roles have been in action films directed by Mexican-American filmmaker Robert Rodriguez. Rodriguez is the most prominent Mexican-American director working in Hollywood, and his films tend to be high action, bordering on parody, with a focus on Mexican themes. The low-budget action film *El Mariachi* (1992) became a cult international success and led to a Hollywood-produced sequel three years later with *Desperado*, which solidified Antonio Banderas's stardom in the U.S. and introduced Salma Hayek to viewers outside of Mexico. Working with Rodriguez reinforces both Jessica Alba's Latina identity and her status as an action heroine. Rodriguez cast Alba as the female lead in *Machete* (2010), his playful homage to 1970s exploitation films, and again in *Spy Kids: All the Time in the World in 4D* (2011), the fourth installment of his children's action-comedy *Spy Kids* franchise. In *Machete*, Alba plays Special Agent Sartana, a Texas immigration and customs officer who switches from deporting illegal Mexican immigrants to rallying them behind Machete (Danny Trejo) and taking down a racist senator, anti-immigration militants, and an evil Mexican drug lord. Sartana is initially portrayed as a fully Anglicized Mexican-American who lives in an upscale yuppy home, orders lattes, and makes notes on migrant laborers from the comfort of her Volvo sedan. Through her adventures with Machete, Sartana comes to realize that "the system" does not work for Mexican immigrants, and she decides to do what is right, rather than what is the law. She also proves to be a deadly and resourceful heroine when she and Machete are attacked in her home, stabbing an armed intruder with a pointy stone carving, punching and kicking another, and killing the last one with her stiletto heels. Sartana may be violent and sexy (the camera often lingers on Alba's beautiful face, and dwells on her naked body in the shower), but she is presented as a strong and proud Latina woman, rather than merely a sexy Latina spitfire. In the fourth *Spy Kids* film, Alba plays Marissa Cortez-Wilson, a newly retired super-spy who has also recently become a mother to her own infant and a stepmother to her husband's (Joel McHale) ten-year-old twin boy and girl. The film does not shy away from displaying Alba in a tight leather bodysuit, but it does not overly fetishize her. *Spy Kids* is cartoony action, featuring Marissa as a calm, incredible fighter. She is an action heroine who learns to balance motherhood with saving the world. She is a loving wife who gains the love and admiration of her initially distant stepchildren. Marissa's ethnicity is not erased, but neither is it an issue. Marissa is undeniably sexy and violent, but she remains outside of the one-dimensional spitfire stereotype; she is also maternal but avoids that other Latina stereotype of being just a nanny for white children or a devoted and saintly maternal figure. Instead, Marissa is a super competent spy, loving wife, mother, and stepmother (she can help the kids with homework, make dinner, and save the world without breaking a sweat), who just happens to be Latina.

MIXPLOITATION AND ACTION HEROINES

The representation of black, Asian, and Latina women in popular culture has been profoundly affected by stereotyping, but these ethnically identified cinematic women also established images of female strength that helped set a precedent for the modern white action heroines that currently dominate the genre. As exotic Others, women in all three of these ethnic categories have been subjected to an excessive form of sexualization, but the stereotypes also permitted the characters to be more physical, more violent, more outspoken, and more likely to use weapons. Historically, women of color have not been treated as reverently as white women; they have not been characterized and idealized as symbols of purity, as chaste, as civilized, as dependent on men, or as deserving or in need of protection. While white heroines have become the standard in action films in the new millennium, the increasing presence of mixed race action heroines indicates the continued importance of ethnic identities. Given the recent popularity and the dramatic increase of mixed race actors, Gregory T. Carter (2008) introduced the idea of "mixploitation" as a term to describe "a set of contemporary movies that forefront mixed race movie stars. They often self-consciously present diverse, conventionally attractive casts, making the exotic looks of the mixed race stars a marketing point" (206). In contemporary culture, "mulatto," "Eurasian," and "mestiza" have lost many of their "tragic" connotations and have become desirable racial identities in Hollywood. As Jane Park argues: "If the tragic mulatto of the past reinforced the incompatibility of two distinct races, the racially ambiguous star of the present epitomizes the desirable compatibility of many races and ethnicities" (2008, 1999). The ambiguity, or liminal status, of mixed race actresses allow films to include different races, and capitalize on the established stereotypes of those ethnicities, without completely jeopardizing an ideal of heroic white womanhood.

The mixed race action heroine bridges the gap between earlier filmic depictions of strong black, Asian and Latina women, and the idealized modern white action heroine. The Orientalist stereotypes that facilitated presentations of minority women as violent, outspoken, hot-tempered, and excessively sexual established a possibility for white women to be depicted as ass-kicking heroines. And while the current white heroines are conventionally beautiful and visually fetishized according to standard Hollywood filming techniques, they are not subject to the dehumanizing stereotypes of being naturally hypersexual and treacherous racial Others in general—or jezebels, dragon ladies, and spitfires in particular. Mixed race actresses exist on the margins of whiteness and the margins of racial Other. They are just ethnic enough to bring to their roles a suggestion of different characteristics—in sexuality, physical skills, and temperament—but white enough to make these racially problematic traits palatable. Physically mixed race performers like Zoe Saldana, Maggie Q, and Jessica Alba are presented as traditionally beautiful with just enough of an exotic look to enhance their desirability. Given their range of more or less European facial features, and skin tones that appear tan or golden rather than white, these mixed race women conform to white beauty ideals at the same time that their appearance suggests a hint of more exotic possibilities. The appeal of the off-white facial features of mixed race actresses is repeated in the depiction of their ethnic, but not *too* ethnic, bodies. Zoe Saldana is extremely thin and her films showcase her tiny frame and "white girl butt," as she herself has referred to it, in direct contrast to popular culture images of black women as "thicker," "bootylicious," or muscular. Likewise, Jessica Alba may be celebrated in men's magazines for her perfect body, but part of that perfection would seem to be because it is thin and modestly curvy unlike the stereotypical exaggerated curves associated with other Latina sex symbols. Consider the description that Guzman and Valdivia (2004) provide of the media's corporeal focus on Jennifer Lopez and Salma Hayek: "While news media images of Lopez foregrounded her buttocks, photographs of Hayek emphasize her bountiful breasts, small waist, and round hips. Hayek's petite yet hyper-curvaceous frame embodies the romanticized stereotypical Latina hourglass shape" (212). In contrast, Alba's body conforms to a more waifish ideal typically associated with young white starlets.

The mixed race identities of Zoe Saldana, Maggie Q, and Jessica Alba allow films to present them as ethnic, sexy, and mysterious, but not *overly* ethnic, sexy, and mysterious. Because these women are seen as being on the margins of whiteness, they are considered by Hollywood to be the best of both worlds. They are appealing, especially as sexual fantasy women, to the widest audiences possible. To put it bluntly, the hope is that mixed race actresses will be found attractive by male viewers regardless of the viewer's own ethnicity. The mainstream sex symbol status of all three of the actresses seems to bear out this assumption about cross-racial appeal. Interestingly, this cross-racial sexual dynamic is played out in almost all of the films starring Saldana, Q, and Alba. As a point of viewer identification for white heterosexual men (the presumed largest market for action movies), these mixed race action heroines are regularly partnered with white male romantic interests—Saldana with such white actors as Sam Worthington in *Avatar*, Zachary Quinto in *Star Trek*, Jeffrey Dean Morgan in *The Losers*, and Michael Vartan in *Colombiana*; Maggie Q with Timothy Olyphant in *Live Free or Die Hard* and Shane West in *Nikita*; Jessica Alba with Bruce Willis in *Sin City*, Ioan Gruffudd in *Fantastic Four*, and Joel McHale in *Spy Kids 4*. In fact, Jessica Alba's final pairing with Mexican actor Danny Trejo in *Machete* was ridiculed by some viewers as unbelievable, but that may have been because of the gap in age and attractiveness between the two performers rather than just his ethnicity. Mixed race actresses paired with white male love interests also afford Hollywood a token feint against any lingering American fears of miscegenation. Interracial romantic relationships have always been a touchy theme in Hollywood movies and were even declared illegal to depict on screen according to the Motion Picture Production Code of 1934, and the official restriction did not wane until the mid-1950s. Mixed race couples have, of course, appeared on-screen, but until recently the topic was so controversial that it had to be handled carefully. As Beltran and Fojas point out: "these portrayals were often mitigated through casting a white (or half-white) actor to portray the nonwhite character, ensuring that audiences were not viewing *actual* miscegenation on screen" (2008, 8). Similarly, actresses like Saldana, Q, and Alba can be depicted in relationships with men of different ethnicities without it being controversial enough to become the focus of the story. Ironically, while these actresses may be "white" enough to offset lingering concerns about miscegenation, their very existence is proof of miscegenation.

The romantic pairing of mixed race actresses with white male actors in these action films shifts the balance of power and the ideological assumptions which often go along with interracial couplings in film. Unlike some of the films mentioned earlier in the chapter that typify a white male messiah complex (*Dances With Wolves, Avatar, The Last Samurai, Pocahontas*, etc.), wherein a heroic white man falls in love with a native woman and her simple culture, ultimately saving her and her people by becoming their champion or leader, these modern mixed race action heroines tend to hold far more power than the white male love interest. These heroines are strong and capable in their own right; they do not need saving from a white male. In fact, characters like Cataleya, Nikita, and Marissa hold all the power in their relationships. They are stronger, smarter, and more resourceful than their male love interests, and they are the ones who dictate the terms of the romantic involvement. Whiteness is not presented as preferable or superior; if anything, it is derided as ineffective because the white male romantic partner is deemed less competent or even humorously incompetent. These are not stories of white male privilege saving the quaint but noble ethnic Others, dabbling among exotic ethnic women, or exerting white ideals. The mixed race heroines control their own fates, fight their own battles, and choose their own romantic partners. The choice of white romantic partners does not imply a disdain for non-white ethnicities or aspirations to idealize whiteness; instead, it is simply presented as unrestricted free choice.

The mixed race action heroine stands in as a generalizable marker for ethnicity in the genre. While female characters who are fully non-white might suggest transgressive behavior and/or are too closely associated with jezebels, dragon ladies, and spitfires, the mixed race action heroine is just off-white enough to fit into the current standard of petite and white heroines. But the mixed race heroine benefits from her touch of visible ethnicity in more ways than merely the hint of exotic beauty and sexuality she embodies. In her discussion of male mixed race action heroes such as Dom (Vin Diesel) in *The Fast and the Furious* series, Mary Beltran (2005) argues that mixed race characters in action movies are granted an assumption of "cultural competence" in ethnic communities whereas white characters have to repeatedly prove their worth in order to garner any respect. "What distinguishes these new heroes," writes Beltran, "is their natural ability to navigate in, command respect in, and, when necessary, handily kick ass in a variety of ethnic communities" (2005, 54.) Like the mixed race male heroes, the mixed heroine's ethnicity grants her validity and access to subaltern groups on the periphery of dominant white society, groups that are also usually portrayed as being on the wrong side of the law. Rather than the tragic mulatto, Eurasian, and mestizo, who were alienated from both sides of their heritage, the modern mixed race heroine can function openly in both dominant and subaltern environments. This cultural competence afforded the mixed race heroine can be race specific or more generalized. For example, in *Machete* Sartana is portrayed as white enough to work as a business-suited immigration agent, and ultimately as specifically Latina enough to rally the Mexican immigrants (legal and illegal) into battle with a speech about racial injustice, with lines like: "I didn't cross the border, the border crossed me!" In a generalized sense, Maggie Q's version of Nikita is Asian enough to appear natural as an exceptional martial artist because the stereotype is so firmly ensconced in action narratives. An even more generalized example occurs with Saldana's role as Uhura in *Star Trek: Into Darkness*, when Kirk, Spock, and Uhura are caught trespassing on the Klingon homeworld, and it is Uhura who marches out on her own to negotiate with the fierce Klingons because she speaks their language and knows their violent customs. While it is ostensibly part of Uhura's job as a communications officer, there is no ignoring the fact that her partial blackness infers an access point to this foreign culture (the actors playing Klingons are all black as well), an access that the white Kirk and even the white-Vulcan Spock are alienated from.

Beltran's concept of "cultural competence" exercised by mixed race action characters can be broken down more specifically to what we might call "subcultural competency" and "dominant cultural competency." The competency that mixed race heroines demonstrate in their ability to navigate within Other ethnic groups (from Mexican laborers to Klingon warriors) is depicted in the narratives as access to specific subcultures. But the mixed race characters also have access to, and can navigate effectively in, dominant culture environments that non-whites have traditionally been denied access to. "More easily than monoracial people of color," Park observes, of mixed race characters being granted a privileged status, "multiracial folks can be regarded as symbolically white because they already contain visible traces of whiteness, which hint at the invisible, historically fetishized biological property of white blood" (Park

2008, 199). Maggie Q's Nikita is as comfortable and effective dressed in an evening gown and mingling with corporate and political bigwigs at a black-tie affair, as she is delivering roundhouse kicks to bad guys. Even on a linguistic level, Zoe Saldana, Maggie Q, and Jessica Alba have an advantage in Hollywood over many foreign-born actresses who are unable to perform American accents. Actresses like Salma Hayek, Sofia Vergara, Michelle Yeoh, and Ziyi Zhang have thick accents that restrict their range of roles in Hollywood. Difficulties with English language serve as a further signifier of racial difference, but for Saldana, Q, and Alba, American English is their first language and thus grants them a wider range of possibilities in Hollywood and greater access to dominant cultural competency. Their accent-free English is not a distraction nor does it remind viewers of their racial Otherness; they can be government agents or American everywomen. In fact, while Saldana speaks both English and Spanish fluently (raised partly in the Dominican Republic), Q and Alba struggled to learn Chinese and Spanish, respectively, for various roles. The lack of ethnically identified accents also helps dissociate these actresses from the roles of jezebel/sapphire, dragon ladies/China dolls, and spitfires.

White heroines dominate the current action genre in overwhelming numbers and in commercial profits, virtually erasing women of color from the genre. Mixed race action heroines represent a bridge between the strong ethnic characters of the past that established a filmic environment where women could be depicted kicking ass. Unfortunately, the contemporary preference for mixed race performers as a way to include ethnicity in action films without subverting the primacy of white heroines means that monoracial actresses/characters have an even greater hurdle to overcome. As Mary Beltran warns: "When multiracial actors replace monocultural actors of color, perhaps for easier consumption by audiences, they erase darker ethnic bodies in the process" (2005, 64). Actresses like Saldana, Q, and Alba have been successful in action film and television because they are relatively close to whiteness, while still carrying a degree of "safe" ethnicity. The trend of mixploitation in popular film and television is a welcome change to the overwhelming whiteness of heroes (both male and female) in popular culture, but it has not replaced whiteness as the dominant race in action narratives. Still, the success of mixed race action heroines may lead to a recognition that ethnicity does not have to limit heroism. If American audiences are willing to embrace lead action heroines who appear somewhat black, Asian, or Latina, it is not unreasonable to believe that women who are monoracial (other than white) can be popular heroines as well. The next chapter explores how specifically black heroines are handled in superhero comic books (where they are more common than in live-action film and television). As the ethnic boundaries of contemporary American culture shift and realign, we may soon have ethnically identified action heroines appearing more regularly on film and television screens.

4

PANTHERS AND VIXENS
Black Superheroines, Sexuality, and Stereotypes in Contemporary Comic Books

COMIC BOOK SUPERHEROES HAVE BEEN AN IMPORTANT PART OF AMERICAN popular culture ever since Superman first appeared in 1938. Though the medium of comic books and the genre of superheroes are typically derided as inconsequential and formulaic children's entertainment, the enduring presence of costumed super beings makes them a useful subject for tracking cultural changes. In fact, it is precisely because superheroes are considered innocuous fantasies that they warrant serious consideration. Everyone knows who Superman, Batman, Spider-Man, and Wonder Woman are. Even if we have never read a comic book, seen their movies, or watched their television series, we know their basic stories. We also know what they look like, know of their never-ending crusades for justice, and are at least familiar with their unique powers. As omnipresent characters in Western culture, superheroes help shape our ideologies. They reveal some of our most basic beliefs about morality and justice, our conceptions of gender and sexuality, and our attitudes towards ethnicity and nationality. The primary focus of this chapter is the depiction of black superheroines in contemporary comic books and how they are portrayed according to specific racial and sexual stereotypes. When looking specifically at recent stories focused on the black superheroines Black Panther and Vixen, it becomes apparent that while many of the superficial ingredients may reinforce racial and sexual stereotypes, they can also present tales that move beyond derogatory stereotypes to provide positive and heroic examples of black women in popular culture.

BACKGROUND: GENDER AND ETHNICITY IN COMIC BOOKS

Despite many cultural advances over the last fifty years, black women in the media, especially within the superhero genre, are still constructed as exotic sexual spectacles, as erotic racial "Others." In contrast to the dominant model of male heroes, and in distinction to non-ethnically identified female characters in the comics, black superheroines are often presented as hypersexual and metaphorically bestial. Moreover, popular black superheroines—like Storm, Vixen, Pantha, and the Black Panther are explicitly associated with exoticized notions of Africa, nature, noble savagery, and a variety of Dark Continent themes, including voodoo, mysticism, and animal totemism. While heroic images of black women challenge the dominant model of superheroes and represent some very real, and very positive changes, the continued use of stereotypes reinforces some of our most rudimentary racial conceptions. In the cases of Black Panther and Vixen, there is a small step forward to representing black superheroines who are more than just a cluster of racial stereotypes.

The colorful stories of comic book superheroes have always been concerned first and foremost with parables of justice and of basic cultural values about heroism, and of good triumphing over evil. But, as a great deal of research over the past two decades demonstrates, issues of gender and sexuality are also central implicit themes played out in superhero tales. Week after week, new issues hit the stands with depictions of perfectly muscled men, what Anthony Easthope (1988) refers to as "super-masculine ideals" (29), ready to defend America against any array of criminals, terrorists, or alien invaders. In addition to teaching lessons about right and wrong, superhero comic books have always provided a clear and rudimentary example of gender ideals. In comic books, women have historically been damsels in distress or—at best—plucky reporters. But men in superhero stories have always been paragons of masculinity. Male superheroes are depicted as incredibly powerful, smart, confident, and always in control. Moreover, the illustrations emphasize the muscles and the stature of the heroes as perfect male specimens. The Clark Kent and Peter Parker side of the characters may exist, but these wimpy secret identities only stress the exceptional nature of Superman and Spider-Man. Alan Klein argues that "comic book depictions of masculinity are so obviously exaggerated that they represent fiction twice over, as genre and as gender representation" (Klein 1993, 267). The conventional superhero is an adolescent fantasy of hegemonic masculinity, either literally or figuratively armored against possible threats. Scott Bukataman points out that in contemporary comics the superhero's body is "hyperbolized into pure, hypermasculine spectacle" (Bukataman 1994, 106). The masculine ideal embodied by heroes such as Superman, Batman, Iron-Man, and Captain America represent a reassuring fantasy about the eminence of patriarchal authority for the genre's mostly young and male readership.

The dominant male superheroes embody masculine ideals and serve as a point of identification for readers. Female superheroines, on the other hand, are primarily depicted as scantily clad and erotically posed fetish objects. Despite some major advancement for female characters, and an increasing presence of female writers and illustrators, women in the comics continue to be portrayed primarily as sexual spectacles.

In his analysis of comic book mutants and bodily trauma, Scott Bukataman argues that "the spectacle of the female body in these titles is so insistent, and the fetishism of breasts, thighs, and hair so complete, that the comics seem to dare you to say something about them that isn't just redundant. *Of course* the female form has absurdly exaggerated sexual characteristics; *of course* the costumes are skimpier than one could (or should) imagine; *of course* there's no visible way that these costumes could stay in place; *of course* these women represent simple adolescent masturbatory fantasies (with a healthy taste of the dominatrix)" (Bukataman 1994, 112). The unequal presentation of gender is certainly not unique to comics. In most forms of popular culture, men are depicted as strong and authoritative figures, while women are, to borrow Laura Mulvey's (1975) famous phrase, valued for their "to-be-looked-at-ness." That this gender dichotomy is taken to an extreme in comics, where men are crafted as hypermasculine heroic ideals and women as scantily clad and extremely curvaceous sexual objects, may not be surprising given the genre's target audience of young males, but it does perpetuate sexist beliefs and is indicative of the medium's reliance on stereotypes.

Just as superhero comics have always relied on gender stereotypes of the most extreme sort, ethnicity in the comics has predominantly been portrayed according to racial stereotypes. In his discussion of shifting forms of black identities within superhero stories, Marc Singer notes that "comic books, and particularly the dominant genre of superhero comic books, have proven fertile ground for stereotyped depictions of race" (Singer 2002, 123). It is this reliance on stereotypes that makes truly progressive depictions of black superhero characters difficult within mainstream comics from industry giants like Marvel and DC Comics. Black male superheroes have come a long way since Blaxploitation-influenced characters like Luke Cage, Black Panther, Black Lightning, and Black Goliath first appeared in the 1960s and 1970s (for a more detailed discussion of black male superheroes, see Brown 2001, Singer 2002, McWilliams 2010, or Cunningham 2010). In the 1960s and 1970s, Blaxploitation-inspired superheroes were mostly stereotypical "black male brutes" who focused on street crime in inner-city ghettos. Contemporary black superheroes have become far more powerful, diverse, and respected. For example, where originally Luke Cage was an ex-convict who fought pimps and drug dealers in Harlem while uttering his trademark expletive "Sweet Christmas!" the current version of Cage is a husband and father, a trusted and revered superhero who fights urban blight in inner cities as well as world-class supervillains and alien invasions; most significantly, he is also the newest leader of Marvel's legendary super-team, the Avengers. While Luke Cage may be the most remarkable example of a black superhero who has risen to prominence within the genre, he is joined by a growing number of other characters who represent a challenge to the traditionally white-dominated heroic landscape. Whether part of a team or headlining their own series, there are a substantial number of black superheroes currently populating the Marvel and DC universes, including such fan favorites as Cyborg, Steel, Blade, Icon, Static, Bishop, Mister Terrific, War Machine, and Deathlok.

While significant advancements have been made with black male superheroes, in both their sheer numbers and the manner in which they are portrayed, the development of black female superheroines has been slower. There are several notable examples of popular black superheroines in mainstream comics, including Marvel's new female version of the Black Panther and DC's Vixen, both of whom will be discussed in detail below, but they are often depicted in a manner that is more problematic than portrayals associated with either white superheroines or black superheroes. Elsewhere (Brown 2011), I contended that ethnically diverse superheroines continue to traffic in Orientalist conceptions of exotic fetishism because their portrayal is dictated by the twin burdens of racial and sexual stereotyping. In my earlier piece, I was concerned with ethnic superheroines as a general type. I argued "the power of exoticism is still a dominant trope played out on the body of the female Other, especially in visual mediums, in a manner that reduces her to a racially charged sex object and a readily consumable body" (Brown 2011, 170). Here, I want to address how the figure of the black superheroine reinforces and challenges specific racial markers. Nearly all comic book superheroines who are identified as ethnic minorities are treated as erotic spectacles, as hypersexual "Others." For example, Latina superheroines like Arana (aka Spider Girl), White Tiger, Fire, Feral, and Tarantula are routinely depicted as seductive and hot-tempered beauties, often referred to in the comics as "hot tamales." Likewise, Asian superheroines such as Lady Shiva, Katana, Hazmat, Psylocke, and Colleen Wing are portrayed as mysterious and alluring dragon ladies. By virtue of their ethnicity and their femininity, black superheroines are presented as exotic beauties in a manner similar to other female characters from different minority backgrounds. It is worth noting that, in addition to black characters, minority representation is restricted in mainstream comics almost exclusively to Asian and Latina (extraterrestrial superheroines may have different skin colors but they are physically depicted as Aryan). In addition to hypersexuality, black superheroines are also specifically aligned with Afro-centric stereotypes related to nature, mysticism, and totemism.

Volumes of research have explored the ways that black women have been constructed and reproduced in the popular imagination as supremely racialized and sexualized figures (see, for example, McClintock 1995, hooks 1992, Collins 2005, and Negra 2001). Based historically in a colonial logic that sought to contain and marginalize non-whites, and thus to valorize whiteness as a cultural category which was personified in the figure of chaste white womanhood, black women in particular became the locus for a specific set of intertwined racist assumptions. In her treatise on the colonial imagination, Anne McClintock notes the centuries-old tradition in Europe of conceptualizing Africans with unbridled sexuality: "popular lore had firmly established Africa as the quintessential zone of sexual aberration and anomaly" (McClintock 1995, 22). Patricia Hill Collins echoes the same sentiments when she argues that "through colonial eyes, the stigma of biological Blackness and the seeming primitiveness of African cultures marked the borders of extreme abnormality" (Collins 2005, 120). And most importantly, as McClintock clarifies, African "women figured as the epitome of sexual aberration and excess. Folklore saw them, even more than the men, as given to a lascivious venery so promiscuous as to border on the bestial" (Collins 2005, 22). Likewise, in his discussion of nineteenth-century depictions of black women, Sander Gilman noted that they were characterized as "more primitive, and therefore more sexually intensive" than white women and that their bodies and sexuality were described as "animal-like" (Gilman 1992, 177). This colonialist and imperialist worldview allowed white Europeans to accept a system of race-based hierarchy as natural. It also facilitated demeaning and dehumanizing practices whereby black bodies were seen as available commodities to be bought and sold in systems of slavery and where black female bodies, especially, could be presented for sexual entertainment or displayed as sexual curiosities.

Contemporary representations of black women are still haunted by the colonialist conception of African females as "animal-like" hypersexual creatures. Bell hooks notes that "representations of black female bodies in contemporary popular culture rarely subvert or critique images of black female sexuality which were part of the cultural apparatus of nineteenth-century racism and which still shapes perceptions today" (hooks 1992, 114). These stereotypes still function, at least in part, as a means to sanctify white female sexuality by contrast. In their discussion of women in modern music videos, Railton and Watson argue that depictions of sexuality are intimately grounded in these long-standing conceptions about race and gender:

> These imperial discourses are only one branch of a long tradition of cultural representation which produces white and black womanhood as very different. Much of this difference turns upon a series of binary oppositions, oppositions which both disguise the complexities of lived experience and structure thinking in ways which tend to mask and shore up hierarchies of power. Simply stated, within this tradition of representation, white women are defined by asexuality in direct contrast to the presumed hypersexuality of black women. On the one hand, black women's "hypersexuality" is seen to derive from a series of apparently natural traits that link them to the animal, the primitive and the "dirty." In defining the black woman first and foremost through a series of physical characteristics, her body is not only made available to both white and black men but the buttocks of that body are figured as emblematic of black womanhood generally and the icon of black female sexuality more precisely. (Railton and Watson 2005, 56)

The colonial tradition which Railton and Watson, Collins, hooks, McClintock, and countless others have documented clearly still informs media representations of black women as hypersexual, "booty-licious," and wild. Recent popular performers continue to present the commodifiable images of the wild black woman, from Grammy-winning singers Beyonce and Nicki Minaj, to award-winning actresses like Halle Berry, to tennis champions Venus and Serena Williams, to reality television stars like New York. Likewise, the variations of this stereotype have been explored in dozens of recent academic studies, including such specific examples as music videos (Railton and Watson 2005), sports (McKay and Johnson 2008), and even video pornography (Miller-Young 2010).

THE MODERN BLACK SUPERHEROINE

The depiction of black women as superheroines in comic books shares many of the same traits associated with black female representations in other media forms. But the very nature of superheroines facilitates a different type of representation than typically occurs when black women appear as singers, actresses, models, porn stars, and even as celebrity athletes. Despite the sexual spectacle that is an inherent aspect of contemporary superheroines, they are also undeniably strong and heroic characters. While the compounded hypersexuality of being both costumed superheroines *and* black women means that black superheroines run the risk of simply reinforcing racial and gendered stereotypes, they also have the potential to embody progressive and empowering concepts about black female strength and heroics. After all, the entire narrative purpose of any superhero is to right wrongs, to defend the weak, and to be a champion for justice. Black female characters in popular culture rarely have the potential to be as explicitly and unabashedly heroic as they do in superhero comic books.

Unfortunately, there are still relatively few black superheroines in mainstream comics. Characters like Marvel's Storm, Misty Knight, and Monica Rambeau (aka Captain Marvel), as well as DC's Thunder, Onyx, and Bumble Bee, may have a devoted following among serious comic book fans, but none of them are considered popular enough to headline their own monthly series. Most of these characters stay in circulation as minor to middling heroines on various super-teams like the Teen Titans, the Outsiders, or Heroes for Hire. Even Storm, who is arguably the most widely recognized black superheroine of all time thanks to the overwhelming popularity of the X-Men comics, cartoons, and movies, remains a character in super-team books with only an occasional one-shot or miniseries of her own. Thus, it was surprising that in 2009 both Marvel and DC chose to feature black superheroines as title characters. Marvel rebooted the *Black Panther* series with a female character taking over the role that had previously been held only by men. The first six issues of the series, in which the African princess Shuri assumes the heroic identity from her fallen brother, proved very popular and was reprinted in the trade paperback collection *Black Panther: The Deadliest of the Species* (Hudlin and Lashley 2009). At DC, the character of Vixen, who has bounced around the DC universe on various super-teams since the early 1980s, was given the opportunity to headline her own miniseries after positive fan reactions to her increased presence as a member of the newly revised Justice League of America. The title won the 2009 Glyph Fan Award (from the East Coast Black Age of Comics Con) for best comic and is available in the trade paperback collection *Vixen: Return of the Lion* (Wilson and Cafu 2009). These two books coincidentally have a lot more in common than just featuring black superheroines. Both characters are African citizens and the stories take place in fictional African settings. Moreover, both of the adventures are about characters coming into their own as superpowered beings and accepting the truth about themselves and their responsibilities. The stories of both Black Panther and Vixen involve mysticism and nature as a central plot point, and both characters have powers closely associated with animals. Though these parallel tales mobilize a range of traditional stereotypes, they each manage to present black superheroines who are ultimately far more than just wild, bestial, or hypersexual spectacles.

BLACK PANTHER'S AND VIXEN'S STORIES

The original Black Panther debuted within the pages of Marvel's *Fantastic Four* #52 in 1966, becoming the first black superhero to appear in mainstream American comic books. The Black Panther was part of the comic book industry's initial wave of Blaxploitation heroes but was popular enough to remain in circulation well after many of his imitators had perished. His biography, powers, and base of operations has been revised many times over the years, but at his core he is T'Challa, the wise ruler of the fictional and technologically advanced African nation of Wakanda. The Black Panther has a mystical connection with the Wakandan panther god that grants him superhuman senses and abilities, including increased strength, speed, agility, and stamina. By the mid-2000s, the T'Challa version of the Black Panther was firmly established as a top-tier hero, with his marriage to Ororo Monroe (aka Storm) treated as a company-wide event.

The events of *Black Panther: Deadliest of the Species* take place shortly after T'Challa's wedding. During a surprise attack by the villainous Dr. Doom, T'Challa is left comatose and Wakanda is rendered vulnerable to an impending assault by the mystical Morlun—Devourer of Totems. Ororo assumes the role of Wakanda's ruler, traveling to the underworld with the help of an ancient witch doctor in order to return her husband's soul to his body. And because Wakanda must have a military leader to survive, T'Challa's sister, Shuri, undertakes a spiritual test to become the new Black Panther. After some physical trials that pose no real challenge to Shuri, she ingests a magical herb that allows her to commune directly with the panther god. When Shuri declares herself worthy to be the next Black Panther and demands the magical gifts that go with the position, the panther god scolds her hubris and rejects her pleas. Shuri is disheartened by her failure but refuses to give up on her people in their hour of need as Morlun destroys Wakanda's army and ravages the city. Despite having no superpowers, Shuri dons the mantle of the Black Panther and sets forth on an apparent suicide mission to battle Morlun. But in the midst of the struggle Shuri's bravery is rewarded and she becomes the one true Black Panther, and destroys Morlun. "The panther god is subtle and wise," explains the witch doctor Zawavari in the final pages. "You threw yourself into the fight . . . not for glory, but for your people. And in doing so, you *became* the Black Panther." *The Deadliest of the Species* is a typical superhero story about bravery and self-sacrifice that both utilizes and challenges centuries-old stereotypes about Africa and black women.

In the DC Comics universe, Vixen was one of the first black superheroines to turn up when she made her initial appearance in the pages of *Action Comics*

#521 in 1981. Vixen is really Mari Jiwe McCabe, who was raised in a small village in the fictional African nation of Zambesi. After Mari's parents are killed, she moves to America and becomes a successful fashion model, but eventually returns to Africa to take back the magical Tantu Totem that her uncle had murdered her father for. The Tantu Totem is a mystical icon that allows Mari to tap into the Earth's "morphogenetic field" and assume the characteristics of any animal she desires—she can fly like a hawk, run with the speed of a cheetah, fight with the strength of a bear, and so on. For two decades, Vixen bounced around the DC universe on various super-teams, such as Suicide Squad, Birds of Prey, and Checkmate, before finally ending up as a core member of the Justice League of America. During his run in the mid-2000s as the writer of the revamped JLA series, Dwayne McDuffie (one of the cofounders of Milestone Media and a leader in the development of ethnically diverse superheroes) raised Vixen's profile within the team and paved the way for her own spin-off miniseries, *Vixen: Return of the Lion*.

Written by G. Willow Wilson and illustrated by Cafu, *Vixen: Return of the Lion* features a heroine who is initially insecure about her place among such superpowered luminaries as Superman, Batman, and Black Canary. The solo adventure begins when Vixen decides to return on her own to Zambesi when new information about her mother's murder comes to light. She returns to her childhood village to visit friends but finds them living in fear. Vixen is soon wounded and left to die on the African plains after an initial fight with the seemingly superpowered villain, Aku Kwesi, who both murdered her mother and continues to terrorize the village. In her weakened state, Vixen's connection to her magical animal powers begins to fade and she seems to be near death until a friendly lion finds her and delivers her to the care of Brother Tabo, a monk who helps her recover both her health and her connection to animal powers. Tabo teaches Vixen that she can have unlimited access to the spirit of the animals, even without the Tantu Totem, if she just frees her mind and soul to accept their mystical gifts. While Vixen was recovering with Brother Tabo, other members of the Justice League discovered that Kwesi was more than just a local warlord: he was helping to organize the super-villains known as "Intergang" so they could gain a foothold on the African continent. Several of the League's top guns travel to Africa but are ambushed by Intergang, who manage to poison Superman and Black Canary and turn them into mindless zombies who attack their own teammates. Vixen arrives with a newfound confidence and sense of purpose and first fights with and then cures Superman moments before he could kill all of the heroes. Vixen then returns to the village and defeats Kwesi on her own before returning to America a renewed superheroine.

RECURRING THEMES

That both *Black Panther: Deadliest of the Species* and *Vixen: Return of the Lion* are set in Africa is atypical for the superhero genre. Stories are usually set in either real or fictional American cities, thus allowing the heroes to explicitly defend "the American way." When Africa, or any other foreign locale, is utilized, the setting characteristically implies an atmosphere of unfamiliar danger. That both Black Panther and Vixen are African lends the setting more authenticity. Africa is not presented in either story as a mysterious or unknowable place for the heroines. They are familiar with the customs, the people, and the landscape. The overall effect, though, does conform to what Edward Said (1979) famously described as Western "Orientalist" notions of Africa as a treacherous Dark Continent. In the colonialist fantasy that Said outlines, the West perceives the East, and in fact all who can be categorized as "Others," as mysterious and exotic mythical places filled with primitive natives, bizarre customs, and dangerous environments. This collective fiction of the "Orient" has long provided a justification for the Western world's domination and subjugation of non-Western nations and people. As in conventional adventure stories, danger lurks around every corner in both *Deadliest of the Species* and *Return of the Lion*, and much of it is presented as specifically wild African dangers. For example, the Black Panther has to fight off real panthers and battle African sorcery, and Vixen is attacked by lions, as well as the warlords who target her village.

In addition to the omnipresence of dangerous wild panthers and lions, it is the presence of voodoo throughout both of the stories that most stereotypically aligns Africa and these black superheroines with ideas of Africa as a mysterious and primitive land. Shuri is granted her Black Panther superpowers by the mystical panther god and eventually defeats the black magic of Morlun with the aid of an ancient witch doctor. Vixen has to reconnect with the magic powers of her amulet totem and is renewed by the faith and teachings of an African monk. In both stories, the people of Africa are depicted as superstitious, resorting to mystical herbs and witch doctors to help save Wakanda, and repeatedly accusing Vixen of being a "voduun" witch for her powers. To their credit, the Black Panther stories also depict Wakanda as a technologically advanced society, complete with supercomputers, hi-tech medical equipment, and flying motorbikes. But since this is a genre in which people can fly, shoot laser beams out of their eyes, and ice from their fingers, voodoo is an accepted reality in superhero comics. The presence of voodoo is never questioned or treated as out of the ordinary in these stories. More specifically, voodoo is not treated as a uniquely African motif. Taken as singular examples, these stories might compound stereotypes of Africa as a dark, mysterious, and mystical place, but for regular readers of superhero comics, it is only part and parcel of the genre itself.

Both Black Panther and Vixen have costumed identities and powers associated with animals. This animalistic association is a clear remnant of colonial stereotypes that characterized African women as the embodiment of an abnormal, voracious, and almost beastial sexuality. The trade paperback covers for both *Black Panther: Deadliest of the Species* and *Vixen: Return of the Lion* depict strikingly similar images that clearly suggest a range of stereotypes about black women as exotic sexual fantasies. The cover illustration for *Deadliest of the Species* shows Shuri in the skintight black leather panther costume that covers her entire body, head, and face. With just a thin belt slung low around her hips and a long necklace hanging across her breasts, the costume seems to be, in typical comic book fashion, simply painted on to her body. Every curve is emphasized as this female Black Panther leans back against a jungle tree with one arm entwined with a branch and her head tilted in an inviting pose (it is difficult to imagine Marvel portraying T'Challa's male version of the character in a similar cheesecake pose). Under her other arm is a large, muscular, and snarling black panther. Similarly, the cover for *Return of the Lion* features Vixen splayed out in the tall grass of the African plains in her signature skintight, mustard-colored body costume complete with clawed gloves and a plunging neckline that shows off much of her chest. Vixen is lying back with one leg flirtatiously pulled up across the other, her head is tilted, and her expression is, like Black Panther's, both confidently challenging and seductive. Accompanying Vixen is a majestic male lion that she is leaning against, with one arm stretched out behind his mane and the other stretched across his torso.

These purely symbolic images (neither depicts a scene that actually occurs in the stories) are typical of the way that superheroines are portrayed as sexual objects on comic book covers. While male characters usually strike heroic action poses, superheroines are far more likely to be illustrated as pinups or centerfolds. Given both the ethnicity of these two specific superheroines and the nature of these adventures, the covers of both *Deadliest of the Species* and *Return of the Lion* symbolically also allude to a level of racial fetishization. The jungle and the plains settings suggest an aura of savage primitivism associated with Africa as the Dark Continent. The costumes, like those of all superheroines, clearly mark the characters as promising the possibility of erotic and/or fetishistic adventures. Or what Bukataman referred to in the earlier quotation as "simple adolescent masturbatory fantasies (with a healthy taste of the dominatrix)" (Bukataman 1994, 112). And the presence of the panther and the lion

Fig. 4.1. *Vixen* cover, © DC Comics.

symbolizes the heroines' powers, but also their affinity with nature and these deadly beasts. That each heroine is posed seductively with an arm around these ferocious African cats further implies that the women's sexuality may be alluring but it is animalistic and threatening as well.

That both Black Panther and Vixen are explicitly associated with big cats is especially noteworthy. Of course, Black Panther's powers are based in those of a real panther and are magically bestowed by a panther god, so her animal association makes sense narratively. But Vixen, whose magical totemic powers grant her access to the abilities of all animals, is repeatedly aligned with lions specifically—as the title, *Return of the Lion*, makes clear. At various points in her story, Vixen is ambushed by a lion, saved by one, and has to fight another that has gone mad and attacked a village. When Vixen slays this rogue beast, she repeats the mantra, "I *am* the lion. I *am* the lion." The strong association of these heroines with wild African cats is easy to interpret as both racial and sexual in nature. This symbolic alignment of superheroic identities with animals is a common convention in comic books, and is not restricted to women or ethnically identified characters. The genre is ripe with this type of hero:

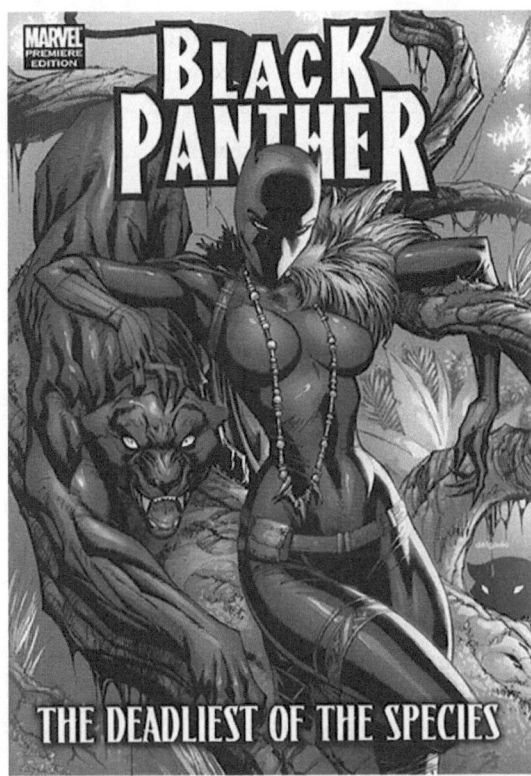

Fig. 4.2. *Black Panther* cover, © Marvel Comics.

Batman, Spider-Man, Hawkman, Animal-Man, the Blue Beetle, the Falcon, etc. But the overloaded sexual symbolism of cats and their specifically feminine connotations is hard to ignore. Male superheroes associated with cats do exist, such as the original Black Panther or the villain Cat-Man, but they are far fewer and much less sexually charged than female-costumed cat characters. The best known may be Catwoman (often described as "the original feline fatale"), but she is joined by the likes of Black Cat, Pantha, Tigra, Cheetah, Hellcat, Shadowcat, Alley Cat, and Feral.

The sexual inference of these various "catwomen" is clearer in some cases than others. Both Tigra and Cheetah, for example, are literally drawn as sexy cats, and sometimes are even called "pussies" by other characters. They each have ideal female bodies but are covered in actual fur, stripes and all, and have tails. To stress the exoticism of their sexy feline/female bodies, Tigra and Cheetah wear only the skimpiest of bikinis as their costumes. As one adolescent superhero in training says of Tigra in *Avengers Academy* #8: "She walks around practically naked." It is worth noting that both Tigra and Cheetah are Latina characters so their sexual depiction also serves to reinforce their ethnic stereotyping. Other feline-costumed characters, like the white women Catwoman and Black Cat, are only symbolically associated with cats through their roles as cat burglars and their cat-themed costumes. Yet Catwoman and Black Cat are both portrayed as eminently erotic—as sex kittens, who flirtatiously and shamelessly flaunt their figures in revealing outfits. All of these fictional catwomen in comics are a modern embodiment of the centuries-old conception of cats as feminine, sexual, and untrustworthy (see, for example, Darnton 1984). Black Panther and Vixen also fit into this catlike sexual iconography, but no more so than any of the other characters. In other words, their identity as black women who are depicted as catlike does have racist stereotype implications, but it is also a formulaic convention of the larger superhero genre. Yes, these feline heroines are eroticized, but their sexualization seems to have less to do with their ethnicity than it does with the genre itself. Black Panther and Vixen may be animal-like but their totemic association is not explicitly linked to their sexuality (as it is with Tigra, Catwoman, and Black Cat); instead, it is tethered to their physical strength. At least in *Deadliest of the Species* and *Return of the Lion*, the heroines' animal nature is not explicitly about sex.

To say that the wild animal nature of both Black Panther and Vixen's superheroine identity is not explicitly linked to their sexuality in these stories is not to say that they are exempt from sexualized depictions. They are both illustrated as extremely attractive, fit women in skintight costumes. And, as the cover illustrations make clear, they are both positioned and sold as erotic spectacles. Yet neither story contains romantic subplots or erotic scenes, and no one comments on their attractiveness or even makes a sexist remark. Furthermore, despite the pinup quality of the covers, the interior artwork does not overtly stress their idealized bodies—certainly no more that any other comic book depiction of women (and far less than most). In these particular stories, Black Panther and Vixen are no more sexualized than white superheroines usually are. Given that the superhero genre routinely depicts women visually in a highly fetishistic manner, and that black women continue to be represented as hypersexual in the media, it would seem logical for these characters to be determined first and foremost by their sexuality. By not overemphasizing Black Panther's and Vixen's sexuality, according to centuries-old racial stereotypes, these stories do not contribute to the accumulative and persistent type of characterization that Railton and Watson argue occurs in other media forms like music videos.

Railton and Watson conclude that "through regular and explicit references to the natural and the animal, the black female body and black sexuality continue to be figured as primal, wild, and uncontrollable" (Railton and Watson 2005, 58). Black Panther and Vixen are clearly associated with animals but not in a manner that links their sexuality to being "primal, wild, and uncontrollable." The stories move the characters beyond such simple classifications. It is unfortunate that the covers still rely on this type of stereotype to promote the books because they do not do justice to the progressive representations of black superheroines that the books offer.

This over-reliance and easy association of black women with animalistic hypersexuality as a way to market black female characters is the persistent problem. Individual stories such as *Deadliest of the Species* and *Return of the Lion* can represent a progressive step away from rudimentary stereotypes, but the stories and the characters still exist within a larger stereotypical context. In other comics, Shuri's version of the Black Panther is lusted after and illustrated to show off her ideal figure to maximum effect. Likewise, Vixen—her very name implies a seductress—is often portrayed as sexually active, physically attractive (she is a supermodel after all) and even a bit of a superheroine homewrecker. But in these two books the heroines' sexuality is downplayed in favor of their heroism. The most sexually evocative moment in either story involves the supporting character of Storm who has to strip naked in order to travel to the underworld to rescue her husband T'Challa in *Deadliest of the Species*. Thus, a black superheroine is displayed as a sexual spectacle, but it is not one of the title characters. And even this minor instance of Storm's disrobing is a far cry from the blatantly erotic way she is normally depicted. It is also very different from the way other black superheroines are routinely hypersexualized, such as Big City Comics' Ant (aka Hannah Washington), who is always illustrated with her butt thrust out evocatively, or Marvel's Misty Knight, who at times seeks out rough-and-dirty recreational sex with other superheroes just to blow off some steam (for a more detailed discussion, see Brown 2011, 178). In contrast to the way most superheroines—black or otherwise—are depicted, these solo adventures of Black Panther and Vixen are remarkably chaste.

DRAWING CONCLUSIONS

As the highest-profile books to feature Black Panther and Vixen, *Deadliest of the Species* and *Return of the Lion* demonstrate that comics featuring black superheroines can be successful without reducing the characters to the most sexist and racist stereotypes associated with black women. I would not go so far as to suggest that black superheroines in general are moving beyond the colonial-influenced jezebel stereotype; it is an unfortunate fact that the superhero genre of comic books continues to rely heavily on stereotypes of all kinds. It is not a medium or a genre that lends itself to mature and nuanced storytelling. But it is a form of mass-mediated popular culture where individual writers and artists can present radically different versions of characters. The fact that both *Deadliest of the Species* and *Return of the Lion* strive to represent black superheroines as fully three-dimensional characters can be attributed to the fact that the books were written and illustrated by creators who are explicitly concerned with the political ramifications of depicting race and gender.

Reginald Hudlin, the author of *Black Panther: Deadliest of the Species*, is an African American writer with a long history of creating progressive black characters. Similarly, G. Willow Wilson, the author of *Vixen: Return of the Lion*, is a woman whose work consistently addresses issues of gender, religion, and Middle Eastern cultures. In a medium where individual creators can have a direct impact on characterization (more so than in mediums like film or television), the increasing presence of writers and illustrators from a diversity of backgrounds bodes well for the future of diverse superheroes and superheroines.

Even within a genre that is typically derided as juvenile, and which traffics predominantly in stereotypical characterizations and extreme portrayals of gender and sexuality, there can be progressive representations of black women. The wild, animal-like hypersexual stereotype of black women that continues to dominate in film, television, music, and even sports exists in superhero comics as well, but as the specific example of Black Panther and Vixen indicate, there is a very real possibility of challenging the one-dimensional racist and sexist logic. Although Black Panther and Vixen may initially appear to simply reinforce the colonialist stereotype of African women (literally "at first glance," given the deceiving erotic come-on of the covers), the stories reveal a message of heroism attributed to these black superheroines. Rarely are black women portrayed in any medium as independent, intelligent, and both physically and spiritually strong. Heroic black women who avoid racist and sexist stereotypes do appear on several police procedural shows on television, but such shows generally feature ensemble casts with white male leads. In headlining their own comic books, Black Panther and Vixen represent rare instances of black heroines taking center stage without resorting to any excessive fetishization of their bodies. While these characters may be costumed in the standard superheroine uniform of revealing skintight outfits, their heroic actions far outweigh the spectacle of eroticism. In these specific cases, Black Panther and Vixen are heroes, first and foremost. They save their families, their villages, and their fictional African nations. They also save themselves from numerous physical and emotional dangers, and model new possibilities for the representation of black women in popular culture.

5

SUPERMOMS?
Maternity and the Monstrous-Feminine in Superhero Comics

DEPICTIONS OF COSTUMED SUPERHEROINES HAVE BEEN DOMINATED BY overt sexualization ever since Wonder Woman first appeared in her high-heeled boots, skirt, and eagle-adorned bustier in 1940. Modern female characters are so thoroughly eroticized that it is nearly impossible to find a superheroine or villainess that is not defined primarily by her sex appeal, all in an attempt to cater to the mostly male comics consumer. Yet, while the illustrations continue to fetishize female bodies at an almost pornographic level, there has been an increased effort by the major publishers to portray superheroines as powerful and legitimate characters in their own right. This double-bind of physical exploitation and narrative legitimization is apparent in Marvel's various celebrations in 2010 of the "Women of Marvel." In a range of special issues, variant covers, miniseries, and collector's magazines, Marvel struggled to position themselves as a female-friendly line with strong feminist characters without sacrificing the central role of heroines as pinups. The irony of showcasing sexy covers of superheroines to celebrate their strength was not lost on most involved with mainstream comics. What is more troubling, and more revealing of gender concerns, is that leading up to, and carrying over into, Marvel's year-long celebration of women was the catastrophic "House of M" event that wiped out or depowered 98 percent of all mutants. In the "House of M" storyline, the Scarlet Witch essentially loses touch with reality and reshapes the universe so that she can magically recreate her lost children. That her maternal desires are portrayed as selfish, destructive, psychotic, delusional, and ultimately villainous is indicative of the genre's conflicting messages about femininity—not just in terms of sexuality but more specifically regarding issues of maternity. The depiction of maternity in recent superhero comics reveals and reinforces cultural fears about female bodies as unstable and uncontrollable agents of abjection. Moreover, this rejection of the maternal in superhero comic books contributes to a greater emphasis on the stability of fatherhood and by extension reaffirms cultural and legal conceptions of paternal authority.

At its core, the superhero genre is about boundaries. In story after story, decade after decade, costumed heroes save the world, solve the crime, thwart the super-villain, and protect the innocent. Specific plots are almost irrelevant; what the superheroes repeatedly enact for readers is a symbolic policing of the borders between key cultural concepts—good and evil, right and wrong, us and them. Intertwined with these abstract concepts are corporeal boundaries between male and female, mind and body, self and other, that are just as obsessively and problematically policed by superheroes as the literal borders between nation states are. Scott Bukataman, in his discussion of mutant superheroes and shifting attitudes towards flesh and society, notes that "superhero bodies, despite their plasticity, are armored bodies, rigid against the chaos of the surrounding disorder" (1994, 103). Conventional superhero bodies tend to be impenetrable (Superman, Power Girl, Luke Cage, Captain Marvel), literally armored (Iron-Man, Hardware, Steel, Cyborg), or symbolically armored with bodies or skin made of substances infinitely more resilient than mere flesh (Collosus, the Thing, Mettle). But superhero bodies are also "plastic" in that they can stretch (Mr. Fantastic, Plastic Man), shrink (the Atom, Ant Man), grow (Giant Man, Stature), change their physical structure (Metamorpho, Veil, Dust), shapeshift (Mystique, Beast Boy, Chameleon), or do anything else that the writers can dream up. It is the boundaries of these fluid and explosive unarmored superhero bodies that Bukataman argues modern comics strive to reinforce. Typified by the ever-popular mutants of the Marvel universe whose "traumatized, eruptive bodies . . . continually threaten to overspill their fragile vessels" (1994, 115) that are situated as "categorical mistakes," these difficult-to-control bodies are easy to understand as metaphorically adolescent entities. The mutants' constant struggle to contain and discipline his body adds an emotional and melodramatic element to the obvious male power fantasy and pubescent metaphor that is an enduring theme for the superhero genre.

The policing of boundaries, especially bodily boundaries, that serves as a fundamental trope in superhero stories takes on added significance with female characters. Like the fascist male military body (see Theweilt 1977) and the hypermuscular male bodybuilder (see Klein 1993), the armoring of the superhero body is fundamentally about the rejection of fluidity and softness, which are traits associated with femininity. The bind for superheroines is that they need to be both an armored, tough, powerful, disciplined body (in essence a masculinized body) *and* a soft, curvaceous, exposed, and inviting body (in essence a feminized body). In retaining a greater emphasis on the sexualized and feminized superheroine body in order to avoid implications of butchness, lesbianism, or any other obvious threats of emasculation that would undermine the masculine fantasy on offer, the genre's depiction and reaction to policing female bodily boundaries reveals a deep-seated fear of female reproductive abilities. That the Scarlet Witch's psychic breakdown over the loss of her children and her subsequent magical recreation of them was the catalyst for a planet-wide mutant genocide is just one of the recent ways that maternity in the comics has been cast as an example of femininity as both literally and figuratively monstrous.

THE PREGNANT SUPERHEROINE

Given the emphasis on origins in superhero narratives, and the increasingly active sexual relations between costumed do-gooders, it is surprising that pregnancy is not a more common occurrence in comics. Then again, the depiction of pregnancy in Western popular culture has always been a mixture of celebration and trepidation. Recent films like *Juno* (2007), *Knocked Up* (2007), *Waitress* (2007), and *The Back-Up Plan* (2010) have been lauded for their humorous and realistic depiction of unexpected pregnancies (as well as their tacit pro-life positions). But these films clearly convey messages about the type of women who can handle unexpected pregnancies (white and middle-class), and that while a traditional nuclear family may no longer be required, the woman is still supposed to be magically transformed by the experience and to sacrifice everything for the good of her baby. As much as we explicitly value pregnancy in our culture as a beautiful and life-affirming event, the media also presents a plethora of warning parables about how maternity should be done. The current tabloid and reality television freak show characterization of women like Kate Gosselin (now a single mother of eight children who seems more intent on maintaining her celebrity status than on being a mother), the various teenage mothers featured on MTV's *16 and Pregnant* and *Teen Moms* (who illustrate the pitfalls of becoming a mother too young), and of course Nadia Suleman (dubbed the Octomom, which certainly sounds like a super-villain) who is derided as crazy and irresponsible for choosing to be artificially inseminated with "too many" fertilized eggs while both unemployed and unmarried. In contemporary culture, pregnancy is a contestable terrain on a number of levels, from birth control and abortion debates, to paternal versus maternal rights, to adoption and medical treatment.

When pregnancies do occur in superhero comics, it is usually treated as a problem for the characters to overcome and is indicative of the genre's

SUPERMOMS? 139

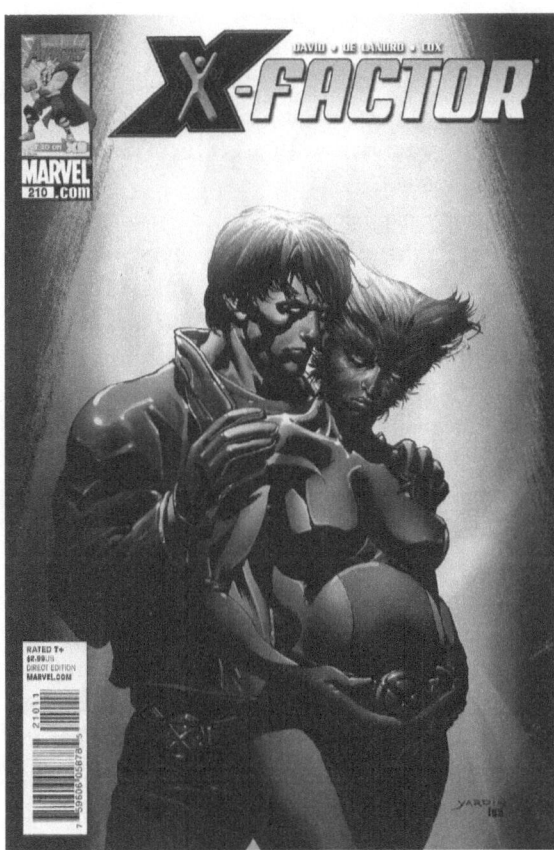

Fig. 5.1. The pregnant superheroine disrupts comic book ideals about perfect and impenetrable bodies (*X-Factor* cover, © Marvel Comics).

overall dismissive attitude regarding the maternal. On a basic level, superheroine pregnancies are used as a narrative device to create tension and to position the woman as exceptionally vulnerable. On a symbolic level, the few pregnancies that do occur are problematic because they challenge the strictly enforced bodily boundaries that are fundamental to the heroic fantasy. In a genre obsessed with armoring, containing, and defending the integrity of self-sufficient and powerful bodies, a pregnant body is troublesome because it evidences the inherent fluidity and penetrability of the superheroine. A 2010 storyline in Marvel's *X-Factor* provides a humorous but clear example of pregnancy characterized as a failure to protect bodily boundaries. When the very visibly pregnant Rahne (a heroic werewolf) catches a cab on her way to a doctor's appointment with her ex-boyfriend Rictor (who mistakenly thinks he is the father), he says, "Hey, [springing for a cab] beats having strangers elbowing you in the gut." Rahne replies, "Ohhh, Ah can take it. Ah'm pretty sturdy these days. Almost impenetrable." But the nosy cab driver points out

"'Almost' being the key word, from the look of things." Rictor is offended by the comment but Rahne finds it funny. It is an odd scene in a subplot outside of the larger heroics of the series but it does reveal how clearly pregnancy is seen as a failure to safeguard bodily boundaries. In a genre all about being impenetrable, "almost" is not good enough.

Pregnancy is a sign that the body has been penetrated. The borders of the body have been breached in some manner, even if the conception is immaculate, magical, psychic, or scientific (all of which are possibilities in comic books). The pregnant body also violates principles of discipline and containment in that it becomes a body that bursts forth with increased mass and with various leaking fluids. This changing body challenges cultural notions of corporeal and social stability. "Pregnant women's body fluids pose a threat to social control and order," writes Robyn Longhurst. "Their border ambiguity may become, for others, a threat to their own borders and they may react with feelings of loathing as the means of restoring the border separating self from other. They may try to confine the pregnant woman in the private realms because of the threat that her leaking, seeping body, her womanly corporeal flows and her splitting self, poses to the rational public world" (2001, 41). Seen from this perspective, the pregnant body undermines some of our most basic beliefs about the importance of corporeal integrity and analogous social rules. Like Longhurst, Mary Anne Doane points out that "it would seem that the concept of motherhood automatically throws into question ideas concerning the self, boundaries between self and other, and hence identity" (1999, 27). This question of stable identity raised by permeable maternal boundaries is particularly threatening within a genre that is premised on safeguarding the body as a means to declare one's own exceptional identity. The readers' identification with superheroes as ideal selves (see Eco 1979) is intimately wrapped up in the fantasy of being undeniably important. To be able to assert one's identity authoritatively and conclusively, at least vicariously through the characters, is part of the pleasure of the genre. Thus, a central cliché in superhero stories is not just the iconic costuming but the opportunity to be identifiable. The importance of empowerment through self-declaration is crystallized in the frequent use of decisive proclamations used in every superhero movie: "I'm Batman!" "Who am I? I'm Spider-man!" "The suit and I are one. I am Iron-Man!" "I'm Kick-Ass!" A firm, uncontestable identity is essential for superheroes. To undermine this all-important sense of identity, as pregnancy seems to do, is downright villainous in superhero narratives.

A pregnant body is what some feminist theorists describe as an abject body or a monstrous-feminine body. In *The Powers of Horror* (1982), Julia Kristeva argues that depictions of the abject are crucial for solidifying the cultural norms that define and delineate the borders between order and that which lies beyond acceptability. In psychoanalytic terms, Kristeva argues there is an association of "the maternal with the abject—i.e., that which is the focus of combined horror and fascination, hence subject to a range of taboos designed to control the culturally marginal" (Doane 1991, 26). The pregnant body in particular can be monstrous precisely because it indicates a collapse between inside and outside, between self and other. At its core, abjection is that which refuses to "respect borders, rules," and it "disturbs identity, system and order" (Kristeva 1982, 4). Through various cultural rituals and personal lessons, societies demarcate a symbolic line between the acceptable and the abject. Elements of abjection are coded as taboo because they violate borders, from sexual prohibitions against incest and bestiality to disgust with corpses and bodily waste. Of course, abject elements can never be fully expunged, and indeed are needed to validate acceptable elements by contrast. As Barbara Creed (1986) has demonstrated, horror is a genre that routinely exercises and reinforces our fear of the abject by transgressing boundaries between features such as life and death (ghosts, zombies), human and animal (werewolves, vampires), and bodily integrity versus vulnerability (all those stabbed, chopped, and mutilated victims). Where the horror genre works to enforce rules against abjection through explicit fear, the superhero genre works by marking the rejection of the abject as a heroic act. Both genres contain bodies that at times erupt and explode beyond their own borders but where horror eradicates those bodies, superheroes struggle to contain them.

A pregnant body is not the ideal well-protected, impervious body valorized in comics with their illustrations of perfectly muscled and toned heroes and heroines in skintight costumes. In contrast, a visibly pregnant body, such as Rahne's in *X-Factor*, is one which is swelling, protruding, and changing. Given the superhero genre's visual emphasis on the standard well-contained, sexy, pinup-like bodies of heroines, a pregnant body stands apart as a disturbing anomaly. In contrast to the other bodies on display, a pregnant body in comics is coded as abject. In superhero stories, bodies may be injured and bloodied in battle, erupt into flames, turn into ice, or shoot energy blasts from eyes or hands—but these bodies are still visually represented as muscular, heroic, and enduring. These bodies may risk being penetrated or torn apart or of losing control, but they never really succumb to these threats. A pregnant body, on the other hand, is no longer a disciplined body. It grows, leaks, consumes, and eventually reproduces. It is a body that is anathema to the perfect figures that constitute the visual terrain of superhero books. The pregnant body is so beyond the norm for comics that creators will often go to great lengths to erase its presence. Some stories may skip over the entire period of a superheroine's pregnancy in order to avoid depicting these sexual fantasy figures with anything less than a perfect body. Children may just pop up from alternate universes (as happened with Power Girl) or the heroine may have a superfast pregnancy (as happened to the Invisible Woman) or they may be alluded to only in flashbacks (as happened to the Black Widow). In a recent storyline, the entire DC universe skipped ahead a full year so that Catwoman suddenly had a baby—but the series managed to avoid illustrating her as anything but her usual flawlessly fit and sexy feline fatale. More than perhaps any other longstanding character, Catwoman's appeal has been predicated on her sexuality. As a temptation for Batman, and as an erotic object for readers, Catwoman embodies a preadolescent type of sexual fantasy that is at once enticing and frightening. Her excessively fetishized body suggests both a promise of sexual penetrability and a refusal of it. The skintight leather body suit that has been Catwoman's costume for the past few decades both reveals her fit body and contains it. To draw this figure of ideal comic book sexuality as a pregnant woman in the third trimester would risk destroying a carefully crafted fantasy. With Catwoman, the abject implications of pregnancy were circumvented, literally erased from view, so that she could still seem a self-contained, hard-body heroine.

SUPERHEROINE MOTHERS

While the pregnant body itself represents a threatening dissolution of bodily boundaries and serves as a symbol of femininity as monstrous, the concept of motherhood is often treated with equal derision in superhero comics. In a genre obsessed with perpetuating a fantasy of hegemonic masculinity, there are very limited options for maternal roles. Few positive examples exist of superheroine mothers. Sue Storm, the Invisible Woman from the Fantastic Four, is the only character with a long-standing history of achieving supermom status. Since she first appeared in 1961, Sue has been depicted as a standard physical ideal and love object (for her husband Reed Richards, aka Mr. Fantastic, and numerous villains such as Dr. Doom and Namor), and eventually balanced superheroics with motherhood after giving birth to twin children, Franklin and Val Richards. Despite a few debatable decisions to leave her children while on adventures, Sue has been portrayed as a loving, competent, and fiercely protective mother. Her success as a mother is a natural character extension from her overriding and initial role as a maternal figure for her superhero team/family. But Sue's ability to balance heroics with maternal responsibilities is not the norm within the genre. At the very least, supermoms are more likely to be portrayed as falling short as mothers and/or restricting their husbands from fulfilling his heroic needs. Outside of comics examples like Elasti-Girl from the animated film *The Incredibles* and Stephanie Powell, the workaholic mother from the television program *No Ordinary Family*, are characters who illustrate negative depictions of would be supermoms. But at least Elasti-Girl and Stephanie Powell are able to redeem themselves somewhat as both parents and heroes. Maternal figures within comics are far more likely to be unable to find an effective balance between motherhood and superpowered adventures. A quick survey of maternity in comics reveals four consistent tropes: 1) the superheroine chooses to give up her child in order to continue her career, 2) she has to give up her heroic calling to assume motherhood as a full-time role, 3) she repeatedly puts her child at risk because she continues her adventures, and 4) mothers are cast as purely monstrous because they are inherently evil, neglectful, or absent. The serial and melodramatic nature of the genre also means that some female characters enact two or more of these negative tropes at the same time.

Several recent storylines in DC Comics demonstrate the tendency of superheroines to give up motherhood in favor of continuing their careers. While having a heroine become pregnant may facilitate some interesting plots, the publishers often jettison the child soon after it is born because babies get in the way of depicting adventures and perhaps because motherhood interferes with the sexual fantasy of ideal latex-wearing women for readers. For example, in a recent storyline the fishnet- and leather-clad Black Canary rescued and then adopted a young girl named Sin who was being raised to become an assassin. Black Canary initially stepped back from superheroing to provide the child with a normal upbringing. But by the end of the miniseries "Living with Sin," Black Canary acquiesces to the plan of her husband, Green Arrow, to fake Sin's death and place the child in a foster home so that she will be safe. In a rather sadistic manner, Green Arrow let his wife think that Sin was really dead so that her emotions would seem genuine to Black Canary's enemies. Similarly, the child born to Stephanie Brown, aka the Spoiler, a teen heroine and one-time girl Robin to Batman, is quietly given up for adoption so that Stephanie is free to continue heroics and eventually assume the mantle of Batgirl in her own series. Yet the most egregious example, and the one that has generated the most debate among fans, is the case of Selina Kyle, otherwise known as Catwoman. In the DC event "One Year Later," Selina reappears coming home from the hospital with her newborn baby girl, Helena. Selina is initially adamant about being a mother and relinquishes her role as Catwoman, even passing her costumed identity along to a friend. Yet within a few days Selina cannot resist the urge to put on her leather costume and head out into the night. After some humorous observations about weight gain and how much tighter her bodysuit is, Selina is drawn into a bit of crime-fighting that convinces her she is still needed as Catwoman. By the time she returns home, villains have broken into her apartment and attempt to kidnap Helena. Because she can never really give up being Catwoman and because it is obvious that her role will always place her infant in danger, Selina enlists Bruce Wayne's assistance in giving Helena up for adoption. Furthermore, Selina even asks the heroic magician Zatanna to erase the memory of Helena from her mind because the knowledge of giving her up is so painful. Although Zatanna refuses to erase Selina's memories because she deems it unethical, the writers manage to enact an amnesia of their own by simply returning Catwoman to her adventures as if nothing had ever interfered with her position as the DC universe's ultimate sexy bad girl heroine.

Giving up the child in order to continue a career as a crime fighter is far more common than the reverse (giving up superheroics to become a full-time parent). For publishers, giving up the child allows superheroine characters to stay in circulation and thus remain profitable properties. It is far more difficult to keep a character involved in the action if she no longer dons a costume. Within the Marvel universe, Jessica Jones, the one-time superheroine Jewel, is one of the few characters to continue appearances despite rejecting the costumed life. The decision to write Jessica as a non-heroing mother was perhaps easier for writers because she had already been established as pursuing a career as a non-costumed investigator in two Brian Michael Bendis-penned series, *Alias* and *The Pulse*. Over the course of both series, Jessica becomes pregnant by her boyfriend and eventual husband, Luke Cage, aka Power Man. After a pregnancy that fans joked literally lasted years, Jessica gave birth to their daughter, Danielle. The birth also coincided with the end of Jessica's own series in *The Pulse* #14. Jessica continues to appear fairly regularly in several Marvel books, most prominently in variations of *The Avengers* also written by Bendis, where her husband is a member of the team. Throughout the Marvel-wide events "House of M," "Civil War," "Secret Invasion," and "Dark Reign," Jessica is depicted as choosing motherhood over heroics, despite repeated pleas from her husband and others, including Iron-Man and Spider-Man, to become an active superheroine again. During the "Civil War" storyline, Jessica even leaves her husband and takes the baby with her to Canada to avoid registering her superpowers and thus becoming a potential target for villains. In fact, Jessica only uses her superpowers when her child's life is at risk, as when Danielle is kidnapped during the events of "Secret Invasion" and the subsequent "Dark Reign." It is Jessica's steadfast refusal to put her responsibilities as a mother in the background that marks her as a strong character rather than a selfish one. As of this writing, though, Marvel has initiated plans to put Jessica back in costume. It remains to be seen what this means for her role as a mother.

As the examples from the first two tropes of supermotherhood suggest, the third pattern of depicting maternity as putting children at risk is a common narrative device in the comics. Both Catwoman's and Jessica Jones's daughters are abducted by villains, as was Sue Storm's daughter, Val, in one of the "Women of Marvel" special miniseries *Heralds*. It is perhaps indicative of the genre's persistent misogyny that it is so often daughters who are kidnapped, further emphasizing a time-honored tradition of females as points of vulnerability, as damsels in distress, no matter how young they are. This third trope of motherhood is taken to an extreme in Top Cow's series *Witchblade*, when the titular heroine Sara Perenzinni becomes magically pregnant with a child who is destined to tip the scales between the mystical forces of lightness and darkness (collected in trade paperback [TPB] *Witchblade*, Volume 5, 2008). When Angelus warriors learn that Perenzinni was impregnated by the spirit of Darkness while she was in a coma, an entire army of Angels sets out to kill her and her unborn child, fearing that the child's birth will allow Darkness to triumph in their eternal battle. With the aid of her friends, and a few enemies, Perenzinni manages to fight off attack after attack until she finally gives birth to her daughter while the battle reaches its zenith outside her bedroom door. Immediately after giving birth, Perenzinni returns to the battle in full Witchblade armor and proudly declares: "I'll kill anyone who touches my baby!" Despite her defiant and protective attitude, however, the baby is taken from her. Fortunately, the minutes-old baby is magical and she herself triggers a massive blast that evaporates all of the warriors around her (except, of course, her mother and allies). Following this epic battle, Perenzinni tries to devote herself to full-time motherhood but is constantly dragged back into adventures as time and again her daughter, Hope, is put in danger. The following six issues of the series all involve attempted kidnappings by various angels, demons, and ghosts. For long stretches, the series equates being a mother and protecting your child with being superheoic. This in itself could be a hopeful metaphor except that Perenzinni and those around her constantly dwell on the possibility that she is the root cause of all the dangers that the infant Hope is exposed to.

The fourth convention of motherhood, and perhaps the most common, is the depiction of mothers as purely monstrous because they are evil, uncaring, or at the very least completely absent from their child's life. Two of the most popular superheroines to emerge in recent years—the Cassandra Cain version of DC's Batgirl and Marvel's X-23, a clone of Wolverine—illustrate this most negative portrayal of motherhood. Both Batgirl and X-23 are teen heroines who were raised and trained by men to become perfect assassins, all the more deadly for their unassuming façade of girlishness. Via flashbacks in her self-titled series *Batgirl*, we learn that David Cain literally bred his daughter Cassandra to follow in his footsteps as the world's top assassin. Seeking the proper genetics, Cain struck a deal with Sandra Wu-San to mother his child in exchange for training her in certain fighting techniques. Sandra gave up any claim to her daughter as soon as she was born and continued on her personal quest to become Lady Shiva, the DC universe's deadliest martial arts villain. Cain raised Cassandra from infancy to be a perfect fighter and adept with every weapon. He even went so far as refusing to speak with her so that the only communication she learned was body language in order to give her an advantage in combat. But after completing her first kill at age nine, Cassandra was repulsed, ran away, and eventually found a new home under the tutelage of Batman. After years of searching to find the truth about who her mother is, Cassandra finally figures it out after being beaten to the edge of death by Lady Shiva. Racked by guilt over the murder she committed at nine, and burdened with the constant worry that she will eventually become evil like her biological parents, Cassandra eventually became the leader of the League of Assassins. The rejection she suffered from her mother is portrayed as the tipping point that led to Cassandra's fall from grace and her abandoning the role of Batgirl. While Cassandra's biological father is clearly cast as the main source of her problems, her absent (and later adversarial) mother is ultimately depicted as responsible for her inability to be purely heroic.

Marvel's X-23, aka Laura Kinney, is similar in many ways to DC's Cassandra Cain version of Batgirl. After decades of trying to clone the mutant Wolverine in order to make an army of obedient super-soldiers, an evil military conglomerate finally succeeds when their lead genetics scientist, Dr. Sarah Kinney, agrees to carry a cloned female fetus to term (collected in *X-23: Innocence Lost* TPB, 2006). Despite some minor misgivings, Dr. Kinney willingly gives over the child immediately after birth so that X-23 can be trained to kill, surgically enhanced with a painful grafting of steel claws onto her hands and feet, and conditioned to fly into an uncontrollable murderous rage whenever she is exposed to a particular chemical scent. At the age of eight, X-23 is forced to kill her sensei (for treating her like a child rather than just a weapon) and then makes millions for her controllers who contract her out to complete assassinations all over the world. X-23's mother does regret what she allows to happen to her daughter and near the conclusion of the X-23 miniseries "Innocence Lost," Sarah laments: "The damage I've done . . . I can never forgive myself." And after realizing "we both used you" and "we're both monsters,"

Sarah helps X-23 escape from the shadowy corporation. But, in a traumatic ending, X-23 viciously murders her own mother who has been tainted with the chemical trigger, and X-23 is left holding her estranged mother's body, pleading, "Please don't leave me." X-23's origin story makes it clear that while she may have been bred, trained, and exploited by a corrupt component of the military industrial complex, the real tragedy of her creation is that she was really nothing more than a science experiment for her mother.

PATERNAL AUTHORITY

The depiction of pregnancy as abject and the predominantly negative portrayal of maternity in superhero comics contradict our romanticized cultural conception of motherhood as a loving and cherished role. Yet, while maternity is suspect in superhero comics, paternity is often glorified. In a genre obsessed with hegemonic masculinity, superheroic male characters almost completely displace mothers as parental figures. Whether literal fathers or (more often) father figures, the central male heroes typically mentor children in adventures and guide them through to maturation. The long-standing rationale for sidekicks is that they allow a point of identification for young readers, but more importantly they facilitate narratives that portray very specific cultural lessons about right and wrong. As fantasy stories about policing borders between good and evil, and of ultimately upholding the law, the rejection of the maternal is tantamount to an acceptance of patriarchal authority, of the Law as the word of the Father. Through the dominant heroic male characters, sidekicks (and other children) are made over in *his* image. They are indoctrinated into the masculine realm of the Law. In their analysis of Batman, Uricchio, and Pearson argue that "the Batman fights crime, and thus serves as an agent of political domination, safeguarding property relations and enforcing the law. Extratextually, the character and the bat-texts serve to gain consent for political authority and the system of property relations it enshrines, and thus supports the dominant hegemonic order" (1991, 207). In general, the same can be said for all superheroes. Their very reason for existing is to stabilize the status quo and to enforce the law. The message may get mixed in with romantic notions of being a "dark knight avenger" or mythical ideas about "a never ending fight for truth, justice, and the American way," but the overall effect is to valorize and validate the hegemonic order. The preeminent male archetypes of the genre provide instruction for young characters—and by extension young readers—as to the value of being dutiful subjects and agents of patriarchal authority.

Where maternity is generally depicted as problematic in superhero comics, symbolic paternity is repeatedly embraced. The most conventional means of paternal influence occurs in the standard convention of costumed sidekicks. Robin proved a successful addition to the Batman comics in the 1940s and gave rise to numerous other sidekicks over the years. Captain America has Bucky Barnes, Green Arrow has Speedy, Aquaman has Aqualad, the Flash has Kid Flash, the Human Torch has Toro, and so on. Mentoring sidekicks seems to be a decidedly male tradition. The introduction of Wonder Girl alongside Wonder Woman in the 1960s is the only case of a major female character fostering a heroic progeny. Moreover, popular male characters can serve as infallible patriarchs to any number of younger heroes in training. The most obvious examples are Batman and Superman. Batman has served as a mentor and father figure for a wide range of characters at different and overlapping times, including five different Robins, three different Batgirls, two Batwomen, Nightwing, Red Robin, Oracle, Spoiler, and the Huntress. Superman has fulfilled the same role for the likes of Superboy, Supergirl, Power Girl, Jimmy Olsen, and Pete Ross. The common reference to these clusters as "The Batman Family" and "The Superman Family" clarifies the conception of these heroes as authoritative patriarchs. Superheroes like Batman and Superman teach their symbolic progeny not just the physical skills required for their adventures, but more importantly they instill a devotion to law and order, and deference to patriarchal authority.

The tendency in superhero comics to valorize the paternal and denigrate the maternal parallels some of Kristeva's further arguments about the role of abjection in cultural logic. In addition to explaining the difficulty inherent in depicting pregnant/maternal bodies which are understood as abject or monstrously feminine bodies in a genre devoted to maintaining bodily integrity, Kristeva's theories of abjection clarify the preferable association of paternity and the law. A key dichotomy in Kristeva's theory is the contrast between maternal authority and the law of the father. Kristeva argues that the semiotic process involved with an individual's contact with authority can be contrasted between the alignment of the abject (e.g., bodily wastes) with maternal authority, and the association of proper social regulation with paternal law. "Maternal authority is the trustee of that mapping of the self's clean and proper body," writes Kristeva. "It is distinguished from paternal laws within which, with the phallic phase and acquisition of language, the destiny of man will take shape" (72). According to this bifurcated model, the superhero that constantly enacts a policing of physical and moral borders represents an exaggerated identification with the masculine domain of paternal laws. If, as Kristeva argues, we are all learning and relearning the cultural rules of maturation which involve negotiating the boundaries between the abject realm of the mother and the proper adoption of paternal social rules, then the genre of superheroes demonstrates for readers the desirability of mastering the law of the father. Because superhero comics are all about fighting crime at one level or another, the character's struggles can be both a literal and metaphorical example of countering the abject. To enforce paternal law is to reject abject chaos. As Kristeva writes, "Any crime, because it draws attention to the fragility of the law, is abject, but the premeditated crime, cunning murder, hypocritical revenge are even more so because they heighten the display of such fragility. He who denies morality is not abject, there can be grandeur in amorality. . . . Abjection, on the other hand, is immoral, sinister, scheming and shady" (1982, 4). The hegemonic message is that to become good, proper, and perhaps even heroic citizens we all must distance ourselves from the fluid and unstable realm of abjection associated with mothers and wholly commit to the rigid and well-controlled level of patriarchal laws.

In some storylines this message about the crucial importance of choosing father's cultural rules over mother's personal ones is blatantly obvious. For example, one of the most interesting changes to occur within Batman mythology in recent years is the revelation that Bruce Wayne has a ten-year-old biological son, Damien (collected in the *Batman and Son* TPB, 2007). As a result of a brief affair with the villainess Talia (daughter to archenemy Rhas Al Ghul), Damien was conceived without Bruce Wayne's knowledge and raised by his mother to be a ruthless assassin who would one day take over his grandfather's criminal empire. While Bruce/Batman had adopted two earlier Robins (Richard Grayson and Tim Drake), thus serving both literally and figuratively as a father for his young sidekicks, the incorporation of Damien as the newest Robin makes clear the genre's preference for patriarchal standards. Where earlier Robins had been parentless before being brought into the Batman fold, Damien must actively reject his mother's evil ways and chooses to pursue life as a crime fighter alongside, and under the guidance of, his father. Raised in secret by Talia within her criminal empire, Damien is at first a wild and uncontrollable brat—a super-villain in the making. Talia's speech when she reveals Damien's existence to Batman makes explicit that transferring the child from mother to father is not just a change of allegiance from evil to good, but from abject chaos to controlled order. "He's been trained by the masters of the League of Assassins, but the boy is growing even beyond my control now," Talia explains. "He lacks discipline and the guiding hand of a great man." Likewise, when Batman is first seen alone with Damien, he tells the child, "If you intend to stay with me, we'll put that training to good use in the fight against crime." Though Damien is at first extremely violent, arrogant, and

Fig. 5.2. Masculinity is often valorized in superhero comic books, both in adventures and in paternal support (From *Batman and Robin* #14 © DC Comics).

out of control (he even tries to kill Robin and beheads a costumed criminal), he gradually learns the value of crime-fighting and protecting lives under the tutelage of Batman. In later adventures, Damien's progress in rejecting the abject in favor of order and social responsibilities in line with his father's ideals is clarified in his repeated refusal to aid his mother in her diabolically terrorist plans.

While a few examples of heroic and responsible maternity exist in superhero comics, the positive examples are far outweighed by problematic or outright negative portrayals of mothers as monstrously feminine. Conceptions of maternity, especially during periods of pregnancy, reflect a deep-seated cultural fear of abjection and all the associated qualities of transgressing borders. In a genre so obsessively concerned with maintaining borders (be they legal, political, bodily, or ideological), the maternal comes to represent the most feared aspects of femininity and/or chaos. Pregnant bodies are seen as violated, out of control, and compromised. Moreover, motherhood is depicted as dangerous to both the heroes and to the children or as actively working against the greater good. Paternity, on the other hand, is portrayed as an essential part of the greater good. To shore up the borders between order and chaos, the superhero must be an agent of authority; whether it is institutionalized state authority or of a higher moral ground is not as relevant as the fact that his or her actions are presented as in the service of communal good. Abject chaos and maternity go hand in hand as that which must be rejected in order for good to triumph over evil. That young characters like Damien often take on this role under the direct tutelage of their fathers or father figures symbolically compounds the association between the law and paternity.

6

SEX, ROMANCE, AND THE TEENAGE SUPERHEROINE

SUPERHEROES ARE AMONG THE MOST WIDELY RECOGNIZED FICTIONAL characters in the world. Most people, particularly in Western cultures, are familiar with the superhero genre—whether from comics, television, or film—and have at least a passing knowledge of key heroes, villains, powers, costumes, origins, and typical plot devices. Given the popularity of the genre, its endurance, and its cultural saturation, it is ironic that it is also one of the most derided forms of popular culture. Superheroes, and the medium of comic books that they are most clearly identified with, are generally considered synonymous with silly childhood fantasies. Personally, I don't see anything wrong with comic books being equated with youthful pleasures. Superhero comic books are fun, escapist, melodramatic, and present a clear, colorful view of the world. They can make you feel like a kid again. Thankfully, the presumption that superhero comic books are immature and undeserving of serious consideration is slowly disappearing in academia. Over the last decade, comics studies has become a vibrant and productive field of research for scholars trained in a variety of disciplines. Numerous critical book-length studies of comics have explored the history of the medium, specific creators, dominant genres, and industrial practices. Several journals are devoted to promoting comic book and cartoon scholarship, and other media and cultural-focused journals now regularly include works about comics. Conferences like the tenth annual University of Florida Conference on Comics and Graphic Novels, entitled "A Comic of Her Own: Women Writing, Reading and Embodying Through Comics," are indicative of the range of interests and the growing academic exploration of a medium that, for most of its history, has been considered unimportant.

Comics, and the dominant genre of superheroes, are anything but unimportant in contemporary society. As a shared reference point, superheroes can reveal a great deal about our cultural beliefs, concerns, and fears. They speak volumes about such important topics as democracy, individualism, civic responsibilities, the legal system, politics, ethnic discrimination, nationalism, and terrorism. My own particular interest in comic studies is the representation of gender. Lessons about masculinity, and to a lesser extent femininity, have always been a key component of comic book superheroes. This chapter considers the often overlooked importance of teenage superheoines and how they facilitate readers' engagement with issues of sex and romance. The teenage superheroine is an anomaly in a genre primarily concerned with hypermasculine men and hypersexualized women. But she is an anomaly that has proven very popular and commercially successful with both male and female readers.

For the conventional young, male audience who makes up most comic book fans, superheroes provide a clear model of ideal masculinity. As the previous two chapters have outlined, comic book superheroes personify hypermasculine fantasies, while the women tend to represent sexualized ideals. Despite cultural changes and an increased awareness of gender politics, the masculine and feminine bodies presented in superhero stories have evolved to ever more ludicrous extremes. In comparing the superheroines from his childhood to more recent ones, the Pulitzer Prize-winning author of *The Amazing Adventures of Kavalier & Clay*, Michael Chabon, notes that

> Boobs were a big part—literally—of the female-superhero package. Almost every superwoman, apart from the explicitly adolescent characters like the original Supergirl or the X-Men's Kitty Pryde, came equipped as if by the nature of the job with a superheroic rack. Furthermore, the usual way of a female-superhero costume was to advertise the breasts of its wearer by means of décolletage, a cleavage cutout, a pair of metal Valkyrie cones, a bustier. Today's female costumed characters tend to sport breasts so enormous that their ability to simply get up and walk, let alone kick telekinetic ass, would appear to be their most marvelous and improbable talent. (Chabon 2008, 198, 201)

These easy and rudimentary stereotypes about gender that continue to circulate in most superhero comic books are rarely challenged and reflect a wider cultural perception of masculinity and femininity, albeit taken to a cartoonish extreme.

It is this reliance on gender stereotypes within mainstream comics that has kept the audience for superheroes an almost exclusively male enclave. In the last ten years, the two major publishers, Marvel and DC Comics, have tried to attract more female readers to their superhero stories but with little success. Perhaps the most notable attempt was Marvel's 2010 "Women of Marvel" campaign that highlighted their roster of superheroines and their female writers and artists. Unfortunately, the reliance on standard pinup-like poses for the heroines undermined any attempts to present these characters as truly powerful women. DC, on the other hand, opted for "cute" instead of "sexy" in one of their recent attempts to lure young female readers to superhero stories. In order to attract younger readers, DC launched a series of kid-friendly titles featuring superheroes including Tiny Titans and Supergirl, and produced several animated shorts to air on the Cartoon Network entitled "Super BFFs" featuring Supergirl, Batgirl, and Wonder Girl. And this summer Marvel is launching a "chick-lit" book series with debut novels *Rogue Touch* and *The She-Hulk Diaries*. Of course, there are women who enjoy superhero comics despite the overwhelmingly masculine bent of the genre and comics fandom. The general assumption, though, is that women who enjoy superhero comics are so rare that they have been dubbed "unicorns." And while these female comic book fans may be fewer in number, they have made their own efforts to promote comics to other women through blogs like Girls-Gone-Geek and When Fangirls Attack and events like "Women Read Comics in Public Day" and "unicorn parties" at comic book stores.

If male superheroes are hypermasculine ideals for young male readers to identify with, and female superheroines are sexual spectacles for male readers to ogle, it is difficult to find any indication of changing gender norms in mainstream comics. But one variation of the superhero archetype may represent a progressive step for comics. Teenage superheroines have flourished with the major publishers over the past ten years despite, or perhaps because, they avoid the most rudimentary sexist logic of superhero gender and identification. Both established and new teen superheroines have headlined their own series, such as Batgirl, Supergirl, Wonder Girl, Spider-Girl, and X-23. Other teen superheroines have been popular and important members of team books, including the Teen Titans, the Runaways, Avengers Academy, Young X-Men, Young Justice, Young Allies, and Young Avengers. The popularity of teen superheroines is curious in a genre that functions primarily as a metaphor for puberty and an adolescent male power fantasy. Teen superheroines are clearly not male ideals for readers to identify with or aspire to be. Nor are they the exaggerated erotic spectacles that are adult superheroines like Wonder Woman, Power Girl, Catwoman, and Black Widow. Richard Gray (2011) refers to the standard portrayal of superheroines as "vivacious vixens and superhotties." As Chabon pointed out, the "explicitly adolescent characters" are not depicted with superheroic racks. By virtue of their youth, teen superheroines are not illustrated in as sexually explicit a manner as adult superheroines are, nor are they portrayed as sexually active. Yes, they are sometimes fetishized ideals, but not nearly as much as mature superheroines, nor are they as explicitly eroticized as are underage females depicted in other media.

Despite their youth, underage girls in film, television, music, and fashion are typically portrayed in just as sexualized a manner as their adult counterparts are. As Valerie Walkerdine points out: "eroticized gazes at the child-woman are everywhere" (166). Teen pop stars sing sexually suggestive songs and perform in revealing outfits; adolescent movie stars are filmed as erotic spectacles; and the high school characters on popular television programs like *Gossip Girl*, *Glee*, and *Pretty Little Liars* are portrayed as sexually aggressive and physically mature pubescents. Though the sexualized teenage girls that dominate representations in popular culture are often referred to as "Lolitas," they are a far cry from the passive victim of Vladimir Nabakov's original novel. "The perception of 'Lolitas' has changed in our society," writes Susan Bordo, "from passive victim to an aggressive, even violent, seductress" (300). So extreme and so commonplace is the sexual portrayal of adolescent girls that Debra Merskin argues that "the message from advertisers and the mass media to girls (as eventual women) is they should always be sexually available, always have sex on their minds, be willing to be dominated and even sexually abused, and to be seen—always and primarily—as sexual objects" (58). In comparison, teenage superheroines in comic books are depicted as far less sexual and are far less objectified. Teen superheroines fight and think on their own, and they control their sexual and romantic interactions with male characters.

The less-sexualized, yet still-heroic teen superheroine can be an obvious object of identification for female readers. These are characters who are eminently powerful and always defeat the villain without a visual focus on their breasts or buttocks. With teen superheroines, female readers can experience the vicarious thrill of wielding great powers, figuring out fantastic mysteries, and saving the world from evil super-villains without having to read around the overtly sexist and objectifying male gaze so often employed in mainstream comics. Teenage superheroines in comic books facilitate a more complex avenue of identification for both female and male readers. Rather than the male superhero which male readers can fantasize being or the female superheroine which male readers can lust after, the appeal of teen superheroines is that they allow identification through a veneer of distance. Because they are clearly feminine and yet only moderately fetishized, male readers can justify the appeal of teen superheroines as objectification but also identify with their exploits. The difference is that the exploits of teen superheroines allow readers to contemplate another set of adolescent concerns. Superman and Captain

America model hegemonic masculinity, and Wonder Woman and Black Widow represent sexual fantasies, but teen heroines allow young readers to explore insecurities about relationships and romance.

Teenage superheroes have been a common convention in comic books ever since Robin first joined Batman as a sidekick in *Detective Comics* #38 in 1940. As Bill Boichel (1991) explains, the inclusion of Robin was conceived as a way to make Batman seem younger without actually changing his age, and create a character who the mostly preteen male audience could easily identify with. Debates have raged for years now about the efficacy of sidekicks as points of identification since most readers seem to identify with the more mature, powerful, and competent Batman than with Robin, the juvenile hero-in-training. But sidekicks have remained popular as helpers and as convenient devices for the hero to explain plot points to. With the initial success of Robin, numerous other superheroes took on teenage sidekicks of their own. Green Arrow added Speedy, Captain America added Bucky, Aquaman added Aqualad, Wonder Woman added Wonder Girl, the Flash added Kid Flash, the Human Torch added Toro, and so on. Over the years, as the genre has evolved, sidekicks have come and gone. Some have matured into full-blown heroes in their own right (Dick Grayson, the original Robin, has become Nightwing; Roy Harper, the original Speedy, has become Red Arrow; and Bucky has become the Winter Soldier), some have been replaced (there have been five different Robins and three different Speedies), and others have been added (Robin begat Batgirl, Superboy begat Supergirl). In the 1960s, Marvel had a number of successes with teenage superheroes like Spider-Man and the original X-Men who were never relegated to being sidekicks. Likewise, DC effectively liberated most of their sidekicks from the shadows of their mentors by placing them on their own independent superhero team, the Teen Titans, starting in 1966. In the modern comic book universes, sidekicks still exist but they are far outnumbered by teen superheroes who operate outside the limitations of direct adult supervision.

With numerous individual and team titles starring teenage superheroes, these characters have become far more complex and well developed than the initial wave of sidekicks ever was. As relatively novice heroes, adolescents are permitted to make mistakes and to wrestle with decisions and the consequences of their actions in a manner that would be unthinkable for icons of hegemonic masculinity like Superman and Batman. In his intriguing article "Gay Sidekicks: Queer Anxiety and the Narrative Straightening of the Superhero" (2011), Neil Shyminski convincingly argues that sidekicks like Robin and Jimmy Olsen (Superman's best pal) function not only to aid the mature male superheroes in their adventures but also to enable their romantic quests.

"Always the bridesmaid to the hero's bride," Shyminski writes, "the ideal sidekick sacrifices or defers sexual and romantic desire so that the hero can realize his or her own" (290–91). "Given the lack of options," Shyminski continues, "the sidekick is made to seem either asexual or, by default, attracted to the same-sexed hero whose company and happiness the sidekick evidently privileges above that of all others—even his own" (291). And while this privileging of the adult hero's romantic pursuits by the sidekick, even to the point of having any homoerotic implications displaced onto the younger hero, may have been true in the past, it is certainly no longer the norm. Now that teenage superheroes have their own stories and lead their own lives, either as sidekicks, team members, or lone heroes, their own romantic pursuits have taken center stage. Teenage superhero stories at times seem more like soap operas than superhero adventures. Teen heroes have boyfriends, girlfriends, same-sex relationships, crushes, flirtations, unrequited loves, and intercourse.

It is ironic, given Shyminski's focus on Robin, that the original Robin, Dick Grayson, is generally considered by fans and critics alike to be the biggest "slut" in comic books. Grayson has had so many intimate relationships and one-night stands that numerous blogs catalogue his sexual adventures and debate his promiscuity. While many of Dick Grayson's sexual activities occurred while he was Robin, it is worth noting that the majority happened after he left Batman's tutelage and became Nightwing. For most teen superheroes, relationships are fairly chaste, but no less emotionally charged. The proliferation of teen superheroines allows writers to explore budding relationships from what they feel is a more feminine and romanticized perspective. The issue of romance is not a new theme for comic books. Until the 1970s, romance comics were a very popular genre aimed primarily at young female readers, producing titles like *Young Romance*, *Teen-Age Romance*, and *Girls' Love*. And ever since Lois Lane pined for Superman, while Clark Kent pined for Lois, romantic subplots have been common in superhero stories. In fact, as the Superman/Lois Lane trope illustrates, sexual desirability is an integral part of the masculine fantasy at the root of the genre. The fantasy is not just about being powerful, heroic, and triumphant; it is also about receiving adoration and being desirable to women. It is a crucial cliché that the hero always gets the girl; even if they do not ride off into the sunset together, the flirtations with romance still demonstrate the hero's masculinity and heterosexuality. The long-running and serial nature of comics mean that adult superhero stories also have something soap opera-esque about them, with characters falling into and out of relationships. An important difference is that adult relationships are often more concerned with sex than just romance and, at times, can venture into fairly kinky areas.

In modern comic books, adult superheroes explore sex in sometimes raunchy and explicit ways. For example, in the first and second issues of DC Comics' "New 52" revision of *Catwoman*, Batman and Catwoman have rough, anonymous sex on a rooftop while wearing their bondage inspired costumes. Batman and Catwoman quickly go from fighting to ripping each other's clothes off (except for masks). Issue #1 of *Catwoman* ends with a scene of her straddling Batman as she reaches under his costume. Issue #2 opens with the two costumed crusaders lying semi-naked on the rooftop in a postcoital embrace under Catwoman's thought bubble, narrating: "Tomorrow there is definitely going to be some bruising." A smug-looking Batman asks, "Are you okay?" and Catwoman replies, "I'm *better* than okay. You couldn't hear how 'okay' I was?" Conversely, superhero teens tend to restrict themselves to loving glances, hand-holding, and first kisses. The stark contrast between adult sex and teen romance is apparent in issue #13 of *Avengers Academy*; while the teens are working up the courage to dance and admit their feelings at a makeshift superhero prom, their adult chaperones, Giant-Man and Tigra, sneak off to have sex. Teen superheroes do not rush into sex, they do not have one-night stands, and if their relationship does eventually evolve into a sexual one, it is depicted as tender, respectful, and caring. For teen superheroes, and for many of the young comics readers, the real mystery explored in their adventures is not how to thwart a crime or defeat a super-villain—the real mystery is romantic relationships.

Most teen romantic couplings in the comics (heterosexual and homosexual) involve partners who are both costumed superheroes. Occasionally heroes may date ordinary people, but the narrative cliché is that only other heroes can understand and accept the superhero lifestyle. Unlike adult superheroes who often have a difficult time expressing their emotions (these are characters of action after all) or opening up to others (these are characters whose safety depends on their defenses), teen superheroes tend to wear their hearts on their colorful sleeves. The fairly insistent discussions about their feelings and expression of their affection that is common for teen superheroes is anathema to the central model of hegemonic masculinity that is at the core of the genre. This may explain the popularity of teen superheroines and their importance to young male readers beyond just their moderate fetishization. In *Men, Women and Chainsaws: Gender in the Modern Horror Film* (1992), Carol Clover argues that the preeminence of the young heroine in horror movies—the Final Girl of slasher films in particular—is an identificatory device that allows male viewers to align themselves with a female protagonist in her fear without bringing into question their masculinity, and then to ultimately identify with her triumphant self-rescue. Clover refers to this slippage of identification as

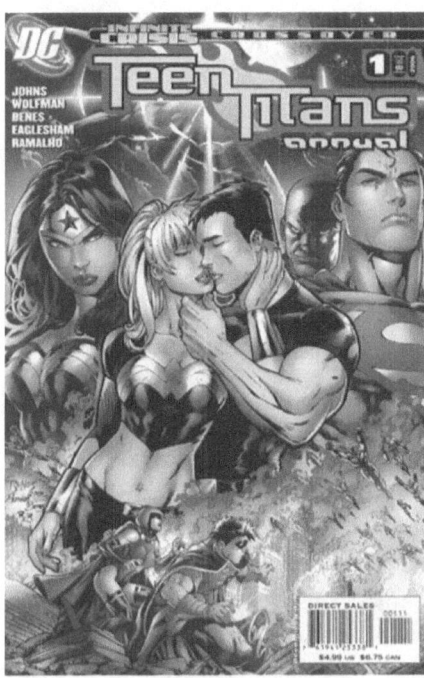

Fig. 6.1. Super-teen romance can blossom even if grown-ups disapprove (*Teen Titans Annual #1*, © DC Comics).

"the politics of displacement," and writes that horror films use women heroes "as a kind of feint, a front through which the boy can simultaneously experience forbidden desires and disavow them on grounds that the visible actor is, after all, a girl" (18). By coding abject terror as feminine, male viewers can identify with the feelings of fear from a safe distance. Likewise, teen superhero romance is typically centered on the figure of the teen superheroine thus allowing young male readers to explore romantic curiosities from a culturally approved distance. Yes, one of the teen superhero partners in most couplings is male, but the superheroine is usually presented as the emotional focus.

Whether the teen superheroines are part of long-running, on-again/off-again romantic couplings, members on superhero teams, or solo adventurers, the superheroine gives voice to romantic struggles, emotional insecurities, and longings. Though two of DC Comics most popular teen superhero relationships involve the iconic Superboy and Robin, the emotional core of the relationships typically rests on the shoulders of their partners, Wonder Girl and the Spoiler, respectively. Through various reboots and reincarnations, Superboy and Wonder Girl have maintained a romantic connection. Yet the highs and the lows of their relationship are primarily presented through Wonder Girl's perspective. She dealt with Wonder Woman's disapproval of the relationship, she dealt with being dumped, and she grieved Superboy's death.

Likewise, the Tim Drake version of Robin has been involved with Stephanie Brown, who transitioned from the Spoiler to being Robin herself and then to being Batgirl, but we often see the relationship primarily from how it affects her: her longing for Robin, her anger for not being his focus, and her desire to maintain a friendly relationship after they have broken up.

The group dynamics of teen superhero teams has led to some of the most popular and well-developed romances in comics. The relationship of the Dick Grayson version of Robin/Nightwing and alien princess Starfire in the Teen Titans, both in the comics and on television, is often rated by fans as the greatest of all superhero love stories. In true soap-opera fashion, team stories also involve a lot of love triangles and shifting romantic interests. In the Teen Titans, the Superboy/Wonder Girl and Nightwing/Starfire couplings may be preeminent, but at various times and in various team configurations Superboy has been romantically linked with Ms. Martian; Robin (I) with Wonder Girl (I); Robin (I and III) with Raven; Raven with Beast Boy; Speedy (I) with Wonder Girl (I); Kid Flash (II) and Onyx; Onyx with Robin (III); and Robin (III) with Wonder Girl (II). And these are just the romances that came to fruition; along the way there are countless moments of crushes and flirtations. The preoccupation with adolescent romance in the Teen Titans is taken to a comical extreme in the two Cartoon Network television variations of the team, *Teen Titans* (2003–2006) and *Young Justice* (2010–current), and then again in the comic books based on these TV series. The exaggerated anime style of *Teen Titans*, in particular, stresses the heroines' externalized romantic longings as when hearts float out of their eyes after they see a hunky hero or when smiles consume their faces as a boy tells them they are pretty.

Not to be outdone, the teen superhero teams in the Marvel universe contain just as much adolescent drama. The *Young Avengers* features two love triangles and a very devoted gay couple (Wiccan and Hulkling). The team's expert female archer, Hawkeye, casually dates both the Young Avenger's leader, the super-soldier Patriot, and the group's resident impulsive speedster and troublemaker, Speed. Of Hawkeye's two suitors, Patriot is presented as the more suitable potential partner. Hawkeye may find Speed attractive and fun, but Patriot is clearly more responsible and genuinely interested in her for more than just casual hookups. Modeling the more appropriate choice of a young romantic partner, Hawkeye eventually chooses to embrace Patriot's advances in *Young Avengers Presents* #6. Hawkeye approaches Patriot and kisses him unexpectedly, telling him, "Give me time, okay? I just—Give me *time*." "Okay," Patriot responds. "I'm not going anywhere." This love triangle clearly portrays the appropriate behavior for teens is to wait until both partners are ready for a real relationship. The team's other, more serious romantic dilemma revolves around the superheroine Stature, who can change her size to be a giant or to be microscopic, and her love for both the robotic shapeshifter, Vision, and the time-traveling super-genius, Iron-Lad. Stature's choice between Vision and Iron-Lad is made all the more difficult because Iron-Lad actually created Vision, so they share the same brainwaves and physical appearance. Vision is basically a sentient clone of Iron-Lad with fully developed emotions. The repeated dilemma of one female having to choose between two male suitors is akin to the *Twilight* and *Hunger Games* love-triangle phenomena, with some fans even jokingly declaring themselves Team Vision or Team Iron-Lad. Ultimately, Stature chooses Vision after she accepts his love despite his being a robot. As Stature tells Iron-Lad after he returns to save her life in *Avengers: The Children's Crusade* #8: "I love you so much. But my place—and my time—is here, with my friends, and my dad . . . and The Vision." Stature and Vision's relationship develops over time as the two increasingly demonstrate their devotion to each other. True love can come from anywhere, and the message is unmistakable: love can overcome any differences, even the boundaries between living flesh and synthetic humanoid.

Likewise, in *Avengers Academy* the young heroes in training seem more confused and frustrated by sexual relations than they do about battling angry gods or super-villains. Reptile and Finesse awkwardly flirt (oddly knowing at one point that their future selves will be unhappily married to each other), Striker crudely makes sexual advances to every woman he meets before admitting he is gay, and Veil has a schoolgirl crush on one of her instructors, Justice. The two remaining team members, Hazmat and Mettle, fall in love over the course of the series, and eventually overcome numerous emotional obstacles before finally having a sexual relationship. Hazmat is a mutant whose body can reproduce any variety of deadly substances, but the uncontrollable nature of her powers make her poisonous to others so she is restricted to a full-body containment suit at all times. Mettle is also a mutant whose body consists of living red iridium metal, which makes him indestructible but has left him cursed with a metallic skull for a face. Both Hazmat and Mettle start out as angry, self-pitying heroes whose powers have made them monstrous and isolated from others. The two teen heroes gradually grow closer after their teammates point out that they can connect with each other because Mettle is the only person immune to Hazmat's poisons when she is out of her suit.

During their time as students at the Avengers Academy, Hazmat and Mettle fall in love as they comfort each other through traumatic events. They also patiently work through each other's insecurities, jealousies, and concerns about having a relationship. When Hazmat decides in issue #21 that she is ready to be intimate with Mettle, they both disrobe, but at the last minute she

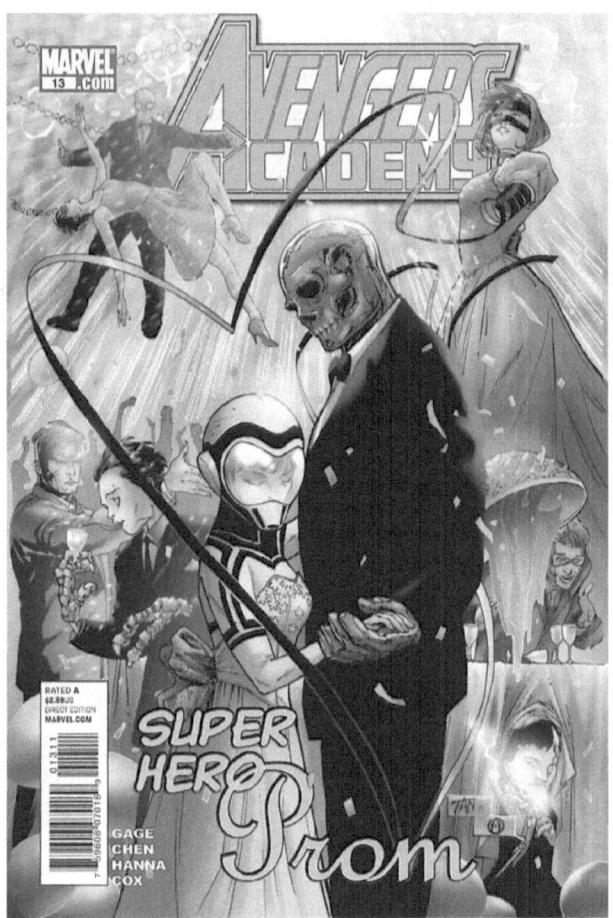

Fig. 6.2. Teenage romance is a superhero-worthy adventure (*Avengers Academy* #13, © Marvel Comics).

panics and cannot go through with it. Hazmat explains that her reluctance is because she almost killed her last boyfriend when they were about to have sex. Mettle is understanding as Hazmat asks for him to wait a little longer, but he believes her panic is because he looks so inhuman. Later, in issue #30, Hazmat confides to X-23: "Ken and I were getting hot and heavy, and I freaked out. Ran. It wasn't him. Ken thinks I'm lying. That it's really about how he looks. . . . He's such a sweet guy. And he really cares about me. Maybe I should just suck it up and—" But X-23 interrupts Hazmat with a clear message for teens about not being pressured into a physical relationship: "No. If it feels wrong you should not do it. Not to please someone else. You will lessen yourself." "What if I lose him?" Hazmat asks meekly. "You will be sad," X-23 sagely advises, "but you will be strong." Adult superheroes may rush into sex, but teen superheroes question their own feelings and motivations.

Fig. 6.3. Hazmat and Mettle demonstrate the value of waiting until sexual partners are ready for sex (© Marvel Comics).

In issues #34–36, an evil scientist cures them of their powers, Hazmat is no longer toxic, and Mettle is a normal, attractive teen with flesh, blood, and hair, but before the two lovers can consummate their relationship they have to reactivate their powers in order to save their teammates from certain death. "We didn't have enough time. It wasn't enough," cries Hazmat. "It was for me," Mettle responds tenderly. "I got to kiss you, to feel your skin against mine. . . . I love you." The tragic young lovers seem doomed to remain distant until, near the end of the series, Hazmat and Mettle decide to go all the way because they love each other too much to worry about their fears. When, in the final issue of *Avengers Academy*, issue #39, Hazmat asks Mettle to spend the night with her, he asks: "Y-You mean . . . Are you sure? You're sure you are ready?" Hazmat explains: "I told you, what I had to work out was about *me*, not you. How I felt about my powers . . . my situation. I'm okay with them now. I'm ready if you are." According to teen superheroines, real intimacy is worth waiting until both parties are ready for it.

While stories like those of Hazmat and Mettle model romantic acceptance and patience as desirable traits for young readers, other storylines present warnings about inappropriate dating behavior. In 2007, during one of the many recent reboots of Supergirl, the sixteen year-old "maid of might" becomes romantically involved with Powerboy, an alien hunk who literally falls out of the sky and into her life. The two begin patrolling together and flirt very suggestively back and forth while saving helpless victims from a number of catastrophes. When her best friend, Wonder Girl, presses her for juicy relationship news about Powerboy in *Supergirl* #13, Supergirl says, "He is confident, but not a jerk. He's nice, but not a boy scout." Wonder Girl appreciatively points out that "the costume hides nothing," and when he flies in the window with a cat, Wonder Girl whispers, "Marry him!" Supergirl and Powerboy begin dating seriously and often canoodle in midair, but Powerboy becomes increasingly possessive of Supergirl. When Supergirl breaks off one particularly passionate make-out session to visit a friend in the hospital, Powerboy screams, "Don't turn your back on me when I'm talking to you!" and savagely beats her unconscious. When Supergirl wakes up in Powerboy's bed in issue #15, he reveals his longstanding obsession with her (he is basically a super-stalker, with thousands of Supergirl pictures on his wall). Powerboy tells her: "You need someone to take care of you, Kara. Someone who loves you to build you up, to make you into something you can be proud of. I love you, Kara. We can be perfect together if you just let me fix you." But Supergirl recognizes the abusive relationship for what it is. "We need to break up," she says as she burns his hands with her heat vision. Then, for seven pages, Supergirl beats the crap out of Powerboy (culminating with an old-fashioned super knee to the groin), while lecturing: "You hit me. You said you loved me, and you hit me! No one who says he loves you, should hit you, ever! Don't call me. Don't talk to me. Don't look at me or I'll break every bone in your body!" This represents a powerful message to teen readers about the unacceptability of abusive relationships: no matter how passionately you feel about someone, if you hit them you are a villain.

The Supergirl example of an abusive relationship is not typical of teen superhero romances. Most are caring and thoughtful situations which may end up in sexual relations if the partners truly love each other. But the dangers of sex are also presented as warnings through teenage superheroines. Just a few weeks after Tim Drake (Robin III) and Stephanie Brown (the Spoiler) officially begin dating, Stephanie confesses that she is pregnant and Robin is not the father. "Relax, boy virgin," Stephanie tells him in *Robin* #58. "You're not the guilty party. A couple of make-out sessions do not a baby make." It turns out that Stephanie had unprotected sex with an ex-boyfriend who had since skipped town. Robin does the right thing and sticks by her through the pregnancy, even going to Lamaze classes. But when Stephanie gives her daughter up for adoption without even seeing her, she is heartbroken and calls off her relationship with Robin. The difficulty of an unwanted teen pregnancy, and the importance of safe sex, is laid bare for readers. Another danger of unprotected sex has been explored in the Green Arrow comics through the teenage superheroine Mia Dearden, who became the archer's third sidekick version of Speedy in 2005. Mia is an orphan who became a street kid at the age of eleven and was forced into a life of prostitution until Oliver Queen, Green Arrow, rescued her and started to train her as his protégé. But in *Green Arrow* #44, Mia, at seventeen, is informed that she is HIV positive during a routine doctor appointment. When Mia breaks the news to Green Arrow, he is shocked and asks, "How . . . How did this happen . . . ?" He thinks her acquiring HIV may have been due to a wound she received while on an adventure with him. "Ollie, I was living on the streets since I was eleven, and I survived by hooking," Mia explains. "There is not a lot of safer sex in prostitution." Though Mia continues her role as Speedy and becomes a spokesperson for HIV awareness, the warning is clear: unsafe sex can be deadly.

The lessons offered throughout teen superhero romances are liberal-minded but still fairly conservative. Overall, the message about love in these comics is conservative. It is the same dominant cultural ideal presented in countless female-oriented genres, including romantic comedies, historical dramas, and romance novels, namely: that true love is rare and hard-earned but blissful—a meeting of two hearts that complete each other. The overarching genre of superhero comics may be sexist and hypermasculine, but when it comes to teen superheroines and romance, it can be downright sentimental and mushy. This conservative intertwining of romance and teenage superheroines runs the risk of perpetuating gendered stereotypes about heterosexual approaches to sexuality. It certainly reinforces the assumption that women value softer, slower, and more emotional aspects of romantic coupling. This assumption might erase the possibility of recognizing female desire in less stereotypical ways, such as physical, aggressive, playful, casual, or non-heterosexual. But the more modest and conservative view of female sexuality presented in these teen-oriented cases is offset by the more lurid depiction of female sexuality in the larger genre of superheroes. In fact, for all of its safe and conservative adolescent stereotypes, this milder view of romance and sexuality is a radical alternative to the typical portrayal of female sexuality offered to male readers in superhero stories. Teen superhero romance is also liberal in that it portrays a world where true love can be achieved between caring individuals, regardless of either's ethnicity, gender, or even species. Loving relationships can be formed with same-sex couples, with aliens, and even with shape-shifting robotic clones of ex-boyfriends from the future. They also profess an acceptance of others no matter how they look. Not everyone has to be a Superboy or a

Wonder Girl—even the kind and sweet giant red metallic boy with a skull for a face, or the toxic mutant girl who has to wear a containment suit, can find love. Teen superhero stories show young readers the "do's and don'ts" of appropriate romantic and sexual relationships. Told primarily through the teen superheroine's perspective, the stories emphasize the importance of honesty, communication, and respect. Being patient about sex and waiting until both parties are ready to become sexually active, in a responsible manner, is presented as paramount. The dangers of sex and relationships are not completely glossed over; pregnancy, sexually transmitted diseases, harassment, and even abusive relationships are addressed. That all of these issues related to sex and romance are presented from the superheroine's point of view, a perspective that even young male readers are encouraged to identify with, allows all young readers to explore the mysterious terrain of relationships without compromising the genre's primary fantasy of an all-knowing and all-powerful ideal of masculinity.

7

GIRL REVOLUTIONARIES
Neoliberalist, Postfeminist, and Feminist Heroines

"She's a warrior. She's this hero who doesn't mean to be a hero. She's a symbol of revolt, and freedom, and hope . . . a futuristic Joan of Arc."
—JENNIFER LAWRENCE ON HER CHARACTER KATNISS FROM *THE HUNGER GAMES* (QUOTED IN MUMFORD, MARCH 16, 2012)

AS THE ACTRESS, JENNIFER LAWRENCE MADE CLEAR WHILE PROMOTING THE first *Hunger Games* film that the character she plays, Katniss Everdeen, has more in common with the mythologized Joan of Arc than she does with contemporary action heroines. The legend of Joan of Arc is a particularly enduring blend of historical fact and fiction. A young peasant girl in the fifteenth century, Joan claimed to have been instructed by angels to lead France's armies into battle against England during the Hundred Years War. Despite having no military background, Joan donned armor and entered the war, winning several key conflicts for France. Dubbed the "Maid of Orleans," Joan of Arc's heroism in battle became the stuff of legend before she was captured, tried for heresy by the Church, and burned at the stake when she was around nineteen years old. Whether Joan of Arc was delusional, a heretic, or a divine warrior has been hotly debated over the years. The Catholic Church's eventual canonization of Joan as a saint in 1920 only increased her popularity and debates about her. The legend of Joan of Arc has inspired fascination for centuries, with thousands of depictions in folktales, songs, art, and literature. Joan of Arc has also been a frequent subject in modern popular culture, appearing in everything from Broadway plays, children's books, advertising, television, video games, and feature films. The idea that a young girl could be a skilled warrior and lead her people to victories against a powerful military force marks Joan of Arc as different than any other historical figure, and provides fodder for a belief in the power of underdogs worldwide. Joan of Arc's unique status as a girl warrior also provides inspiration for contemporary fictions centered on young action heroines that fight their own battles against oppressive political systems.

The enduring popularity of Joan of Arc-type characters can be seen in the success of several contemporary blockbuster films featuring teenage girls who fight for their lives and inspire sweeping revolutions in their respective fictional worlds. Powerful young heroines abound in recent films like *The Hunger Games* series (2012, 2013, 2014, 2015), the *Divergent* series (2014, 2015), *Snow White and the Huntsman* (2012, 2015), *Mortal Instruments: City of Bones* (2013), and *Alice in Wonderland* (2010), as well as television series like *Revolution* (2012–current) and *The 100* (2014–current). Even comic books have gotten into the act with series like Brian Michael Bendis's *Scarlet* (2011–current) and Greg Rucka's *Lazarus* (2012–current). Moreover, even before the record-breaking *Hunger Games* films, the success of Suzanne Collins's trilogy of *Hunger Games* books inspired a flood of young adult stories featuring teenage heroines set in dystopic worlds. Some, like Veronica Roth's *Divergent* series and Cassandra Clare's *Mortal Instruments* series, have already followed *The Hunger Games* to the big screen hoping to reproduce its accomplishments. Other similar young adult book series have been hurriedly released hoping to capitalize on the remarkable thirst for this type of heroine, and perhaps to eventually replicate feature film franchise profits. Literary series like Ally Condie's *Matched*, Marie Lu's *Legend*, Moira Young's *Dust Lands*, Kiera Cass's *Selection*, and Janelle Stadler's *New World* have all been optioned by Hollywood studios even before the books have proven their marketability. The modernized versions of Joan of Arc featured in these stories are worth considering as more than just an unconventional image of female adolescence. Yes, these young heroines are permitted to be strong, smart, resourceful, and violent in a manner that was unthinkable for teenage girls in the media of past generations, but they also reveal a melding of class-based, anti-authoritarian resistance within a gendered context. The heroines of these tales combine a progressive idea of adolescent girlhood with a cultural critique of patriarchal systems of oppression.

The theme of rebellion that is so central to this new wave of girl revolutionaries plays out not just as a resistance to patriarchal control, but also as a mediation of feminist and postfeminist principles within a larger cultural climate of neoliberalism. Since the mid-1980s, there has been a gradual ideological shifting in Western nations that reflects a distinctly neoliberal attitude in politics, commerce, and social life. This overarching shift to neoliberalism is characterized by a belief in the "deregulation, privatization, and withdrawal of the state from any areas of social provision" (Harvey 2005, 3). As Wendy Brown (2005) has convincingly argued, the current political landscape of neoliberalism functions hegemonically to produce "subjects, forms of citizenship and behavior, and a new organization of the social" (37). More than simply an extension of free-market capitalism, or a political-economic mandate reducing government responsibility, neoliberalism as an ideology extends to individuals and "assumes that social subjects are not and should not be subject to direct forms of State control" (Hay 2000, 54). This shift in responsibility fosters an internalization of a new form of individualism: the belief that every person is required to become increasingly self-reliant and self-governing. As Wendy Larner (2000) phrases it, neoliberalism "encourages people to see themselves as individualized and active subjects responsible for enhancing their own well-being" (13). The neoliberal assumption is that each of us is responsible for our own happiness, our success, and our failures. We exercise a freedom of choice on an individual level, often tied-up with consumerism, and individual happiness/success is measured out in pros and cons, advantages and disadvantages, in order to maximize our own personal advancement.

A range of feminist scholarship in recent years has detailed the role that neoliberalism has played in the tenuous and often conflicting relationship between the ideologies and practices of second-wave feminism and postfeminism (see Duggan 2003, McRobbie 2009, Butler 2013, and Rottenberg 2014). The extreme, self-oriented individualism at the heart of neoliberalism is anathema to the collective call to action against systemic social injustices that characterized much of second-wave feminist politics. Who cares about others when we are each responsible only for governing ourselves? Some critics, like Nancy Fraser (2013), go so far as to suggest that feminism's privileging of identity politics over economic redistribution has contributed to the current climate of neoliberalism. Several early commentators on neoliberalism, such as Anthony Giddens (1991) and Ulrich Beck (1992), believed that the destabilization of an established political and social order would result in a desirable increase in an individual's freedom of choices and a sense of agency. More recently, critics like Duggan (2003) and Gill and Scharff (2011), have argued that neoliberal beliefs about individualism and personal autonomy have only reinforced inequalities of gender, race, and class. Not everyone has the same access to financial or technological resources to improve their lives. Others still face social limitations and expectations based on the color of their skin or the sex of their bodies. Still, the intrinsic belief in the primacy of individualism and the power of personal choices is an influential philosophy that recontextualized how many young women think of feminism. Thanks in part to "the ever-expanding neoliberal celebrations of autonomy, individualism, and consumer choice," observes Jess Butler (2013), "postfeminism surfaces as a more attractive alternative to previous forms of gender politics" (41). It is this neoliberal underpinning that contributes to some of postfeminism's greatest limitations and restricts its political agency in deference to what are deemed simplistic self-interests and rationalized capitulations to misogyny.

One of the problems with postfeminism as a descriptive tool is that it does not entail a clear ideology. Postfeminism is more of a mood, a tone, or a shifting worldview utilized by many women to understand their own particular preferences and practices in our current media-saturated culture. Rosalind Gill (2007) notes that the "notion of postfeminsim has become one of the most important and contested terms in the lexicon of feminist cultural analysis" (147). Gill also notes that the indistinct nature of postfeminism means that "after nearly two decades of argument about postfeminism, there is still no agreement as to what it is and the term is used variously and contradictorily to signal a theoretical position, a type of feminism after the Second Wave, or a regressive political stance" (2007, 147–48). In an attempt to clarify what exactly postfeminism is, and how it can be usefully analyzed via media representations, Gill suggests that postfeminism should be though of as a "sensibility," rather than as an epistemological shift or simply a backlash against earlier feminist principles. As a "sensibility," postfeminism, Gill argues, is composed of several specific features: "the notion that femininity is a bodily property; the shift from objectification to subjectification; the emphasis upon self-surveillance, monitoring, and discipline; a focus upon individualism, choice and empowerment; the dominance of a makeover paradigm; a resurgence in ideas of natural sexual difference; a marked sexualization of culture; and an emphasis upon consumerism and the commodification of difference" (Gill 2007, 149). These factors that constitute a postfeminist sensibility intersect with neoliberal beliefs that emphasize personal choices as inherently empowering. Thus, women can choose to present themselves as sexual beings, even getting breast implants or Brazilian waxes, not because they are capitulating to misogynistic desires, but because they choose to feel sexy for themselves. Postfeminism assumes that any choice a woman makes is a feminist choice so long as she is making herself happy. While postfeminism does encapsulate a number of positive features which permit women to enjoy and benefit from their choices without feeling guilty about participating in traditionally "girly" activities and pursuits, it also runs the risk of simply reframing cultural sexism as the woman's choice. The association of postfeminism with young women and girls in the media may just be rationalizing an internalization of traditional beliefs that female happiness can only be found by being beautiful and sexy, by shopping, and by catching the hunky guy. This anachronistic message of postfeminist empowerment through sexiness and romance is at the forefront of many films and television programs targeted at teenage female viewers like *Confessions of a Shopaholic* (2009), *Bride Wars* (2009), *Friends with Benefits* (2011), the *Bring It On* series (2000, 2004, 2006, 2007, 2009), *Gossip Girl* (2007–2012), and *Pretty Little Liars* (2010–current). But the current wave of girl revolutionary heroines in action genres manages to avoid the limiting pitfalls of postfeminist characters while still appealing to young female audiences informed by postfeminist sensibilities.

Several of the highest-grossing films in the last ten years featuring female leads have cast the young action heroine as a type of revolutionary leader. Focusing on such globally successful (in terms of worldwide box office) films as *The Hunger Games* ($692 million) and its sequel *The Hunger Games Catching Fire* ($865 Million), *Alice in Wonderland* ($1.025 billion), *Snow White and the Huntsman* ($397 million), and *Divergent* ($300 million)—and in the case of *The Hunger Games* and *Divergent*, the popular books they are based on—this chapter considers the teenage heroines as a complicated embodiment of neoliberal feminist principles. The bulk of this chapter will address *The Hunger Games* series because it is the most popular and culturally pervasive of the narratives. Some portrayals of postfeminist, "girl power" characters in popular culture have typically reduced political agency and feminist ideology to mere slogans of token empowerment. Even depictions of action heroines risk undermining female strength when the visual focus is as much, or more, on the beauty and desirability of the heroine than on her accomplishments. Infamously hypersexualized action heroines like those found in *Barb Wire* (1996), *Lara Croft: Tomb Raider* (2001), *Catwoman* (2004), and *Sucker Punch* (2011) have far more to do with sexploitation than empowerment. In her critique of the hollow dangers of assuming that women who kick ass are automatically feminist characters, Christina Lucia Stasia (2004) argues that "the new female action hero thus manifests the girl power mantra 'girls can do anything!' without acknowledging how this action is mitigated by race, class, sexuality and, yes, gender . . . the danger is in believing that image is equal to politics and material change. The new female action hero films manifest this danger as they provide attitudinal feminist heroes who spout feminist rhetoric and kick ass, but who neither acknowledge that oppression exists at an institutional level, nor that its forms are diverse" (181). However, the heroines of the stories dealt with in this chapter—Katniss, Alice, Snow White, and Tris, respectively—provide more than just the visceral thrills usually offered in action films and a few perfunctory moments of "girl power." These heroines eschew overt sexualization, and their narratives offer sustained critiques of oppressive patriarchal systems under the guise of pure entertainment. These more recent young action heroines "do acknowledge that oppression exists at an institutional level" and "that its forms are diverse." Katniss, Alice, Snow White, and

Tris present a model of young women as agents of systemic change. They are powerful and strong, good with weapons and strategic thinking, and inspire those around them—all without sacrificing or relinquishing their femininity, and perhaps more importantly, without having to rely on their femininity.

Countless media reviews about Katniss, Alice, Snow White, and Tris have jubilantly described these heroines as postfeminist warriors. The fashionable label of "postfeminist" seems appropriate at first glance with each of these heroines conforming to a simple and superficial media image of postfeminism's presumed subject. As Sarah Projansky (2001) summarizes: "the central figure of postfeminist discourse is a white, heterosexual, middle-class woman" (12). The youthfulness, independence, and prettiness of these heroines further compounds their supposed status as typically postfeminist characters. The association of contemporary action heroines with a postfeminist perspective whose default figure is assumed to be young, middle-class, and white may also explain the current lack of racially diverse heroines in action narratives (see Chapter Three). But the respective narratives of these girl revolutionaries tell a far different story than previous assumptions about postfeminist characters who are intertwined with an acceptance of "girl pleasures," including material consumption, media awareness, beauty practices, and sexual activity. Katniss, Alice, Snow White, and Tris present a more serious and responsible neoliberal feminist ideal for young women. These characters interact with feminism and postfeminism, they adhere to principles found in both ideologies, but they move beyond both to a more all-encompassing status as not just a female heroine but a revolutionary hero not defined by gender. These heroines are founded on the neoliberal belief in self-reliance and self-governing, a right of freedom from state and social control, that is a crucial lynchpin for postfeminism. But they also fight for equality and measure their self worth through their actions instead of their appearance or ability to attract a man, both of which are basic ideals of feminism. Katniss, Alice, Snow White, and Tris are not the postfeminist "heroines" from sexual comedies like *Sex and the City* (1998–2004) and *Bridget Jones Diary* (2001), who are so often discussed in media studies (for example, on *Sex and the City* see Arthurs 2003, Hermes 2006; and on *Bridget Jones* see McRobbie 2009, Genz and Brabon 2009, Negra 2009). These are *action* heroines who are redefining feminine representations, and feminism, for the new millennium.

In an era where "feminism" and "feminists" have been thoroughly demonized or reduced to joyless, man-hating stereotypes in the popular imagination, and where postfeminism is often used in media representations as an excuse for embracing "girlishness" as a form of empowerment, creating strong female characters who appeal to young women can be a difficult task. Many young women bristle at the idea of being labeled as, or declaring themselves, "feminists." The marketing of these girl revolutionary films (and the various young adult book series) promotes the central female protagonists but carefully avoids presenting her explicitly as a feminist character. Figures like Katniss, Alice, Snow White, and Tris model a neoliberalist type of feminism to a contemporary audience for whom feminism has become a dirty F-word, associated with outdated and undesirable alternative femininities not suitable for supposedly enlightened young women. What the narratives about these girl revolutionaries offer is a complex blend of feminism, postfeminism, and an image of civil disobedience against patriarchal/totalitarian control, all presented in appealing terms for a neoliberal minded audience. The stories allow young female audience members to experience heroic female empowerment without aligning with feminism, to identify with romantic desirability without being pressured to capitulate to standard postfeminist beauty makeovers, to vicariously fight a totalitarian state safely displaced in time and space, and to witness the efficacy of personal choices as heroic and rewarding actions.

MAKING CHOICES

Like Joan of Arc, each of these four young heroines become a symbolic figurehead and leads an oppressed group into battle, and victory, against overwhelmingly superior forces. Unlike Joan of Arc, these heroines achieve a happy ending, finding love for themselves and liberation for their followers. Katniss, Alice, Snow White, and Tris do not set out to inspire people or to lead revolutions, but find themselves thrust into the role of a heroine by forces beyond their control. And while their stories share a great deal in common, they each emphasize different tropes related to gender and political issues that appeal to contemporary audiences, most interestingly to a presumed core audience of young women. The achievement of a wide-sweeping cultural and military revolution by each of these heroines is central to the overall fantasy of revolutionary possibilities at the heart of these youth-oriented narratives. The figure of an otherwise unassuming adolescent girl acting as a revolutionary catalyst gives hope to the belief that individual women can overcome great odds in an oppressive patriarchal world like our own.

As one of the tag lines for *The Hunger Games: Catching Fire* declared: "Every revolution begins with a spark." Katniss, Alice, Snow White, and Tris provide this spark in their respective stories. In *The Hunger Games* series, the sixteen-year-old Katniss Everdeen (Jennifer Lawrence) goes from a surprising victory in the games in defiance of the Capitol's rules to a symbol of political resistance for the oppressed districts to rise up against the totalitarian rule of President Snow (Donald Sutherland) and the Capitol. Katniss eventually joins forces with the resistance fighters and leads an overthrow of Panem's oppressive regime. In director Tim Burton's reimagining of *Alice in Wonderland*, a now-nineteen-year-old Alice (Mia Wasikowska) returns to the magical realm of Wonderland to find it dilapidated under the rule of the evil Red Queen (Helena Bonham Carter). Alice finds her own strength and rallies resistance forces against the queen, and in a final victorious battle Alice slays the gargantuan Jabberwocky dragon and restores happiness to the land. The revisionist telling of the fairy tale in *Snow White and the Huntsman* portrays Snow White (Kristen Stewart) as a relatively plain princess who escapes imprisonment by her evil stepmother, Queen Ravenna (Charlize Theron), and braves the dark forest with the assistance of a down-and-out Huntsman (Chris Hemsworth) and seven dwarfs. In the end, Snow White rallies an army of displaced citizens to overthrow the queen's castle and kills the queen herself. And in the *Divergent* series, the sixteen-year-old Tris (Shailene Woodley) must choose which faction she will commit her life to even though she is secretly "divergent," exhibiting an affinity for all five of the social factions. Tris chooses the fearless Dauntless faction and undertakes harsh physical and psychological training to become a warrior, and eventually Tris uncovers a plot by the leader of the Erudite faction, Jeanine Matthews (Kate Winslet), to enslave all of the other factions. Matthews mind-controlling drug does not work on Tris because she is divergent, and Tris manages to defeat Matthews and goes on to undermine the entire system of social stratification.

The dystopic settings of these girl revolutionary stories include near futures, fictional pasts, other worlds, alternate realities, and magical realms. What all of the dystopia's share in common, however, is a vision of totalitarian state control over the disenfranchised: President Snow and the Capitol's exploitation of the lower districts in *The Hunger Games*; Jeanine Matthews, the leader of the Erudite faction, instituting mind control in order to enslave the other factions in *Divergent*; and the evil queen's dictatorial rule in both *Snow White and the Huntsman* and *Alice in Wonderland*. The vilification of totalitarian systems is nothing new in American popular culture. Resistance to tyrannical control is a founding cultural belief glorified in everything from the repeated mythologizing of the American Revolutionary War to the Allies battle against Nazis in World War II to the Cold War against Russia and the spread of communism to the Rebels versus the Empire in *Star Wars* (1977). But the current cultural climate of neoliberalism frames the fantasy of rebellion as a personal responsibility and as a right to freedom from state governance. Part of the appeal of these films for young female viewers is undoubtedly the image of someone like themselves who successfully battles against great odds. These heroines appear to be ordinary girls, more or less, who are swept into world changing adventures. Katniss, Alice, Snow White, and Tris do not set out to be revolutionary leaders. Their initial concerns are primarily for themselves and their loved ones—not any need to confront social injustices. As President Snow says about Katniss in *Catching Fire*: "She's not who they think she is. She's not a leader. She just wants to save her skin. It's as simple as that." Yet, despite their initial reluctances, these characters make a conscious choice to lead revolutions. President Snow may initially be correct about Katniss not wanting to spark a revolution, but she ultimately proves him wrong and ably assumes the role of the "Mockingjay," a symbol of the revolution and one of its leading warriors.

While, in a sense, every fictional character has to make a choice to be heroic, the primary decisions made by the girl revolutionaries that set their adventures in motion are given a great deal of narrative weight and are turned into public spectacles. With most of District 12 looking on in person and the rest of Panem watching on television, Katniss volunteers to take her younger sister's place in the games during the reaping ceremony. Tris has to choose which of the five factions she will devote her life to during a formal ceremony in front of a large audience of other teenagers, their families, representatives from each of the factions, and the senior officials of the city. Alice decides to go back down the rabbit hole while she is at her own elaborate engagement garden party. These initial choices made by the heroines, and the many smaller ones they make later, indicate their independence and their bravery, as well as their willingness to do things that go against the grain of social expectations. This emphasis on the heroines' shocking and very public choices positions her as a brave model for the neoliberal influenced audience of young women. Here is a teenage girl willing to make the hard choices and risk her life for change, someone who takes control of her situation and creates a new world order for it. For an audience raised and mired in neoliberal and postfeminist beliefs about the personal efficacy of "choice," the decisions made by girl revolutionaries reinforce the value of individual decisions. That these choices led to the eradication of an oppressive regime, and benefit not just the heroine herself but an entire community, only strengthens the heroic principle that could be dismissed as merely self-serving in neoliberalism and postfeminism.

But the dystopic settings of these stories are at odds with the underlying neoliberal beliefs that shape our real world. One of the foundational notions of neoliberalism is that everyone is equally free to make choices about their own lives. The very concept of "freedom" is at the core of this disjuncture between the oppressive states inhabited by fictional heroines, most obviously with the characters of Katniss and Tris, and our own supposedly liberated Western world. Eva Chen (2013) rightly points out that instead of the traditional humanist concept of freedom as unlimited, universal, and absolute, neoliberalism constructs freedom as an individual's ability to exercise agency to achieve material wealth and emotional happiness. "Rather than viewing freedom as an ultimate and yet-to-be-reached goal," argues Chen, "neoliberalism posits a new type of subject as *already* free and rational, a *homo economicus* who freely deliberates every action based on a rational cost-benefit calculation" (2013, 443, italics in original). The illusion that we are all free to make choices in the real world—an illusion initially reinforced by these girl revolutionary stories—is complicated by the explicit recognition in the narratives that the heroines are not free. Katniss, Tris, Snow White, and Alice live in worlds where true freedom does not exist. The powers that be watch the heroines' every move and rule with an iron fist; even small attempts at freedom are punishable by death. Even as fictional dystopias go, these stories are far more like George Orwell's *1984* (1949) than Aldous Huxley's *Brave New World* (1932). In fact, the neoliberal belief in individuated freedom to choose constructs Western culture in line with Huxley's parable about controlling the populace through the artifice of satisfaction and the erasure of needs. In the real world, the belief that we all are free to choose whatever we desire may only reinforce existing inequalities. For example, numerous criticisms of postfeminism argue that the belief in an individual's unfettered freedom and agency in the pursuit of immediate gains persuades women into voluntary self-objectification and a willing complicity with misogynistic norms under the guise of "innocent" fun or "empowered" sexuality. Given the principles of neoliberalism, power does not need to be directly enforced since norms are hegemonically reproduced as freely chosen. As Chen notes, the state may not dictate choices but it does impact the conditions (i.e., financial costs, personal rewards) that make certain decisions more desirable: "As a new form of self-governance, where the only guiding principle is marketization and self-interest, neoliberalism encourages individuals to willingly and freely choose to follow the path most conducive to their self-interest: the path which often turns out to be the normative one, the one for which the state has provided the best conditions" (2014, 443). This chimera of one's right and freedom to choose may apply to the young consumers of the girl revolutionary tales, but it is in direct opposition to the fictional world of the stories.

The Orwellian narratives of the girl revolutionary stories resignify choice and freedom as things that are not assumed but need to be fought for. Unlike their viewers, Katniss, Tris, Snow White, and Alice do not have any false impressions about their freedom to choose. Decisions are made for them by the ruling elite and are enforced with imprisonment or corporal punishment. In order to achieve freedom, these young women have to pick up bows, knives, and swords to fight for it. As a result of their actions, these heroines achieve freedom not just for themselves but for all of those who have been oppressed. They achieve freedom in the classical humanist sense as complete and total, rather than merely in the neoliberal sense of individual freedom to make personal and commercial choices. As heroic fantasies, these stories appeal to young audiences on a number of levels. The successful rebellions and personal empowerment played out through the figures of Katniss, Tris, Snow White, and Alice provide a vicarious fantasy that any young audience member can identify with. As exciting and melodramatic parables, these stories appeal to the imagined rebel in all of us, whether we believe we are being oppressed by parents, the government, the rich, the education system, corporate structures, or systems of discrimination. For example, Mark Fisher (2013) points out that "*The Hunger Games* was published in 2008, at the very moment that the financial crisis was pitching the world into panic and confusion. . . . The film and the novel have no doubt resonated so powerfully with its young audience because it has engaged feelings of betrayal and resentment rising in a generation asked to accept that its quality of life will be worse than that of its parents" (27). Youth in Western cultures has always been characterized by a rebellious spirit, as the motorcycle gang leader Johnny Strabler (Marlon Brando) said when asked what he is rebelling against in *The Wild Ones* (1953): "Whadda you got?" It was widely reported in the press that when the creators of the movie version of *Divergent* were looking for inspiration for Tris they turned to the image of "James Dean's Jim Stark, the rebellious protagonist who defies his parents and his peers in 1955's *Rebel Without a Cause*" (Clark, March 22, 2014, para. 1). The modern girl revolutionary stories tap into that same classic spirit of ambiguous youthful rebellion embodied by Brando and Dean with heroines fighting against tyrannical forces that can metaphorically stand in for any number of perceived oppressors.

The specific allegories of these girl revolutionary tales are not as important as their spirit of rebellion. The fictional dystopias are a Rorshach inkblot for any number of contemporary issues. For example, the popularity of *The Hunger Games* films has led to a range of media speculations regarding what the story is really about. An article in the *Los Angeles Times*, entitled "What *The Hunger Games* Really Means" (Zeitchik, March 24, 2012), notes that the film "is without question, a parable of the Occupy Wall Street movement. It's also a cautionary tale about Big Government. And undeniably a Christian allegory about the importance of finding Jesus. Or maybe a call for campaign-finance reform?" (para. 1). Conservative pundits at Fox News described the film as "a furious critique of our political system, in which the central government grows rich from the toil of the masses," and conclude that the subversive message is that "ordinary folks are good, government is bad—really bad" (Pinkerton, March 22, 2012, paras. 3 and 17). *Maclean's* magazine argued that, among other reasons, *The Hunger Games* is appealing because it "taps into our fascination—and unease—with reality TV (particularly the intimate, purportedly behind-the-scenes parts)" (Bethune, April 2, 2012, 33). A feature article on media critique website Slate.com claimed that *The Hunger Games* and other similar films and books are metaphors for high school: "dystopias externalize the turmoil that's already taking place in adolescent minds, hearts and bodies. The social, interpersonal, and biological phenomena that define teenage life—competition and jealousy, anxiety about exclusion and belonging, shifting alliances, first crushes, wet dreams. . . . The cutthroat race for high-school popularity becomes an annual televised fight to the death" (Stevens, March 21, 2014, para. 3). In the *New York Times*, reviewer Manohla Dargis claimed much of the appeal of the film depends on Katniss as a modern version of the archetypal Western hero: "there's something of the American frontiersman in her, as if she were Natty Bumpo reborn and resexed" (March 22, 2012, para. 1). And in his review of the film, Roger Ebert noted that "the old folks in the Capitol are no doubt a right-wing oligarchy," but "my conservative friends, however, equate the young with the Tea Party and the old with decadent Elitists." Ebert recognized that "*The Hunger Games*, like many parables, will show you exactly what you seek in it" (March 20, 2012, para. 5). Rather than trying to nail down exactly what the rebellious appeal of these heroines is for contemporary audiences, what the stories are "really" about, I am interested in how the popularity of these formulaic storylines might shift viewers'—especially young female viewers'—understanding of feminism from an implicitly neoliberal and postfeminist assumption to an active feminist political belief.

One of the biggest disjunctures between neoliberal postfeminism and second-wave feminism is the ideological chasm between a myopic focus on the self and the belief in collective agency. Where feminism famously argued that "the personal is political," the reverse is more typical of postfeminism: the political is reduced to the personal. Rottenberg (2014) describes the shift away from even the possibility of collectivity under neoliberalism: "Collective forms of action or well-being are eroded, and a new regime of morality comes into being, one that links moral probity even more intimately to self-reliance and efficiency, as well as to the individual's capacity to exercise his or her own autonomous choices" (421). The neoliberal and postfeminist emphasis on personal goals and pleasures is antithetical to second-wave feminism's call for sisterhood and the need for women's united defiance against

Fig. 7.1. Revolutionary heroines inspire and unite the disenfranchised.

sexist principles and practices. As Chen (2014) argues, the notion of collective action becomes undesirable, almost unthinkable, for many young women raised under the pervasive logic of neoliberalism: "Perhaps the most crucial area where freedom and agency are resignified is where the neoliberal project of individual gratification has threatened to replace the feminist politics of collective emancipation. Emancipation in the political sense of women gaining strength and abolishing restrictions through solidarity and collectivity is shunned and distrusted increasingly, as young women today turn to small changes in one's personal life" (444–45). While the girl revolutionary heroine does make bold individual choices, especially at the onset of her adventures, the fact that she becomes a leader of a rebellion models the value of collective action for young viewers. The personal becomes the political again in these tales. The importance of heroic individualism is never completely lost as the girl revolutionaries are still singled out as the most important person within the story. As Plutarch Heavensbee (Philip Seymour Hoffman), one of the masterminds behind organizing the rebellion of the districts, informs Katniss in *Catching Fire* after rescuing her from the arena: "You have been our mission from the beginning. The plan was always to get you out. Half the tributes were in on it. This is the revolution, and you are the Mockingjay." But no matter how important the individual heroine is, she ultimately wins because she joins forces with other subjugated people. The girl revolutionary's personal experiences inspire collective political action.

The collective action of rebellion found in these narratives may not be explicitly feminist in tone but the efficacy of group action is demonstrated. Change happens because of both individual actions and through the joining of forces. And the participants in the revolution do not have to be women to model the power of communal resistance. Like-minded men, be they other tributes, divergents, huntsmen, or Mad Hatters, are as welcome as anyone else. Like Joan of Arc, these heroines inspire others to follow them through their actions and their call to arms. No longer the passive Snow White presented in classic fairy tales and Disney films, the new Snow White raises an army to battle the wicked queen with a stirring speech:

> We have rested long enough. Frost to fire and fire to frost. Iron will melt. But it will writhe inside of itself! All these years, all I've known is darkness. But I have never seen a brighter light than when my eyes just opened. And I know that light burns in all of you! Those embers must turn to flame. Iron into sword. I will become your weapon! Forged by the fierce fire that I know is in your hearts! For I have seen what she sees. I know what she knows. I can kill her. And I'd rather die today than live another day of this death! Who will ride with me? Who will be my brother?

The downtrodden citizens rally behind Snow White and literally ride into battle with her. Likewise, the subjugated people of the lower districts, the various factions and factionless, and the creatures of Wonderland join forces with Katniss, Tris, and Alice.

And if popularity is any indication, these girl revolutionary heroines have the potential to inspire young audience members as well. Young women, in particular, are devouring the books and turning the films into blockbusters. Numerous media stories have appeared documenting the unprecedented popularity and influence of these girl revolutionary characters. Katniss has been especially influential, inspiring young women to volunteer in the fight against hunger and illiteracy, and even being credited with an increase of girls signing up for archery lessons. As *Entertainment Weekly* (Staskiewicz, April 6, 2012) declared on its cover, we are in a moment of "Katniss Fever!" The feature was subtitled "How a Fierce Female Fighter Became a Global Obsession." Many of the 99 percenters who participated in the Occupy Wall Street and Occupy Main Street protests against the unequal distribution and control of wealth in America displayed signs bearing such *Hunger Games* slogans as "The Odds Are Never in Your Favor" and "Down With the Capitol," as well as the image of the Mockingjay. Whether the girl revolutionary heroines are inspiring a sense of political activism, reflecting a climate of youthful frustration and rebellion, or providing a symbolic fantasy for themes to coalesce around is not as relevant as the fact that something is happening beyond the self-interests of neoliberalism and the shallow sexist conformity of postfeminism.

CHALLENGING POSTFEMINIST IDEALS

The figure of the dystopic girl revolutionary bridges the gap between the solipsism of postfeminism that influences young women in the audience and the desirability of collective action for political purposes. The foregrounding of each of the heroines' brave choices invites female fans to identify with the characters long before shifting into parables of cultural revolution. The use of young female protagonists, played in the films by attractive but not overly sexualized actresses, further facilitates adolescent identification with the characters in a postfeminist sense of idolizing beauty as an ideal and an undeniable asset. These popular girl revolutionary figures may at first glance seem to conform to postfeminist ideals of womanhood; after all, each of them is young, pretty, desired, successful, and independent. But the narratives complicate some of the very basic concepts of postfeminism, in addition to demonstrating the importance and compatibility of personal choices and collective action. In particular, the girl revolutionary narratives recontextualize or consciously critique postfeminist ideas about consumerism, beauty, fashion, makeovers, romance, and normative femininity. As Katha Pollitt wrote in her review in the *Nation* of *The Hunger Games*: "We're worlds away from the vicious-little-rich-girls of *Gossip Girl* and its many knockoffs, where everything revolves around looks, clothes, consumerism, social status and sexual competition" (April 23, 2012, para. 4). Similarly, Sheri Linden of the *Los Angeles Times* argued that "Katniss, a character defined by her unwavering inner compass and not her appearance, stands in opposition to those who worship at the church of fashionable conformity and celebrity-branded consumerism. It's not merely because she lacks the means to indulge, but because she has the intelligence and self-possession to see through the vanity" (April 5, 2012, para. 9). All of these girl revolutionary stories seem to reinforce postfeminist notions while ultimately critiquing them and offering new alternatives. In a way, the films get to have their postfeminist cake and eat it too.

As profit-driven corporate properties, the heroines are literally commodities to be purchased at the box office and the bookstore. Moreover, the worldwide fascination with a character like Katniss has led to a range of ancillary products available for purchase, including Katniss Barbie dolls, blankets, shirts, phone cases, video games, jewelry, mugs, notebooks, and so on. At an extratextual level, these girl revolutionaries run the risk of reinforcing consumerism as a means to personal happiness and a marker of pseudo-individual identity choices. Yet, within the narratives, the message is often an overt warning about the dangers and inequity inherent in conspicuous consumption. The contrast between the abject poverty of Katniss's District 12 and the spectacular excess of the Capitol presents a clear denunciation of wanton consumerism. In the districts, starvation is a constant threat, and Katniss has to poach squirrels and other small game just to keep her family alive. The few clothes and material things they have are hard won and need constant repair. But in the Capitol, ridiculous fashions and frivolous presentations of wealth and privilege are the norm. When Katniss and Peeta (Josh Huthcherson), her co-tribute, first leave District 12 to visit the Capitol before the games, they are amazed and offended by the ostentatious lifestyle enjoyed by citizens of the Capitol. While attending a lavish reception in *Catching Fire* when Peeta claims to be too full to continue eating, he is offered a drink that will make him sick so he has room to taste everything. Peeta bitterly tells Katniss: "People are starving in 12. Here they just throw it up so they can stuff more in." Likewise, both the humble clothing and appearance of Tris's initial Abnegation faction and the sparse, utilitarian uniforms and lifestyle of the Dauntless, her chosen faction in Divergent, are in stark contrast to the privileged and fashionable look of Jeanine Mathews and the rest of the corrupt Erudite faction. And in *Snow White and the Huntsman*, Snow White's plain appearance and the grimy poverty of the average citizens is presented as more desirable than the extravagant clothing and wealth of the wicked queen.

The disjuncture between the condemnation of commercial excess within the narratives and the merchandising of the officially licensed products related to the girl revolutionaries seems hypocritical. In an editorial for *Bitch* magazine, Emily Prado (2013) points out the duplicity between the narrative of *The Hunger Games* and its marketing. "*The Hunger Games* is different from other lucrative book franchises, as its main character is a strong-willed and explicitly anti-authoritarian rebel who is specifically fighting the oppressive policies that go hand-in-hand with consumerism and the exploitation that results from a minority's luxurious lifestyles," writes Prado. "She is also vocal about her disdain for the Capitol and its people who lavish luxury on themselves while the rest of Panem suffers. The whole series ridicules the Capitol-dwellers' garish costumes, gluttonous foods, and the cruel entertainment they receive from watching the Hunger Games" (2013, paras. 2 and 4). This message of disdain for consumerism is undercut by the excessive merchandising of Katniss. Perhaps most disturbing are the series of advertisements for CoverGirl makeup and Subway sandwiches that were tied into the film series. CoverGirl launched the Capitol Collection makeup for young girls in flashy and extravagant colors. The print advertisements for the Capitol Collection featured models in over-the-top clothing and hairstyles typical of denizens of *The Hunger Games* ruling elite, as well as each of the lower districts. After reviewing CoverGirl's campaign, Alexandra Petri of the *Washington Post* admitted to being shocked by its tacky commercialization and concluded: "Even if it's trying to be self-aware, the result is a deeply awkward series of 'looks' inspired by each of the twelve districts, assuming all the districts resemble a sexy robot mime without eyebrows" (November 27, 2013, para. 6). Not to be outdone in missing the point of the stories, the fast-food chain Subway featured a "Fiery Footlong Collection" that included five different spicy sandwiches. Heather Long of the *Guardian* ridiculed the choice of the Subway promotion: "Yes, someone honestly thought that a story about food shortages and massive inequalities between the Capitol and the rest of the nation would make good inspiration to advertise new lunch sandwich flavors" (November 22, 2013, para. 4). That the film studio, Lionsgate, and the series' author, Suzanne Collins, both praised these marketing campaigns as a playful tongue-in-cheek satire of the Capitol while still profiting from the products, lead Prado to sarcastically conclude: "So essentially, its all just a joke, people."

Still, the message of the narratives (and the viewers' identification with the young protagonists) has the potential to trump the commercial interests of the studios who are trying to capitalize (*Capitolize?*) on the series' popularity. Properties like *The Hunger Games* appeal to audiences because of the stories and the morals they present within the narrative, not the marketing campaigns for related products. The merchandising may be playfully consumed by postfeminist-minded audiences, but it also creates a link to a more feminist-minded protagonist. CoverGirl's Capitol Collection of makeup and Subway's *Hunger Games* sandwich deals may have been in bad taste, but the public response to these campaigns demonstrated that many fans aligned with the anti-consumerist message of the narrative more than with the consumption promoted through the marketing tie-ins. In addition to the outraged editorials that appeared in *Bitch* magazine, the *Washington Post*, the *Guardian*, and other news outlets, young fans started movements to boycott CoverGirl and Subway. As CBC News reported, "fans are starting to revolt against the seemingly endless marketing tie-ins that have come along with *Catching Fire*" (O'Neil, December 6, 2013, para. 1). Numerous fan-run websites appeared on which people could post their criticisms and parodies of the offending promotional tie-ins. Hundreds of *Hunger Games* fans contributed sarcastic comments and pictures of themselves parodying CoverGirl's Capitol Collection to the popular tumblr blog "Capitol Cuties." Similar ridicule was heaped on the CoverGirl marketing via Twitter with the popular hashtag #CapitolCovergirl.

In an op-ed piece for the *Los Angles Times* concerning the discrepancy between the message of the books/films and the ancillary promotions, activist Andrew Slack (November 25, 2013) points out that "to its credit, Lionsgate and *Hunger Games* do have antipoverty partners—Feeding America and The World Food Program," and notes that if "the studio's marketing was even a fraction as creative in pushing those group's messages as it has been in crafting its orgy of conspicuous consumption, it might be achieving something true to the film's themes" (para. 10). But, Slack argues, "even if Lionsgate has dropped the ball, a coalition of fan activists is taking up the cause" (para. 11). "Wherever the studio and its promotional partners post an advertisement for the movie," Slack continues, "you'll see our members posting pictures of themselves doing the three-finger salute—the Districts' symbol for solidarity in the face of the Capitol. Instead of letting the studio's campaign silence or distort the film's message, activists will draw attention to the reality of economic inequality in America and to organizations that are working to end it" (para. 13). The larger neoliberal economic logic that enables businesses to pursue profits on any and all media properties does not necessarily trump the narrative message of *The Hunger Games* and other girl revolutionary films about class warfare and anti-consumerism. And while "playful" cosmetics campaigns like the Capitol Collection that encourage young women to "choose your district" fits perfectly with a postfeminist notion of unlimited and unconditional free choice, it does not mean audiences are not adopting a more activist and feminist point of view about consumption.

The marketing partnership between *The Hunger Games* and CoverGirl is an odd fit not only because it alluded to the garish aesthetics of the Capitol and promotes conspicuous consumption. Nor is this the only case of a no-nonsense young heroine used to market cosmetics. A *Divergent* makeup line was featured at Sephora; *Alice in Wonderland* inspired a collection of Urban Decay eye shadows, lipsticks, and nail polish; and *Snow White and the Huntsman* was aligned with Benefit cosmetics. These types of partnerships are also counterintuitive because the films do not present female beauty as a pleasurable pursuit. Unlike so many other media representations of young women which glorify the beauty and sexiness of female protagonists, the girl revolutionary has more serious things on her mind than cosmetics and is dismissive of beauty standards in general. When Katniss is forced to undergo a beauty makeover upon first arriving in the Capitol, the process is depicted as torturous instead of fun and empowering, as makeovers are depicted in standard postfeminist films like *Ms. Congeniality* (2000), *The Princess Diaries* (2001), *The Devil Wears Prada* (2006), and *The House Bunny* (2008). In the film version of *The Hunger Games*, the makeover scene is set in what looks like a sinister operating room. In the book, Katniss's description makes the physical violation and the absurdity of the beautification process clear:

>*R-i-i-i-p!* I grit my teeth as Venia, a woman with aqua hair and gold tattoos above her eyebrows, yanks a strip of fabric from my leg, tearing out the hair beneath it . . . I've been in the Remake Center for more than three hours and I still haven't met my stylist. Apparently he has no interest in seeing me until Venia and the other members of my prep team have addressed some obvious problems. This has included scrubbing down my body with a gritty foam that has removed not only dirt but at least three layers of skin, turning my nails into uniform shapes, and primarily, ridding my body of hair. My legs, arms, torso, underarms, and parts of my eyebrows have been stripped of the stuff, leaving me like a plucked bird, ready for roasting. I don't like it. My skin feels sore and tingling and intensely vulnerable. (Collins 2009, 86)

In *Divergent*, Tris's original faction, Abnegation, shuns vanity and personal adornment. In Abnegation, people are only permitted to look in a mirror for a few seconds at a time in order to avoid vanity. Even when Tris leaves behind her plain beige and off-white Abnegation clothes to join the Dauntless faction, her clothes remain completely utilitarian black and grey pants and tanktops. In Dauntless, makeup appears subtle-to-nonexistent, and Tris's hair is almost exclusively tied back in a simple ponytail.

Part of the balancing act these girl revolutionary tales struggle with is between the narratives' explicit condemnation of beauty as a pathway to happiness or empowerment and the media promotions and the climate of celebrity worship that dominate external framings of the films and the actresses who embody the heroines. Jennifer Lawrence, Kristen Stewart, Shailene Woodley, and Mia Wasikowska are all very attractive young women. They are all thin and have conventionally pretty faces, perfect complexions, and beautiful long hair. The heroines are not glamorized within the films, but the actresses are presented as Hollywood-perfect in promotional and red carpet appearances. In particular, Jennifer Lawrence's turn as Katniss catapulted her to the top of the list for hot young celebrities. Lawrence has proven herself as a performer, winning the Best Actress Oscar for her role in *Silver Linings Playbook* (2012). She has also become a darling of entertainment reports and the paparazzi for her playful, every-girl antics. And Lawrence has become a sex symbol despite resisting overly sexy roles. A cover feature in *Rolling Stone* trumpeted Lawrence as "America's Kick-Ass Sweetheart" (April 2012); when she made the cover of *Vanity Fair* the headline described her as "The World's Most Desirable Woman!" (February 2013); and *FHM Magazine* declared Lawrence "The Sexiest Woman in the World!" (May 2014) in its annual ranking of the hottest

100 women. While the girl revolutionary narratives stress a more feminist belief in the heroine's empowerment through strength of character, the culture of celebrity worship promotes a more postfeminist ideal of success through glamour and beauty.

In an interesting reversal of the typical fairy tale that places a great deal of value on women's natural beauty, *Snow White and the Huntsman* offers a poignant critique of the power and meaning of beauty. This dark reimagining of the Snow White tale explores the history and motivation of Queen Ravenna's thirst for beauty and power. Ravenna leverages the control over men that her appearance grants her. She is a heartless femme fatale and a formidable sorceress who literally consumes the hearts and blood of others in order to maintain her youth and beauty. Appearing first in the guise of a helpless victim held captive by a magical army, Ravenna easily seduces the widowed King Magnus, who saves her, and then murders him on their wedding night. She assumes the throne and has the princess, Snow White, locked away in a tower. Snow White, in contrast to Ravenna (and in contrast to the pretty and helpless version made famous in Disney's classic animated feature *Snow White and the Seven Dwarfs* [1937]), does not rely on her physical beauty for her power. As played by Kristen Stewart, Snow White is certainly attractive but she is depicted as plain, with straggly hair and a simple tattered dress. Where the camera lingers on Charlize Theron's strikingly beautiful face as Ravenna, Snow White is treated as unremarkable. No one is enamored by Snow White's appearance when meeting her. The Huntsman is unimpressed, sneering at Snow White, "Don't flatter yourself," when she is surprised that he cuts her dress to a shorter more practical length for the forest. Even the dwarves are unmoved by Snow White until they see how the forest animals respond to her. In the film's prologue, we see Snow White's mother wish for a child like a rose she finds blooming in the winter—beautiful, but, more importantly, strong and resilient. This Snow White is defined by her inner beauty, her strength, and her ability to persevere.

In her *Time* magazine review entitled "*Snow White and the Huntsman*: The Fairest Feminist of Them All" (May 31, 2012), Mary Pols points out that the underlying message of the film "is that focus on and insecurity over one's physical appeal to men is poison to a woman's soul. That's hardly a news flash—feminists and good mothers have been preaching this for ages, but movies, with their emphasis on genetic lottery winners, tend to steadily undermine the message even when supposedly celebrating it" (para. 1). Beauty may be the source of Ravenna's power, but it is also her curse. She hates how she has been sought after and abused by men her entire life; she sees the world around her as fools for so easily falling for her beauty; she slaughters any women who may rival her status as the most desirable woman; and she is desperate to maintain her youth and perfect appearance through dark magic. That the film constructs Snow White as less beautiful—but still the heroine of the story—is a remarkable condemnation for Hollywood to make of our fascination with female appearances. As Pols notes: "For Ravenna, beauty translates to power" (para. 7). But that type of power is depicted as corrupted, illusory, and evil. The film's criticism of physical beauty as a form of female power makes the advertising campaign for Benefit cosmetics associated with the film particularly anachronistic; heavily made-up models were featured alongside large text which declared "Beauty is Power." Instead, true strength is favored within the narrative in the form of Snow White's inner beauty, her strength of character, her compassion, her self-confidence, and her ability to unite the commoners to resist the queen's tyranny. In the end, she also wins the heart of the hunky Huntsman—not because she is the most beautiful but because of her character. This message of inner strength as more beautiful than external appearance is an important one for young women to hear. It may be a message that is nominally conveyed in postfeminist-leaning films like *The Princess Diaries* and *The House Bunny*, but those films undermine the validity of it by featuring undeniably beautiful actresses like Anne Hathaway and Emma Stone as the ugly ducklings turned into pretty girls. Kristen Stewart's Snow White does not have to undergo a beauty makeover in order to best Charlize Theron's Queen Ravenna; she does not have to become the "fairest in the land."

In fact, the makeover, which is such an important part of postfeminist narratives, does exist in the girl revolutionary stories, instead functioning in a different manner. The current popularity of makeover narratives in fictional films and television programs, as well as on reality television series such as *How To Look Good Naked*, *What Not To Wear*, and *Ten Years Younger*, coincides with the rise of postfeminist thinking and reinforces the cultural and personal logic of neoliberalism. Genz and Brabon (2009) identify the makeover as "a crucial feature of postfeminism whereby the 'idiom of reinvention' can be applied to every aspect of our social world" (127). The makeover implies that by learning to dress appropriately, groom properly, and act correctly, any individual (particularly a woman) can achieve personal, professional, and social success. Sarah Gilligan (2011) notes that "the makeover narrative is an endlessly repeated and eagerly consumed staple of popular culture" (167). Gilligan describes the structure and function of the makeover as

> Prevailingly structured around three key components—namely the make-under, the makeover, and the final revelation/affirmation—the

> makeover narrative implies that through the processes of consumption and feminization, the female protagonist will achieve social mobility, popularity, and the "prize" of (a new or rekindled) heterosexual romance. Through their formulaic structure, such texts work to establish the parameters of acceptable feminine appearance, while also offering viewers the vicarious visual pleasure of witnessing the protagonist's transformation from frump to bombshell. (Gilligan 2011, 167)

The women who undergo the makeover, whether fictional characters or real people, gleefully embrace their newfound feminine power and are rewarded with social acceptance and praise. The transformation is characterized as freeing the women from the burdens of not being properly feminine and from not conforming to cultural expectations. Numerous critics have pointed out how the logic of the makeover paradigm promotes consumption and gender conformity under the guise of personal empowerment. The instructive lesson for young women exposed to the endlessly repeated makeover reinforces and naturalizes neoliberal and postfeminist beliefs about the efficacy of conforming to ideals of feminine beauty.

The beauty makeover that liberates postfeminist female characters from frumpiness and empowers them as sexual beings is replaced in girl revolutionary tales with a sense of being made over as physically and mentally strong rather than simply pretty. *The Hunger Games* treats Katniss's beauty makeover in the Capitol as a sadistic and shallow exercise for the cameras, but the narrative valorizes her development from a capable but unremarkable citizen of the poorest district to a champion in the games and a leader of the revolution. When Tris chooses to leave behind the modest and peaceful Abnegation faction for life among the Dauntless faction in *Divergent*, she undergoes an intense and brutal training regimen. Acceptance into Dauntless is not automatic, and Tris has to battle her way into the faction. She struggles at first, but then through hard work, Tris learns to excel at hand-to-hand combat, marksmanship, military strategy, and knife-throwing. Snow White develops from an innocent child and a princess locked away in a castle tower to a general leading her troops into battle against an army. Along the way, Snow White demonstrates her strength and resolve against hardships in the dark forest, impressing the warrior huntsman with her character far more than with her beauty. And the adult Alice, who resists the corset and elaborate dress that her mother makes her wear at the beginning of *Alice in Wonderland*, gradually regains her confidence and her inner strength (what the film refers to as her lost "muchness") through her increasingly dangerous adventures in Wonderland. By the climax of the film, Alice has traded in pretty dresses for a suit of armor

Fig. 7.2. In *Divergent*, the conflict between totalitarian control and revolution is framed as a generational conflict between strong women.

and a sword, slays the dreaded Jabberwocky dragon on her own, and defeats the evil Red Queen.

Instead of beauty makeovers, the girl revolutionary undergoes a transformation more akin to the training montage usually associated with male characters. Whether showing the preparation for military battles or for a sporting event, training montages illustrate the hard work that the protagonist, a perpetual underdog, must complete in order to take on a seemingly undefeatable foe. To the beat of an inspiring anthem, we witness Rocky Balboa go from an out-of-shape thug to a title bout-ready boxer in all the *Rocky* films. Or we see Arnold Schwarzenegger's characters loading up on weapons and preparing traps in any Schwarzenegger movie. In mere minutes, we observe the character become more powerful, developing the necessary strength and skill to defeat his enemies. While it may not always be seen in a clichéd montage sequence, the girl revolutionary characters undergo the same sort of development, transitioning from weak to strong, from hesitant to forceful, from powerless to powerful. This empowerment is not based on the postfeminist notion of empowerment through beautification, but upon a less restrictive idea of becoming more confident and stronger, both mentally and physically. And while this type of makeover avoids coding feminine strength as something that can be found by simply giving in to cultural ideals about female beauty, it also resists merely reducing empowerment to a form of symbolic gender crossdressing. In other words, the heroines' empowerment is not conceived as a type of masculinization.

In the 1980s and 1990s, it was common for film critics to describe female characters who took on the traditionally masculine role of action hero as "masculinized." According to the logic of gender binarism, women were

Fig. 7.3. Revolutionary heroines are capable of being their own knights in shining armor.

overwritten by conventions of passivity, frailty, and beauty, whereas men in action genres were overdetermined by violence, muscles, and lethal abilities. Thus, as Elizabeth Hills (1999) summarized: "From this perspective [gender binarism], active and aggressive women in the cinema can only be seen as phallic, unnatural or figuratively male" (39). The increasingly common depiction of female characters as action heroines over the years has helped rewrite cultural perceptions about gender when it comes to kicking ass in films. The figure of the girl revolutionary, in particular, carefully avoids aligning gender with heroism. Her strength does not come from developing visible muscularity, a clear symbol of masculinity, nor does it come from behaving in a macho or excessively gruff manner, another convention of the male action star. Both men and women in these stories can be strong and heroic, and the heroine does not have to trade in her femininity in order to emerge triumphant. Even the costuming of the girl revolutionary films implies a more gender-neutral approach to empowerment. In *The Hunger Games*, the tributes all wear identical and practical outfits when in the arena. Though a male and female tribute is selected from each district, the game costumes do not emphasize gender differences (unlike the gaudy dresses and suits the tributes are forced to wear during the pre-games promotional broadcast). Likewise, in *Divergent* the utilitarian black shirts, cargo pants, and military boots worn by both genders in Dauntless function to efface gender difference. Male and female members of Dauntless dress, train, fight, and live in the exact same manner.

Interestingly, in the updating of both fairy tale princesses Snow White and Alice, the heroine trades in her initial dress for full armor by the end of the film. The donning of armor clarifies that both Snow White and Alice have been made over from damsel in distress to their own shining knight, and could in this sense carry connotations of being masculinized. But the armor they each wear is practical and ungendered, worn by both male and female characters. Snow White and Alice are certainly not the first female characters to wear armor in contemporary action movies, but other films have often used the armor to emphasize the wearer's femininity at the same time they stress her fortitude. Women's armor all too often includes pronounced metal breastplates, a corset-like shape, a miniskirt-looking bottom, and thigh-high metal boots. This "sexy armor" implies the character's willingness to engage in battle while simultaneously fetishizing her attractive figure and femininity. Made famous by the likes of Wonder Woman and Xena, this look has appeared recently on characters like Princess Isabelle (Eleanor Tomlinson) in *Jack the Giant Slayer* (2013), the Asgardian warrior Lady Sif (Jaimie Alexander) in *Thor: The Dark World* (2013), or in the full robotic armor variation worn by Mako Mori (Rinko Kikuchi) in *Pacific Rim* (2013). The armor of Snow White and Alice does not emphasize their curves or leave vulnerable flesh exposed simply for the sake of titillation or confirming the wearer's femininity. For example, the character posters featuring Snow White in her armor and Lady Sif in hers may both imply strong action heroines. But where Snow White's armor covers her entire body with no emphasis of her feminine features and a practical shield, Lady Sif's outfit accentuates her beauty and her curves—she has only the tiniest of shields and her chest, arms, and legs are left vulnerable.

NEOLIBERAL, POSTFEMINIST, AND FEMINIST

The important trick for these girl revolutionary tales is the incorporation of feminist principles under the guise of neoliberal informed postfeminism. Explicit feminism may be seen as an outdated political ideology for many young women today, but the principles that have been lost under the fun-and-flashy presentation of postfeminism are still of value. The girl revolutionary narratives do present an affirming message about resisting oppression, the efficacy of collective action, the demeaning effects of beauty standards, and women's genuine empowerment. But these narratives also include just enough of the features that appeal to postfeminist fantasies to be palatable to a wide audience. Themes of heterosexual romance, individuality and rule-breaking, vicarious female agency, and resistance to maternal authority all contribute a postfeminist aura to what are essentially feminist tales.

Perhaps the most obvious pandering to the enculturated longings of young women in the audience is the inclusion of heterosexual romance within these stories, even if the romantic subplot seems an awkward fit. The blockbuster series *Twilight* (2008, 2009, 2010, 2011, 2012), which just predated the girl revolutionary tales, masterfully marketed the choice Bella (Kristen Stewart), the romantic heroine, has to make between two romantic rivals, vampire Edward (Robert Patinson) and werewolf Jacob (Taylor Lautner). With *The Hunger Games* following in the page-to-screen footsteps of *Twilight*, and hoping to replicate its financial success with young female viewers, part of its promotion was devoted to the story's tenuous love triangle with Katniss as the object of affection for both Gale (Liam Hemsworth), her childhood companion, and Peeta, her co-tribute. Mirroring the *Twilight* phenomena, fans and official promotions have aligned as "Team Gale" or "Team Peeta." T-shirts, posters, notebooks, and other merchandise are available depending on which hunky suitor you think Katniss should choose. Similarly, the romantic relationship in *Divergent* between Tris and her Dauntless trainer and eventual boyfriend, Four (Theo James), is as important to the story's success as is the revolution. Pretty much every media description of Theo James in reviews of *Divergent* described him as a "hunk" of the first order. *Entertainment Weekly* claimed that "the camera flat-out loves the guy" (Vilkomerson, March 7, 2014, 35), and described him as a cross between Montgomery Clift, James Dean, George Clooney, and Steve McQueen. And while the romance between the two titular characters only emerges near the climax of *Snow White and the Huntsman*, it was expected because the actor playing the Huntsman, Chris Hemsworth, is considered one of the most attractive men in Hollywood. Even Mary Pols's *Time* magazine piece about the exceptional feminism of the film admitted that the actor is so sexy that "Hemsworth could have chemistry with a potted plant" (May 31, 2012, para. 4). The inclusion of super-hunky suitors who long for the heroines and assist them in their adventures plays to the adolescent female fantasy of romantic desirability. *Alice in Wonderland* is the only film that rejects the goal of heterosexual romance and avoids concluding with the happy union of the heroine and a hunky paramour. Instead, Alice returns to the real world, refuses to marry, and is last seen going into business and boarding a ship to engage in foreign trade with China.

The romantic subplots found in most of the girl revolutionary narratives bridge the gap between pure action stories and more contemporary postfeminist "Chick Flicks" and "Chick Lit." In modern postfeminist films and books, romantic coupling is a central goal for the female protagonist as she navigates between numerous suitors and the pleasures of career, friends, and shopping. For all the postfeminist rhetoric about freedom, independence, and abundant choices, the ultimate conclusion of finding Mr. Right reinforces very traditional conceptions about gender and heterosexual coupledom. The fantasy of living happily ever after once the postfeminist heroine chooses the right man equates personal fulfillment and success with romantic union. Nothing else matters if the heroine is with the right man. As Diane Negra and Yvonne Tasker (2013) argue, "The chick flick typically generates an affective economy in which the achievement of romantic intimacy forecloses all other concerns" (351). Romance is certainly not the central issue for the girl revolutionary—she has her hands full fighting for her life and leading a rebellion, but the romantic subplot does directly appeal to postfeminist-influenced audiences who believe in the necessity of coupledom. The romance angle serves several important functions: the burgeoning attractions between the hunky leading men and the girl revolutionary works to confirm the female characters' heterosexuality and desirability, it allows young female readers/viewers to indulge in vicarious longings for male characters and actors, and it reconfirms the comforting fantasy of achieving romantic bliss as at least part of the reward for the protagonists.

The inclusion of a romantic subplot and hunky young actors for viewers to swoon over is standard Hollywood operating procedure. Certainly male-centered action movies do the same thing when they regularly include a beautiful love interest for the hero to be rewarded with by the closing credits. But the excessive Team Peeta- or Team Gale-type of publicity that surrounds the texts plays directly into the postfeminist concern with romantic coupling as the ultimate goal. The more insidious postfeminist theme that runs throughout many of the girl revolutionary stories, however, is the vilification of older female characters. Susan Faludi (1992) famously described the backlash against second-wave feminism to appear in various forms since the 1980s. Wittingly or not, postfeminism has been characterized as a major contributor to the feminist backlash through its conception of a specifically defined version of feminism as outdated. In her critique of postfeminism, Angela McRobbie (2004) argues that "postfeminism actively draws on and invokes feminism as that which can be taken into account in order to suggest that equality is achieved, in order to install a whole repertoire of meanings which emphasize that it is no longer needed, a spent force" (4). Building on this observation, Tasker and Negra (2007) note that "postfeminism draws on and sustains an invented social memory of feminist language as inevitably shrill, bellicose, and parsimonious. Thus, while feminism is constituted as an unwelcome, implicitly censorious presence, it is precisely *feminist* concerns that are silenced within postfeminist culture. Reference to 'the F word' underscores the status of feminism as unspeakable within contemporary popular culture" (3). This postfeminist conception of feminism as a spent force and an unwelcome, silencing, and censorious presence is parlayed into a battle between the girl revolutionary and older female villains.

McRobbie also points out that postfeminism presents "a gendered, generational fault line, where young women are championed as a metaphor for social change" (2004, 6). This generational fault line is made explicit in the girl revolutionary narratives, playing out a postfeminist fantasy of young women overcoming the stifling and misguided control of older women. In *The Hunger Games* stories, Katniss's defiance of the Capitol and President Snow eventually combines in her ideological conflict with Alma Coin (Julianne Moore), the older female leader of District 13 and chief architect of the rebellion. Coin is portrayed as heartless, power-hungry, and manipulative, and she looks down on Katniss and exploits her merely as a symbol of rebellion in order to gain support. Coin also bombs her own medics, killing Katniss's sister, Prim, in the process, in an attempt to frame President Snow. In a live broadcast in which Katniss is supposed to execute Snow, she turns her arrow on Coin instead and kills her before Coin can become ruler of all Panem. In *Divergent*, Jeanine Mathews, the older female leader of the Erudite faction, is cold, calculating, and ruthless. Jeanine makes a deal with the leaders of Dauntless and subjects them to mind control in order to use the Dauntless as an army to enslave all the other factions. Jeanine also attempts to capture Tris and any other divergents because they are resistant to the mind control and represent the only challenge to her total domination. Tris battles Jeanine in *Divergent* and both overpowers her and outsmarts her before going on the run to lead the rebellion against Jeanine and her forces. As mentioned earlier, in *Snow White and the Huntsman* the central conflict is between Snow White and Queen Ravenna. Snow White is characterized as brave, noble, and kind, while Ravenna is older, vain, evil, and despotic. When Snow White kills Ravenna, her youth and beauty turns to dust, as she literally turns into a haggard carcass of an old woman, a female grotesque inside and out. And in *Alice in Wonderland*, the villainous Red Queen who rules with an iron fist is a CGI-rendered caricature of a female grotesque, with an enormously bulbous head and garish makeup, hair, and costuming. The queen is violent and temperamental, enslaving or killing all who stand in her path. Alice, in contrast, is young, pretty, brave, and compassionate. Once Alice slays the Jabberwocky, the Red Queen loses all authority and Wonderland is freed from her control.

It is alarming that the girl revolutionary narratives so often cast older, power-mad women—caricatures of earlier feminists—as symbols of domination which the heroines must defeat. This postfeminist trope potentially undermines the stories' repositioning of the young heroines as more feminist than postfeminist. In particular, the villainesses' attempts to silence the young heroines are analogous to feminist oppression. Like President Snow before her, Alma Coin tries to script Katniss's speeches and public presentations before trying to kill her to silence Katniss for good. Jeanine Mathews wants to silence Tris before she can warn the factions about her nefarious plot. Queen Ravenna locks Snow White away in a tower and then tries to kill her. And in the most absurd case, when Alice says anything the Red Queen does not like, she is met with the immediate command, "Off with her head!" This type of censorious control makes explicit the implied silencing of young women that McRobbie describes as part of the way postfeminism preempts the possibility of cultural critique. As McRobbie observes, "The new female subject is, despite her freedom, called upon to be silent, to withhold critique, to count as a modern sophisticated girl, or indeed this withholding of critique is a condition of her freedom" (2004: 8). McRobbie is speaking of silencing any criticisms young women might have about the normalization of their sexual, social, and commercial exploitation. In order to been seen as liberated women and to enjoy the perceived freedoms they participate in, young women must remain silent about the sexist underpinnings of their roles. The narratives sidestep this issue by reframing silencing as a battle not over sexist exploitation but political resistance. Importantly, though, the young heroines refuse to be silenced. They deliver impassioned speeches, question authority, give three-finger salutes, and shoot arrows through those who would control them. The girl revolutionary narratives also sidestep depicting the conflict between older women as villains and younger women as heroines as simply a struggle between feminist and postfeminist ideologies by framing the conflict as a larger political battle. The villainesses represent the state, the faction, the districts, and the kingdom, and as such are aided and aligned with a whole host of other oppressors, male and female, young and old, black and white. Likewise, the heroines align with a diverse group of fellow rebels. What the heroines are fighting against is political oppression; that the struggle takes on the veneer of a postfeminist renunciation of older versions of feminism only allows an access point for young viewers from a postfeminist generation to vicariously feel aligned.

Still, the fact that the ultimate symbol of evil in these narratives is an older woman is undeniably an unfortunate cliché from a feminist perspective. For strong, young and, yes, feminist characters like Katniss, Tris, Snow White, and Alice to have to kill off authoritarian older women potentially conveys a message tantamount to feminist backlash. But just because there is a gendered and generational fault line between older and younger women in these narratives does not necessarily equate to a postfeminist dismissal of feminism. In fact, given the ages of the protagonists—and, more importantly, the female antagonists and the length of time postfeminism has now been around—the generational conflict can be read as exactly the opposite. The young girl revolutionary who utilizes collective action, who eschews the beauty paradigm and makeover ideals, and who is strong rather than girly, is more akin to second-wave ideals of feminism. The older women, on the other hand, are by-and-large still young enough to be informed by postfeminist ideology. The relative ages of the actresses in the movies is revealing: Julianne Moore, who plays Alma Coin, is the oldest at fifty-two; Helena Bonham Carter was forty-three when she starred as the Red Queen; and Charlize Theron and Kate Winslet were both born in 1975, making Theron only thirty-six when she played Queen Ravenna and Winslet thirty-eight when she played Jeanine Mathews. Moreover, Theron is famous for her youthful beauty, and Winslet is best known for her performance as the heroine Rose in *Titanic* (1997), which Kathleen Rowe Karlyn (2011) describes as "among the first films identified with Girl Culture, and it valorized a model of unruly femininity that spoke to teen girls . . . it is also an exemplary postfeminist text" (21). Characteristics like Queen Ravenna's ruthless pursuit of beauty and the precarious power it provides—as well as the pursuit of personal power at any cost by Jeanine Mathews, Alma Coin, and the Red Queen—are far more symbolic of neoliberal and postfeminist ideology than they are of feminism.

In a sense, what we are seeing in these girl revolutionary stories is not a postfeminst repudiation of feminism, but a new, younger, politically aware version of feminism overthrowing the shallow, self-serving, and corrupting principles of neoliberalism and postfeminism. These heroines are a type of feminist wolf in postfeminst clothing. They may be pretty, they may get the hunky boy, they may have a veneer of platitudes about female empowerment, but within the narrative they are feminists through and through. They are attractive enough to young female audiences that have grown up in a postfeminist world with messages of girl power and the beauty imperative, but they also appeal to audiences who have simultaneously experienced a worldwide economic collapse and a growing disparity between the few elite and wealthy members of Western culture and the rest of us. Joan of Arc would be proud.

8

PRETTY LITTLE KILLERS

SHELDON: "Okay, then, riddle me this: Assuming all the good Terminators were originally evil Terminators created by Skynet but then reprogrammed by the future John Connor, why would Skynet, an artificial computer intelligence, bother to create a petite, hot, 17-year old killer robot?"
LEONARD: "Skynet is kinky? I don't know."
SHELDON: "Artificial intelligences do *not* have teen fetishes."
—*THE BIG BANG THEORY*, SEASON 1, EP. 10 (2008)

THIS HUMOROUS EXCHANGE BETWEEN THE GEEK ROOMMATES SHELDON Cooper and Leonard Hofstadter of the top-rated sitcom *The Big Bang Theory* (2007–current) points out the absurdity of creating "a petite, hot, 17-year old" girl as the fearsome cyborg in the short-lived television series *Terminator: The Sarah Connor Chronicles* (2008–2009). And, while Sheldon observes that "artificial intelligences do *not* have teen fetishes," it would seem that the rest of the world does. By casting the beautiful and young actress Summer Glau as the sexy cyborg Cameron, the *Terminator* series catered to a presumed male audience that would find a hot, young robot more appealing to watch than a hulking male one. But this emphasis on youth and beauty is not restricted to sexy cyborgs like Cameron. Violent teenage action heroines have become the new norm, and while their beauty may not always be crucial to the story (as with some of the revolutionary heroines addressed in the previous chapter), their physical attractiveness is often a crucial part of their persona. There has been a shift in action genres to younger and younger heroines who are every bit as lethal as their adult and/or male counterparts. As film reviewers have observed: "Our action thrillers right now seem to be awash in young girls who are stone cold killers" (Lin, April 6, 2011); "The era of teenage action heroine is fully upon us" (Hynes, April 6, 2011). Teenage (or even preteen) action heroines embody a unique combination of innocence, violence, and sexuality.

In films like *Serenity* (2005), *Hard Candy* (2006), *Kick-Ass* (2010), *True Grit* (2010), *Winter's Bone* (2010), *Hanna* (2011), *Sucker Punch* (2011), *Kick-Ass 2* (2013), *Violet & Daisy* (2013), and *Barely Lethal* (2014), young heroines do not hesitate to kill their enemies in the most spectacular of ways. The same can be said for countless young female characters in comic books, video games, and young adult literature series. While this extreme toughening up of girls in action narratives is sometimes heralded as an exaggerated model of "girl power," or "postfeminist" ideals, the emphasis on their remarkable feats of violence reveals a peculiar fetishization of young women. These "lethal Lolitas," as they are often described in the media, meld together cultural preconceptions about female innocence and predatory sexuality with fantasies of male control, all disguised within a narrative that parallels more conservative coming-of-age stories.

The trend of young girls as action heroines occurs across a range of genres, from straight action to westerns to dystopian science fiction to superheroes and comedy. Elsewhere (Brown 2011), I explored the rise of girls as action heroines as an expression of the cultural shift from second to third wave feminism and the media's embrace of, and capitalizing on, popular notions of girl power as a literalization of postfeminist ideology. Here, I am less concerned with how young action heroines reflect neofeminist ideas, but with how the use of young female characters who can kick ass also raises a variety of issues about gender, violence, and sexual development. In this chapter, I want to look specifically at several key young action heroines from recent films and literature and how each of them were received by critics in relation to themes of feminism and sexualization. Though the young girl as action heroine is quickly becoming a stock figure, the character is still novel enough to inspire a great deal of public debate about whether or not the roles are appropriate and whether or not they can represent a type of empowerment for young women. The controversial and violent Hit-Girl from the films *Kick-Ass* and *Kick-Ass 2*, based on the comics by Mark Millar, shocked critics and viewers with the sight of an eleven-year-old girl gleefully cussing like a sailor as she brutally shot, stabbed, and disemboweled bad guys. In a different vein, the scantily clad heroines of writer/director Zack Snyder's *Sucker Punch* were shocking for the excessive and gratuitous ways they were displayed as teenage sexual fantasies. Conversely, the character of Hanna from director Joe Wright's film *Hanna* was widely praised as a truly feminist figure because she struggled with emotional development while she efficiently dispatched numerous villains. And finally, I want to briefly discuss the contemporary subgenre of spy girls in young adult literature for the way these books handle many of the same themes of violence, sexuality, and puberty that the cinematic versions do, but also emphasize the metaphor of the young girls' sexual maturation through mystery and heroic actions.

"WE CAN KICK ASS!"—HIT-GIRL

Director Matthew Vaughn's *Kick-Ass* was a surprise hit at the 2010 box office, grossing over $50 million, earning cult film status, and meriting a sequel in 2013. Based on an extremely graphic revisionist comic book miniseries by Mark Milllar, *Kick-Ass* was an independently produced film that strived to remain as faithful to the source material as possible, even though that meant retaining an exaggerated level of violence and vulgar language. The film centers on Dave Lizewski (Aaron Taylor-Johnson), a relatively plain nobody in high school who decides to put on a costume and fight crime as the hero Kick-Ass, even though he has no powers, skills, or training. Despite being brutally beaten several times, Kick-Ass eventually becomes a media phenomenon and is embroiled in a battle against Frank D'Amico (Mark Strong), the head of a crime syndicate, and his nerdy son, Chris D'Amico (Christopher Mintz-Plasse), who takes on the persona of an inept super-villain named the Red Mist. Along the way, Dave partners up with the lethal super-team of Big Daddy (Nicholas Cage) and his daughter, Mindy Macready, aka Hit-Girl (Chloe Grace Moretz). Mindy is only eleven years old, but is a master of numerous weapons and fighting styles. When Dave first meets her, Hit-Girl gleefully and bloodily kills an entire room of armed gang members after challenging them with: "OK you cunts. . . . Let's see what you can do now!" Hit-Girl has been trained her entire life by Big Daddy so they can exact revenge against D'Amico for the death of Hit-Girl's mother. Where other girls are excited about makeup and boys, Hit-Girl cares only for swords and sniper rifles. After Big Daddy is tortured and killed by D'Amico's thugs, Hit-Girl teams up with Kick-Ass to finally take down the criminal empire through an all-out assault. In the finale, it is Hit-Girl, not the ridiculous Kick-Ass, who expertly and ruthlessly kills dozens of armed guards and fights to the death with D'Amico himself. At every turn, the film reminds us that the real hero, the skilled killer, is the preadolescent whirling dervish Hit-Girl.

For most viewers and critics, Hit-Girl steals the movie. As *Bitch* magazine's review asked: "Why on earth wasn't *Kick-Ass* called *Hit-Girl*?" (Johnson, 2010); meanwhile, the *Globe and Mail* review was simply entitled: "*Kick-Ass*: It's Hit-Girl Who Packs the Real Punch" (Groen, April 16, 2010). Chloe Grace Moretz's performance as Mindy/Hit-Girl was singled out as touching, exuberant, and exciting. Likewise, the character of Hit-Girl was described as

Fig. 8.1. Hit-Girl's combination of childhood and violence challenged assumptions about girlish innocence.

unprecedented and oddly gratifying. "It is the plucky Moretz who dazzles," Claudia Puig wrote in *USA Today*. "Even as she wields outlandish weaponry, she comes off as adorable. Her devotion to her father adds a touching note amid the bloodletting and whacked-out mayhem" (Puig, April 16, 2010). And the *New York Times* declared: "Ms. Moretz is by far the best thing about the film: she holds the screen as gracefully as she executes a running backflip" (Dargis, April 15, 2010). But the real reason Hit-Girl stole the movie is her outrageously violent actions and vulgar language. Never before had an eleven-year-old girl been depicted happily killing baddies in the most brutal ways imaginable, while casually spouting expletives that would make a dive-bar full of sailors blush. For example, in the final assault on D'Amico's well-guarded penthouse, Hit-Girl kills dozens of armed henchmen in a brutal flurry. She stabs, cuts off limbs, shoots (and reloads on the run), and even uses a rope to make one henchman shoot himself in the face. Blood flies everywhere while Hit-Girl leaps and flips around, killing everyone in her path. Hit-Girl's violence is well-choreographed excess set to the tune of upbeat pop songs, and she causes more bloodshed than James Bond or even Rambo ever did. The anachronism of such levels of violence being dealt out by a cute pixie of a girl is surprising. Likewise, her constant use of profane language was jarring coming from an innocent-looking girl. In addition to the controversial "cunts" line, Hit-Girl revels in language usually deemed inappropriate for minors, especially preadolescent girls. When Dave asks her how he can contact Big Daddy and Hit-Girl, she sarcastically says, "You just contact the mayor's office. He has a special signal he shines in the sky; it's in the shape of a giant cock." And after killing the villains who tortured her father on a live video feed, she looks into the camera and deadpans, "Show's over, motherfuckers!"

Hit-Girl's shocking violence and language was intentionally controversial. *Rolling Stone* called Hit-Girl "deliciously unsuited for mass consumption" and "a nightmare for the Christian right" (Travers, April 15, 2010). And, perhaps not unexpectedly, the violence and language coming from a character (and actress) so young was divisive. Legendary film critic Roger Ebert called the film "morally reprehensible," primarily because "it shows deadly carnage dished out by an 11-year-old girl, after which an adult man brutally hammers her to within an inch of her life. Blood everywhere" (Ebert, April 14, 2010). And Kenneth Turan, in the *Los Angeles Times*, wrote that Hit-Girl's "language is so astonishingly crude that it has taken people's attention away from all the killing she does, which is mind-boggling as well" (Turan, April 15, 2010). Many other critics enjoyed Hit-Girl's antics. Tricia Olszewski of the *Washington City Paper*, for example, wrote that "the sensitive will surely faint in horror, but there's something incredibly thrilling about a little girl who's always armed with throwing stars and a butterfly knife and can mow down a room full of big men with big guns" (Olszewski, April 16, 2010). And Emily M. Gray declared: "I loved her because she is such an antidote to the women we usually see in movies of the genre who are usually posited as the appendage of (and inevitably in need of rescue by) the superhero. . . . I also loved her because she is a girl in the literal sense and rarely in film do we see girl protagonists. . . . She challenges what we think about girls, and about girls and violence and the viewer is left in awe as she spins around the screen finishing off bad guys" (Gray, December 3, 2010). Love her or hate her, Hit-Girl made an impression on everyone who saw the film.

The much-publicized controversy that circulated around the figure of Hit-Girl was primarily due to her age. The character was only eleven, and perhaps more importantly, so was Moretz at the time of filming the movie. In numerous interviews, Moretz clarified that she would never be allowed to use language like Hit-Girl's in real life, and that her parents forbid her from watching any of the violent action heroine movies that preceded *Kick-Ass*, like *The Professional* (1994) or *Wanted* (2008). The disjuncture is that Hit-Girl looked like, and was, a prepubescent child, which was not the case with most portrayals of underage girls in Hollywood films (often by women in their twenties). Examples of the latter include Megan Fox as a sultry high-school teenager in the *Transformer* movies (2007, 2009); Emma Stone as a rumored promiscuous teen in *Easy A* (2010); or any of the leggy and buxom teen heroines of *Sucker Punch*. During the early stages of developing the film, all of the major studios refused to sign on unless Hit-Girl was revamped as an eighteen-year-old character. Vaughn and Millar decided to produce the film independently because they felt that Hit-Girl's youth was what made the character truly progressive and unique. It was Hit-Girl's age, more than the actual violence or language, that was alarming. When adult women behave as Hit-Girl does, there is celebration rather than controversy. When Uma Thurman slices and dices her way through dozens of henchmen during the Tokyo nightclub scene in *Kill Bill* (2003)—a scene that Hit-Girl's carnage clearly is inspired by—the film is praised for its choreography and adrenaline rush. Likewise, when Melissa McCarthy plays extremely foul-mouthed and aggressive women in movies like *Bridesmaids* (2011) and *The Heat* (2013), she is applauded as a standout character and wins numerous awards. The difference is that both Thurman and McCarthy are adult women, while Hit-Girl is clearly just a child. Culturally, we have a deep-seated belief in childhood as a time of innocence that needs to be safeguarded.

Childhood has been romanticized as a golden age of innocence that needs to be protected from the vile world of adult concerns ever since the eighteenth century when French philosopher Jean-Jacques Rousseau postulated that childhood is a natural, pure, perfect, and thus innocent state. "In contemporary Western societies," observes Affrica Taylor in her article reviewing the debates about childhood sexualization, "the compulsion to essentialise, de-historicise and universalize childhood as a natural state of innocence is incredibly powerful" (Taylor 2010, 52). Hit-Girl's proficiency in both violence and profanity challenges our dominant beliefs about acceptable childhood behaviors. Violence and profanity can be entertainment when performed by mature actresses like Thurman and McCarthy because they are only slightly taboo topics for adults. The outrage over Hit-Girl's "morally reprehensible" depiction is rooted in the belief that the filmmakers failed to protect a cherished ideal of innocent childhood, and failed to protect a young actress specifically. And, by extension, anyone who enjoys Hit-Girl's antics does not endorse a more proper conception of children. As Robinson and Davies have argued, the Western belief in childhood innocence is complexly intertwined with a perceived need to protect the very concept of childhood from volatile and serious topics deemed as adult-only issues:

> Within hegemonic discourses of childhood, innocence is viewed as natural, and moral panic is often associated with a perceived risk of the child's innocence being compromised. Within these discourses, stemming from philosophy and developmental psychology, childhood is perceived as a universal natural state of human development, epitomized by angelic purity and innocence. Adulthood and childhood become mutually exclusive polarized worlds with the child becoming the powerless "other" in the world of adults, a world in which adults become the

> "gate-keepers" of knowledge and experience in an effort to preserve the perceived essence of childhood; that is "innocence." Adults often have a nostalgic longing for childhood, reminiscing that it is a time of carefree fantasy that is too quickly lost. Within this constructed dichotomy, certain kinds of knowledge become the exclusive rights of adulthood. Politics, sex and death, for instance, become adult knowledge from which children are excluded. (Robinson and Davies 2008, 343)

Hit-Girl confounds the boundaries between childhood innocence and adult knowledge. She demonstrates a knowledge of "sex and death" that is beyond her years. Hit-Girl's casual use of sexually charged curse words and her proficient killing are troublesome because they reveal her transgressive status as a child behaving as an adult. The very behaviors that are a staple of the action genre, and a pleasurable part of most action heroes and heroines, are surprisingly shocking when embodied in a little girl.

The fact that Hit-Girl is a *girl* seems to only compound the objectionable clash between her vulgar attributes and her youth. Girls are still seen in our culture as more vulnerable and more quintessentially innocent than boys are. As the nursery rhyme says, girls are "made of sugar and spice, and everything nice," while boys are more naturally rough-and-tumble, made of "snips and snails, and puppy dog tails." The opening credits of Cartoon Network's *The Powerpuff Girls* (1998–2005) directly alludes to this gendered belief when it explains that the Professor used these specific ingredients (sugar, spice, everything nice) to concoct "perfect little girls." The ingredients for Hit-Girl seem to have skipped "sugar" and "everything nice" altogether. Numerous critics wondered if the same public outcry would have occurred if the character had been Hit-Boy. "We would never be having this whole conversation about Hit-Girl if the character would have been Hit-Boy," wrote Melissa Silverstein on the website Women and Hollywood. "No one would care in the same way if an 11-year-old boy said the c-word" (April 12, 2010). We expect boys to be more vulgar and violent than girls; after all, they are men in training. Even for children, we have a sexist double standard that categorizes girls as more passive, more vulnerable, and more in need of protection from the world around them. When a reporter for the *Washington Post* asked Jane Goldman, the co-screenwriter of *Kick-Ass*, if the controversy would even exist if the character had been Hit-Boy, Goldman responded: "I think there is something about [a girl in this role] that makes people uncomfortable. It amazes me that the traditional view of little girls as being innocent and sweet still holds true. I'm personally fed up with people seeing women and girls cast as victims, so I feel it is refreshing" (Chaney, April 14, 2010). Hit-Girl may be a shocking character but that is the case only because she presents such a challenge to deep-seated presumptions about appropriate behavior for young girls. She resists the dual double standards (a quadruple standard?) of age and gender expectations.

The film's atypical portrayal of Hit-Girl as a young girl who can verbally and physically kick ass better than any of the boys or male adults makes her, possibly, one of the most progressive female film characters in recent years. Though the film is primarily a comedic spoof of superhero conventions, the creator's feminist leanings for Hit-Girl were even self-consciously evoked in one of her character posters. Posed like Rosie the Riveter from the iconic "We Can Do It!" World War II propaganda poster, Hit-Girl is featured rolling up her tiny sleeve as she holds a gun, declaring "We Can Kick Ass!" For those who could look past, or who enjoyed, Hit-Girl's language and violence, the character represented a vision of female empowerment unlike anything ever seen before. The review in the feminist magazine *Bitch* argued: "Hit-Girl is empowered, non-sexualized, and capable of defending herself—she's the one that comes to the rescue, and only needs assistance from others in the most dire of situations" (Johnson, April 20, 2010). The feminist website Gender Across Borders wrote that "in many ways, Hit-Girl is an empowering character for young girls . . . the idea of superhero and action movies creating space for girls to play aggressive, powerful characters is innovative and refreshing" (Nelson, April 20, 2010). An article in *California Literary Review* bluntly declared that "Hit-Girl is a feminist character" (Rhodes, April 19, 2010). Other critics had trouble reconciling Hit-Girl's outrageous behavior with feminist ideals. The *New York Times*, for example, argued that *Kick-Ass* gives "the false impression that because Hit-Girl is a powerful figure she's also an empowering one" (Dargis, April 15, 2010). The debates about Hit-Girl's legitimacy as a feminist icon depended on each commentator's belief in how a feminist character would look and act. As an eleven-year-old character, Hit-Girl is not sexualized, which most critics agreed was a rare and welcome step—her superhero costume is not skintight and she is not flirtatious. Her language and violence was regarded as liberating to many viewers since neither is usually the provenance of female characters in action movies. But some saw it as inappropriate and corrupting to align such profanity and bloodletting with an otherwise innocent little girl. Some regarded her training by Big Daddy as manipulative and controlling, taking away her decision-making abilities. Others focused on her decisive and kinetic actions as a symbol of independence and self-control. Perhaps Hit-Girl's greatest achievement was not her defeat of all those villains, nor was it critics celebrating her as a feminist icon for the twenty-first century, but instead that she sparked a wide-ranging public debate about feminism and media depictions of girls.

"YOU WILL BE UNPREPARED"—BABYDOLL

Critics and fans were conflicted about Zack Snyder's *Sucker Punch*, his CGI-heavy entry into the subgenre of teenage ass-kicking heroines. The promotional tag line, "You will be unprepared," was a reference to the elaborate visual effects used throughout the film, but it could just as easily be applied to the way the five young female characters are visually depicted. A few critics/viewers saw *Sucker Punch* as a visually stunning tale of female empowerment. Most, however, regarded it as merely hyper-stylized sexual exploitation of underage girls. In *Sucker Punch*, Snyder indulges the same preference for stunning visuals that he demonstrated in his previous films, *300* (2006) and *Watchmen* (2009). But where those films were based on successful graphic novels, *Sucker Punch* is an original story by Snyder and co-writer Steve Shibuya ostensibly about fighting back against sexism, or as the *Time* magazine review described it: "a pastiche of every lubricious girl-power film ever made" (Corliss, 2011). The complicated narrative focuses on the plight of the teenage Babydoll (Emily Browning), who is locked up in an asylum and is scheduled for a lobotomy after being framed for the murder of her sister who Babydoll was trying to save from her lecherous stepfather after her mother's death. Babydoll joins forces with four other imprisoned young women—Blondie (Vanessa Hudgens), Amber (Jamie Chung), Rocket (Jena Malone), and her sister, Sweet Pea (Abbie Cornish)—all of whom are desperate to escape. The film rotates between three different narrative levels—the dank and despondent real world of the asylum; a fantasy level that Babydoll imagines wherein the asylum is a sleazy brothel run by the orderly, Blue (Oscar Isaac), who forces her and the other inmates to function as dancers/prostitutes for the pleasure of powerful and disgusting male visitors; and a third, even more extreme level of fantasy where the women must battle giant stone samurai warriors, zombie Nazis, robots, and dragons, in order to secure five different objects that they need to escape the asylum/brothel. While in the third level the girls are guided through their missions by the lone helpful male character, an older mysterious figure simply referred to as the Wise Man (Scott Glenn). The different narrative levels are a visual representation of Babydoll's heroic imagination that meld together escapism and attempts to escape. In order to access the elaborate CGI battles of the third level, Babydoll must perform a mesmerizing erotic dance for the brothel patrons in the second level (we never see the actual dance), and it is implied that she is being raped on the first level.

An ambitious film that was vehemently defended by some critics and fans, nonetheless the heavily promoted *Sucker Punch* was a relative failure at the box office and was harshly reviewed as visually impressive but ultimately a vapid mishmash of fan-boy fantasies. The review in the *Chicago Sun-Times* claimed that *Sucker Punch* is "a green-screen, mash-up video game with an indecipherable plot; scantily clad, busty women giving flat performances, and the least interesting villains and monsters in recent memory" (Roeper 2011). The review in *Variety* called the film "fantasy fodder for 13-year-old-guys," with the women costumed in "demeaning fetish gear" (Debruge, March 24, 2011). The most obvious and repeated criticism of *Sucker Punch* focused on this fetishistic depiction of the five young heroines. *Slant* magazine described the women as "barely legal hotties in stripper-schoolgirl outfits" (Schager, March 24, 2011). Similarly, *Time* magazine referred to lead heroine Babydoll as the one "who with the giant eyes, puffy lips and fake eyelashes could be her own anime doll, the whole package dressed in a Japanese schoolgirl outfit as retailored by Victoria's Secret" (Corliss, 2011). In response to the numerous accusations of sexism, the film's creators defended *Sucker Punch*, claiming that it is actually a deeply feminist story. The *Sydney Morning Herald* quoted Australian actress Emily Browning's (Babydoll) comments to the BBC, where she claimed: "I find the idea that it is sexist really bizarre. The sexism is within the story of the film. Within the brothel, the girls are being objectified but that does not mean the film is doing the same. It's really about these girls breaking free" (quoted in Wenn, April 4, 2011). Director Zack Snyder repeatedly argued that *Sucker Punch* was a critique of the male gaze so common in films and that his intention was to empower the heroines and to frustrate the viewer's gaze by substituting action fantasies in the moments when Babydoll dances erotically. In an interview with *Movieline*, Snyder said, "Someone asked me, 'Why are they dressed so provocatively? Why would you dress them like that in their fighting sequences?' The girls are in a brothel performing for men because men are the audience, so when they go into the action sequences, that's us—we, the viewer in the theatre. We are the people in the brothel who want the girls to perform for us. We want them in those costumes—I didn't put them in those costumes." When the interviewer surmises that the point of the film is that "these young women are taking back the submissive, fetishized female archetypes," Snyder rather passively agrees: "Well, in the end, I hope that is what happens. In the end, you put them in those costumes and now they are using them against you—That's basically what Babydoll does to Blue in a lot of ways. The metaphor there is he puts her in that role and she starts knocking the dominoes over that lead to his destruction" (Yamato, March 23, 2011).

Still, for all of Snyder's rationales about empowering women, the emphasis on stunning visuals featuring beautiful young women going into battle in sexy costumes, means the eroticism overrides any of *Sucker Punch*'s intended criticism of sexploitation. Instead, what *Sucker Punch* presents is a very stylized

Fig. 8.2. The fetishized heroines of *Sucker Punch* equate kicking-ass with being sexy.

fantasy of fetishized young women who kick ass only in a dream world. For all their heroics, Babydoll, Blondie, Amber, Rocket, and Sweet Pea are prime examples of contemporary popular culture's continued sexualization of girlhood. As feminist scholars have been arguing for decades, our youth- and sex-obsessed culture thoroughly eroticizes young women. We teach girls that they should strive to be sexually attractive, we depict girls in the media as sexual spectacles, and we infantilize adult women. Both popular and academic discussions about the sexualization of girls have been reinvigorated in recent years thanks in large part to high-profile reports on the issue released by the Australian, American, and UK governments, and due to several shocking performances by young female celebrities. The Australian report (Rush and La Nauze 2006) described an atmosphere of "Corporate Paedophilia" where adolescent and preadolescent girls are systemically fashioned as sexual objects. The American study conducted by the American Psychological Association (APA) in 2007 was entitled "The Sexualization of Girls," and stressed the omnipresent pressure brought to bear on girls through the media, peers, and family that leads girls to sexualize themselves and to perceive themselves only in objectified terms. The United Kingdom report, entitled *The Sexualisation of Young People Review* (Papadopoulos 2010), emphasized how pervasive sexual pressures are and the harmful affects they have on young people, particularly girls. In their review of these reports, and the wealth of literature they spawned, Vares, Jackson, and Gill (2011) summarize: "The growth in sexualized images and products targeted at young girls, as well as the increasing pervasiveness of media technologies, is seen to encourage girls to 'grow up too fast' and become 'too sexy too soon'" (140). Meanwhile, public and media debates have continued about the acceptability of sexualizing young women due to several scandalous performances. Just as the image of a teenage Britney Spears gyrating in a skimpy schoolgirl uniform in the video for "Hit Me Baby, One More Time" was fading from public memory, Miley Cyrus created a furor by pole dancing at the Teen Choice Awards in 2009, and then again for her twerking against adult Robin Thicke's crotch during a performance at the Video Music Awards in 2013. While Miley's spectacular antics have garnered the most attention, other contemporary young female singers like Selena Gomez, Ariana Grande, Pixie Lott, and Hyuna have pushed sexual boundaries even though the bulk of their audience is tween girls.

The pervasive sexualization of young girls in contemporary culture, and the popular/scholarly debates about it, is nothing new. In our misogynistic world, girls have always been fetishized. Contemporary media forms have accelerated this ever-present fetishization and communicate a very clear message. In her discussion of fashion magazines and advertisements, Debra Merskin argues that "the message from advertisers and the mass media to girls (as eventual women) is they should always be sexually available, always have sex on their minds, be willing to be dominated and even sexually abused, and to be seen—always and primarily—as sexual objects" (2008, 58). Images of eroticized girls in modern mass media, like the heroines of *Sucker Punch*, normalize an association of young girls with sexuality. In her book *The Lolita Effect* (2008), M. Gigi Durham describes the recent acceleration of sexualized images of girls in popular culture: "The turn of the new millennium has spawned an intriguing phenomenon: The sexy little girl . . . with preternaturally voluptuous curves, and whose scantily clad body gyrates in music videos, poses provocatively on teen magazine covers, and populates cinema and television screens around the globe . . . she is Lolita" (p.22). That the figure of Lolita, the tragic victim of pedophilia from Vladimir Nabokov's infamous novel *Lolita* (1955), is so often used as a symbol of sexualized girlhood reveals how our cultural impression of these girls has changed. Susan Bordo (2000) correctly points out that fluctuating depictions of girlhood and different adaptations of the original novel means that currently "we may not be inclined to think of *Lolita* as a story of child abuse. For in the years since *Lolita* was published, Nabokov's creations have been usurped by cultural archetypes with a life of their own" (300). Countless portrayals of young girls as sexual spectacles, from Elizabeth Taylor to Brooke Shields to Megan Fox, have naturalized a belief that girls are active sexual subjects rather than merely fetishized objects. "For many people," Bordo continues, "the very word 'Lolita' no longer denotes Nabokov's fictional twelve-year-old but exists as an all-purpose signifier for the underage sexual temptress" (2000, 300). Young girls are not only eroticized in the media, they are coded as flirtatious, sexually aggressive, even predatory.

That the modern Lolita is perceived as a "sexual temptress" can best be understood as a gradual shifting away from a belief in girls as sexual innocents, in need of protection from lecherous older men, to a popular image of girls as gleefully wielding sexual power over men. In her analysis of the public reception of eroticized girls in film between 1962 and 1996, Kristen Hatch charts a concern that over time girls have been recategorized from victims to victimizers: "If *Pretty Baby* (1978) was perceived to pose a danger to girls' sexual development, positioning pubescent girls as the object of a sexualized male gaze, *Lolita* (Adrian Lyne's 1997 remake) was understood to be a threat to the stable sexuality of adult men who were imagined to be at risk of being transformed, en masse, into pedophiles" (Hatch 2002, 176). While girls, especially teenage girls, have always been sexualized to various degrees in popular culture, the 1990s clearly marked a shift to being sexy *and* dangerous. In an era of burgeoning Riot Grrl and third-wave feminist politics, a rising AIDS epidemic, an increasingly common acceptance of porno-chic images, and drastic changes in media dissemination, teenage girls were increasingly presented as alluring but threatening. For example, the public fascination with the story of seventeen-year-old Amy Fisher, who shot the wife of her adult lover Joey Buttafuoco in 1992, gave real world credence to a fear of sexually aggressive teenage girls. This bizarre scandal was almost immediately adapted for film and television exploitation in *Amy Fisher: My Story* (1992), *Casualties of Love: The Long Island Lolita Story* (1993), and *The Amy Fisher Story* (1993). The depiction of sexualized young girls in the media went from being perceived as prey to being perceived as predators.

The 1990s also saw the start of a film trend about deadly and sexy teenage girls, a trend which continues today with films such as *The Crush* (1993), the *Poison Ivy* series (1992, 1996, 1997, 2008), the *Wild Things* series (1998, 2004, 2005, 2010), *Devil in the Flesh* (1998) and its sequel, *Teacher's Pet* (2000), *Cruel Intentions* (1999), *Swimfan* (2002), *Pretty Persuasion* (2005), *Jennifer's Body* (2009), and *Spring Breakers* (2012). Katherine Farrimond describes this change in how teenage girls are depicted as deadly sirens in films from the 1990s on as a new type of adolescent femme fatale:

> Throughout the history of Hollywood cinema, teenage girls have been variously presented as tearaways, Lolitas, coquettes, high-school bitches, and jailbait. Until the 1990s, however, these bad girls were not approximate to the sexy-but-deadly femme fatales of classic American noir. Indeed, it is only in the last two decades that the femme fatale's cruel single-mindedness and erotic allure has been transferred to the figure of the teenage girl. . . . The combination of sexuality, criminality, and

> youthful femininity is interpreted in a way that emphasizes the teenage girl's seductive danger, while playing down any concern for her personal well-being. The femme fatale in these films thus functions primarily as the object of desire: her motivations go unquestioned and the threats she poses to the family (and to adult masculinity in particular) are neutralized through her death or incarceration. (Farrimond 2011, 77, 79)

Though the action heroine of modern cinema is a different character type than the femme fatale of noir, the boundaries between the two are permeable. Action heroines are independent, physically strong, and skilled with weapons, while femme fatales are seductive schemers who are typically concerned with their own financial rewards, but the two figures overlap in their irresistible beauty and the danger they pose to masculinity. The teen heroines of *Sucker Punch* are visually depicted in a manner that relates them as much to the "sexual temptress" stereotype of deadly, teenage femme fatales as it does to ass-kicking action heroines. These overly fetishized heroines risk being just sexy young objects, like every other depiction of hot young girls in the media, rather than self-determining active subjects.

Part of the difficulty with the depiction of sexy young action heroines like Babydoll, Blondie, Sweet Pea, Amber, and Rocket is the problematic muddling of notions about sexualization and sexual empowerment. Scholarly debates still continue about whether or not increased sexualization of girls and women is progressive or regressive. Rosalind Gill, in her review article "Media, Empowerment and the 'Sexualization of Culture' Debates" (2012), accurately summarizes the dilemna: "On one side of the argument are those who mobilize women's 'choice,' 'agency' and 'empowerment' to champion aspects of 'sexualized' culture such as pornography, burlesque or the popularity of pole dancing as a recreational activity—these activities can be defended (or even celebrated) because they are 'empowering.' On the other, empowerment is regarded merely as a cynical rhetoric, wrapping sexual objectification in a shiny, feisty, postfeminist packaging that obscures the continued underlying sexism" (736–37). Moreover, in popular culture itself the progressive sex-positive themes of third-wave feminism were often misunderstood, and mutated into a rationale for ratcheting up sexual portrayals. "Girl power" became a hollow catchphrase for the likes of the Spice Girls, and suggested that women, no matter how young, should embrace sexuality as a means to control one's own life. But in commercial media forms, "sexiness" rarely equals "empowerment." All too often empowerment is just a narrative illusion used as an excuse to continue portraying women as erotic objects. Farrimond goes on to describe how this feint applies to the modern femme fatale in terms that are just as applicable to films like *Sucker Punch*: "While she is prevailingly presented as an icon of female empowerment, then, the teenage femme fatale—with her outwardly conventional 'sexiness' and apparent sexual availability—is best understood as a figure that occupies the liminal territory between sexual empowerment and patriarchal objectification. . . . In other words, the dominating patriarchal gaze is likely to read the teenage 'sexy vamp' as anything but powerful" (2011, 79–80). When action heroines, particularly teenage action heroines, are overwrought with sexual symbolism, any pretense to their being empowered is undermined.

For Snyder to claim that his teenage heroines in *Sucker Punch* are empowered because they wield guns and swords while dressed like slutty schoolgirls and underage dominatrices is a hard pill to swallow. Though a few critics and bloggers agreed that the girls' sexuality helped empower them, most reviews were offended by the idea that *Sucker Punch* was anything more than expensive and stylish sexploitation. As Dodai Stewart put it in her column on the feminist website Jezebel.com: "*Sucker Punch* is a two-hour $82 million fetish film examining how hot and sad schoolgirls look when holding weapons. Snyder should have just made a porn movie—It might have been better, and it definitely would have been cheaper and more honest" (March 25, 2011). In the *Chicago Sun-Times*, Richard Roeper bemoaned that "*Sucker Punch* wants us to sympathize with the plight of these oppressed women even as it delights in showcasing their assets. The voiceover speaks of empowerment and finding your inner strength, but the screen is filled with highly digitized images of young women in high heels and short skirts wielding gigantic guns as they mow down the opposition" (March 24, 2011). In the *Huffington Post*, Jessica Massa argued that "*Sucker Punch* fails to be empowering because it takes such a caricatured stance on what female empowerment actually entails. It's a male-driven version of empowerment, where machine guns and powerful right hooks take the place of more nuanced displays of strength and confidence and accomplishment. . . . For starters, they do all of their fighting dressed as burlesque dancers or Japanese schoolgirls" (March 23, 2011). Many critics took umbrage with Snyder claiming in interviews that the film is actually a feminist parable. "Snyder's conception of his heroines—who are asked to do little more than pout, strut, glare, and look fierce—is pure nonsense," argued Nick Schager in *Slant* magazine, "since like the story's villains, his film reduces them to mere objects of carnal desire, and ones whose physical prowess and take-no-shit attitude is less a face-slapping rejoinder to sexism than a manifestation of amalgamated male desires. A zoom into Babydoll's miniskirt hemline as she wraps her hand around a sword's handle epitomizes Snyder's true aim here, teen-boy titillation, and any ensuing message about feminist liberation—and any expository efforts to own up to said titillation—is just so much disingenuous lip service aimed at masking the proceedings' wet-dream pandering" (March 24, 2011). Likewise, Angie Han at Slashfilm.com declared that "Snyder's claim that Sucker Punch is empowering isn't just false, but damaging. It reframes feminism—or 'female empowerment,' if you prefer not to use the F-word—in terms of male fantasy. In other words, it's OK for ladies to kick ass and shit, so long as they do it in a way that turns men on" (March 26, 2011).

"YOUNG. SWEET. INNOCENT. DEADLY."—HANNA

Director Joe Wright's film *Hanna* arrived in theatres just months after *Sucker Punch* in 2011, but with far less publicity. While *Sucker Punch* was poorly received by critics and audiences alike, *Hanna* was generally praised by reviewers, going on to earn a surprising $42 million at the box office. *Hanna* has more of a European art-house-film-style to it than most Hollywood action movies, but still presents a strong, young, girl who can kick ass with the best of them. While the heroines of *Sucker Punch* were overdetermined by sexual display, *Hanna* stressed the naïve innocence of its gun-wielding heroine. Promotional posters featured stark close-ups of Hanna (Saoirse Ronan) holding a gun or bow with one of three different tag lines: "Adapt or Die," "Innocence can be deadly," or "Young. Sweet. Innocent. Deadly." Rather than linking Hanna's youthful sexuality to her lethal nature, the film associates her innocence with her deadliness. The plot for *Hanna* is essentially a Grimm fairy tale or coming-of-age story refashioned for the twenty-first century—and with a lot of action and adventure tossed in for good measure. Hanna is a sixteen-year-old girl who has been raised in an isolated cottage in the frozen wilds of Finland by her ex-CIA father, Erik Heller (Eric Bana). Erik has extensively trained her with a range of weapons, fighting styles, and survival skills, turning her into a lethal assassin. Hanna is curious about the outside world and Erik feels she is prepared for her mission, so he leaves and allows her to be captured by shadowy black-ops soldiers after she activates a homing beacon. Taken into custody, the tiny and frail-looking Hanna almost immediately snaps the neck of the woman interrogating her, Marissa Weigler (Cate Blanchett), who Hanna believes is her nemesis. Hanna escapes the bunker and goes on a cross-Europe adventure while being pursued by the ruthless Weigler and her creepy henchmen. Hanna is befriended by a well-meaning family and bonds with their teenage daughter, Sophie (Jessica Barden), who exposes Hanna to a normal teenage life, including popular music and cute boys. Gradually Hanna learns about herself and the real world, and she eventually dispatches her pursuers. Hanna finds out that she was part of a government experiment run by Weigler to produce genetically enhanced soldiers, and that Erik recued her from that fate while she was just an infant. Erik is killed when he tries to meet up with Hanna at a rendezvous point in Berlin, and in the final showdown Hanna executes Weigler.

Where reviewers debated the feminist possibilities of Hit-Girl despite her being perceived by some as too violent and crude, and where Babydoll and her friends were generally dismissed for being too sexualized, Hanna was almost exclusively embraced as a legitimately feminist teenage action heroine. From the outset, *Hanna* director Joe Wright made it clear that his depiction of a strong young heroine was intentionally in opposition to the routine sexualization of female violence. Wright's response to a question at the Los Angeles Wondercon about how his heroine would differ from the girls of *Sucker Punch* was widely repeated in the press:

> For me, one of the main issues in terms of women's place in society and feminism is the sexual objectification of women . . . that is something that feminists in the '70s tried to fight against but has been totally lost in the 21st century consumer-celebrity world. So for me, when I look at the poster for *Sucker Punch* it seems actually incredibly sexist, because it is sexually objectifying women regardless of if they can shoot you or not. I have a kind of immediate, knee-jerk reaction to such iconography. I remember when the Spice Girls came out in the mid-'90s and it was all about Girl Power, but one of them was dressed as a baby doll, do you know what I mean? That isn't Girl Power, that isn't feminism. That's marketing bullshit. And I find it very, very alarming.

For critics, Wright's approach to Hanna and his self-conscious avoidance of Hollywood action heroine clichés translated into a genuinely feminist character. "After watching *Hanna*, I tried to figure out what made it so vastly different—and superior—to *Sucker Punch*," wrote Dodai Stewart on the feminist blog Jezebel.com. "Both stories involved young women being incredibly, graphically violent . . . but unlike Babydoll, Hanna, is a well-drawn, fully realized character, not just an avatar for an idea" (Stewart 2011). Matt Smith claimed that *Hanna* "provides a strong feminist outlook," and that "Wright has crafted a feminist take on assassination tales that rivals the best any director has to offer" (Smith, April 9, 2011). In *Bitch* magazine, Marina DelVecchio praised Hanna as "so unsexy, and yet so powerful. A small girl, she is smart, fast, and logical" (May 4, 2011). And James Worsdale declared that, upon

Fig. 8.3. Hanna is a lethal young feminist coming of age.

seeing *Hanna*, he "was in awe of how well it fulfilled the need for feminist reclamations in both the action and fairytale genres, artfully choreographed a tale of determination despite violent chaos and crushing disillusionment, and created a desexualized, brilliant and focused heroine" (April 13, 2011).

In desexualizing Hanna, the film presented not just a young action heroine but an action heroine who is not defined in any way by her beauty. In addition to rewriting some of the rules of action films, *Hanna* also reworks conventions about gender in fairy tales, one of the few genres where ideas about masculinity and femininity are even more dichotomous and firmly ensconced than in contemporary action. From the Brothers Grimm and Hans Christian Andersen to the modern influence of Disney princesses, fairy tales and fairy tale-inspired entertainments have defined conventional gender roles for centuries. As much as *Hanna* is an action movie, it is also a revisionist fairy tale. *Total Film* magazine called Hanna "a woozy mix of hard-as-nails actioner and modern-day fairytale" (Mottram 2011), and *New York* magazine described the film as "The Black-Ops Fairy Tale" (Edelstein, April 6, 2011). From the gingerbread-inspired forest cottage where Hanna initially lives with her father—their only reading material being an encyclopedia and a collection of Grimm fairy tales—to Hanna's final showdown with Marissa Weigler, the evil witch/stepmother, at a rundown fairy tale theme park, the film positions Hanna as a modern fairy tale princess. But Hanna is no damsel in distress waiting for her prince to come and save the day or sleeping beauty in need of a kiss or Rapunzel locked in a tower; Hanna, rather, is a thoroughly feminist character who can vanquish her enemies all on her own. Other films and television series have also sought to update fairy tale women in recent years, to varying degrees of success. Feature films like *Alice in Wonderland* (2010),

Tangled (2010), *Red Riding Hood* (2011), *Snow White and the Huntsman* (2012), *Hansel and Gretel* (2013), and *Maleficent* (2014)—and television programs like *Alice* (2009–2010), *Once Upon a Time* (2011–current), *Once Upon a Time in Wonderland* (2013–current), and *Sleepy Hollow* (2013–current)—have all updated centuries old legends. Moreover, all of these revisionist tales have tried to rework their classically passive heroines as modern action heroines. According to Hollywood, princesses are now as likely to wield a sword as they are to be beautiful.

As an action movie and a revisionist fairy tale, *Hanna* was often misleadingly described as postfeminist rather than feminist. While the concept of postfeminism is notoriously problematic given the different ways it has been used by cultural commentators, the media, journalists, and academics, there are a few key concepts that help contextualize *Hanna*'s melding of action and fairy tale. In her discussion of *Enchanted* (2007), itself a postmodern revision of fairy tale romance and Disneyesque princesses, Yvonne Tasker describes postfeminism as emphasizing "women's achievements—physical, educational, professional—and places particular emphasis on individual choice. Contemporary women are imagined by postfeminist discourse to be free to choose; free of both old-fashioned, sexist ideas about women's limits and feminism's supposed imposition of an asexual, unfeminine appearance. . . . While postfeminism insists on female strength and the primacy of the self (for which choice stands as the marker), that strength can, it seems, only be celebrated when figured in appropriately feminine terms" (Tasker 2011, 68–69). In general, postfeminism is also aligned with young women and their knowing/ironic pleasurable embrace of consumerism, popular culture, diversity, sexual freedom, and personal ideas of empowerment. It is this muddled understanding of postfeminism that allows the concept to be used as a rationale for categorizing films like *Sucker Punch* as empowering. The girls are sexy because the film is "postfeminist," not exploitative. *Hanna* avoids this misinterpretation of postfeminism by not fetishizing the young heroine. The film still retains a feminist voice in that it addresses Hanna's ability to make her own choices and to be an active subject. Choice for Hannah is better understood as the foundational principle of second-wave feminism because she exercises the right to make decisions about her life. Where postfeminism emphasizes choice through the lenses of popular culture and consumerism, Hanna has very little time or concern for these more superficial types of choices. It could, however, be argued that, like Hit-Girl in *Kick-Ass*, Hanna's early training by her father in effect determined many of her choices before she was old enough to decide on her own. But the film focuses on her adventures after she leaves her father's nest, and we repeatedly witness her navigating a violent world all on her own. The skills that her father taught Hanna allow her to protect herself (and others), but she is free to make her own choice of what to do with her lethal skills. The emphasis on her free will is set out from the very beginning of the film when Erik allows her to decide if she is ready to activate the beacon that will attract Marissa Wiegler's vengeful attention and set the entire plot in motion.

Given *Hanna*'s feminist intentions as set out by director Joe Wright, it is unfortunate that to complete the fairy tale revisionism of the film, the wicked witch has to be slain by a younger feminist princess. The film coyly avoids revealing too much background information about the villainous Marissa, but we do learn that she was the senior CIA agent in charge of a project in genetic experimentation to create super-soldiers out of children still in their unsuspecting mothers' wombs. When the project was scuttled, Erik absconded to the forest with baby Hanna, and Marissa has spent years trying to find and kill Hanna in order to tie up loose ends. In many ways, the stern Marissa is all the more evil because she is a ruthless female. In her tailored suits and helmet-like red hair, middle-aged Marissa is a caricatured depiction of the failures of second-wave feminism. Marissa is a woman who has chosen to pursue her own interests and her own career at the expense of compassion or maternal feelings. What kind of a monstrous woman tries to turn babies into weapons? The kind of woman who puts her job before all else. In a pivotal scene where Marissa is questioning an old woman, trying to figure out where Hanna may run to, the older woman rather judgmentally asks Marissa if she has children of her own. Marissa replies that she does not because she "made certain choices," and then coldly shoots the old woman. Clearly we understand that Marissa made the wrong choices. Where the heroine, Hanna, chooses to fight for freedom and for her family (her father, as well as her momentarily adopted English family), Marissa chose success in the highly competitive and male-dominated profession of the CIA. Hanna's innocent and youthful postfeminism is celebrated, while Marissa's careerist and outdated feminism is vilified. The transformation of the wicked witch/evil stepmother into a crimson-haired career woman may be essential to the fairy tale metaphor, but it has the incidental consequence of dismissing earlier feminist politics as misguided and dehumanizing. Despite any flaws, real or perceived, with earlier feminist practices and decisions, older generations of feminists paved the way for today's postfeminist girls. Even in a narrative sense, Hanna would not have her amazing lethal skills if Marissa had not been so career-minded.

"THEY'RE ARMED. SHE IS DANGEROUS."

Kick-Ass, *Sucker Punch*, and *Hanna* are three very different movies that raise different issues around the increasingly common figure of the young action heroine. While the girls of these three films have the highest profiles among young action heroines, they are joined by dozens more of their kin in other movies, on television, in comics, and in popular literature. And despite the noticeable differences between these young killers, they do share several key narrative conventions that can help contextualize their emergence in popular culture. The first, and most obvious, trait that all young action heroines share is their incredibly lethal abilities. Hit-Girl easily and joyfully mows down dozens of armed men; Babydoll and her team destroy fantastical creatures from giant samurai statues to robotic Nazis to dragons; and Hanna snaps necks and shoots to kill without any hesitation. These young heroines leave a trail of bloody bodies behind them that would shock Rambo. The idea that excessive violence in action genres is the sole provenance of grizzled men is quickly becoming a thing of the past in popular entertainments. Women have been kicking fictional ass for quite a while now, and younger and younger heroines are upping the ante. The level of violence may be unsettling; nonetheless, these remarkable characters are a fantasy challenge to the notion that women, especially young girls, need to be protected by men. As the petite teenage girl River Tam (Summer Glau) tells her wounded big brother in the film *Serenity*: "You have always taken care of me. My turn." River then jumps into lone battle with dozens of brutal, barbarian-like "Reavers," and slays them all in a spectacular fashion. Indeed, there is no reason why fictional young women should not have their turn to kick ass. As disturbing as some viewers and critics may find it, the concept of young action heroines holding their own, in a genre that has always been very closely associated with masculine fantasies of empowerment, broadens our cultural perceptions of what girls may be able to do if we do not hold them to a stereotype of passivity.

Part of the pleasure of the young action heroine is the surprising sight of a petite and innocent-looking girl easily beating up numerous hulking adversaries. Everyone loves an underdog, and to see macho men or superior forces beaten to a pulp by an unassuming character is vicariously satisfying. In Joss Whedon's 2005 film *Serenity*, which continued the adventures of his science fiction/western television series *Firefly*, it is revealed that the mentally disturbed waif, River Tam, is actually an incredibly gifted fighter who was turned into a killing machine by evil government scientists. The film's promotional tag line bluntly clarifies the difference between River and the rest of the Serenity crew: "They're armed. She is dangerous." When River hears a

Fig. 8.4. River Tam is a ninety-eight-pound girl programmed to kill.

subliminal trigger message while in a seedy bar full of really mean outlaws, she suddenly trounces all of them in a beautifully choreographed ballet of violence. Upon returning to their ship, a shocked Captain Malcolm Reynolds (Nathan Fillion) asks, "What in the hell happened back there?" And the ship's pilot, Walsh (Alan Tudyk), mirrors viewers' pleasure from the scene when he giddily adds, "Start with the part where Jayne gets knocked out by a ninety-pound girl 'cause . . . I don't think that is ever getting old." Jayne (Adam Baldwin) may be part of Walsh's own crew, but he is a large, muscular tough-guy jerk, and the irony of his being knocked out by a tiny teenage girl is a funny comeuppance. Whether presented for humor or shock, this type of visual dissonance is played out in every instance of young action heroines. When Hit-Girl first saves Kick-Ass by literally slicing up an apartment full of drug dealers, all Kick-Ass can do is cower from her in fear and wonder, or when Hanna snaps her interrogator's neck with no warning, we share in Marissa Weigler's shock as she observes the event through a two-way mirror. These tiny heroines seem to be the perfect disguise for strength and violence. They are the quintessential "ninety-pound weaklings" from the legendary Charles Atlas advertisements from the comic books. While the weakling male from those advertisements clearly pandered to insecure adolescent boys, and built his muscles to seek revenge on the beach bully, the young action girl remains safely disguised as unthreateningly petite. She is a perfectly innocent-looking visual proxy for both male and female viewers that would like revenge on powerful forces.

The diminutive physical stature of the young action heroine is a crucial part of her character. Either she is clearly a preadolescent (like Hit-Girl or Mattie Ross [Hailee Steinfeld] in *True Grit*) or she is a teenager who looks prepubescent (like Hanna or Hayley Stark [Ellen Page] in *Hard Candy*). And even when the young action heroine is a teenager who is either moderately or excessively sexualized like in *Sucker Punch* and *Violet and Daisy*, her "tininess" is noticeable. They are each essentially "ninety-pound girls" like River in *Serenity*. The trend of petite ass-kickers is so common that commentators and fans have dubbed it "waif fu." In addition to the narrative humor/shock capitalized on by the absurd image of a tiny girl trouncing countless tough guys, the young heroines' small size stresses her youth, innocence, and conformity to feminine physical ideals. The young action heroine is a case of extreme gender dimorphism wherein cultural standards dictate that men are supposed to be big, while women are supposed to be petite. A wealth of feminist literature has explored the cultural imperative of a petite body as the ideal female form. Most of the literature focuses on the issue of women's weight and efforts to regulate it, that is, to reduce body mass. Kim Chernin refers to this condition as a "tyranny of slenderness" (1981), and Susan Bordo analyzes the overdetermined nature of "slenderness as a contemporary ideal of a specifically *feminine* attractiveness" (1993, 205). As Chernin, Bordo, and numerous other scholars have argued, the cultural presumption is that ideal female bodies are not supposed to take up space, are not supposed to be loud, and are not supposed to be hungry or voracious. Tiny is the ideal physical form for women and implies the social ideals of innocence, passivity, and conformity. In contrast, women whose bodies (and by extension their personalities) are too much—too large, too muscular, too mouthy, too sexual, etc.—are considered grotesques (see Rowe 1995). Conforming to this logic of gender mutual exclusivity, earlier landmark action heroines like Ellen Ripley (Sigourney Weaver) in *Aliens* (1986) and Sarah Connor (Linda Hamilton) in *Terminator 2: Judgment Day* (1991) were often criticized (despite their box-office success) for being too masculine because they were noticeably muscular (see Brown 1996, Hills 1999). As Lisa Purse (2011b) observes about the shift from muscular to tinier heroines since the 1980s, current "female heroes combine their readily apparent strength and skill with a more traditionally feminine, and often emphatically sexualized, physique" (187). But the twenty-first century adolescent action heroine is the epitome of current feminine, and racialized, ideals: tiny, thin, usually blonde, cute, and fair-skinned.

Though visible muscles would make sense for physically strong female characters, adult action heroines have become, for the most part, significantly smaller in size in the new millennium in order to conform to binary gender expectations. For example, in Angelina Jolie's most recent action films—*Mr. and Mrs. Smith* (2005), *Wanted* (2008), and *Salt* (2010)—she appears even thinner than she was in the *Tomb Raider* films (2001, 2003). Likewise, other actresses routinely featured in tough-women roles—like Milla Jovovich from the *Resident Evil* series (2002, 2004, 2007, 2010, 2012), Kate Beckinsale from the *Underworld* series (2003, 2006, 2009, 2012), Zoe Saldana from *The Losers* (2010) and *Columbiana* (2011), and Olga Kurylenko from *Quantum of Solace* (2008), *The Assassin Next Door* (2009), and *Centurion* (2010)—are incredibly petite. The preteen and teen action heroine carries this cultural preference for women who are strong but still look tiny and traditionally feminine to an even further extreme. Our rigid expectations of what women should look like in the media, even women who kick ass, reveals a clear preference for tiny over big. While eleven-year-old heroines like Hit-Girl can become phenomenal successes, the few recent attempts to launch action heroine franchises featuring physically strong actresses have failed miserably. Academy Award-winning director Steven Soderbergh tried to turn real-life mixed martial arts champion Gina Carano into a believable action heroine in the star-studded film *Haywire* (2011) without much success. Despite Carano's beauty and her proven ability as an exceptional fighter, audiences appeared to be uninterested in a woman with visible muscularity who actually looks like she could, and in fact can, beat up men. Likewise, lower-budget attempts to turn WWE wrestling superstar Trish Stratus into a voluptuous but muscular action heroine in *Bounty Hunters* (2011) flopped. That petite adult heroines and pint-sized young heroines are more popular at the box office than credibly tough and muscular women only confirms age-old gender norms. Visibly muscular women are still considered "unfeminine" even if, like Carano and Stratus, they are otherwise conventionally beautiful. Muscular bodies are assumed to be indicative of masculinity and the antithesis of femininity. "Muscles have chiefly symbolized and continue to symbolize masculine power as physical strength," writes Bordo, "frequently operating as a means of coding the "naturalness" of sexual difference" (1993, 193). And, as Laurie Schulze (1990) argued about female bodybuilders, muscular women are perceived in general as disturbing because they confound deep-seated beliefs about nature and sexual difference, and because they resist easy categorizations. Petite action heroines are easier to categorize as ideally feminine in order to temper the threat their ass-kicking may represent.

The petite figure of the young action heroine signifies her conformity to traditional physical gender norms, but it also specifically symbolizes her youthful innocence as an integral component of that feminine ideal. While young action heroines are extremely knowledgeable about weapons and martial arts, they are almost uniformly naïve about everything else, especially sex. Women have long been faced with the conundrum of being valued for their sexual desirability while simultaneously expected to be virtuous. Men are presumed to have carnal knowledge and appetites; women are supposed to be naïve and virginal. In Hollywood, the virginal and/or chaste female character has always been the Holy Grail of ideal femininity. Young female characters typically represent the innocence of childhood and a feminine ignorance or indifference to sexuality. The importance of feminine naiveté is so idealized that it is routinely incorporated into some of our culture's most recognizable sex symbols. In the case of adult actresses, the stereotypical dumb blonde character—that favorite of popular-culture clichés—is used to maintain a pretense of innocence within a clearly sexualized figure. Moreover, the naïve stupidity of the blonde caricature infantilizes actresses, regardless of how mature and well developed her body is. Actresses like Judy Holliday, Jayne Mansfield, Goldie Hawn, Suzanne Somers, Pamela Anderson, Jessica Simpson, and Ana Farris have all crafted successful careers by embodying a combination of childlike innocence and adult sexual appearance. For example, as Richard Dyer (1979) argued, even Marilyn Monroe, the most preeminent sexual icon in Western culture, is appealing in large part because of her perceived innocence: "She is certainly aware of her sexuality, but she is guiltless about it and it is presented moreover primarily in terms of narcissism . . . her motivations were taken to be 'spiritual,' either in the magic, 'little-girl' aspirations to be a movie star or in the 'pretentious' interests in Acting and Art" (130). Monroe's hypersexual appearance was only enhanced in desirability by her many roles (and stories about her real-life persona) that presented her as wide-eyed, vapid, and innocent. The infantilized image of the dumb blonde is indicative of a misogynistic cultural fetishization for youth and innocence. Naïve and innocent women are vulnerable, unsullied, unchallenging—ripe for male domination. While the young action heroine's lethal skills may represent a potential threat to masculinity, her youthfulness implies an alluring innocence.

In her fascinating historical analysis of teenage girls in American popular culture, Ilana Nash (2006) argues that these young females can be both appealing and problematic for patriarchy. "The liminality of the adolescent girl makes her simultaneously disturbing and attractive to patriarchy," observes Nash. "Poised between innocence and experience, her combination of a womanly body and a childlike mind offers male authorities the best of both worlds: a female both pure and ripe, young enough to leave unchallenged the dominance of mature men, but old enough to be 'hot'" (23). It is in this context that the innocence of the young action heroine is an important factor, whether they are explicitly "hot" like the women of *Sucker Punch*, a prepubescent looking teenager like Hanna, or clearly a childlike Hit-Girl. The narratives emphasize their innocence (or their innocence-in-danger-of-being-lost, as is the case of the aptly named Babydoll), and the heroines' slow exposure to the world of sexuality. For example, Hanna's secluded upbringing left her ignorant of the world beyond her snow-swept cabin, especially in regards to interpersonal relationships. When Hanna tags along with a British family of tourists and strikes up a close friendship with their teenage daughter, Sophie, she is baffled by almost everything they do and say. Hanna seems particularly clueless about the superficial elements of girlhood that Sophie gleefully introduces her to. Makeup, fashion magazines, celebrity gossip, and boys are a complete mystery to the innocent Hanna. When Sophie exposes Hanna to the world of boys and romance during an impromptu double date, Hanna's lethal background and ignorance of courtship collide to humorous effect. When the boy leans in to kiss Hanna, she reflexively punches him in the throat, hurls him to the ground, and puts him in a chokehold. Confused by romance and desires, Hanna also experiments with kissing Sophie later in the tent they share, not so much as a demonstration of same-sex desires as a need for human connection. Similarly, Hit-Girl's unfamiliarity with sexual longings is twice played for comedic purposes in *Kick-Ass 2*. When Mindy attends a sleepover with some of the popular girls from her high school in an attempt to fit in, they show her a music video of a generic boy band to teach her about "those" feelings that girls get. Mindy is visibly stirred and her body involuntarily convulses for a moment. The usually composed Mindy is left gasping: "What the fuck was that?" And later in the film, when she is training Dave Lizewski (aka Kick-Ass), she notices his muscular body doing chin-ups and becomes flush with excitement and is clearly embarrassed by her own arousal. In instances such as these, viewers bare witness to the young heroine's innocence and her halting progress towards sexual maturity.

Nash describes this common type of scene in narratives about adolescents as a "chrysalis moment." As Nash argues, this chrysalis moment is a central part of the voyeuristic appeal of female adolescence, a "carefully manipulated scenario in which an adolescent female is shown crossing a threshold to sexual maturity, like a caterpillar's transition to butterfly" (23). But this ritualized transition to sexual awareness is indicative of more than just voyeuristic pleasures. This emerging female sexuality can be as threatening as Hanna's archery or Hit-Girl's swords. As Nash explains: "chrysalis moments bespeak not merely men's desire, but also their anxiety; one might see in these carefully orchestrated scenarios an effort to control and contain teen-girl sexuality by ritualizing it, subjecting it to the interpretation and narration of patriarchal ideology" (24). A female who becomes sexually aware wields a type of potentially disruptive power. How will she use her body? Who can she control with it? Who will she reject? Her precarious innocence might be lost forever. Sexual maturity, and an awareness of the power that comes with it, can result in full-blown subjectivity. While the young action heroine's façade of innocence is, ironically, part of her lethal persona and a source of her power, she is always on the verge of losing her innocence and embracing a type of power that men really fear: female sexual agency. "What might the *girl* do with it, once she learns how to wield the power it grants her?" observes Nash. "A girl who consciously deploys her sexuality can create chaos that threatens her own father as well as her societal Father" (24). In her discussion of teen-girl films from the mid-twentieth century, Nash argues that the potential threat suggested by the girl's blossoming sexuality is countered by worried fathers, and father figures, who help guide the teenager into a proper maturation. The overall message is that adolescent female sexuality is not really threatening because it is still subject to patriarchal authority and control.

While worried fathers and father figures in classic female coming-of-age films like *Junior Miss* (1945), *The Bachelor and the Bobbysoxer* (1947), *Tammy and the Bachelor* (1957), and *Gidget* (1959) may ultimately exercise patriarchal authority over the girls' behavior, characters like Hit-Girl, Babydoll, and Hanna have a very different relationship with fathers. Rather than trying to protect the girls from suitors, Big Daddy, Wise Man, and Erik Heller train and assist the girls to be super fighters, to protect them from violence by becoming masters of it. In a sense, patriarchal authority is not so much exerted over Hit-Girl, Hanna, and Babydoll as it is bequeathed to them. The girls are indoctrinated into a world of weapons and fighting skills—of phallic authority—that more than prepares them to take care of themselves. Among these three young heroines, the only character who ultimately fails to protect herself from villains and lecherous men is Babydoll. Not coincidentally, Babydoll is also the heroine with the weakest link to a father figure since the Wise Man, who guides her on the fantastical missions, is really just a figment of her imagination; she is also the most overtly eroticized character, even lusted after by her despicable stepfather. Hit-Girl and Hanna, on the other hand, are trained from birth to become perfect little killers by their fathers. In essence, Hit-Girl and Hanna become phallic extensions of their fathers, a next generation of warriors who are prepared to carry on the good fight. As coming-of-age stories, the young girl action heroine is also a version of the Pygmalion myth, but instead of learning traditionally feminine skills she learns masculine traits (for a detailed discussion of Pygmalion traditions among action heroines, see Brown 2011). Hit-Girl and Hanna also finally replace and avenge their fathers who both die at the hands of the films' villains. They internalize and assume patriarchal authority in the realm of action, if not in the realm of sexuality. The added lethal component of the young girl action heroine presents her burgeoning sexuality as all the more potentially destructive to individual men, and to patriarchal standards as a whole, within the narrative. Hit-Girl, Babydoll, and Hanna may not yet be the sexually threatening femme fatale-inspired figure that fully mature and eroticized heroines like Lara Croft, Catwoman, and Nikita are, but they are on the cusp of that power.

The threat of the young action heroines' gender-transgressive violence may not be countered by patriarchal authority figures, but it is offset through the containment strategy that presents these characters as safely fictional. The threat of female strength, particularly adolescent female strength is demarcated in these films as the stuff of pure fantasy. It is a fun, and perhaps even inspiring fantasy, but the message of the film seems to be that "it could never happen in the real world." *Kick-Ass* is ultimately a costumed superhero movie, and a parody of the genre at that, despite all of the promotional claims, presents what superheroes would be like in the real world. Hit-Girl's incredibly choreographed fight scenes have as much to do with reality as Iron Man's flying armor or Thor's magic hammer. The stylized, anime- and video game-inspired, CGI world of *Sucker Punch* never lets viewers forget that the story is just a fevered dream. Likewise, the narrative of *Hanna* stresses the fairy tale aspects of the story. The exotic locales of *Hanna* may be real places, and the violence may be more realistic than in *Kick-Ass* and *Sucker Punch*, but the constant references to fairy tales make it clear that Hanna's adventure is an imaginative fiction along the lines of Snow White, Alice in Wonderland, Hansel and Gretel, and Little Red Riding Hood (all of which have also been turned into young action heroine films in recent years). The young action heroine is systemically presented as unthreatening to cultural standards because she is so thoroughly contained as mere fantasy.

"I'D TELL YOU I LOVE YOU, BUT THEN I'D HAVE TO KILL YOU."—SPY GIRLS

One area that has often been overlooked in considerations of action heroines is the genre of young adult literature. Book series marketed to teens, especially teen girls, have undergone a significant growth in the publishing industry in recent years. Many of these books explore stories about young girls coming of age in fantasy settings ranging from the milieu of the super rich to average high schools populated by cliques of vampires, witches, and zombies. Less fantastical in tone are the numerous young adult book series about seemingly normal girls who lead double lives as super-spies. The preteen and teen girl characters featured in these spy series are clearly indebted to the surge of action heroines in other mediums, as well as to the older (and usually more serious) literary female detectives found in novels by Janet Evanovich, Sue

Grafton, and Patricia Cornwell, and the larger male-dominated spy genre. But these literary spy girls manage to transcend the limitations of their influences, and are indicative of new fantasies of empowerment embraced by young female readers because they are heroic stories with a postfeminist sensibility that allow girls to envision their own agency without sacrificing or demeaning their capitulation to heteronormative feminine ideals. The spy girl books meld sexual curiosity and physical development with a belief that, underneath it all, even relatively average girls can save the world. While many of these books are clearly rooted in fantasy settings, the heroic actions of the female characters seem more realistic than those of Hit-Girl, Babydoll, Hanna, and their cinematic sisters because they are not visually represented as fetishized physical ideals or superpowered, gravity-defying, fighters.

J. K. Rowling's enormously popular *Harry Potter* books (about a downtrodden boy who discovers he is actually a legendary wizard progeny and goes off for a more exciting life of battling evil at Hogwarts magical school) have become a literary phenomenon. Likewise, Stephenie Meyer's *Twilight* series (about the romantic entanglements of the average teen heroine Bella Swan who gets swept up in a world of vampires and werewolves) has achieved an unprecedented level of popularity in the realm of young adult fiction—as has Suzanne Collins's *Hunger Games* series (discussed in the previous chapter). But packed tightly beside the *Harry Potter*, *Twilight*, and *Hunger Games* titles on most bookstore shelves are dozens of series that offer action-driven adolescent fantasies tailor-made for young girls. No doubt inspired by the *Harry Potter*, *Twilight*, and *Hunger Games* book-to-film phenomena, and hoping to repeat them, numerous series about normal young girls whisked into an intriguing and action-packed world of international espionage have emerged. Some of these books are meant for very young readers and feature heroines of grade-school age, such as Jill Marshall's *Jane Blonde: Sensational Spylet* series (seven books from 2008 to 2011) and Christine Harris's *Undercover Girl* series (five books from 2005 to 2008), as well as Kim Harrington's *Sleuth or Dare* series (four books from 2012 to 2014). Other characters have had an extreme longevity, such as those in Francine Pascal's popular series of *Fearless* books, which followed the heroine Gaia from high school through college and into her early years as an FBI recruit (forty books from 1999 to 2012). But the bulk of the books feature high-school girls who become super-spies, including Elizabeth Cage's *Spy Girls* series (six books from 1998 to 2014), Shannon Greenland's *The Specialists* series (five books from 2005 to 2012), Jennifer Lyn Barnes's *The Squad* series (2008 and 2009), Michael P. Spradlin's *Spy Goddess* series (2006, 2009, 2013), Carol Hedges's *Spy Girl* series (four books from 2005 to 2008), and Ally Carter's *Gallagher Girl* series (seven books between 2006 and 2013).

All of these book series about teen spies feature intelligent, beautiful, and innocent heroines who find themselves recruited into an exciting and glamorous world of espionage. They are the younger, more tween-audience-friendly versions of adult characters like Sydney Bristow (Jennifer Garner) of *Alias* (2001–2006), Nikita (Anne Parillaud, Bridget Fonda, Peeta Wilson, Maggie Q) from the various versions of *La Femme Nikita* (1990), Evelyn Salt (Angelina Jolie) of *Salt* (2010), and Annie Walker (Piper Perabo) of *Covert Affairs* (2010–current).

While the narrative emphasis in young action heroine films is on the spectacular stunts, special effects, and fighting sequences, in the spy girl books there is more attention devoted to the central character's emotional development as she transitions from ordinary girl to teen super-spy. In *The Squad: Perfect Cover* (2008), Tobey Klein is a high school sophomore with a nonconformist attitude, a black belt in karate and formidable computer-hacking skills. Tobey is shocked when she receives an invitation to join the elite cheerleading squad consisting of all the most popular and beautiful girls in the school. These are just the kind of vapid bimbos that Tobey despises, but she soon learns that these cheerleaders are really secret government agents who undertake harrowing missions of national importance in between cheerleading competitions. Tobey joins up with, and is made over into, one of the popular girls, fights terrorists, bonds with her teammates, meets a cute boy who may or may not be a villain, and ultimately helps save America. Similarly, in the first book of *The Specialists* series, *Model Spy* (2007), readers are introduced to sixteen-year-old Kelly James, an incredibly intelligent but socially awkward computer expert who is already flying through college. Kelly is invited to join a top-secret government spy agency that uses a team of teenage experts to carry out important undercover operations. Kelly is trained in weapons and hand-to-hand combat before being assigned her first mission: posing as a supermodel in order to infiltrate a foreign espionage ring that uses a fashion company as cover. Along the way, Kelly makes friends with the other operatives on her team and develops a romantic connection with David, her trainer and field partner. One of the best-selling spy girl series is Ally Carter's *Gallagher Girl* books, which follow the exploits of Cammie Morgan and her friends at the Gallagher Academy for Exceptional Young Women, a secretive all-girls private school tasked with producing the nation's next generation of female super-spies (think Hogwarts for spy girls). In the first book, *I'd Tell You I Love You, But Then I'd Have to Kill You* (2006), Cammie and her friends attend classes about code-breaking, martial arts, and covert operations. During a practice mission in the surrounding town, Cammie meets Josh, a handsome and sweet local boy. Cammie starts dating Josh even though it is forbidden and she has to lie about what really goes on at the Gallagher Academy. Unfamiliar with boys and romance, Cammie and her friends treat Josh as a mission: going through his garbage for clues to his activities, discretely following him when he is with his friends, and questioning his family. In the end, the girls have to save Josh when he is swept up in a (fake) kidnapping, and Cammie has to reveal that she is actually a spy in training.

These popular young adult book series blend together James Bond- or *Mission: Impossible*-style adventures with the contemporary genre of "Chick Lit." Seminal Chick Lit targeted to women, like Helen Fielding's *Bridget Jones Diary* series and Candace Bushnell's *Sex and the City* series, typifies the genre's focus on women navigating their way in the modern world of romance and friendships, with a great deal of attention given to the pleasures of shopping and beauty regimens. Cecilia Konchar Farr (2009) describes this relatively recent genre as "rooted in consumerism and nurtured by a certain neofeminist consciousness" (201). Even more specifically, the spy girl books fall under the umbrella young adult category of what Joanna Webb Johnson (2006) describes as "Chick Lit Jr.," which stresses issues like "coming of age, identity, sexuality, and material culture" (141), from a teenager's perspective. "The girl characters are typically in a borderland between childhood and adulthood," argues Johnson, "and the novels show how to move through this difficult transition. At the very least, they use humor to realistically portray emotionally difficult adolescent and preadolescent development and maturation, usually featuring a character whose search for identity is less than graceful, and thus, easily identifiable to the young reader . . . the genre usually features stages of emotional and sexual maturity for their protagonists or, at their best, a grand moment of self-realization" (2006, 142). In the case of spy girl books, casting the young heroines as secret agents trying to solve a mystery and/or complete a perilous mission, allows for an exciting and well-disguised metaphor about girls coming of age. The heroine's search for her own identity, and the discovery of truths about herself, is blended with her mission to discover the identity of a villain and the truth of the villain's nefarious plot. Like most literature marketed to young readers, the spy girl books are relatively conservative parables about growing up. Amid token clichés about being true to oneself and valuing friends, the stories also profess the virtues of being good girls, being interested in safe, heterosexual crushes, working hard in school, and the advantages of being attractive and girly.

In all of these spy girl books, the heroine's mission comes second to the real story of finding out who she really is as a person. Tobey, Kelly, and Cammie each develop close friendships with other girls, and learn to value people who they may have initially thought they had nothing in common with. They learn how to fit in with their friends without losing their individual personalities. Most importantly in the stories, all three of the young spy heroines learn to navigate their social world and to deal with being attractive to boys, and being attracted to them. For example, after Tobey is made over into a glamorous cheerleader in *Perfect Cover*, she reluctantly attends parties and trips to the mall and is forced to figure out how to rebuff unwanted attention, as well as how to approach and understand the boy she is attracted to. Likewise, in *Model Spy* Kelly struggles to understand her flustered behavior around David and is surprised at the power her appearance gives her when she goes undercover as a model. Kelly eventually grasps that what she feels for David is mutual and that he has not been giving her attention because she is incompetent but because he likes her. The real mystery to be solved in these spy stories is not where the microchip is hidden or what the code is to defuse the bomb, the real mystery to be figured out is romance. The analogy of spying as akin to finding out about boys is made most explicit in the *Gallagher Girl* books. In *I'd Tell You I Love You But*, Cammie is completely ignorant about romance and turns to her newest roommate, Macey McHenry, a recent transfer from a real school who has valuable experience with boys. Cammie says she is confused and asks Macey for her opinion: "'Now you can't stop thinking about him. . . . You always want to know what he's doing. . . . You'd kill to know if he is thinking about you . . .' Macey said, like a doctor reeling off symptoms. 'Yes!' I cried. 'That's soooo it!'" (132). Cammie concludes: "I wasn't exactly sure what was happening, but one thing was becoming obvious: Macey McHenry had intel I desperately needed" (133). And later, as Cammie prepares to go on a date with Josh, with the help of her friends and her newly discovered intel, she reflects: "I looked at everything I was supposed to carry and thought about all the things I was supposed to know, I had to wonder: Do all girls go through this? Is every girl on a date really in deep cover?" (143). Knowledge about boys and romance is recast as "intel," and the performance of courtship rituals, like a simple pizza-and-movie date, is framed as going "undercover"—appropriate and useful analogies for young readers who may also be struggling to understand the world of adolescence, and looking for their own clues about romance.

Since the playful spy fantasies presented in these various book series combine action and mystery, the young spy heroine is clearly indebted to the larger tradition of literary girl detectives (see Cornelius and Gregg 2008). The most obvious archetype is Nancy Drew, the iconic girl sleuth first made famous in the 1930s in the book series written by various women under the pseudonym of Carolyn Keene. Nancy Drew has appeared in countless radio, film, and television reincarnations over the years, most recently revamped in the feature film *Nancy Drew* (2007). In many ways, the young heroines featured in these spy girl books are as much Nancy Drew as they are James Bond. Characters like Tobey, Kelly, and Cammie are smart and adventurous Nancy Drews for the twenty-first century, armed with spy gadgets, martial arts skills, and incredible computer abilities. The element of mystery at the core of the spy girl literature encourages exploration and discovery far more than the kinetic physical events focused on with young heroines in action film. The adventures of these modern spy girls are more explicitly concerned with heterosexual romance than the thoroughly chaste Nancy Drew ever was, but even the earliest Nancy Drew stories subtly associated mystery with sexual knowledge. As Bobbie Ann Mason (1975) first pointed out in her historical analysis of Nancy Drew: "But as it is in anything that interests adolescents, sex is subtly present. Mysteries are a substitute for sex, since sex is the greatest mystery of all for adolescents" (63). Like Nancy Drew, Tobey, Kelly, and Cammie explore the mysteries of sex under the relatively safe camouflage of a spy adventure. Even if it is not technically "carnal knowledge" that the heroines seek, it is their pursuit of romantic knowledge that marks their coming of age more clearly than their adventures in espionage. For young readers, these books explore romance, sexual insecurities, and a sense of identity as things to be negotiated and grappled with. As Johnson argues, Chick Lit Jr. can function as "an engaging guide book" for girls, one that presents "a world that cannot be *controlled* but can be *negotiated*" (2006, 148, 149).

In addition to more fully exploring the young spy heroines' emotional coming of age through learning about romance, and learning about themselves, the literary heroines are also not subjected to eroticization in the same way their filmic counterparts often are. As book characters, Tobey, Kelly, and Cammie are presented very differently than Hit-Girl, Babydoll, and Hanna. Where young heroines in film need to be attractive and risk being objectified by the camera, literary characters are, by their very nature, not visually defined. Though Tobey, Kelly, and Cammie are described as pretty and conform to specific cultural fetishes as cover identities (cheerleader, model, private-school girl), their appearances are left up to the imagination of the reader, and the first-person narration reveals their disinterest in traditional expectations of beauty. The characters navigate and respond to being perceived as beautiful, they use it as a way to distract boys when needed, but they are not objectified by a male gaze or by a male assumption of control. Even the book covers obfuscate objectification by picturing generically attractive teens relatively devoid of any possible sexual overtones. The spy girl covers tend to employ the same, or similar, visual strategy of many Chick Lit Jr. books. As Johnson describes it: "Cover art often offers real life photos of teens without revealing the person. The photo always chops off below the eyes and sometimes only features a body from the neck down. This method . . . allows the reader to impose herself into the story. She could, with a small stretch of the imagination, be that girl on the cover and in the story" (2006, 153). Young female readers can identify with these heroines, and perhaps imagine themselves as these heroines, without the distance or comparisons created by visual representations. Moreover, where the films emphasize spectacular action, whether it is Hit-Girl laying waste to dozens of bad guys or Babydoll toppling giant stone monsters with her sword, as a necessary part of their box-office draw, the books may describe moments of intense action but their emphasis is on the heroines' personal interactions and internal emotional development.

Admittedly, comparing spy girl heroines from young adult literature to young action heroines in feature films is unfair. The literary heroines are written for, and promoted to, a niche market of young female readers, whereas Hollywood films need to appeal to as wide an audience as possible in order to generate a profit. Moreover, the difference between fictional characters who exist only through printed words and in the minds of the readers, and celluloid heroines who are embodied by flesh and blood actresses, creates a marked contrast in how we envision characters physically according to our own beliefs or mass media standards. Of course, literary heroines are more pliable for readers' imaginations, and cinematic action heroines conform to genre and cultural expectations. But the comparison is not exactly "apples and oranges" either. Fictional young heroines like Hit-Girl, Babydoll, Hanna, Tobey, Kelly, and Cammie share a lot of common traits. They are all extremely smart, resourceful, violent, tenacious, and noble. They are also adolescent, socially awkward with other girls, romantically confused with boys, and transitioning from daughters to their own person. And—not coincidentally, given how the media represents girlhood rather monolithically—they are all white, economically middle-class or higher, thin, heterosexual, and conventionally pretty. By juxtaposing the spy girls alongside cinematic young action heroines, I do not want to suggest that the literary characters are better. But the young adult spy girls do indicate a clear function that action heroines can fulfill as cyphers for dealing with particular adolescent concerns. The unconventional image of girlhood that is presented with young action heroines, whether on screen or in novels, suggests a range of new possibilities for female characters, and perhaps for real girls as well. These figures raise the possibility that young women can kick ass, can solve mysteries, can have exciting lives, can make their own choices, and can save themselves and others . . . even males. But the increasing use of young action heroines also raises some longstanding practices such as the overt fetishization of young females, assumptions about childhood innocence, tropes of violence and vulgarity, and access to knowledge, especially that of a sexual nature. The value of the young action heroine, in whatever form she is presented, is easily contestable; it really is in the eyes of the beholder or in how she is interpreted, depending on which part of the narrative audiences focus on.

CONCLUSION

STILL WONDERING ABOUT WONDER WOMAN

AT THE CONCLUSION TO *DANGEROUS CURVES,* I DISCUSSED THE FAILURE OF Joss Whedon's 2006 script about Wonder Woman to be turned into a feature film. Unfortunately, despite the general increase in the number and profitability of action heroine-led films, we are still left to wonder about a Wonder Woman movie. As an iconic character in popular culture, recognizable well beyond the confines of the comic book page or the campy 1970s television series, Wonder Woman represents an archetype of female strength but she is also burdened with an image as a sexualized male fantasy. Finding the balance between strength and eroticism is a difficult task for a live-action version of Wonder Woman or any other superheroine. Over fifty superhero movies have been released in the last decade and only three of them have focused on superpowered women. Of these three films, *Catwoman* (2004) and *Elektra* (2005) were critical and financial flops, and *My Super Ex-Girlfriend* (2006) was a lighthearted comedy that went pretty much unnoticed. The failure of these three films to recoup their expenses has made studio executives wary of bankrolling the extravagant budget of a superhero movie featuring another woman in the title role. Still, superhero films have become the most reliable of blockbusters, and Hollywood has rushed dozens of costumed characters into production to cash in on the craze. At least a dozen *male* characters are being rushed into action. In addition to superhero heavyweights like Batman, Superman, Iron-Man, and Captain America, other more obscure characters such as Ant-Man, Deadpool, and Dr. Strange are in feature film production or development. Likewise, on television, Green Arrow and the Flash have recently been turned into live-action series. The occasional box-office disappointment of male superhero films—such as *Daredevil* (2003), *Hulk* (2003), *Ghostrider* (2007), and *Green Lantern* (2011)—have not scared Hollywood away from costumed men. In fact, the Hulk was quickly and successfully revisioned in *The Incredible Hulk* (2008), Ghostrider was granted a sequel in 2011, and reboots are planned for both Daredevil and Green Lantern.

Of course, a select few superheroines have appeared in recent movies, but primarily as minor characters next to the male lead or as part of male-dominated super-teams. Rogue, Storm, and Jean Grey appeared in *The X-Men* films (2000, 2003, 2006), and will be involved in their reimagining through the *X-Men: First Class* series (2011, 2014); the Invisible Woman was part of the mildly successful *Fantastic Four* films (2005, 2007), and will appear again in their 2015 rebooted version; the Black Widow fought alongside the male leads in *Iron-Man 2* (2010) and *Captain America: The Winter Soldier* (2014), and as part of the otherwise all-male group in *The Avengers* (2012); Catwoman played as Batman's sexy adversary/helper/love interest in *The Dark Knight Rises* (2012); and the alien warrior Gamora gets to kick a lot of ass alongside her male teammates in *Guardians of the Galaxy* (2014). Yet, as of this writing, there is still no Wonder Woman movie. In fact, in the few years since Whedon's version of the character failed to entice the studio executives at Warner Bros., Wonder Woman has suffered two other live-action failures. Famed television creator David E. Kelly (*Ally McBeal, The Practice, Boston Legal, Chicago Hope*, etc.) wrote and produced a Wonder Woman pilot in 2011 amid a flood of publicity, but the series was ultimately turned down by the networks and never aired. Similarly, the CW network commissioned a Wonder Woman series entitled *Amazons* in 2013 but has put the project on indefinite hold. Bringing Wonder Woman to life again, on the big or small screen, has proven remarkably difficult for Hollywood despite the possibility of huge financial returns.

In the meantime, the general public and media critics alike have become impatient with the apparent sexism behind decisions about which superhero projects get approved and which do not. The November 26, 2010, issue of *Entertainment Weekly* ran a feature article entitled "What About Wonder Woman?" (Svetkey), detailing frustrations with attempts to bring the Amazon princess to life again. The headline of a *Time* article asked: "Why *Don't* We Have a Wonder Woman Movie?" (McMillan, August 30, 2013). And the popular science fiction magazine *SciFiNow* (March 2014) ran the article "Where on Earth 1 is the Wonder Woman Movie?" (Ward), detailing the film industry's dismissal of the character and the frustration of fans. Other reports wondered about the dearth of feature film superheroines in general. Headlines in major media outlets repeatedly ask: "Where are all the movies starring female superheroes?" (*New York Post*—Tucker 2014), "Why won't cinema embrace female superheroes?" (*BBC News*—Moloney 2013), and "Why are there no female superhero blockbusters?" (*Daily News*—Sacks, 2013). In the *American Prospect* (August 15, 2008), Alyssa Rosenberg wondered: "Why is it that a film industry will cast lovably schlubby Seth Rogen as The Green Hornet and will take a serious chance on an Ant-Man movie but can't get it together to make a Wonder Woman flick? Or any true superheroine movie at all?" (39–40). An article in *USA Today*, "In Superhero Genre, Movie Girl Power is in Short Supply" (Truitt, August 26, 2013), complained: "While dudes headline big-budget films, the likes of Wonder Woman and Black Widow bide their time" (para. 1). And an article in the *Atlantic*, entitled "Earth to Hollywood: People Will Pay to See a Female Superhero Film" (Funkhouser, December 6, 2013), argued: "Wonder Woman was originally meant to replace Superman, not back him up. Why not give her, or any female superhero for that matter, her own film?" (para. 2).

Even Hollywood heavyweights have started to express their concerns over the testosterone bias in superhero movies. For example, after Whedon directed *The Avengers*, which became second highest-grossing film of all-time, he publicly complained about the difficulties of convincing studios that audiences can accept superheroines if they are done right. Whedon acknowledged the lack of superheroines and vowed to introduce more female characters in *Avengers* sequels. Whedon agrees that superheroines are needed and that their visibility should not be dependent on their sexuality. He explained his frustrations with Hollywood's lack of superheroines in an interview with the *Daily Beast*: "Toymakers will tell you they won't sell enough, and movie people will point to the two terrible superheroine movies that were made and say, 'You see? It can't be done.' It's stupid, and I'm hoping *The Hunger Games* will lead to a paradigm shift. It's frustrating to me that I don't see anybody developing one of these movies. It actually pisses me off. My daughter watched *The Avengers* and was like, 'My favorite characters were the Black Widow and Maria Hill,' and I thought, 'Yeah, of course they were'" (Stern, June 5, 2013, para. 9). Whedon is a Hollywood power player, creator of *Buffy the Vampire Slayer*, among other popular television programs, and a director of blockbuster movies, yet even he finds it difficult to convince studios of the potential value of superheroines. That Whedon is willing to publicly comment about the absurdly sexist nature of excluding superheroines from equal representation in films may help pressure Hollywood into developing female properties like Wonder Woman.

While the press repeatedly wonders why female superheroes are so absent from the current wave of big-budget films, fans have taken to the Internet to express their desire for a female-driven super movie. As the archetype of all superheroines, Wonder Woman has been the main subject of online petitions and blog posts desperately encouraging Warner Bros. to develop a feature film about the Amazon. Fans have created hundreds of lists about which actresses could best embody Wonder Woman, and they have produced thousands of images of actresses, models, and ordinary people in Wonder Woman costumes in an attempt to envision a modern real-life version of the character. Most notably, in the fall of 2013 Rainfall Films, a small production company, released a stunning three-minute video on the Internet that featured a realistic battle between Wonder Woman and numerous armed mercenaries, all interwoven with a flashback of Wonder Woman slaying a gargantuan mythological monster alongside her Amazon sisters. Directed by Sam Balcomb and starring Rileah Vanderbilt, this Wonder Woman short film became a media sensation, and was reviewed and shown on numerous network newscasts. The film depicts Wonder Woman as strong, confident, and beautiful but not eroticized. Fans and critics wondered loudly and widely: "If a small video company can do this, why can't Hollywood make a feature film?"

But, thanks to public demand and the proven success of action heroine franchises like *The Hunger Games* and *Divergent*, things may finally be looking up for big-screen superheroines. Marvel films has announced they will be making a stand-alone Black Widow film after a great deal of pressure from the media, fans, and the actress herself, Scarlett Johansson. Part of the pressure on Marvel Films reportedly came from Johansson's frustrations with waiting for a Black Widow film of her own, which resulted in Johansson taking on the lead in Luc Beeson's film *Lucy* (2014) as a drug courier who develops superpowers. The success of *Lucy* (grossing over $330 million worldwide) has helped to dispute any fears that female lead superhero movies are box-office poison. Rumors are also circulating that Katee Sackhoff of *Battlestar Galactica* (2004–2009) and *Longmire* (2012–current) fame has been approached to play Ms. Marvel, and that Anne Hathaway has been asked to reprise her role as Catwoman for her own film. And, perhaps most importantly, Wonder Woman herself is set to appear as part of Zack Snyder's upcoming *Man of Steel* (2013) sequel, *Batman vs. Superman: Dawn of Justice*, which is scheduled for a 2016 release. Gal Gadot, a little-known actress/model and former Miss Israel beauty queen, has been cast as the iconic Amazon. According to *Variety* (Kroll, January 23, 2014), Gadot has signed a three-picture deal to reprise the role in a team-based Justice League movie and then possibly in her own Wonder Woman feature. The announcement that Wonder Woman will appear in *Batman vs. Superman: Dawn of Justice*, and the casting of Gadot in the role, quickly resulted in a media frenzy that eclipsed even the excitement about Batman and Superman appearing in a film together. Fans are enthusiastic that Wonder Woman will finally appear on the big screen, and if all goes well, in her own movie eventually. But fans are also understandably nervous about exactly how Wonder Woman will be depicted. Will she be sexualized? (After all, Snyder also directed *Sucker Punch*, which reduced young heroines to fetishized objects.) Will she just be a love interest? Will she be reduced to a glorified sidekick? Is Gal Gadot a good enough actress to bring substance to the character? One of the main concerns is that while Gadot is undeniably beautiful, she is also extremely skinny. Fans have argued that Gadot's thinness will undercut the need for Wonder Woman to be seen as believably strong. To counter this concern, Gadot has spoken to the press about the strenuous workout routine she is undertaking in order to bulk up. Gadot has even taken to regularly tweeting pictures of herself downing protein shakes to gain weight, and flexing her developing muscles while at the gym with professional trainers. As of now, it remains to be seen if Snyder and Gadot can pull off a version of Wonder Woman that satisfies critics, fans, and studio heads enough to warrant her own film.

Unfortunately, one of the few live-action formats where superheroines have had success lately is, perhaps not surprisingly, in pornography. Video porn production companies have tapped into the current popularity of superheroes by releasing countless X-rated parodies of almost every character imaginable, including Batman, Superman, Spider-Man, Captain America, the Avengers, and the Justice League. Vivid Entertainment, the world's leading adult film company, has even created their own special imprint line, "Vivid-Superhero," dedicated to producing pornographic superhero parodies. Like high-end Tijuana Bibles or well-funded slash fiction, these porn parodies are an excuse to explore the sexual exploits of all these attractive characters running around in skintight fetish costumes. Now we can see Batman, Robin, and Catwoman having a threesome, or Spiderman getting a blowjob from Mary-Jane while he hangs upside down from his web in an alley. Focusing on the sexual fantasy rather than the heroic fantasy, superheroines seem better suited to headline porn films than mainstream summer blockbusters. There are three pornos starring Wonder Woman, as well as her appearances in the *Justice League of Pornstar Heroes* and *Superman: Man of Steel* pornos. Others, like Batgirl, Supergirl, Catwoman, She-Hulk, and the Birds of Prey, have also starred in their own XXX films. And a wide range of lesser-known superheroines have been featured in some of the super-team pornos including Spider-Woman, Ms. Marvel, Zatanna, Hawkgirl, the Black Cat, and the Scarlet Witch. These pornographic versions of superheroines are sophomoric parodies, and proof that the porn industry never misses an opportunity to cash in on a popular trend. But these pornographic spoofs also reveal just how rooted in sexual display these characters are. It is not really that big a step from the teasing displays of Anne Hathaway's Catwoman and Scarlet Johansson's Black Widow to the hardcore action of porn starlet versions like Tori Black's Catwoman and Brooklyn Lee's Black Widow. According to many fans and critics, the porn industry may even being taking superheroines more seriously than mainstream films do. When promotional images were released of adult actress Kimberly Kane dressed as Wonder Woman for yet another porn film, the Internet immediately lit up with talk about how Kane and her costume looked better than actress Adrianne Palicki did in stills for David E. Kelley's Wonder Woman television pilot.

The traditionally exaggerated physical forms, hypersexual bodies, and erotic costuming of comic book superheroines, which was discussed in Chapters Four and Five, lends itself easily to pornography. This emphasis on the sexual desirability of the heroines as a defining characteristic in the male-dominated world of comic books makes it difficult to adapt superheroines to serious feature films. In his discussion of the superheroines who have appeared on screens over the last decade, Richard J. Gray argues:

> When the superheroine is brought to film, if the creators are truly going to tap into that male sexual desire that will bring men to watch such films, she must be portrayed in a way that the male of the species (and parts of the female audience, for that matter) finds sexually appealing: lots of flesh, or in leather jumpsuits, fishnet stockings, spiked heels, etc. We must continue to point out, however, that men do not want to feel physically threatened by women, or by superheroines, for that matter. Whether attainable or not, women must remain approachable. (Gray 2011, 78)

The rudimentary logic that superheroines in film have to be "hot" in order to attract a male audience, the logic apparently subscribed to by studio executives, shifts the focus from potentially strong female characters to standard Hollywood fetish objects. It is this logic that director Joss Whedon is critical of when he points to examples like Katniss in *The Hunger Games*, who appeals to a wide audience of women and men despite not being sexualized. Just because superheroines have been unequally burdened as fantasy sexual ideals for a presumed adolescent male audience does not mean that sexuality has to be their defining characteristic. Moreover, as the male superhero films have demonstrated, sexual attractiveness can be part of a superhero character without overwhelming his power or bravery. Certainly, the Hollywood hunk status of Chris Evans as Captain America, Chris Hemsworth as Thor, and Hugh Jackman as Wolverine is part of their popularity for a large number of viewers. Their square jaws, chiseled features, and bulging muscles visually reinforce their heroic stature, but these features also make them contemporary sex symbols. The problem is that culturally we still tend to think along mutually exclusive gender lines that permit handsome men to be strong, but limits the strength of beautiful women.

To date, however, Hollywood has offered very few live-action superheroines not defined by their gender and not over-defined by their sexuality. As was discussed in Chapter Eight, Hit-Girl in the *Kick-Ass* films (2010, 2013) is one of the few heroines who is not presented for fetishistic appeal, and that is primarily due to her being only a child. The titular characters of *Elektra* and *Catwoman*—as well as earlier comics-to-screen heroines like those in *Barbarella* (1968) and *Barb Wire* (1996)—were promoted and filmed as erotic spectacles that just also happened to be heroic. In the case of *Catwoman*, as many critics pointed out, the sole purpose of the film seemed to be to put reigning sex symbol Halle Berry in a costume that amounted to essentially a leather bikini and chaps while she slinks around the city brandishing a whip. Yet even the presence of Berry's celebrated sex appeal and ideal body was not enough to make the film a success. Nor was Berry's physical beauty enough on its own to embody the eroticized figure of a comic book superheroine. Throughout much of the film, when Catwoman appears in her costume, Berry's body is digitally enhanced to a level of unattainable perfection. At times, the flesh-and-blood actress is actually absent from the screen, replaced by an entirely computer-generated likeness that leaps, catlike, from building to building and struts along narrow rooftops. The use of CGI technology in contemporary superhero films is a common way to visually represent the comic book-inspired body doing things that would be impossible in real life, like flying, turning to fire, or shooting lasers out of your eyes. Likewise, male superheroes are often completely digitally rendered figures when they appear on screen. When Spider-Man swings through the streets of New York, when the enormous and green-skinned Hulk hurls tanks around, or when Iron-Man flies through the air to intercept a missile, living actors in costumes are wholly replaced by computer-generated images. But where the CGI Spider-Man, Hulk, and Iron-Man are rendered as active, powerful, armored, and muscular in these moments, Catwoman is simply made curvier, prettier, and sexier.

The use of CGI in superhero movies elevates traditional cultural norms about men as strong and powerful, and women as sexy, to a ridiculous level. As Sabine Lebel (2009) observes in her discussion of special effects and superhero movies: "What become obvious in watching these films is that they are not only traditional in terms of the superhero narrative but they are positively regressive in terms of their portrayal of male and female bodies, and gender relations" (56). The gigantic muscles of the Hulk are obvious representations of hypermasculinity, but so are the stylized metallic muscles of Iron-Man's armor and Batman's Kevlar costume. Even the thin, adolescent Spider-Man is constructed as powerfully masculine through CGI technology. "There is an insistence on the traditionally masculine aspects of the Spider-Man construct's body—namely his muscles," Lebel argues, "even though Spider-Man is not necessarily coded as 'hypermasculine,' his construction as heroic figure is signified, and emphasized, through built muscles" (2009, 61). The male cinematic superhero body is powerful and resilient; it can withstand torture, incredible wounds, and remarkable physical transformations. But, as Lebel describes the contrast especially apparent in the ensemble *X-Men* films, female superhero bodies remain beautiful at all costs. "In these films," Lebel argues, "the female body consistently remains surprisingly 'intact.' Neither the mutation nor special effects work to visually disrupt, dismantle, or change the surface of the female form. The powers attributed to female superhero bodies are linked to traditional notions of female power, including manipulation, sexuality, and masquerade (rather than brute physical or muscular strength)" (2009, 65). And while the "mutation and special effects" do not disrupt the female form, they do enhance it in purely sexual terms as in the case of Berry's CGI Catwoman or the blue-skinned and strategically scaled nude bodies of Mystique, played by the already-celebrated bodies of Rebecca Romijn in the original *X-Men* films and by Jennifer Lawrence in the *X-Men: First Class* series.

Male superheroes receive digital enhancements to make them appear more masculine and thus heroic. Female superheroes similarly receive digital enhancements, too, but for the purposes of appearing more feminine, which is equated with being sexualized. Nor does the situation seem to have improved dramatically since the heavily eroticized heroines of *Catwoman* and *Elektra* failed to attract audiences or impress critics in 2004 and 2005. The marketing of Scarlett Johansson's Black Widow, who has now appeared prominently in three different Marvel films (*Iron-Man 2*, *The Avengers*, and *Captain America: Winter Soldier*), is a clear example of what the studio thinks is the appeal of the character. Within the narrative of all three films, Black Widow is a capable super-agent; she is a master fighter, an expert marksman, and excels at extracting information from villains. Black Widow holds her own alongside the male superheroes as they battle mercenaries, Nazis, Norse gods, and invading alien warriors. The male superheroes are attracted to Black Widow, but for the most part they treat her with respect and value her as an ally. The films do, however, also establish Black Widow as a sexy femme fatale with questionable motives. In *Iron-Man 2*, Black Widow is first seen as an undercover S.H.I.E.L.D. agent posing as a personal assistant for Tony Stark (Robert Downey Jr.). She is sexy, and flirtatiously fends off Stark's standard playboy banter. Similarly, in Chapter One, I used the example of Black Widow's stylized torture scene, her first appearance in *The Avengers*, as emblematic of the cinematic eroticization of violence against women. And in Chapter Two, I mentioned Black Widow's status as the lone female team member who must fulfill the "Honeypot" role when needed. The films present her as strong and a hero in her own right, but they do not resist capitalizing on the sex symbol status of Scarlett Johansson (twice named *Esquire* magazine's "Sexiest Woman Alive") and the cliché of a sexy spy in a skintight black body suit. Regardless of all of her strengths as a live-action character, Black Widow is still burdened with sexual overrepresentation in a manner that the men are not.

Chapter Two also briefly described the condemnation the group poster for *The Avengers* received because the male heroes were all posed facing forward ready for battle, while Black Widow was posed with her butt thrust out as she looked seductively back over her shoulder. Despite criticism of the blatantly obvious way in which Black Widow was framed as a sexual object while her male teammates were depicted as heroic subjects, the Marvel films' marketing division committed a similar mistake with the character-specific posters for *Captain America: Winter Soldier*. Just prior to the film's opening in the spring of 2014, the studio released a series of individual posters featuring each of the main characters. Two of the posters were of Captain America; in the first he appears brooding and contemplative, while in the second he is springing into action. In other posters, Nic Fury (Samuel L. Jackson) is posed behind his desk glaring into the camera; Sam Wilson, aka the Falcon (Anthony Mackie), is in full battle gear ready to take flight; the central villain, Alexander Pierce (Robert Redford), is posed sternly in his office with the Washington Monument and menacing-looking S.H.I.E.L.D. hellicarriers visible through the window behind him; and the mysterious Winter Soldier (Sebastian Stan) stares angrily at the viewer while holding a massive machine gun, a ship exploding in the air behind him. The Black Widow is featured on her poster posed almost Christlike with her arms extended from her sides, a pistol in each hand, her hair blowing in the wind as fighter planes launch in the background.

This Black Widow character poster sparked a flurry of media attention—not because of her pose (which some fans applauded as looking like a descending angel of vengeance), but because of the fairly obvious photoshop alterations it had been subjected to. Many fans and critics were incensed that the image drastically narrowed her waist and exaggerated her curves. The *Daily Mail* (January 31, 2014) reported that "she's famous for her curvy and voluptuous figure. So it is understandable that fans would be surprised to see Scarlett Johansson's highly coveted body undergo what appeared to be extensive photoshopping for a new *Captain America: Winter Soldier* poster. The 29-year-old's waist looked to have been dramatically shrunk in the promo image along with her entire physique undergoing a slimming down . . . Scarlett's naturally full and well-rounded figure is clearly pulled in and slimmed down to almost make her look surgically altered." The entertainment news website The Wrap ran an article about the public's reaction to the Black Widow poster over social media and included sample Twitter comments like, "You know there is no helping the world when even Scarlett-Jo's already little waist is shopped to an impossible width;" "Seriously though. Scarlett Johansson is already curvy. There is zero need to photoshop more curves. None"; and "Shame on the people @Marvel and @Captain America that felt you had to photoshop Scarlett Johansson until she is barely recognizable." While this digital alteration of Black Widow on the poster is not as extensive as the CGI manipulation of Catwoman in the Halle Berry film, it still reveals the double standard that movie superheroines face.

If the planned stand-alone Wonder Woman and Black Widow movies do materialize, and if the filmmakers can resist gratuitously sexualizing the characters, the films will represent a huge step in the depiction of action heroines. Ticket sales have proven that audiences will pay to see heroic narratives, regardless of the main protagonists gender. Devoted fans have demonstrated that action heroines appeal to them on numerous levels and influence our understanding of acceptable gender roles and increased possibilities for female characters. Action heroines have become enormously popular in a range of contemporary media forms, from young adult literature, comic books, and video games to blockbuster film series and television programs. A female superheroine successfully headlining her own movie, however, is the holy grail of action heroines in contemporary popular culture. As action genres have developed, the genre of superheroes has become the biggest in the world. For the most part, superhero films depict icons who are unquestionably courageous, valiant, noble, and self-sacrificing. They are altruistic gods with powers and abilities far beyond us mere mortals, the stuff of fantasy and wish fulfillment come to life. Superheroes on the screen are at once nostalgic and comforting in a world rocked by terrorism and economic collapse, and hopeful about a future where anything is possible. These movie superheroes also circulate within culture, and across national boundaries, as fantasy ideals for children and adults alike. For a female character to ascend to the heights of Superman or Captain America fame would represent a genuine advancement in how we understand women in general. Despite Wonder Woman's worldwide recognition, despite her long history as an image of female strength, and despite all her fictional battles and victories, Wonder Woman still has one hurdle to overcome.

WORKS CITED

Alcoff, Linda, and Laura Gray. 1993. "Survivor Discourse: Transgression or Recuperation?" *Signs: Journal of Women in Culture and Society* 18, no. 2, 260–90.
Alter, Ethan. 2010. "Film Review: *The Loser*." *filmjournal.com*, April 22.
American Psychological Association Task Force. 2007. "Report of the APA Task Force on the Sexualization of Girls." American Psychological Association.
Anon. 2011. "Right on Q." *Time Out Hong Kong*, January 19.
Arogundade, Ben. 2002. "'I'm Black, and I Believe in the "One Drop" Theory': Halle Berry on Race, Ethnicity and her Daughter Nahla." *arogundade.com*, November 21.
Arons, Wendy. 2001. "'If Her Stunning Beauty Doesn't Bring You to Your Knees, Her Deadly Drop Kick Will': Violent Women in the Hong Kong Kung Fu Film." In *Reel Knockouts: Violent Women in the Movies*, eds. Martha McCaughey and Neal King. Austin, TX: University of Texas Press.
Arthurs, Jane. 2003. "*Sex and the City* and Consumer Culture: Remediating Postfeminist Drama." *Feminist Media Studies* 3, no. 1, 83–98.
Banet-Weiser, Sarah. 2004. "Girls Rule!: Gender, Feminism, and Nickelodeon." *Critical Studies in Media Communication* 21, no. 2 (June), 119–39.
Barrera, M. 2000. "Hottentot 2000: Jennifer Lopez and her Butt." In *Sexualities in History: A Reader*, eds. K. Phillips and B. Reay. New York: Routledge, 110–33.
Beck, Ulrich. 1992. *Risk Society: Towards a New Modernity*. Thousand Oaks, CA: Sage Publications.
Bellafante, Ginia. 2009. "Lusting After Guns, and the Affections of an Ex-Boyfriend." *New York Times*, January 30.
Beltran, Mary. 2002. "The Hollywood Latina Body as Site of Social Struggle: Media Constructions of Stardom and Jennifer Lopez's 'Cross-over Butt.'" *Quarterly Review of Film and Video*, no. 19, 71–86.
———. 2005. "The New Hollywood Racelessness: Only the Fast, Furious, (and Multiracial) Will Survive." *Cinema Journal* 44, no. 2, 50–67.
———. 2008. "Mixed Race in Latinowood: Latino Stardom and Ethnic Ambiguity in the Era of *Dark Angels*." In *Mixed Race Hollywood*, eds. Mary Beltran and Camilla Fojas. New York: New York University Press.
———. 2013. "Fast and Bilingual: *Fast & Furious* and the Latinization of Racelessness." *Cinema Journal* 53, no. 1, 75–96.

Beltran, Mary, and Camilla Fojas, eds. 2008. *Mixed Race Hollywood*. New York: New York University Press.
Bethune, Brian. 2012. "*The Hunger Games*: Your Kids are Angrier Than You Think." *macleans.ca*, April 2.
Bianco, Robert. 2010. "Maggie Q Brings Killer Looks to a Killer Role in *Nikita*." *USA Today*, September 9.
Bogle, Donald. 1973. *Toms, Coons, Mulattoes, Mammies, and Bucks: An Interpretive History of Blacks in American Films*. New York: Viking.
Boichel, Bill. 1991. "Batman: Commodity as Myth." In *The Many Lives of the Batman: Critical Approaches to a Superhero and his Media*, eds. R. E. Pearson and W. Uricchio. New York: Routledge.
Bordo, Susan. 1993. *Unbearable Weight: Feminism, Western Culture and the Body*. Los Angeles: University of California Press.
———. 2000. *The Male Body: A New Look at Men in Public and Private*. New York: Farrar, Straus and Giroux.
Bradshaw, Peter. 2011. "The Girl with the Dragon Tattoo—Review." *Guardian*, December 22.
Brady, Miranda J. 2009. "The Well-Tempered Spy: Family, Nation and the Female Secret Agent in *Alias*." In *Secret Agents: Popular Icons Beyond James Bond*, ed. Jeremy Packer. New York: Peter Lang Publishing.
Brody, Jennifer DeVere. 1999. "The Returns of Cleopatra Jones." *Signs: Journal of Women in Culture and Society* 25, no. 1, 91–121.
Brown, Jeffrey A. 2001. *Black Superheroes: Milestone Comics and Their Fans*. Jackson: University Press of Mississippi.
———. 2002. "The Tortures of Mel Gibson: Masochism and the Sexy Male Body." *Men and Masculinities* 5, no. 2, 123–43.
———. 2011. *Dangerous Curves: Action Heroines, Gender, Fetishism, and Popular Culture*. Jackson: University Press of Mississippi.
Brown, Wendy. 2005. "Neo-Liberalism and the End of Liberal Democracy." *Theory & Event* 7, no. 1, 37–59.
Brunsdon, Charlotte. 2013. "Television Crime Series, Women Police, and Fuddy-Duddy Feminism." *Feminist Media Studies* 13, no. 3, 375–94.
Bukatman, Scott. 1994. "X-Bodies (The Torment of the Mutant Superhero)." In *Uncontrollable Bodies: Testimonies of Identity and Culture*, eds. Rodney Sappington and Tyler Stallings. Seattle, WA: Bay Press, 92–129.
Butler, Jess. 2013. "For White Girls Only? Postfeminism and the Politics of Inclusion." *Feminist Formations* 25, no. 1 (Spring), 35–58.
Butler, Judith. 1990. *Gender Trouble: Feminism and the Subversion of Identity*. New York: Routledge.
Carter, Gregory T. 2008. "From Blaxploitation to Mixploitation: Male Leads and Changing Mixed Race Identities." In *Mixed Race Hollywood*, eds. Mary Beltran and Camilla Fojas. New York: New York University Press.
Caveder, Gray, and Nancy C. Jurik. 2012. *Justice Provocateur: Jane Tennison and Policing in Prime Suspect*. Urbana: University of Illinois Press.

Cepeda, Esther J. 2012. "Opinion: Stop the Sexy Latina Stereotype." *nbclatino.com*, August 8.
Chabon, Michael. 2008. "Designing Women." *Details*, March, 196–201.
Chaney, Jen. 2010. "Wait 'til They Get a Load of Hit-Girl." *Washington Post*, April 14.
Chen, Eva. 2013. "Neoliberalism and Popular Women's Culture: Rethinking Choice, Freedom and Agency." *European Journal of Cultural Studies* 16, no. 4, 440–52.
Chernin, Kim. 1981. *The Obsession: Reflections on the Tyranny of Slenderness*. New York: Harper and Row.
Clark, Noelene. 2014. "*Divergent* Shailene Woodley in Warrior Mode for Dystopian Adventure." *herocomplex.latimes.com*, March 22.
Clover, Carol. 1992. *Men, Women and Chainsaws: Gender in the Modern Horror Film*. Princeton, NJ: Princeton University Press.
Collins, Patricia Hill. 2004. *Black Sexual Politics: African Americans, Gender, and the New Racism*. New York: Routledge.
———. 2005. *Black Sexual Politics: African Americans, Gender, and the New Racism*. New York: Routledge.
Cook, Pam. 1976. "'Exploitation' Films and Feminism." *Screen* 17, no. 2, 122–27.
Corliss, Richard. 2011. "*Sucker Punch*: Don't Drink the Kool-Aid." *Time*, March 25, 34.
Cornelius, Michael G., and Melanie E. Gregg, eds. 2008. *Nancy Drew and Her Sister Sleuths*. Jefferson, NC: McFarland.
Creed, Barbara. 1986. "Horror and the Monstrous-Feminine: An Imaginary Abjection." *Screen* 27, no. 1, 44–70.
Cunnigham, Phillip Lamarr. 2010. "The Absence of Black Supervillains in Mainstream Comics." *Journal of Graphic Novels and Comics* 1, no. 1 (June), 51–62.
Dargis, Manhola. 2010. "*Kick-Ass* Review." *New York Times*, April 15.
———. 2012. "Tested by a Picturesque Dystopia." *New York Times*, March 22.
Darnton, Robert. 1984. *The Great Cat Massacre and Other Episodes in French Cultural History*. New York: Vintage Books.
Debruge, Peter. 2011. "Review: *Sucker Punch*." *variety.com*, March 24.
Deleyto, Celestino. 2003. "Between Friends: Love and Friendship in Contemporary Hollywood Romantic Comedy." *Screen* 44, no. 2 (Summer), 167–82.
Delvecchio, Marina. 2011. "Girl Power in *Sucker Punch*, *Hanna*, and *Winter's Bone*." *bitchflicks.com*, May 4.
Denby, David. 2011. "Lisbeth Salander: The Movies Have Never Had a Heroine Quite Like Her." *New Yorker*, December 27.
Doane, Mary Ann. 1991. *Femme Fatales, Film Theory, Psychoanalysis*. New York: Routledge.
———. 1999. "Technophilia: Technology, Representation, and the Feminine." In *Cybersexualities: A Reader on Feminist Theory Cyborgs and Cyberspace*, ed. Jenny Wolmark. Edinburgh: Edinburgh University Press.
Dole, Carol M. 2001. "The Gun and the Badge: Hollywood and the Female Lawman." In *Reel Knockouts: Violent Women in the Movies*, eds. Martha McCaughey and Neal King. Austin: University of Texas Press.

Douglas, Susan J. 1994. *Where the Girls Are: Growing Up Female with the Mass Media*. New York: Penguin.
Driscoll, Catherine. 2002. *Girls: Feminine Adolescence in Popular Culture and Cultural Theory*. New York: Columbia University Press.
Duggan, Lisa. 2003. *The Twilight of Equality? Neoliberalism, Cultural Politics, and the Attack on Democracy*. Boston: Beacon Press.
Dunn, Stephane. 2008. *"Bad Bitches" and Sassy Supermamas: Black Power Action Films*. Chicago: University of Illinois Press.
Durham, M. G. 2008. *The Lolita Effect: The Media Sexualization of Young Girls and What We Can Do About It*. London: Gerald Duckworth Press.
Dyer, Richard. 1986. *Heavenly Bodies: Film Stars and Society*. New York: St. Martin's Press.
Easthope, Antony. 1988. *What a Man's Gotta Do: The Masculine Myth in Popular Culture*. New York: Routledge.
Ebert, Roger. 2010. "Kick-Ass." *rogerebert.com*, April 14.
———. 2011. "The Girl with the Dragon Tattoo." *Chicago Sun-Times*, December 19.
———. 2012. "The Hunger Games." *rogerebert.com*, March 20.
Eco, Umberto. 1979. *The Role of the Reader: Explorations in the Semiotics of Texts*. Bloomington: Indiana University Press.
Edelstein, David. 2011. "The Black-Ops Fairy Tale: *Hanna* is a Very Strange Mix of Paranoia, Pyrotechnics, and Fable." *New York*, April 8.
Edwards, Tim. 2008. "Spectacular Pain: Masculinity, Masochism and Men in the Movies." In *Sex, Violence and the Body: The Erotics of Wounding*, eds. Viv Burr and Jeff Hearn. New York: Palgrave Macmillan.
Evans, Martin. 2011. "Dame Helen Mirren: I'd Love to be an Action Hero." *telegraph.co.uk*, September 23.
Faludi, Susan. 1992. *Backlash: The Undeclared War Against Women*. New York: Chatto and Windus.
Farr, Cecilia Koncha. 2009. "It Was Chick Lit All Along: The Gendering of a Genre." In *You've Come A Long Way, Baby: Women, Politics, and Popular Culture*, ed. Lilly J. Goren. Louisville: University of Kentucky Press.
Farrimond, Katherine. 2011. "Bad Girls in Crisis: The New Teenage Femme Fatale." In *Women on Screen: Feminism and Femininity in Visual Culture*, ed. Melanie Waters. New York: Palgrave Macmillan.
———. 2013. "The Slut That Wasn't: Virginity, (Post) Feminism and Representation in *Easy A*." In *Postfeminism and Contemporary Hollywood Cinema*, eds. Joel Gwynne and Nadine Muller. New York: Palgrave Macmillan.
Fisher, Mark. 2013. "Precarious Dystopias: *The Hunger Games*, *In Time*, and *Never Let Me Go*." *Film Quarterly* 65, no. 4, 27–33.
Fraser, Nancy. 1997. *Justice Interruptus: Critical Reflections on the "Postsocialist" Condition*. New York: Routledge.
Fregoso, Rosa Linda. 2007. "Lupe Velez: Queen of the B's." In *From Bananas to Buttocks: The Latina Body in Popular Film and Culture*, ed. Myra Mendible. Austin: University of Texas Press.

Fuchs, Cynthia J. 1993. "The Buddy Politic." In *Screening the Male: Exploring Masculinities in the Hollywood Cinema*, eds. Steve Cohan and Ina Rae Hark. New York: Routledge.

Funkhouser, Kathryn. 2013. "Earth to Hollywood: People Will Pay to See a Female Superhero Film." *theatlantic.com*, December 6.

Funnell, Lisa. 2011a. "Assimilating Hong Kong Style for the Hollywood Action Woman." *Quarterly Review of Film and Video*, no. 28, 66–79.

———. 2011b. "'I Know Where You Keep Your Gun': Daniel Craig as the Bond-Bond Girl Hybrid in *Casino Royale*." *Journal of Popular Culture* 44, no. 3, 455–72.

Gates, Philippa. 2004. "Always a Partner in Crime: Black Masculinity in the Hollywood Detective Film." *Journal of Popular Film and Television* 32, no. 1, 20–29.

———. 2010. "Acting His Age? The Resurrection of 80s Action Heroes and their Aging Stars." *Quarterly Review of Film and Video*, no. 27, 276–89.

Genz, S., and B. A. Brabon. 2009. *Postfeminism: Cultural Texts and Theories*. Edinburgh: Edinburgh University Press.

Giddens, Anthony. 1991. *Modernity and Self-Identity: Self and Society in the Late Modern Age*. Palo Alto, CA: Stanford University Press.

Gill, Rosalind. 2007. "Postfeminist Media Culture: Elements of a Sensibility." *European Journal of Cultural Studies* 10, no. 2, 147–66.

———. 2012. "Media, Empowerment and the 'Sexualization of Culture' Debate." *Sex Roles*, no. 66, 736–45.

Gill, Rosalind, and Christina Scharff, eds. 2011. *New Femininities: Postfeminism, Neoliberalism and Subjectivity*. New York: Palgrave Macmillan.

Gilligan, Sarah. 2011. "Performing Postfeminist Identities: Gender, Costume, and Transformation in Teen Cinema." In *Women on Screen: Feminism and Femininity in Visual Culture*, ed. Melanie Waters. New York: Palgrave Macmillan.

Gilman, Sander. 1992. "Black Bodies, White Bodies: Toward an Iconography of Female Sexuality in Late 19th Century Art, Medicine and Literature." In *Race, Culture & Difference*, eds. James Donald and Ali Rattasni. London: Sage/The Open University.

Glock, Allison. 2005. "The Body and Soul of Jessica Alba." *rollingstone.com*, June 30.

Goldman, Andrew. 2008. "Don't Mess With Jess." *elle.com*, January 4.

Goodwin, Christopher. 1998. "Bum's the Word." *Sunday Times*, September 20.

Grant, Barry Keith. 1996. "Taking Back the *Night of the Living Dead*: George Romero, Feminism, and the Horror Film." In *The Dread of Difference: Gender and the Horror Film*. Austin: Univeristy of Texas Press.

Gray, Emily M. 2010. "Does Hit Girl Kick Ass?" *genderandeductation.com*, December 3.

Gray, Richard J. 2011. "Vivacious Vixens and Scintillating Superhotties: Deconstructing the Superheroine." In *The 21st Century Superhero: Essays on Gender, Genre and Globalization in Film*, eds. Richard J. Gray and Betty Kalamaniduo. Jefferson, NC: McFarland.

Groen, Rick. 2010. "*Kick-Ass*: It's Hit-Girl Who Packs the Real Punch." *Globe and Mail*, April 16.

Guerrero, Ed. 1993. *Framing Blackness: The African American Image in Film*. Philadelphia: Temple University Press.

Guzman, Isabel Molina. 2007. "Salma Hayek's *Frida*: Transnational Latina Bodies in Popular Culture." In *From Bananas to Buttocks: The Latina Body in Popular Film and Culture*, ed. Myra Mendible. Austin: University of Texas Press.

Guzman, Isabel Molina, and Angharad N. Valdivia. 2004. "Brain, Brow, and Booty: Latina Iconicity in U.S. Popular Culture." *Communication Review*, no. 7, 205–221.

Hale, Mike. 2013. "Asian Actresses Challenge Stereotypes." *Columbus Dispatch*, December 6.

Hallam, Julia. 2005. *Lynda La Plante*. Manchester: Manchester University Press.

Han, Angie. 2011. "On Zack Snyder's *Sucker Punch*: Why Ass-Kicking and Empowerment Aren't Always the Same Thing." *slashfilm.com*, March 26.

Harris, Mark. 2012. "Enter the Dragon." *Entertainment Weekly*, January 6.

Harvey, David. 2005. *A Brief History of Neoliberalism*. New York: Oxford University Press.

Hassel, Holly. 2008. "The 'Babe Scientist' Phenomenon: The Illusion of Inclusion in 1990s American Action Films." In *Chick Flicks: Contemporary Women at the Movies*, eds. Suzanne Ferriss and Mallory Young. New York: Routledge.

Hatch, Kristen. 2002. "Fille Fatlae: Regulating Images of Adolescent Girls, 1962–1996." In *Sugar, Spice, and Everything Nice: Cinema of Girlhood*, eds. Frances Gateward and Murray Pomerance. Detroit, MI: Wayne State University Press.

Hay, James. 2000. "Unaided Virtues: The (Neo-)Liberalization of the Domestic Sphere." *Television & New Media* 1, no. 1, 53–73.

Hedeggard, E. 2005. "Eva Longoria: A Year of 'Sex' for the *Desperate Housewives* Star." *rollingstone.com*, December 15.

Hermes, Joke. 2006. "'Ally McBeal,' 'Sex and the City' and the Tragic Success of Feminism." In *Feminism in Popular Culture*, eds. Joanne Hollows and Rachel Moseley. New York: Berg Publishers.

Hills, Elizabeth. 1999. "From 'Figurative Males' to Action Heroines: Further Thoughts on Active Women in the Cinema." *Screen* 40, no. 1, 38–50.

Holmlund, Chris. 2005. "Wham! Bam! Pam! Pam Grier as Hot Action babe and Cool Action Mama." In *Quarterly Review of Film and Video*, no. 22, 97–112.

hooks, bell. 1992. *Black Looks: Race and Representation*. Boston: South End Press.

Hudlin, Reginald. 2009. *Black Panther: The Deadliest of the Species*. New York: Marvel Comics.

Hunt, Leon. 2003. *Kung Fu Cult Masters: From Bruce Lee to Crouching Tiger*. New York: Wallflower Press.

Hynes, Eric. 2011. "Tracking a Teenage Mutant Ninja in *Hanna*." *Village Voice*, April 6.

Inness, Sherrie, ed. 2004. *Action Chicks: New Images of Tough Women in Popular Culture*. New York: Palgrave Macmillan.

Jeffords, Susan. 1994. *Hard Bodies: Hollywood Masculinity in the Reagan Era*. New Brunswick, NJ: Rutgers University Press.

Jenkins, Mark. 2011. "La Femme *Colombiana*." *Washington Post*, August 26.

Jermyn, Deborah. 2003. "Women With a Mission: Lynda La Plante, DCI Jane Tennison and the Reinvention of British TV Crime Drama." *International Journal of Cultural Studies* 6, no. 1, 46–63.

Jerven, Taraneh Ghajar. 2010. "The Girl Who Doubted Stieg Larsson's Feminism." *Bitch*, no. 48 (Fall), 9.

Johnson, Audrey D. 2009. "Male Masochism in Casino Royale." In *Revisioning 007: James Bond and Casino Royale*, ed. Christoph Linder. New York: Wallflower Press.

Johnson, Joanna Webb. 2006. "Chick Lit Jr.: More Than Glitz and Glamour for Teens and Tweens." In *Chick Lit: The New Woman's Fiction*, eds. Suzanne Ferriss and Mallory Young. New York: Routledge.

Johnson, Kjerstin. 2010. "Why on Earth Wasn't *Kick-Ass* called *Hit-Girl*?" *bitchmagazine.org*, April 20.

Johnson, Naomi R. 2010. "Consuming Desires: Consumption, Romance, and Sexuality in Best Selling Teen Romance Novels." *Women's Studies in Communication*, vol. 33, 54–73.

Karaminas, Vicki. 2006. "'No Capes!' Uber Fashion and How 'Luck favors the Prepared': Constructing Contemporary Superhero Identities in American Popular Culture." *International Journal of Comic Arts* 8, no. 1 (Spring), 498–508.

Klein, Alan M. 1993. *Little Big Men: Bodybuilding Subculture and Gender Construction*. Albany, NY: SUNY Press.

Knee, Adam. 2008. "Race Mixing and the Fantastic: Lineages of Identity and Genre in Contemporary Hollywood." In *Mixed Race Hollywood*, eds. Mary Beltran and Camilla Fojas. New York: New York University Press.

Kord, Susanne, and Elisabeth Krimmer. 2011. *Contemporary Hollywood Masculinities: Gender, Genre, and Politics*. New York: Palgrave Macmillan.

Kristeva, Julia. 1982. *Powers of Horror: An Essay on Abjection*. New York: Columbia University Press.

Kroll, Justin. 2014. "Wonder Woman Gal Gadot Signs Three-Picture Deal with Warner Bros." *variety.com*, January 23.

Larner, Wendy. 2000. "Neo-Liberalism: Policy, Ideology, Governmentality." *Studies in Political Economy*, vol. 63, 5–25.

Larsson, Stieg. 2005. *The Girl with the Dragon Tattoo*. New York: Vintage Press.

Lebel, Sabine. 2009. "Tone Down the Boobs, Please! Reading the Special Effect Body in Superhero Movies." *Cineaction*, no. 77, 56–68.

Lehman, Peter, and William Luhr. 2008. *Thinking About Movies: Watching, Questioning, Enjoying*. New York: Wiley-Blackwell.

Lin, Kristian. 2011. "*Hanna* and the Company." *fwweekly.com*, April 6.

Linden, Sheri. 2012. "Katniss, Hermione, *Brave*: Defiant Girls with Old Souls Rule." *herocomplex.latimes.com*, April 5.

Lipworth, Elaine. 2013. "'I Love Being a Badass': Helen Mirren on Playing with Guns and Encouraging Girls to Swear at Men." *dailymail.co.uk*, July 20.

Lockwood, Dean. 2009. "All Stripped Down: The Spectacle of Torture Porn." *Popular Communication*, vol. 7, 40–48.

Long, Heather. 2013. "Total Misfire: Brands Like CoverGirl and Subway Miss Point of *Hunger Games*." *theguardian.com*, November 22.

Longhurst, Robyn. 2001. *Bodies: Exploring Fluid Boundaries*. New York: Routledge Press.

Lowenstein, Adam. 2011. "Spectacle Horror and *Hostel*: Why 'Torture Porn' Does Not Exist." *Critical Quarterly* 53, no. 1, 42–60.
Luscombe, Belinda. 2005. "25 Most Influential Hispanics in America." *content.time.com*, August 22.
Mason, Bobbie Ann. 1975. *The Girl Sleuth*. Athens: University of Georgia Press.
Massa, Jessica. 2011. "Why *Sucker Punch* Isn't as Empowering as It Wants to Be." *Huffingtonpost.com*, March 3.
McCaughy, Martha, and Neal King, eds. 2001. *Reel Knockouts: Violent Women in the Movies*. Austin: University of Texas Press.
McClintock, Anne. 1995. *Imperial Leather: Race, Gender, and Sexuality in the Colonial Contest*. New York: Routledge.
McKay, James, and Helen Johnson. 2008. "Pornographic Eroticism and Sexual Grotesquerie in Representations of African American Sportswomen." *Social Identities* 14, no. 4 (July), 491–504.
McMillan, Graeme. 2013. "Why *Don't* We Have a Wonder Woman Movie?" *entertainment.time.com*, August 30.
McNair, Brian. 2002. *Striptease Culture: Sex, Media and the Democratisation of Desire*. New York: Routledge.
McRobbie, Angela. 2004. "Notes on Postfeminism and Popular Culture: Bridget Jones and the New Gender Regime." In *All About the Girl: Culture, Power, and Identity*, ed. Anita Harris. New York: Routledge.
———. 2009. *The Aftermath of Feminism: Gender, Culture and Social Change*. London: Sage Publications.
McWilliams, Ora. 2010. "Not Just Another Racist Honkey: A History of Racial Representation in Captain America and Related Publications." In *Captain America and the Struggle of the Superhero: Critical Essays*, ed. Robert G. Weiner. Jefferson, NC: McFarland.
Merskin, Debra. 2007. "Three Faces of Eva: Perpetuation of the Hot-Latina Stereotype in *Desperate Housewives*." *Howard Journal of Communication*, vol. 18, 133–151.
———. 2008. "Lolita Lives! An Examination of Sexual Portrayals of Adolescent Girls in Fashion Advertising." In *Women in Popular Culture: Representation and Meaning*, ed. Marian Meyers. New Jersey: Hampton Press.
Meslow, Scott. 2012. "The Rise of the Female-Led Action Film." *Atlantic*, January 20.
Miller-Young, Mireille. 2010. "Putting Hypersexuality to Work: Black Women and Illicit Eroticism in Pornography." *Sexualities* 13, no. 2, 219–35.
Mizejewski, Linda. 2004. *Hardboiled and High Heeled: The Woman Detective in Popular Culture*. New York: Routledge.
Moloney, Al. 2013. "Why Won't Cinema Embrace Female Superheroes?" *bbc.com*, September 11.
Morris, Wesley. 2011. "*Colombiana* Review." *Boston Globe*, August 27.
Mottram, James. 2011. "*Hanna* Review." *totalfilm.com*, April 8.
Mulvey, Laura. 1975. "Visual Pleasure and the Narrative Cinema." *Screen* 16, no. 3, 6–18.
Mumford, Gwilym. 2012. "*The Hunger Games*: Jennifer Lawrence on Katniss, a 'Futuristic Joan of Arc.'" *Guardian*, March 16.

Nash, Ilana. 2006. *American Sweethearts: Teenage Girls in Twentieth-Century Popular Culture*. Bloomington: Indiana University Press.
Neale, Steve. 1983. "Masculinity as Spectacle: Reflections on Men and Mainstream Cinema." *Screen* 24, no. 6, 2–16.
———. 1992. "The Big Romance or Something Wild?: Romantic Comedy Today." *Screen* 33, no. 3 (Autumn), 284–99.
Negra, Diane. 2009. *What a Girl Wants? Fantasizing the Reclamation of Self in Postfeminism*. New York: Routledge.
Negra, Diane, and Yvonne Tasker. 2013. "Neoliberal Frames and Genres of Inequality: Recession-Era Chick Flicks and Male-Centred corporate Melodrama." *European Journal of Cultural Studies* 16, no. 3, 344–61.
Nelson, Carrie. 2010. "Girls and Guns: Understanding the Politics of *Kick-Ass*." genderacrossborders.com, April 20.
Nishime, Leilani. 2008. "*The Matrix* Trilogy, Keanu Reeves, and Multiraciality at the End of Time." In *Mixed Race Hollywood*, eds. Mary Beltran and Camilla Fojas. New York: New York University Press.
O'Day, Marc. 2004. "Beauty in Motion: Gender, Spectacle and Action Babe Cinema." In *Action and Adventure Cinema*, ed. Yvonne Tasker. New York: Routledge.
Olszewski, Tricia. 2010. "*Kick-Ass*: A Cultish Super Hero Flick About Misfits. And Ass-Kicking." *Washington City Paper*, April 16.
Orange, Michelle. 2011. "Zoe Saldana, *Colombiana* Impress With Crisp, Eye-Popping Action." *movieline.com*, August 25.
Ovalle, Priscilla Pena. 2011. *Dance and the Hollywood Latina: Race, Sex, and Stardom*. New Brunswick, NJ: Rutgers University Press.
Papadopoulos, L. 2010. "Sexualisation of Young People Review." London: Home Office.
Park, Jane. 2008. "Virtual Race: The Racially Ambiguous Action Hero in *The* Matrix and *Pitch* Black." In *Mixed Race Hollywood*, eds. Mary Beltran and Camilla Fojas. New York: New York University Press.
———. 2010. *Yellow Future: Oriental Style in Hollywood Cinema*. Minneapolis: University of Minnesota Press, Minneapolis.
Patches, Mark. 2014. "The *Veronica Mars* Movie: A Momentous Return from Retirement—SXSW Review." *theguardian.com*, March 9.
Petri, Alexandra. 2013. "This Covergirl Makeup Makes a Statement!" *Washington Post*, November 27.
Pinkerton, James P. 2012. "*Hunger Games* Shoots Arrows at Big Government, Big Media, Hits Bullseye." *foxnews.com*, March 22.
Piper, Helen. 2009. "How long since you were last alive?: Fitz and Tennison Ten Years On." *Screen* 50, no. 2, 233–50.
Pollitt, Katha. 1991. "Hers; The Smurfette Principle." *nytimes.com*, April 7.
———. 2012. "*The Hunger Games*' Feral Feminism." *Nation*, April 23, 8–10.
Pols, Mary. 2012. "*Snow White and the Huntsman*: The Fairest Feminist of Them All." *Time*, May 31.

Prado, Emily. 2013. "The Hunger Games' Anti-Consumerism Message is No Match for Cover Girl." *bitchmagazine.org*, November 19.
Projansky, Sarah. 2001. *Watching Rape: Film and Television in Postfeminist Culture*. New York: New York University Press.
Puig, Claudia. 2010. "The Real Hero of *Kick-Ass* is a Little Girl: Chloe Moretz." *USA Today*, April 16.
Purse, Lisa. 2011a. *Contemporary Action Cinema*. Edinburgh: Edinburgh University Press.
———. 2011b. "Return of the 'Angry Woman': Authenticating Female Physical Action in Contemporary Cinema." In *Women On Screen: Feminism and Femininity in Visual Culture*, ed. Melanie Waters. New York: Palgrave Macmillan.
Railton, Diane, and Paul Watson. 2005. "Naughty Girls and Red Blooded Women: Representations of Female Heterosexaulity in Music Videos." *Feminist Media Studies* 5, no. 1, 51–63.
Ray, Robert B. 1985. *A Certain Tendency of the Hollywood Cinema, 1930–1980*. Princeton, NJ: Princeton University Press.
Reid, Mark A. 1993. *Redefining Black Film*. Los Angeles: University of California Press.
Rhodes, Julia. 2010. "*Kick-Ass* and the Hit-Girl Debacle." *California Literary Review*, April 19.
Riviere, Joan. 1929. "Womanliness as Masquerade." In *Formations of Fantasy*, eds. Victor Burgin, James Donald, and Cora Kaplan. London: Routledge.
Robinson, Kerry H., and Cristyn Davies. 2008. "'She's Kickin' Ass, That's What She's Doing!': Deconstructing Childhood 'Innocence' in Media Representations." *Australian Feminist Studies* 23, no. 57, 343–58.
Roeper, Richard. 2011. "*Sucker Punch* a Confusing House-of-Horrors Story with Busty Women." *Chicago Sun-Times*, March 24.
Rosenberg, Alyssa. 2008. "The Invisible Woman." *American Prospect*, September.
Rosenberg, Robin S. 2011. "Salander as Superhero." *Psychology Today*, December 9.
Rottenberg, Catherine. 2014. "The Rise of Neoliberal Feminism." *Cultural Studies* 28, no. 3, 418–37.
Rowe, Kathleen. 1995. *The Unruly Woman: Gender and the Genres of Laughter*. Austin: University of Texas Press.
Rowe, Kathleen Karlyn. 2003. "*Scream*, Popular Culture, and Feminism's Third Wave." *Genders Online Journal*, no. 38.
Rush, E., and La Nauze A. 2006. *Corporate Paedophilia: Sexualisation of Children in Australia*. Australian Institute Working Paper #90.
Sacks, Ethan. 2013. "Why There are No Female Superhero Blockbusters." *nydailynews.com*, September 19.
———. 2014. "Scarlett Johansson's Black Widow Poster Does Justice to Captain America: The Winter Soldier." *nydailynews.com*, January 31.
Said, Edward. 1979. *Orientalism*. New York: Random House.
Satran, Joe. 2012. "Brave, Prometheus, and the Rise of Female Action Heroes." *huffingtonpost.com*, July 2.

Savran, David. 1992. *Taking it Like a Man: White Masculinity, Masochism, and Contemporary American Culture*. Princeton, NJ: Princeton University Press.
Schager, Nick. 2011. "Sucker Punch Film Review." *slantmagazine.com*, March 24.
Schneider, Michael. 2010. "CW's *Nikita* Ads Too Sexy?" *variety.com*, August 18.
Schubart, Rikke. 2007. *Super Bitches and Action Babes: The Female Hero in Popular Cinema, 1970–2006*. Jefferson, NC: McFarland.
Schulze, Laurie. 1990. "On the Muscle." In *Fabrications: Costume and the Female Body*, eds. Jane Gaines and Charlotte Herzog. New York: Routledge.
Schwartz, Missy. 2010. "Did Larsson Have a Problem With Women?" *Entertainment Weekly*, June 25.
Scodari, Christine. 2012. "'Nyota Uhura is Not a White Girl': Gender, Intersectionality, and *Star Trek* 2009's Alternate Romantic Universes." *Feminist Media Studies* 12, no. 3, 335–51.
Scott, A. O. 2012. "Hollywood's Year of Heroine Worship." *New York Times*, December 6.
Scott, A. O., and Manohla Dargis. 2012. "A Radical Female Hero from Dystopia." *New York Times*, April 4.
Shimizu, Celine Parrenas. 2007. *The Hypersexuality of Race: Performing Asian/American Women on Screen and Scene*. Durham, NC: Duke University Press.
Shyminski, Neil. 2011. "'Gay' Sidekicks: Queer Anxiety and the Narrative Straightening of the Superhero." *Men and Masculinities* 14, no. 3, 288–308.
Silverman, Kaja. 1992. *Male Subjectivity at the Margins*. New York: Routledge.
Silverstein, Melissa. 2010. "The Politics of Hit Girl." *womenandhollywood.com*, April 12.
Simpson, Catherine. 2014. "*Veronica Mars*: Kristen Bell Gets Back on the Case." *totalfilm.com*, March 10.
Sims, Yvonne D. 2006. *Women of Blaxploitation: How the Black Action Film Heroine Changed American Popular Culture*. Jefferson, NC: McFarland.
Singer, Marc. 2002. "'Black Skins' and White Masks: Comic Books and the Secrets of Race." *African American Review*, vol. 36 (Spring), 107–119.
Slack, Andrew. 2013. "Ad Campaign (Lip) Glosses Over *Hunger Games* Message." *Los Angeles Times*, November 25.
Smith, Paul. 1994. *Clint Eastwood: A Cultural Production*. Minneapolis: University of Minnesota Press.
Stabile, Carol A. 2009. "'Sweetheart, This Ain't Gender Studies': Sexism and Superheroes." *Communication and Critical/Cultural Studies* 6, no. 1, 86–92.
Staiger, Janet. 2008. "Film Noir as Male Melodrama: The Politics of Film Genre Labeling." In *The Shifting Definitions of Genre: Essays on Labeling Films, Television Shows and Media*, eds. Lincoln Geraghty and Mark Jancovich. Jefferson, NC: McFarland.
Stasia, Cristina Lucia. 2004. "Wham! Bam! Thank You Ma'am!: The New Public/Private Female Action Hero." In *Third Wave Feminism: A Critical Exploration*, eds. Stacy Gillis, Gillian Howie, and Rebecca Mumford. New York: Palgrave Macmillan.
Staskiewicz, Keith. 2012. "Hunger Strikes." *Entertainment Weekly*, April 6.
Steenberg, Lindsay. 2011. "A Pathological Romance: Authority, Expert Knowledge and the Postfeminist Profiler." In *Women On Screen: Feminism and Femiinity in Visual Culture*, ed. Melanie Waters. New York: Palgrave Macmillan.

Stern, Marlow. 2013. "Joss Whedon on Shakespeare, Female Superheroes, and Feminism." *newsweek.com*, June 5.
Stevens, Dana. 2014. "Why Teens Love Dystopias: Brutal, Highly Factionalized Worlds Governed by Remote Authoritarian Entities? That's Basically High School." *slate.com*, April 16.
Stewart, Dodai. 2011. "Why *Sucker Punch* Really, Truly Sucks." *jezebel.com*, March 25.
Stringer, Rebecca. 2011. "From Victim to Vigilante: Gender, Violence, and Revenge in The *Brave One* (2007) and *Hard Candy* (2005)." In *Feminism at the Movies: Understanding Gender in Contemporary Popular Cinema*, ed. Hilary Radner and Rebecca Stringer. New York: Routledge.
Studlar, Gaylyn. 1992. "Masochism and the Perverse Pleasures of the Cinema." In *Film Theory and Criticism: Introductory Readings*, 4th edition, ed. Gerald Mast, Marshall Cohen, and Leo Braudy. New York: Oxford University Press.
Sturtevant, Victoria. 2005. "Spitfire: Lupe Velez and the Ambivalent Pleasures of Ethnic Masquerade." *Velvet Light Trap*, no. 55, 19–32.
Svetkey, Benjamin. 2010. "What About Wonder Woman?" *Entertainment Weekly*, November 26.
Sydney Smith, Susan. 2007. "Endless Interrogation: *Prime Suspect* Deconstructing Realism Through the Female Body." *Feminist Media Studies* 7, no. 3, 189–202.
Tasker, Yvonne. 1993. *Spectacular Bodies: Gender, Genre and Action Cinema*. New York: Routledge.
———. 1997. "Fists of Fury: Discourses of Race and Masculinity in the Martial Arts Cinema." In *Race and the Subject of Masculinities*, eds. Harry Stecopolous and Michael Uebel. Durham, NC: Duke University Press.
———. 1998. *Working Girls: Gender and Sexuality in Popular Culture*. New York: Routledge.
———. 2011. "*Enchanted* (2007) by Postfeminism: Gender, Irony, and the New Romantic Comedy." In *Feminism at the Movies: Understanding Gender in Contemporary Popular Cinema*, eds. Hilary Radner and Rebecca Stringer. New York: Routledge.
Taylor, Affrica. 2010. "Troubling Childhood Innocence: Reframing the Debate Over the Media Sexualisation of Children." *Australasian Journal of Early Childhood* 35, no. 1, 48–57.
Thornham, Sue. 1994. "Feminist Interventions: *Prime Suspect 1*." *Critical Survey* 6, no. 2, 226–33.
———. 2003. "'A Good Body': The Case of/for Feminist Media Studies." *European Journal of Cultural Studies* 6, no. 1, 75–94.
Tierney, Sean M. 2006. "Themes of Whiteness in *Bulletproof Monk*, *Kill Bill*, and *The Last Samurai*." *Journal of Communication*, vol. 56, 607–624.
Tolchin, Karen R. 2007. "'Hey, Killer': The Construction of a Macho Latina, or the Perils and Enticements of *Girlfight*." In *From Bananas to Buttocks: The Latina Body in Popular Film and Culture*, ed. Myra Mendible. Austin: University of Texas Press.
Travers, Peter. 2010. "*Kick-Ass*." *Rolling Stone*, April 15.
———. 2011. "*Sucker Punch*." *Rolling Stone*, March 25.

Truitt, Brian. 2013. "In Superhero Genre, Movie Girl Power is in Short Supply." *usatoday.com*, August 26.
Tucker, Reed. 2014. "Where Are All the Movies Starring Female Superheroes?" *nypost.com*, April 3.
Turan, Kenneth. 2010. "Movie Review: *Kick-Ass*." *Los Angeles Times*, April 15.
Uricchio, William, and Roberta Pearson, eds. 1991. *The Many Lives of the Batman: Critical Approaches to a Superhero and his Media*. New York: BFI Publishing.
Valdivia, Angharad. 2007. "Is Penelope to J. Lo as Culture is to Nature? Eurocentric Approaches to 'Latin' Beauties." In *From Bananas to Buttocks: The Latina Body in Popular Film and Culture*, ed. Myra Mendible. Austin: University of Texas Press.
Vares, Tina, Sue Jackson, and Rosalind Gill. 2011. "Preteen Girls Read 'Tween' Popular Culture: Diversity, Complexity and Contradiction." *International Journal of Media and Cultural Politics* 7, no. 2, 139–54.
Vilkomerson, Sara. 2014. "Diverge & Conquer." *Entertainment Weekly*, March 7.
Walkerdine, Valerie. 1997. *Daddy's Girl: Young Girls and Popular Culture*. Cambridge: Harvard University Press.
Walton, Priscilla L., and Manina Jones. 1999. *Detective Agency: Women Rewriting the Hard-Boiled Tradition*. Berkeley: University of California Press.
Ward, Hazel. 2014. "Where on Earth 1 is the Wonder Woman Movie?" *SciFiNow*, March.
Weitzman, Elizabeth. 2014. "*Veronica Mars*: Movie Review." *New York Daily News*, March 13.
Wenn. 2011. "Browning Defends 'Sexist' *Sucker Punch*." *Sydney Morning Herald*, April 4.
Wilkinson, Eleanor. 2009. "Perverting Visual Pleasure: Representing Sadomasochism." *Sexualities* 12, no. 2, 181–98.
Wilson, G. Willow. 2009. *Vixen: Return of the Lion*. New York: DC Comics.
Wittstock, M. 2005. "Mothers of Suburbia." *observer.guardian.com*, March 8.
Worsdale, James. 2011. "More Than a Woman: Hanna as a Post-Female Feminist Heroine." *thecanonball.wordpress.com*, April 13.
Yamato, Jen. 2011. "Zack Snyder on Male Moviegoers and His Subversive Sucker Punch." *movieline.com*, March 23.
Zeitchik, Steven. 2012. "What the *The Hunger Games* Really Means." *Los Angeles Times*, March 24.

INDEX

9 and ½ Weeks, 32
16 and Pregnant, 138
48 Hours, 66, 67, 81
100, The, 22, 168

Abjection, 21, 136, 140, 141, 142, 147, 148, 149, 150, 159, 181
Abrams, J. J., 56, 57, 76
Accused, The, 38, 74
Adoption, 95, 138, 143, 144, 149, 164
Aeon Flux, 96
African American heroines, 20, 66, 78–89, 92, 134
After the Sunset, 106, 108
Aisha, 90, 91, 92
Alba, Jessica, 20, 32, 80, 82, 103, 108–17
Alcoff, Linda, and Laura Gray, 34
Alias, 15, 30, 35, 56, 61, 144, 226
Alice in Wonderland, 168, 171, 174, 184, 188, 192, 194, 214, 224
Aliens, 15, 78, 96, 219
Alma Coin, 194, 196
Alter, Ethan, 90
Anaconda, 108
Angela Mao Ying, 94
Ant-Man, 232
Anwar, Gabrielle, 4, 56
Arons, Wendy, 95
A-Team, The, 58
Austin Powers in Goldmember, 87
Avatar, 80, 87, 89, 92, 108, 114, 115

Avengers, The, 18, 30, 31, 55, 56, 144, 233, 234, 239, 240
Avengers Academy, 11, 131, 154, 158, 161, 163

Babydoll, 205, 206, 207, 210, 211, 213, 217, 221–25, 229, 230
Back-Up Plan, The, 138
Bad Boys, 66
Baise Moi, 38
Banderas, Antonio, 8, 12, 111
Bandidas, 64, 106, 108
Barb Wire, 171, 238
Barbarella, 238
Barely Lethal, 109, 198
Basic Instinct, 32
Batgirl, 6, 21, 31, 143, 145, 146, 154, 156, 160, 236
Batman, 119, 120, 127, 131, 140–43, 146–50, 156–58, 232–38
Beart, Emmanuelle, 60
Beautiful Creatures, 8
Beck, Ulrich, 169
Beckett, 65, 69, 72, 73, 74
Beckinsale, Kate, 11, 15, 19, 79, 220
Bell, Kristen, 9, 252
Bellafante, Ginia, 4
Beltran, Mary, 81, 106, 108, 111, 115, 116, 117
Bendis, Brian Michael, 144, 168
Berry, Halle, 79, 80, 87, 88, 109, 124, 238, 239, 241
Besson, Luc, 91

255

Bethune, Brian, 178
Beyonce, 87, 124
Bianco, Robert, 102
Big Bang Theory, The, 197
Big Boss, The, 93
Big Daddy, 199, 200, 204, 223
Birds of Prey, 63, 127, 236
Black Caesar, 82
Black Canary, 127, 143
Black Goliath, 121
Black Lightning, 121
Black Panther, 20, 119–34
Black Widow, 30, 31, 34, 56, 57, 142, 154, 233–41
Blacklist, The, 6
Blaxploitation, 19, 78–93, 103, 121, 126
Blomkvist, Mikael, 17, 37, 39
Bloodrayne, 80
Blue Steel, 74
Bodily Harm, 74
Bogle, Donald, 84
Boichel, Bill, 156
Bones, 19, 55, 65, 69, 71, 75
Bordo, Susan, 155, 208, 219, 220
Bradshaw, Peter, 40
Brady, Miranda, 61
Brave One, The, 44
Braveheart, 27
Breakout Kings, The, 55
Bridesmaids, 202
Bridget Jones Diary, 172, 227
Brosnan, Pierce, 49
Brown, Jeffrey A., 6, 28, 36, 82, 92, 121, 122, 133, 198, 219, 223
Brown, Wendy, 76
Browning, Emily, 205, 206
Bruce Wayne, 144, 149
Brunsdon, Charlotte, 14, 15
Buddy-cop stories, 19, 64–70, 72, 74, 81
Buffy the Vampire Slayer, 32, 56, 110, 234
Bukataman, Scott, 120, 121, 129, 137
Bullock, Sandra, 64
Burn Notice, 4, 5, 18, 55, 56, 58, 62, 63

Butler, Judith, 61, 169
Butterfly and Sword, The, 96

Cafu, 125, 127
Cagney and Lacey, 63
Captain America, 56, 120, 148, 156, 232–41
Captain James T. Kirk, 57, 92, 116
Captain Marvel, 6, 125, 137
Carano, Gina, 8, 12, 220
Carter, Gregory T., 58, 60, 80, 89, 113, 174
Casino Royale, 25, 26, 27, 28, 48–53
Cassandra Cain, 145, 146, 168
Castle, 19, 32, 55, 65, 68, 69, 71–75
Cataleya, 91, 92, 115
Catching Fire, 7, 171, 173, 175, 179, 182, 183
Catwoman, 21, 31, 79, 131, 132, 142–45, 154, 158, 171, 232–39, 241
Cell, The, 108
CGI, 89, 194, 205, 224, 238, 239, 241
Chabon, Michael, 153, 154
Chaney, Jen, 203
Charlie's Angels, 8, 63, 80, 85, 96
Charmed, 63
Cheetah, 131
Chen, Eva, 176, 179
Chernin, Kim, 219
Chick lit, 192, 227, 229
Childhood innocence, 202, 203, 231
China O'Brien, 95
Chinese Connection, The, 93
Chrysalis moment, 222
Chuck, 19, 55, 65, 68, 69, 75, 81, 93
Chung, Jamie, 205
City of Bones, 6, 8, 168
Civil rights, 82, 83
Clark Kent, 120, 157
Cleopatra Jones, 78, 83, 84
Client List, The, 32
Closer, The, 72
Clover, Carol, 51, 158
Coffy, 78, 83, 84
Collins, Patricia Hill, 83, 86, 123, 124
Collins, Suzanne, 8, 168, 183, 185, 225

Colombiana, 38, 80, 90, 91, 92, 114
Colonialism, 85, 93, 95, 123–34
Coming of age, 23, 214, 224, 227, 229
Commando, 67
Cooper, Gary, 26, 105
Copycat, 64
Cornish, Abbie, 205
Cornwell, Patricia, 225
CoverGirl, 182–84
Covert Affairs, 6, 226
Craig, Daniel, 26, 40, 48, 49, 50
Criminal Minds, 55
Crouching Tiger, Hidden Dragon, 96
Cruise, Tom, 15, 59, 71, 98
Crush, The, 209
CSI, 55, 65
Cunningham, Phillip, 121
Curtis, Jamie Lee, 76
Cyborg, 122, 137

Damien Wayne, 149–51
Damsels in distress, 5, 120, 145
Dances with Wolves, 90
Daredevil, 232
Dark Angel, 80, 109, 110
Dark Continent, 120, 128, 129
Darnton, Robert, 132
Dauntless, 174, 182, 185, 188–94
Dave Lizewski, 199, 200, 222
Davis, Geena, 30
Dawson, Rosario, 80, 109
DC Comics, 20, 63, 121, 126, 143, 153, 159
Deadpool, 232
Deaf and Mute Heroine, The, 94
Debruge, Peter, 206
D.E.B.S., 63, 80
Deleyto, Celestino, 69
DelVecchio, Marina, 213
Denby, David, 44, 244
Desperado, 31, 106, 108, 111
Desperate Housewives, 32, 106
Dexter, 53
Diaz, Cameron, 31, 80

Diesel, Vin, 81, 89, 115
Disney, 180, 186, 214
District 12, 175, 181, 182
Divergent, 6, 8, 11, 22, 80, 168, 171, 174, 177, 184–94, 235
Doane, Mary Ann, 61, 140, 141
Dobson, Tamara, 84, 85, 92
Dole, Carol, 64, 65
Dominatrix, 121
Douglas, Susan, 85
Dr. Strange, 232
Dragon Lady, 20, 95, 96, 98, 100, 101, 102, 103
Dragon Squad, 97
Dragon Tattoo, 17, 18, 24, 36, 39, 41
Duggan, Lisa, 169
Dunn, Stephane, 60, 84, 85, 87
Durham, M. Gigi, 208
Dustlands, 6
Dyer, Richard, 27, 221
Dystopia, 8, 22, 168, 174, 175, 181

Easthope, Anthony, 120
Eastwood, Clint, 12, 29
Easy A, 201
Ebert, Roger, 36, 39, 178, 201
Eco, Umberto, 140
Edelstein, David, 214
El Mariachi, 111
Elektra, 96, 232, 239
Elementary, 55, 65
Ellen Ripley, 15, 78, 96, 219
Enchanted, 215, 253
Enter the Dragon, 93
Ethan Hunt, 59, 60, 94, 95, 98, 99
Evanovich, Janet, 224
Evans, Chris, 90, 237
Everly, 108
Expendables, The, 12, 58
Extremities, 38

Fall, The, 17
Faludi, Susan, 193

Fantastic Four, The, 55, 80, 109, 111, 114, 126, 142, 233
Farr, Cecilia Koncha, 227
Farrimond, Katherine, 209, 210
Fast and the Furious, 81, 108, 115
Fatherhood, 15, 137
Fearless Defenders, 63
Feminists, 4, 5, 11–14, 18, 24, 25, 38, 39, 43–46, 52–57, 64, 84, 136, 140, 168–79, 183–86, 191–98, 204–16
Feminization, 26, 28, 51, 69, 137, 138
Ferngully, 90
Fetishization, 7, 23, 27, 98, 129, 134, 158, 198, 208, 221, 230
Fifty Shades of Gray, 33
Fight Club, 28, 40
Fillion, Nathan, 65, 218
Fincher, David, 39, 40, 41
Fiona Glenanne, 4, 5, 18, 56, 58, 62, 63
Firefly, 217
Firelight, 6, 8
Fisher, Mark, 177, 209
Fools Rush In, 106
Ford, Harrison, 11, 12
Foster, Jodie, 44, 64
Fox, Megan, 11, 201, 208
Fox, Vivica A., 79, 80
Fraser, Nancy, 169
Fregoso, Rosa Linda, 105
Frida, 106
Friday Foster, 83
From Dusk Till Dawn, 106
Fuchs, Cynthia J., 70
Funkhouser, Kathryn, 234
Funnell, Lisa, 48, 96

Gadot, Gal, 235, 236
Gale Hawthorne, 192, 193
Gallagher Girls, 225, 226, 228
Gamora, 89, 233
Garner, Jennifer, 30
Gates, Philippa, 12, 67
Gen-X Cops, 2, 97

Get Christie Love, 83
G.I. Jane, 35
Ghost Protocol, 18, 55, 60, 80
Ghost Squad, 14, 17
Gibson, Mel, 12, 25, 26, 27, 28, 81
Giddens, Anthony, 169
Gilda, 11, 31
Gill, Rosalind, 169, 170, 207, 210
Gilligan, Sarah, 187, 188
Gilman, Sander, 123
Girl Fight, 108
Girl power, 171, 196, 198
Girl Who Kicked the Hornet's Nest, The, 17, 43
Girl Who Played with Fire, The, 17, 43
Girl with the Dragon Tattoo, The, 5, 16–18, 24, 25, 30, 36–41, 42, 45–55
Girlhood, 168, 208, 222, 230
Glau, Summer, 197, 217
Glock, Allison, 110
Golden Swallow, 78, 94
Goldfinger, 25, 49
Goldman, Andrew, 111, 203
Good Day to Die Hard, A, 11
Gossip Girl, 155, 171, 181
Grant, Barry Keith, 59
Gray, Richard J., 154, 237
Green Arrow, 143, 148, 156, 165, 232
Grier, Pam, 12, 84–86, 87, 92
Grind House, 80
Groen, Rick, 199
Grotesque, 21, 194
Guardians of the Galaxy, The, 55, 80, 89, 233
Guerrero, Ed, 82
Guzman, Isabel Molina, 104, 106, 107, 114

Hale, Mike, 103
Hallam, Julia, 13
Hamilton, Linda, 12, 15, 219
Hannah, 5, 133, 215
Hansel and Gretel, 215, 224
Hapkido, 94
Hard Candy, 44, 198, 219

Harlow, Jean, 11
Harris, Mark, 36
Harry Potter, 225
Hart to Hart, 65, 75
Harvey, David, 168, 247
Hathaway, Anne, 40, 187, 235, 236
Hawaii Five-O, 55
Hawkeye, 56, 160
Hawksian professionalism, 59, 65
Hay, James, 169
Hayek, Salma, 11, 31, 103, 106, 108, 111, 114, 117
Haywire, 8, 38, 220
Hayworth, Rita, 11, 31
Hazmat, 122, 161, 162, 163
Heat, The, 64, 66, 202
Hegemonic masculinity, 29, 50, 142, 147, 156, 158
He-Man and the Masters of the Universe, 57
Hemsworth, Chris, 174, 192, 237
Heralds, 145
Heroes for Hire, 31, 32, 125
Heroic Trio, The, 63, 96
Hills, Elizabeth, 190, 219
Hit-Girl, 23, 198–204, 213, 215, 217, 218, 220–25, 229, 230, 238
HIV positive, 22, 165
Holmlund, Chris, 78, 84
Homeland, 6, 71
Honey Pot, 18
Hong Kong, 16, 17, 63, 79, 93–100, 102
hooks, bell, 123
House Bunny, The, 184, 187
House of Flying Daggers, The, 96
Hu, Kelly, 80
Hudgens, Vanessa, 205
Hudlin, Reginald, 125, 134
Hulk, 56, 154, 232, 236, 238
Hunger Games, The, 5, 8, 11, 15, 22, 161, 167–74, 177, 178, 180–84, 188, 190, 192, 194, 225, 234, 235, 237
Hynes, Eric, 197
Hypermasculinity, 15, 48, 238

Hypermuscularity, 137
Hypersexuality, 20, 21, 38, 83, 86, 104, 108, 122–25, 132–34, 153, 171, 237

I Spit on Your Grave, 38
Icon, 122
In Plain Sight, 6, 65
Incredibles, The, 143
Indiana Jones, 5, 12
Indiana Jones and the Kingdom of the Crystal Skull, 12
Individualism, 54, 67, 152, 169, 170, 179
Inness, Sherrie, 5
Invisible War, The, 45
Invisible Woman, 109, 142, 233
Iron-Man, 56, 120, 137, 140, 144, 232, 233, 238, 239

Jackman, Hugh, 237
James, Theo, 192
James Bond, 5, 25–27, 40, 48–51, 61, 65, 76, 83, 96, 200, 227, 229
Jane Blonde, 225
Jane Tennison, 13, 14, 15, 16
Jason Bourne, 65, 67
Jeffords, Susan, 11, 26, 27
Jenkins, Mark, 92
Jennifer's Body, 38, 209
Jermyn, Deborah, 13
Jerven, Taraneh Ghajar, 38, 248
Jessica Jones, 144, 145
Jezebel stereotype, 20, 86, 87, 92, 104, 117, 134
Jimmy Olsen, 148, 156
Joan of Arc, 22, 167, 168, 173, 180, 196
Johansson, Scarlett, 11, 30, 31, 40, 56, 235, 239–41
Johnson, Audrey, 48, 49
Johnson, Dwayne, 81, 89
Johnson, Joanna Webb, 227, 229
Johnson, Kjerstein, 199, 204
Jolie, Angelina, 15, 19, 30, 44, 75, 76, 78, 219, 226

Jovovich, Milla, 11, 19, 79, 220
Judd, Ashley, 16
Juno, 138
Justice League of America, The, 125, 127

Katniss Everdeen, 6, 15, 167, 171–85, 188, 192–95, 237
Kelley, David E., 237
Kick-Ass, 22, 23, 140, 185, 198–204, 215–18, 222, 224, 238
Kick-Ass 2, 198
Kickstarter, 9, 10
Kill Bill, 5, 15, 30, 38, 44, 79, 80, 202
Killers, The, 67
Killing, The, 17, 65, 68
Kinky Boots, 32
Klein, Alan M., 120, 137, 226
Knee, Adam, 81
Knight and Day, 19, 55, 67, 80
Knocked Up, 138
Kord, Susanne, and Elisabeth Krimmer, 48, 76
Kristeva, Julia, 21, 140, 141, 148, 149
Kung Fu, 5, 16, 20, 36, 78, 79, 80, 82, 93–103
Kurylenko, Olga, 220

La Femme Nikita, 100
Lady Cocoa, 83
Lady Sif, 191
Lady Whirlwind, 78, 94
Larner, Wendy, 169
Larsson, Stieg, 17, 18, 24, 25, 42, 46, 53
Last Boy Scout, The, 66, 81
Last House on the Left, The, 38
Last Samurai, The, 90, 115
Last Stand, The, 12
Latina, 78–82, 89, 103–17, 122, 131
Latinadad, 104, 107, 108
Lawrence, Jennifer, 19, 79, 167, 173, 185, 239
Lebel, Sabine, 238, 239
Lee, Bruce, 93

Lethal Weapon, 26, 66, 67, 69, 70, 81
Lin, Kristian, 197
Linden, Sheri, 68, 181
Lionsgate, 183, 184
Lipworth, Elaine, 13
Lisbeth Salander, 16–25, 30, 36–52
Liu, Lucy, 79, 80, 97
Live Free or Die Hard, 11, 97, 98, 99, 103, 114
Lives of a Bengal Lancer, 26
Lois Lane, 157
Lolita, 38, 155, 198, 208, 209
Long, Heather, 183
Long Kiss Goodnight, The, 29, 34
Longhurst, Robyn, 140
Longoria, Eva, 103, 106, 108
Lopez, Jennifer, 3, 103, 105, 106, 108, 114
Losers, The, 55, 87, 90, 92, 114, 220
Loving v. Virginia, 81
Lowenstein, Adam, 32
Lt. Uhura, 57, 87, 89, 92, 116
Lucy, 235
Luke Cage, 121, 122, 137, 144

Machete, 80, 108–12, 114, 116
Makeover, 170, 184, 187–89, 196
Maleficent, 215
Malone, Jena, 205
Manga, 32
Manhattan Midnight, 97
Mara, Rooney, 40
Marissa Weigler, 212, 214, 218
Marvel Comics, 20, 32, 63, 131, 139, 162, 163
Masculinization, 28, 96, 108, 137, 189, 191
Mask, The, 31
Masochism, 28, 33, 34
Mason, Bobbie Ann, 229
Masquerade, 61, 239
Maternity, 15, 20, 21, 136, 138, 143, 145, 147, 148, 150, 151
Matrix, 79, 81, 96
McCarthy, Melissa, 64, 202

McCaughy, Martha, and Neale King, 5
McClintock, Anne, 123
McDuffie, Dwayne, 127
McMillan, Graeme, 233
McMillan & Wife, 75
McNair, Brian, 33
McRobbie, Angela, 169, 172, 193, 194, 195
McWilliams, Ora, 121
"Meet cute," 72, 73
Mentalist, The, 55, 58, 65, 68, 69
Merskin, Debra, 107, 155, 208
Meslow, Scott, 7
Mettle, 137, 161–63
Mexploitation, 103, 104
Michael Westen, 4, 62
Milestone Media, 127
Millar, Mark, 198
Millennium Trilogy, 37, 45, 46, 51, 52
Miller-Young, Mirielle, 124
Mirren, Helen, 12–14
Missing, 16
Mixed race heritage, 20, 80–99, 102, 103, 108–17
Mixploitation, 113, 117
Mizejewski, Linda, 5
Mockingjay, 175, 179, 180
Modern Family, 107
Monroe, Marilyn, 11, 221
Monster, 41
Moonlighting, 65, 71, 75
Moore, Demi, 35, 71
Moore, Julianne, 194, 196
Moretz, Chloe-Grace, 200, 201
Morris, Wesley, 25
Mortal Instruments, 8, 168
Mottram, James, 214
Mr. and Mrs. Smith, 19, 219
Mr. Fantastic, 142
Ms. Congeniality, 184
Ms. 45, 38
Ms. Marvel, 32, 235, 236
Mulatto, 81, 86, 88, 93, 110, 113, 116
Mulvey, Laura, 26, 28, 30, 121

Muppets, The, 57
Murder in Suburbia, 14, 17, 64
My Super Ex-Girlfriend, 232
Mystique, 137, 239

Naked Weapon, 97, 98
Nancy Drew, 228, 229
Nash, Ilana, 221–23
NCIS, 55, 58
Neale, Steve, 26, 27, 72–74
Neeson, Liam, 11, 16
Negra, Diane, 111, 123, 172, 193
Neoliberalism, 168, 169–80, 184, 187, 188, 191, 196
Newton, Thandie, 60, 80
Nightwing, 148, 156, 157, 160
Nikita, 6, 30, 35, 38, 64, 80, 97, 100–103, 114–17, 224, 226
Nishime, Leilane, 81

Occupy Wall Street Movement, 177, 180
O'Day, Marc, 36
Olszewski, Tricia, 201
Oplev, Niels, 39, 41
Orientalists, 20, 95, 107, 113, 122, 128
Otherness, 80, 117
Out of Sight, 108

Page, Ellen, 44, 219
Paranormalcy, 6
Park, Grace, 59
Park, Jane, 81, 113, 116
Patches, Mark, 10
Paternalism, 12, 137, 138, 148–50
Patriarchal control, 22, 23, 168
Patton, Paula, 60, 80
Peeta Mellark, 182, 192, 193, 226
Peter Parker, 120
Petri, Alexandra, 182
Pitt, Brad, 76
Point of No Return, 100
Poison Ivy, 209
Pollitt, Katha, 57, 181

Pols, Mary, 186, 187, 192
Pornography, 32, 33, 39, 43, 136, 210, 236, 237
Postfeminism, 11, 169–81, 187, 191, 193–96, 215, 216
Postmodernism, 33, 215
Power Girl, 31, 137, 142, 148, 154
Powerboy, 164
Powerpuff Girls, 63, 203
Prado, Emily, 182, 183
Pregnancy, 15, 21, 138–42, 144, 147, 150, 165, 166
President Snow, 174, 175, 194
Pretty Little Liars, 155, 171
Priest, 80, 97
Prime Suspect, 8, 13, 14, 16, 72
Princess Diaries, The, 184, 187
Professional, The, 91, 201
Projansky, Sarah, 172
Protector, The, 64
Pulse, The, 144
Puig, Claudia, 200
Purse, Lisa, 41, 79, 219

Q, Maggie, 12, 20, 30, 60, 80, 82, 95, 97–103, 114, 117, 226
Quantum of Solace, 49, 220

Rahne, 139, 140, 141
Railton, Diane, and Paul Watson, 123, 124, 132
Rambo, 5, 12, 26, 27, 28, 200, 217
Rambo III, 27
Rapace, Noomi, 39
Rape, 7, 18, 24, 25, 28–53
Ravenna (Queen), 174, 186, 187, 194, 195, 196
Ray, Robert, 66, 67
Rebel Without a Cause, 177
Red, 12, 13
Red 2, 12, 13
Red Heat, 66, 67
Red Queen, 174, 189, 194, 195, 196

Red Riding Hood, 215, 224
Reeves, Keanu, 81
Reid, Mark A., 84
Remasculinization, 48, 93, 94
Remington Steele, 65, 71, 75
Resident Evil, 5, 108, 220
Revolution, 6, 22, 59
Richard Grayson, 149, 156, 157, 160
Rihanna, 33, 87
River Tam, 217
Robin, 36, 68, 143, 148–60, 164, 165, 208, 236
Rocky, 11, 12, 189
Rodriguez, Robert, 104, 111
Roeper, Richard, 206, 211
Ronan, Saoirse, 212
Rosenberg, Alyssa, 233
Rothrock, Cynthia, 95
Rottenberg, Catherine, 169, 178
Roundtree, Richard, 83
Runaways, The, 154
Rush, E., and A. La Nauze, 207
Rush Hour, 66, 96, 97

Sackhoff, Katee, 12, 235
Sadomasochism, 27, 33
Said, Edward, 128
Saldana, Zoe, 20, 57, 80, 82, 87–92, 99, 103, 113–17, 220
Salt, 5, 7, 15, 30, 38, 219, 226
Sam Axe, 4, 56
Sapphire stereotype, 86, 87, 117
Sarah Connor, 15, 96, 197, 219
Satran, Joe, 7, 251
Savran, David, 26, 28
Scarlett Witch, 136
Schager, Nick, 206, 211
Schneider, Michael, 101
Schubart, Rikke, 5, 84
Schwartz, Missy, 25
Schwarzenegger, Arnold, 11, 25, 76, 81, 189
Scodari, Christine, 89, 252
Scott, A. O., 7, 17, 64, 75, 120, 121, 137, 205

Second-wave feminism, 14, 169, 178, 193, 215
Secretary, 32
Self-rescue, 32, 50, 158
Serenity, 96, 198, 217, 219
Se7en, 40
Sex and the City, 172, 227
Shaft, 82, 83
She-Hulk, 154, 236
Shyminski, Neil, 156, 157
Sidekicks, 67, 156, 157, 165, 236
Silence of the Lambs, 64
Silver Linings Playbook, 185
Silverman, Kaja, 26, 28, 34
Silverstein, Melissa, 44, 203
Sims, Yvonne D., 84, 85, 88
Sin City, 12, 80, 109, 111, 114
Singer, Marc, 121
Skyfall, 49
Slack, Andrew, 183, 184
Sleuth or Dare, 225
Smith, Paul, 29
Smurfette, 57, 58, 59, 250
Snipes, Wesley, 12, 81
Snow White, 172–77, 180, 184, 186–92, 194, 195, 224
Snow White and the Huntsman, 5, 7, 22, 78, 168, 171, 174, 182, 186, 192, 194, 215
Snyder, Zack, 8, 198, 205, 206, 211, 212, 235, 236
Soderbergh, Steven, 8, 220
Spears, Britney, 33, 208
Specialists, The, 225, 226
Speedy, 148, 156, 160, 165
Spice Girls, The, 210, 213
Spider-Girl, 6, 11, 154
Spider-Man, 57, 119, 120, 131, 144, 156, 236, 238, 239
Spider-Man and his Amazing Friends, 57
Spider-Woman, 31, 236
Spitfire stereotype, 20, 78, 104, 105, 106, 107, 108, 112
Spock, 92, 116

Spook Who Sat by the Door, 82
Spy Girl, 225
Spy Goddess, 225
Spy Kids, 80, 109, 111, 112, 114
Squad, The, 225, 226
Staiger, Janet, 46, 252
Stallone, Sylvester, 11, 12, 25, 26
Stana, Katic, 65
Star Trek, 55, 56, 57, 80, 87, 89, 90, 92, 114, 116
Starfire, 57, 160
Starsky and Hutch, 66
Stasia, Cristina Lucia, 171
Staskiewicz, Keith, 180
Steenberg, Lindsay, 75
Stephanie Brown, 143, 160, 164
Stereotypes, 18–20, 76, 80–87, 93–95, 100–108, 111–13, 119–29, 132–34, 153, 165, 172
Stevens, Dana, 178
Stewart, Kristen, 174, 185, 186, 187, 192
Stone, Emma, 187, 201
Storm, 109, 111, 120, 125, 126, 133, 142, 145, 233
Stringer, Rebecca, 44
Sturtevant, Victoria, 105
Sucker Punch, 8, 11, 22, 23, 44, 63, 171, 198, 201, 205–19, 221, 224, 235
Sugar Hill, 83
Super Fly, 82
Super Friends, The, 57
Superboy, 148, 156, 159, 160, 165
Supergirl, 6, 11, 21, 31, 148, 153–56, 164, 236
Superheroines, 21, 31, 32, 109, 122, 125–44, 153, 155, 159, 161, 165, 166, 232, 234, 237, 238
Superman, 27, 119, 120, 127, 137, 148, 155–57, 232–36, 241
S.W.A.T., 108
Sweet Sweetback's Baadasssss Song, 82
Swimfan, 209
Sydney Bristow, 30, 35, 61, 226
Sydney Smith, Susan, 13

Taken, 15, 16
Taking Lives, 75
Tango and Cash, 65, 66
Tarantino, Quentin, 79, 87
Tasker, Yvonne, 11, 67–71, 74, 76, 81, 86, 93, 193, 215
Teen Moms, 138
Teen Titans, 125, 154, 156, 159, 160
Terminator, The, 15, 28, 96, 197, 219
Terminator 2, 15, 96, 219
Theweilt, Klaus, 137
Thin Man, The, 65, 75
Thomas, Rob, 9
Thornham, Sue, 13
Three The Hard Way, 82
Tierney, Sean M., 79
Tigra, 131, 132, 158
Tim Drake, 149, 160, 164
Titanic, 196
T.N.T. Jackson, 83
Torture, 7, 18, 24–38, 41–53, 239
Totally Spies, 63
Transformers, 201
Trejo, Danny, 112, 114
Tris Prior, 6, 171–85, 188, 192, 194, 195
True Grit, 198, 218
True Lies, 67, 76
Truitt, Brian, 234
Turan, Kenneth, 201
Twilight, 161, 192, 225
Twisted, 74

Undercover Brother, 87
Undercover Girl, 225
Undercovers, 55, 76, 80
Underworld, 5, 15, 96, 220
Unfaithful, 32
Unforgettable, 55
Uricchio, William, and Roberta Pearson, 147

Vampire Academy, The, 8
Van Damme, Jean-Claude, 93

Van Peebles, Melvin, 83
Vaughn, Matthew, 199, 201
Velez, Lupe, 104, 105
Velvet Smooth, 83
Vergara, Sophia, 103, 107, 108, 117
Veronica Mars, 9, 10
Victoria Winslow, 12, 13
Vilkomerson, Sara, 192
Violet & Daisy, 198
Vixen, 20, 119–34
Voodoo, 20, 120, 128

Wakanda, 126, 128
Walkerdine, Valerie, 155
Walton, Priscilla, and Manina Jones, 14
Wanted, 55, 201, 219
War of the Worlds, 15
Ward, Hazel, 233
Warner Bros., 9, 233, 234
Wasikowska, Mia, 174, 185
Watchmen, 205
Way of the Dragon, The, 93
Weaver, Sigourney, 12, 15, 64, 78, 219
Weitzman, Elizabeth, 10
Wenn, 206
Werewolf, 139, 192
Whedon, Joss, 56, 57, 217, 232–34, 237
Whistleblower, The, 45
White Collar, 70
Wild Ones, The, 177
Wild Things, 209
Wilkinson, Eleanor, 33
Willis, Bruce, 11, 81, 99, 114
Wilson, Willow, 125, 127, 134
Wing Chun, 94, 96
Winslet, Kate, 174, 196
Winter's Bone, 198
Witchblade, 21, 145
Without a Trace, 55
Wittstock, M., 106
Wolverine, 145, 146, 237
Wonder Girl, 148, 154, 156, 159, 160, 164, 166

Wonder Woman, 7, 31, 57, 80, 85, 119, 136, 148, 154–59, 191, 232–37, 241
Woodley, Shailene, 174, 185
World Is Not Enough, The, 49
Worsdale, James, 213
Wright, Joe, 198, 212, 213, 216

X-23, 22, 145, 146, 147, 154, 162
Xena: Warrior Princess, 15, 63, 191
X-Factor, 139, 141
X-Files, The, 55, 65, 71, 77
X-Men (comic), 125, 153, 156
X-Men, The (films), 55, 63, 79, 233, 239

Yamato, Jen, 206, 254
Yeoh, Michelle, 95, 96, 117
Yes, Madam, 95
Young Allies, 154
Young Avengers, 11, 154, 160
Young Justice, 11, 154, 160
Young X-Men, 154

Zeitchik, Steven, 177
Zhang, Ziyi, 95, 96, 117

www.ingramcontent.com/pod-product-compliance
Lightning Source LLC
Chambersburg PA
CBHW030339240426
43661CB00052B/1679